I0528445

www.ingramcontent.com/pod-product-compliance
Lightning Source LLC
Chambersburg PA
CBHW051313120626
46547CB00015B/2217

בראשית

THE
ISRAEL
BIBLE

GENESIS

EDITED BY

Rabbi Tuly Weisz

The Israel Bible: Genesis

First Edition, 2021

The Israel Bible was produced by Israel365 in cooperation with Teach for
Israel and is used with permission from Teach for Israel. All rights reserved.
The English translation was adapted by Israel365 from the JPS Tanakh.
Copyright © 1985 by the Jewish Publication Society. All rights reserved.

Cover image used under license from Shutterstock.com

ISBN 978-1-957109-26-8

A CIP catalogue record for this title is available from the British Library

The Israel Bible: Genesis is a holy book that contains the
name of God and should be treated with respect.

Table of Contents

Introduction

The Hebrew Bible is commonly known as the *Tanakh* which stands for *Torah* (the Five Books of Moses), *Neviim* (the Prophets) and *Ketuvim* (the Writings). The *Tanakh* consists of 24 books that are considered by Jews to be the word of God. While these books have been referred to as the "Old Testament," many Jews reject this label since it implies the replacement of the Hebrew Bible with something newer and prefer the more authentic Jewish name.

The *Tanakh* is not only the most important book known to man, it is God's word that is perfect and absolute. It is therefore a daunting undertaking to publish an edition of the *Tanakh*, and the responsibilities are awesome. There is no room for error or carelessness in dealing with the eternal word of God. Further, upon embarking on such a serious initiative, we ask ourselves if our efforts are gratuitous. Considering the many editions of the Bible in print, is there truly a need for yet another one?

While there are numerous Bibles in circulation today, its most central aspect – the Land of Israel – has often been overlooked. References to Israel appear on nearly every page, and the city of Jerusalem is specifically referred to hundreds of times throughout the Bible. The essential link between Israel and *Torah* is emphasized repeatedly in verses such as, "For instruction (*Torah*) shall come forth from *Tzion*, the word of *Hashem* from *Yerushalayim*" (Micah 4:2).

The miraculous return of the People of Israel to the Land of Israel in our own generation provides the perfect moment for a new volume to fill this void in biblical literature. *The Israel Bible* includes many special features elucidating God's focus on Israel throughout *Tanakh* and there are many additional, multimedia features available on our website **www.theisraelbible.com**.

Ordering and Presentation – In presenting *The Israel Bible*, our goal is to spread awareness of the biblical significance of the Land of Israel as well as the Jewish people's eternal connection to the land, based on the text of the *Tanakh*, the Hebrew Bible. We aim to honor "the God, the People and the Land of Israel" from an Orthodox Jewish perspective. To that end, *The Israel Bible* follows the traditional Jewish ordering of the books and the customary Hebrew division of chapters. Therefore, for example, we count 24 books of *Tanakh* with *Sefer Divrei Hayamim* (Chronicles) appearing last. It is our hope that our rich content will speak to all Jews and non-Jews who appreciate Israel as the God given land of the Jewish people.

English Translation – Throughout history, Jews have studied the Bible in Hebrew, as any form of translation would miss much of the nuance of the original holy tongue in which *Torah* has been transmitted since the days of Moses. However, as many Jews settled in America in the 19th Century, the need for an English translation became necessary. To be sure, there were already English translations prepared over the centuries by Christians, but in the words of the original editors of the Jewish Publication Society (JPS), "The Jew cannot afford to have his Bible translation prepared for him by others. He cannot have it as a gift, even as he cannot borrow his soul from others."

JPS set out in the late 1800s to publish an authoritative English translation "in the spirit of Jewish tradition." It was compiled over decades by some of the leading Jewish scholars of the time. They formed committees and subcommittees to compare existing English versions, considering medieval and modern Jewish commentators. The monumental JPS translation, originally published in 1917, has been updated in recent years, and *The Israel Bible* is proud to utilize the 1984 New Jewish Publication Society (NJPS) version with its modern, clear language, as well as its wide-ranging acceptance as an accurate and high-quality translation. We applied the NJPS translation verbatim, except for a select list of nouns which we replaced with their traditional Hebrew names. This is true even when we found the NJPS translation to be different than the popular translation of a word or phrase and when the NJPS switched the order of the text for the sake of clarity (see, for example, Ezekiel 24:22–24).

Hebrew Transliteration – To give our readers an authentic *Tanakh* experience, every verse that has commentary is transliterated from Hebrew into English. The Hebrew alphabet chart includes our standards for transliteration and pronunciation of Hebrew verses, enabling readers of *The Israel Bible* to decipher key biblical passages in the holy language. Readers can hear the entire Bible read in Hebrew on our website **www.theisraelbible.com**.

There are various standards when it comes to transliterating Hebrew words into English letters. While we have relied primarily on the classical Hebrew transliteration, we have occasionally deviated for the sake of simplicity, clarity and to reflect common usage.

In addition to whole verses, we have also transliterated many proper nouns in the English translation so that our readers can learn the names of key biblical figures and locations in their Hebrew form. As a rule, we chose to transliterate names of people that were central in the establishment and functioning of the nation of Israel, as well as significant places in the Holy Land. Therefore, regarding Adam's sons, for example, only *Shet* (Seth) is transliterated since it was from him that *Noach* (Noah), and ultimately *Avraham* (Abraham), descended. For this reason, there might be verses or sections of *The Israel Bible* that contains multiple names and only some of them are transliterated.

For the same reason, we have transliterated the names of the books of *Tanakh* when referring to them in our introductions and commentary. When referencing a specific chapter or verse, however, we use the English names of the books in our citations for clarity. We also transliterated ideas and concepts that are central to Judaism such as *Shabbat* (Sabbath), the names of the Jewish holidays and the *Beit Hamikdash* (Temple), as well as biblical measurements. Finally, the name of God is transliterated. Out of respect, Orthodox Jews generally refer to the Lord as *Hashem*, which literally means 'the Name.' Referring to God as *Hashem* reminds us that we feel close to Him but also recognize our distance at the same time. To stress this moniker, we transliterated both the Tetragrammaton as well as the name *Elohim* as *Hashem*.

Study Notes – Our unique commentary was compiled by Orthodox Jewish scholars who live in Israel. It is an anthology in the sense that most of the commentary is not original, but draws from traditional teachings of early Jewish Sages and modern rabbinic commentators. We also include quotations from individuals who have played a significant part in the past century of modern Israeli history including Israeli prime ministers, poets and military leaders.

Our commentary can be broken into four categories, three of which are identified by an icon at the beginning of the study note:

 Israel lessons are indicated with an icon bearing the map of Israel and focus on the Land of Israel and the modern State of Israel.

 Jewish lessons are indicated with a *Torah* scroll and teach a concept in Judaism or a classic idea from rabbinic thought.

 Hebrew lessons are represented by an icon bearing the letter *aleph* and focus on the meaning of a Hebrew word or phrase.

All other comments are considered general comments and are not assigned an icon.

Supplemental Material – In addition to our unique translation and original commentary, *The Israel Bible* offers supplementary material to enrich the learning experience of our readers. Before every book of *Tanakh*, we provide an introduction, as well as information, generally in the form of a map, a chart or a list, which is central to the specific book.

Maps – As the purpose of *The Israel Bible* is to highlight the biblical significance of the Land of Israel, significant time was spent researching and preparing maps to bring the physical contours of the holy land to life with great accuracy. However, since there is a lack of information regarding the precise locations of certain ancient cities, some of the places on our maps are approximate or subject to debate. In these cases, we followed the opinion that we are most comfortable with, but acknowledge that there is room for disagreement. We continue to produce new maps, which are available on our website **www.theisraelbible.com/maps**.

Torah **Readings** – The *Torah* is not just a work that is studied privately, it is also read out loud in synagogue. Every *Shabbat* and holiday a portion of the *Torah* is read, as well as a related section from *Neviim*, the prophets, called the *haftarah*. We included the blessings recited before and after the reading of the *Torah*, a list of the weekly *Torah* portions and their corresponding *haftarot*, and a chart of the *Torah* readings for special days with their corresponding *haftarot*. Readers can always find the current week's *Torah* portion by visiting **www.theisraelbible.com/weekly-torah-portion**. In this volume, we indicate where a new *Torah* portion begins by highlighting the Hebrew verse number with a gray box so readers can follow along with the communal *Torah* readings. Furthermore, we have included prayers for the State of Israel and the soldiers of the Israel Defense Forces (IDF) that are generally recited following the *Torah* reading in synagogue. It is our constant prayer that God watch over the State of Israel and the members of the IDF, who defend Israel every hour of every day.

In 1948, the State of Israel was created providing a modern answer to Isaiah's ancient question, "Is a nation born all at once?" (Isaiah 66:8). *The Israel Bible* was first published in the 70th year of God's miraculous restoration of the People of Israel to the Land of Israel. Jewish wisdom teaches that 70 is a significant number: *Moshe* (Moses) translated the *Torah* into 70 languages for all 70 nations of the world. From our very origins, the Jewish people were meant to be a light unto the 70 nations, spreading God's truth to the masses.

In the seven decades since the modern rebirth of the State of Israel, God's plan has been unfolding with unprecedented speed, dramatic highs and heartbreaking lows. Never has Israel been at the forefront of the world's attention as it is in our generation. Efforts to vilify the Jewish State seem to spread every day across the globe. At the same time, so does the growing movement of millions of non-Jewish biblical Zionists who stand with the nation of Israel as an expression of their commitment to God's word. As we seek to understand the clash of these two conflicting worldviews, the need for *The Israel Bible* has never been so important.

Standing on the great shoulders of those who came before us and emanating from the land that has always served as the birthplace for the Bible, we conclude with a heartfelt prayer: May the Almighty bless our efforts in offering this *Tanakh* to influence the hearts, minds and actions of its readers. In this way, it is our hope to spread God's name so that the publication of *The Israel Bible* brings us one step closer to the final redemption of Israel and the entire world.

Rabbi Tuly Weisz
Editor, *The Israel Bible*

Foreword

The mandate to study God's word daily is interestingly not found in the Five Books of Moses (Pentateuch), but rather in the first book of our prophetic writings: "Let not this Book of the Teaching cease from your lips, but recite it day and night, so that you may observe faithfully all that is written in it. Only then will you prosper in your undertakings and only then will you be successful" (Joshua 1:8). Charged with bringing the Israelites into the land covenantally promised to Abraham, Isaac and Jacob, God ensures Joshua of His protection if the nation observes His ways as dictated in the Divine constitution known as the *Torah*.

In Jewish tradition, Joshua (1:8) is directly linked with Deuteronomy (11:14), "You shall gather in your new grain and wine, and oil."[1] Our Sages deduced from this scriptural combination the importance of merging *Torah* study with a profession. Completely dedicating oneself to the study of *Torah* without having the financial means to sustain this lifestyle can lead one to eventually straying from observance of God's will. Poverty and crime can have an intimate relationship.

We must also be careful that our work does not affect our daily study of Scripture. The addiction of becoming a workaholic and not making *Torah* study a priority can also lead one into temptations that can violate our personal relationship with Him as well as our fellow human beings. The goal is to achieve a healthy balance between our study of God's word and our daily work.

The Deuteronomic verse quoted above is part of the second section of the Shema[2] that discusses the concept of reward and punishment. Sanctifying God by fulfilling His commandments results in the Land of Israel practically benefitting from rains that occur in the right season and reaping the abundance from the fields. However, if the nation follows pagan gods and practices, the consequences are devastating – famine and death. The Land of Israel is intrinsically linked with the keeping of the *Torah*. Covenant Land comes with covenant responsibility.

---

1. Talmud Bavli Berachot 35b
2. Consisting of three sections within the Five Books of Moses (Deut. 6:4–8; 11:13–22 and Numbers 15:37–42), the *Shema* is proclamation of accepting God's Kingdom in our lives, loyalty to His commandments and remembering His redemptive act of liberating us from Egypt. Jews recite the *Shema* twice a day as stated in Deut. 6:7.

Born into slavery, Joshua is now leading His people into the Promised Land. More than 500 years separates him from his ancestral forefather Abraham. The historical narratives that took place between Abraham leaving everything behind to follow God in Genesis 12 and the death of Moses in the last chapter of Deuteronomy are filled with intrigue, suspense, joy, sorrow and hope. What began as a family is now a nation actualizing its mission to be a kingdom of priests to the world. However, for the Israelites to succeed in the Land of Israel, they must see the *Torah* as the only compass to direct their lives.

The biblical episodes after our first entry into the land are well known. Our ancestors' triumphs and sins are all on public record. We learned the harsh reality of Leviticus (18:28) "So let not the land spew you out for defiling it as it spewed out the nation that came before you." Twice, we lost the privilege to be stewards of the Land of Israel and to fulfill our nation state mandate to be a light to the world. However, when the annals of history were ready to archive the Jewish people after the Holocaust, God kept His covenantal promise and gathered us from the four corners of the globe to come home. The year 1948 was a game changer. Biblical prophecies were and are being realized. We are now living in the birth pangs of the messianic era.

In our morning prayers, we recite a series of blessings over the *Torah* that include petitioning God to have a sweet tooth for His word, to study it without any ulterior motive and to have Him to teach it to us. They are some congregations that invoke the following liturgical prayer after the completion of these blessings: *May the Torah be my faith and El Shaddai my help. Blessed be the name of His glorious kingdom forever and all time.*

According to Jewish tradition, the neglect of not blessing the *Torah* before engaging in its study was one of the reasons for the destruction of the Temple.[3] This is deduced from the redundancy of words in Jeremiah (9:12) that talks about Israel not following God: "... Because they forsook the teaching I had set before them. They did not obey Me and they did not follow it [did not make a blessing before studying it]." Our inability to properly cherish God's greatest gift to the world, the *Torah*, led to our eventual exile from our land.

On Israel's Independence Day, Jews around the world recite Psalms 113–118 to express our gratitude to God for His Divine hand in helping establish the State of Israel. We have learned from our past and realize the privilege to see firsthand the land, people and *Torah* operating all together in our generation.

---

3. Babylonian Talmud Nedarim 81a

When Rabbi Tuly Weisz approached me about his intent to publish *The Israel Bible* that would highlight commentary about the special relationship between the land and people, I saw this project as another way to publicly demonstrate our appreciation to God for having the State of Israel. In addition, it is another educational tool to ensure biblical literacy. If we are to truly enjoy the Land of Israel, it is incumbent upon us to continually study the *Torah*. Isaiah once prophesied that the Jewish people would return to Zion with songs, "crowned with everlasting joy" (35:10). *The Israel Bible* provides us the lyrical content to express our joy in living in the land that God calls holy.

Rabbi Shlomo Riskin
Chief Rabbi of Efrat
Founder of the Center for Jewish-Christian
Understanding & Cooperation (cjcuc)

Introduction to Sefer Bereishit
The Book of Genesis

Introduction and commentary by Rabbi Tuly Weisz

Sefer Bereishit (Genesis) is the first of the Five Books of *Moshe. Sefer Bereishit* begins with a detailed description of the creation of the world, and continues with a brief account of the generations from *Adam* through *Avraham*. The remainder of the book focuses on the lives of the matriarchs and patriarchs, culminating with the story of the departure of the family of *Yaakov* from the land of Israel and their descent to Egypt.

Rabbi Shlomo Yitzchaki, the famed medieval commentator known by his acronym *Rashi*, asks a compelling question. If the *Torah* is essentially a book of law, why did God choose to start it with the stories of creation? Would it not have made more sense to begin with the first commandment given to the Jewish people? Quoting the verse from *Sefer Tehillim* (Psalms 111:6), "He revealed to His people His powerful works, in giving them the heritage of nations." *Rashi* explains that the Lord began His *Torah* with the account of the creation of the world in order to give the People of Israel a response to anyone who would accuse them of stealing the Land of Israel: Since *Hashem* is the Creator of the world, it is His prerogative to give it to whomever He chooses. Though He initially gave it to the seven nations of Canaan, when they were no longer worthy He chose to take it from them and to give it to the Children of Israel.

This theme of choice and choosing is present throughout the book. *Sefer Bereishit* is known as the book of creation. Most obviously, this refers to the description of the creation of the world, but beyond that it is about the creation of a people, the nation chosen by *Hashem* to be His representatives in the world and to carry out His mission of being a light unto the nations. In every generation described in *Sefer Bereishit*, there is a person or a group that stands out from the rest, and is chosen by God due to their morality and recognition of God. Once a person is chosen, the continuation of the narrative focuses on him and his offspring, often emphasizing their positive qualities. Thus, *Shet* is the chosen son of *Adam, Noach* is chosen to survive his entire generation, and the Bible then focuses on the descendants of *Noach*'s son *Shem*. Ultimately, *Hashem* chooses *Avraham*, his son *Yitzchak* and *Yitzchak*'s son *Yaakov*. With *Yaakov*, the process of choosing is complete and a nation is born.

As *Rashi* implies, the *Torah* is much more than a book of laws; it is the legacy of the Jewish people. It tells of the creation of a nation, chosen by God to be His emissaries of kindness, justice, goodness and recognition of the one true Creator. It starts with the creation of the world so that there would be no question that *Eretz Yisrael* belongs to them. From the very beginning of the world, *Hashem* intended for the People of Israel to be holy, to do His holy work in the holy Land of Israel, and from there, for their light to emanate to the entire world. May our study of *Sefer Bereishit* strengthen the chosenness within each of us and our appreciation for *Eretz Yisrael*.

Map of *Avraham*'s Journey

This map features *Avraham*'s journey to, and throughout, the Promised Land, as described in *Sefer Bereishit* (11:31–23:20).

1. *Avraham* is born in Ur of the Chaldeans (Genesis 11:26–31).
2. From Ur of the Chaldeans, *Avraham* travels with his family to Haran (Genesis 11:31–32).
3. From Haran, Avraham travels to Canaan, where he builds an altar to God in **Shechem** (Genesis 12:6–7).
4. In **Beit El**, Avraham builds an altar to God and calls out in His name (Genesis 12:8).
5. *Avraham* travels to Egypt in order to escape famine in Canaan (Genesis 12:10–20).
6. Upon returning from Egypt, Avraham moves to **Elonei Mamre**, just north of Chevron (Genesis 13:18).
7. *Avraham* moves once again and settles in Gerar (Genesis 20:1).
8. In **Be'er Sheva**, Avraham plants a tree and again calls out in God's name. He returns to Be'er Sheva after the binding of Isaac (Genesis 22:19).
9. When Sarah dies, Avraham buys the Cave of Machpelah, in **Chevron**, as a burial plot (Genesis 23:1–20).

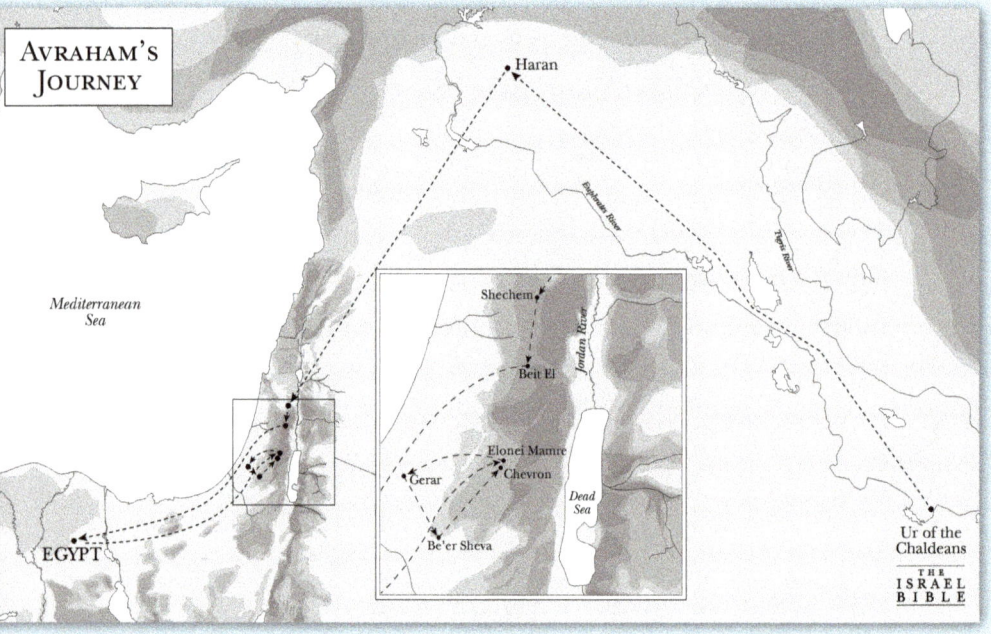

1 ¹ When *Hashem* began to create heaven
and earth –

א  בְּרֵאשִׁ֖ית בָּרָ֣א אֱלֹהִ֑ים אֵ֥ת הַשָּׁמַ֖יִם
וְאֵ֥ת הָאָֽרֶץ:

b'-ray-SHEET ba-RA e-lo-HEEM AYT ha-sha-MA-yim v'-AYT ha-A-retz

² the earth being unformed and void, with darkness
over the surface of the deep and a wind from
Hashem sweeping over the water –

ב וְהָאָ֗רֶץ הָיְתָ֥ה תֹ֙הוּ֙ וָבֹ֔הוּ וְחֹ֖שֶׁךְ עַל־פְּנֵ֣י
תְה֑וֹם וְר֣וּחַ אֱלֹהִ֔ים מְרַחֶ֖פֶת עַל־פְּנֵ֥י
הַמָּֽיִם:

³ *Hashem* said, "Let there be light"; and there was
light.

ג וַיֹּ֥אמֶר אֱלֹהִ֖ים יְהִ֣י א֑וֹר וַֽיְהִי־אֽוֹר:

⁴ *Hashem* saw that the light was good, and *Hashem*
separated the light from the darkness.

ד וַיַּ֧רְא אֱלֹהִ֛ים אֶת־הָא֖וֹר כִּי־ט֑וֹב וַיַּבְדֵּ֣ל
אֱלֹהִ֔ים בֵּ֥ין הָא֖וֹר וּבֵ֥ין הַחֹֽשֶׁךְ:

⁵ *Hashem* called the light Day, and the darkness He
called Night. And there was evening and there was
morning, a first day.

ה וַיִּקְרָ֨א אֱלֹהִ֤ים ׀ לָאוֹר֙ י֔וֹם וְלַחֹ֖שֶׁךְ קָ֣רָא
לָ֑יְלָה וַֽיְהִי־עֶ֥רֶב וַֽיְהִי־בֹ֖קֶר י֥וֹם אֶחָֽד:

⁶ *Hashem* said, "Let there be an expanse in the midst
of the water, that it may separate water from water."

ו וַיֹּ֣אמֶר אֱלֹהִ֔ים יְהִ֥י רָקִ֖יעַ בְּת֣וֹךְ הַמָּ֑יִם
וִיהִ֣י מַבְדִּ֔יל בֵּ֥ין מַ֖יִם לָמָֽיִם:

⁷ *Hashem* made the expanse, and it separated the
water which was below the expanse from the water
which was above the expanse. And it was so.

ז וַיַּ֣עַשׂ אֱלֹהִים֮ אֶת־הָרָקִיעַ֒ וַיַּבְדֵּ֗ל בֵּ֤ין
הַמַּ֙יִם֙ אֲשֶׁר֙ מִתַּ֣חַת לָרָקִ֔יעַ וּבֵ֣ין הַמַּ֔יִם
אֲשֶׁ֖ר מֵעַ֣ל לָרָקִ֑יעַ וַֽיְהִי־כֵֽן:

⁸ *Hashem* called the expanse Sky. And there was
evening and there was morning, a second day.

ח וַיִּקְרָ֧א אֱלֹהִ֛ים לָֽרָקִ֖יעַ שָׁמָ֑יִם וַֽיְהִי־עֶ֥רֶב
וַֽיְהִי־בֹ֖קֶר י֥וֹם שֵׁנִֽי:

⁹ *Hashem* said, "Let the water below the sky be
gathered into one area, that the dry land may
appear." And it was so.

ט וַיֹּ֣אמֶר אֱלֹהִ֗ים יִקָּו֨וּ הַמַּ֜יִם מִתַּ֤חַת
הַשָּׁמַ֙יִם֙ אֶל־מָק֣וֹם אֶחָ֔ד וְתֵרָאֶ֖ה
הַיַּבָּשָׁ֑ה וַֽיְהִי־כֵֽן:

¹⁰ *Hashem* called the dry land Earth, and the gathering
of waters He called Seas. And *Hashem* saw that this
was good.

י וַיִּקְרָ֨א אֱלֹהִ֤ים ׀ לַיַּבָּשָׁה֙ אֶ֔רֶץ וּלְמִקְוֵ֥ה
הַמַּ֖יִם קָרָ֣א יַמִּ֑ים וַיַּ֥רְא אֱלֹהִ֖ים כִּי־טֽוֹב:

לב
ישראל
בראשית

1:1 When *Hashem* began to create heaven and earth If the Bible
is essentially a book of law, why does it begin with stories of
Genesis? Would it not make more sense to skip the stories and
start with the legal sections of the *Torah*? *Rashi*, the famed medieval
commentator, answers this question with an es-
sential lesson that should inform our reading of
the entire *Tanakh*. According to *Rashi*, one day the
nations of the world would accuse the Jewish
People of stealing *Eretz Yisrael*. In response, the
Jews will point to the *Torah* which begins by telling us that God created the heaven and the earth.
Since *Hashem* is the Creator of the world, He may
give the land to whomever He wishes, and it is the
divine will that the Land of Israel will belong
to the People of Israel.

1:1 When *Hashem* began The
first word in the *Torah* is *Berei-*
shit (בראשית), which begins
with the letter *bet* (ב), while the last
word in the *Torah* is *Yisrael* (ישראל), 'Israel,' which ends with the letter *lamed* (ל).
Together, these two letters spell the
word *lev* (לב), which means 'heart' in
Hebrew. The first lesson hinted at in the
very first letter of the *Tanakh* is that
Torah is the heart of the People of Israel,
and the ultimate expression of *Hashem's*
love for us. By studying the *Torah*, from
the first letter through the last, we can
access the 'heart' of *Hashem*.

"Heaven and Earth" – Dead Sea landscape

11 And *Hashem* said, "Let the earth sprout vegetation: seed-bearing plants, fruit trees of every kind on earth that bear fruit with the seed in it." And it was so.

יא וַיֹּאמֶר אֱלֹהִים תַּדְשֵׁא הָאָרֶץ דֶּשֶׁא עֵשֶׂב מַזְרִיעַ זֶרַע עֵץ פְּרִי עֹשֶׂה פְּרִי לְמִינוֹ אֲשֶׁר זַרְעוֹ־בוֹ עַל־הָאָרֶץ וַיְהִי־ כֵן:

12 The earth brought forth vegetation: seed-bearing plants of every kind, and trees of every kind bearing fruit with the seed in it. And *Hashem* saw that this was good.

יב וַתּוֹצֵא הָאָרֶץ דֶּשֶׁא עֵשֶׂב מַזְרִיעַ זֶרַע לְמִינֵהוּ וְעֵץ עֹשֶׂה־פְּרִי אֲשֶׁר זַרְעוֹ־בוֹ לְמִינֵהוּ וַיַּרְא אֱלֹהִים כִּי־טוֹב:

13 And there was evening and there was morning, a third day.

יג וַיְהִי־עֶרֶב וַיְהִי־בֹקֶר יוֹם שְׁלִישִׁי:

14 *Hashem* said, "Let there be lights in the expanse of the sky to separate day from night; they shall serve as signs for the set times – the days and the years;

יד וַיֹּאמֶר אֱלֹהִים יְהִי מְאֹרֹת בִּרְקִיעַ הַשָּׁמַיִם לְהַבְדִּיל בֵּין הַיּוֹם וּבֵין הַלָּיְלָה וְהָיוּ לְאֹתֹת וּלְמוֹעֲדִים וּלְיָמִים וְשָׁנִים:

15 and they serve as lights in the expanse of the sky to shine upon the earth." And it was so.

טו וְהָיוּ לִמְאוֹרֹת בִּרְקִיעַ הַשָּׁמַיִם לְהָאִיר עַל־הָאָרֶץ וַיְהִי־כֵן:

16 *Hashem* made the two great lights, the greater light to dominate the day and the lesser light to dominate the night, and the stars.

טז וַיַּעַשׂ אֱלֹהִים אֶת־שְׁנֵי הַמְּאֹרֹת הַגְּדֹלִים אֶת־הַמָּאוֹר הַגָּדֹל לְמֶמְשֶׁלֶת הַיּוֹם וְאֶת־הַמָּאוֹר הַקָּטֹן לְמֶמְשֶׁלֶת הַלַּיְלָה וְאֵת הַכּוֹכָבִים:

17 And *Hashem* set them in the expanse of the sky to shine upon the earth,

יז וַיִּתֵּן אֹתָם אֱלֹהִים בִּרְקִיעַ הַשָּׁמַיִם לְהָאִיר עַל־הָאָרֶץ:

18 to dominate the day and the night, and to separate light from darkness. And *Hashem* saw that this was good.

יח וְלִמְשֹׁל בַּיּוֹם וּבַלַּיְלָה וּלְהַבְדִּיל בֵּין הָאוֹר וּבֵין הַחֹשֶׁךְ וַיַּרְא אֱלֹהִים כִּי־טוֹב:

19 And there was evening and there was morning, a fourth day.

יט וַיְהִי־עֶרֶב וַיְהִי־בֹקֶר יוֹם רְבִיעִי:

20 *Hashem* said, "Let the waters bring forth swarms of living creatures, and birds that fly above the earth across the expanse of the sky."

כ וַיֹּאמֶר אֱלֹהִים יִשְׁרְצוּ הַמַּיִם שֶׁרֶץ נֶפֶשׁ חַיָּה וְעוֹף יְעוֹפֵף עַל־הָאָרֶץ עַל־פְּנֵי רְקִיעַ הַשָּׁמָיִם:

21 *Hashem* created the great sea monsters, and all the living creatures of every kind that creep, which the waters brought forth in swarms, and all the winged birds of every kind. And *Hashem* saw that this was good.

כא וַיִּבְרָא אֱלֹהִים אֶת־הַתַּנִּינִם הַגְּדֹלִים וְאֵת כָּל־נֶפֶשׁ הַחַיָּה הָרֹמֶשֶׂת אֲשֶׁר שָׁרְצוּ הַמַּיִם לְמִינֵהֶם וְאֵת כָּל־עוֹף כָּנָף לְמִינֵהוּ וַיַּרְא אֱלֹהִים כִּי־טוֹב:

22 *Hashem* blessed them, saying, "Be fertile and increase, fill the waters in the seas, and let the birds increase on the earth."

כב וַיְבָרֶךְ אֹתָם אֱלֹהִים לֵאמֹר פְּרוּ וּרְבוּ וּמִלְאוּ אֶת־הַמַּיִם בַּיַּמִּים וְהָעוֹף יִרֶב בָּאָרֶץ:

23 And there was evening and there was morning, a fifth day.

כג וַיְהִי־עֶרֶב וַיְהִי־בֹקֶר יוֹם חֲמִישִׁי:

24 *Hashem* said, "Let the earth bring forth every kind of living creature: cattle, creeping things, and wild beasts of every kind." And it was so.

כד וַיֹּאמֶר אֱלֹהִים תּוֹצֵא הָאָרֶץ נֶפֶשׁ חַיָּה לְמִינָהּ בְּהֵמָה וָרֶמֶשׂ וְחַיְתוֹ־אֶרֶץ לְמִינָהּ וַיְהִי־כֵן:

25 *Hashem* made wild beasts of every kind and cattle of every kind, and all kinds of creeping things of the earth. And *Hashem* saw that this was good.

כה וַיַּעַשׂ אֱלֹהִים אֶת־חַיַּת הָאָרֶץ לְמִינָהּ וְאֶת־הַבְּהֵמָה לְמִינָהּ וְאֵת כָּל־רֶמֶשׂ הָאֲדָמָה לְמִינֵהוּ וַיַּרְא אֱלֹהִים כִּי־טוֹב:

26 And *Hashem* said, "Let us make man in our image, after our likeness. They shall rule the fish of the sea, the birds of the sky, the cattle, the whole earth, and all the creeping things that creep on earth."

כו וַיֹּאמֶר אֱלֹהִים נַעֲשֶׂה אָדָם בְּצַלְמֵנוּ כִּדְמוּתֵנוּ וְיִרְדּוּ בִדְגַת הַיָּם וּבְעוֹף הַשָּׁמַיִם וּבַבְּהֵמָה וּבְכָל־הָאָרֶץ וּבְכָל־הָרֶמֶשׂ הָרֹמֵשׂ עַל־הָאָרֶץ:

27 And *Hashem* created man in His image, in the image of *Hashem* He created him; male and female He created them.

כז וַיִּבְרָא אֱלֹהִים אֶת־הָאָדָם בְּצַלְמוֹ בְּצֶלֶם אֱלֹהִים בָּרָא אֹתוֹ זָכָר וּנְקֵבָה בָּרָא אֹתָם:

28 *Hashem* blessed them and *Hashem* said to them, "Be fertile and increase, fill the earth and master it; and rule the fish of the sea, the birds of the sky, and all the living things that creep on earth."

כח וַיְבָרֶךְ אֹתָם אֱלֹהִים וַיֹּאמֶר לָהֶם אֱלֹהִים פְּרוּ וּרְבוּ וּמִלְאוּ אֶת־הָאָרֶץ וְכִבְשֻׁהָ וּרְדוּ בִּדְגַת הַיָּם וּבְעוֹף הַשָּׁמַיִם וּבְכָל־חַיָּה הָרֹמֶשֶׂת עַל־הָאָרֶץ:

29 *Hashem* said, "See, I give you every seed-bearing plant that is upon all the earth, and every tree that has seed-bearing fruit; they shall be yours for food.

כט וַיֹּאמֶר אֱלֹהִים הִנֵּה נָתַתִּי לָכֶם אֶת־כָּל־עֵשֶׂב זֹרֵעַ זֶרַע אֲשֶׁר עַל־פְּנֵי כָל־הָאָרֶץ וְאֶת־כָּל־הָעֵץ אֲשֶׁר־בּוֹ פְרִי־עֵץ זֹרֵעַ זָרַע לָכֶם יִהְיֶה לְאָכְלָה:

30 And to all the animals on land, to all the birds of the sky, and to everything that creeps on earth, in which there is the breath of life, [I give] all the green plants for food." And it was so.

ל וּלְכָל־חַיַּת הָאָרֶץ וּלְכָל־עוֹף הַשָּׁמַיִם וּלְכֹל רוֹמֵשׂ עַל־הָאָרֶץ אֲשֶׁר־בּוֹ נֶפֶשׁ חַיָּה אֶת־כָּל־יֶרֶק עֵשֶׂב לְאָכְלָה וַיְהִי־כֵן:

31 And *Hashem* saw all that He had made, and found it very good. And there was evening and there was morning, the sixth day.

לא וַיַּרְא אֱלֹהִים אֶת־כָּל־אֲשֶׁר עָשָׂה וְהִנֵּה־טוֹב מְאֹד וַיְהִי־עֶרֶב וַיְהִי־בֹקֶר יוֹם הַשִּׁשִּׁי:

2 ¹ The heaven and the earth were finished, and all their array.

ב א וַיְכֻלּוּ הַשָּׁמַיִם וְהָאָרֶץ וְכָל־צְבָאָם:

2 On the seventh day *Hashem* finished the work that He had been doing, and He ceased on the seventh day from all the work that He had done.

ב וַיְכַל אֱלֹהִים בַּיּוֹם הַשְּׁבִיעִי מְלַאכְתּוֹ אֲשֶׁר עָשָׂה וַיִּשְׁבֹּת בַּיּוֹם הַשְּׁבִיעִי מִכָּל־מְלַאכְתּוֹ אֲשֶׁר עָשָׂה:

3 And *Hashem* blessed the seventh day and declared it holy, because on it *Hashem* ceased from all the work of creation that He had done.

ג וַיְבָרֶךְ אֱלֹהִים אֶת־יוֹם הַשְּׁבִיעִי וַיְקַדֵּשׁ אֹתוֹ כִּי בוֹ שָׁבַת מִכָּל־מְלַאכְתּוֹ אֲשֶׁר־בָּרָא אֱלֹהִים לַעֲשׂוֹת:

4 Such is the story of heaven and earth when they were created. When *Hashem* made earth and heaven –

ד אֵלֶּה תוֹלְדוֹת הַשָּׁמַיִם וְהָאָרֶץ בְּהִבָּרְאָם בְּיוֹם עֲשׂוֹת יְהֹוָה אֱלֹהִים אֶרֶץ וְשָׁמָיִם:

5 when no shrub of the field was yet on earth and
no grasses of the field had yet sprouted, because
Hashem had not sent rain upon the earth and there
was no man to till the soil,

ה וְכֹל שִׂיחַ הַשָּׂדֶה טֶרֶם יִהְיֶה בָאָרֶץ
וְכָל־עֵשֶׂב הַשָּׂדֶה טֶרֶם יִצְמָח כִּי לֹא
הִמְטִיר יְהֹוָה אֱלֹהִים עַל־הָאָרֶץ וְאָדָם
אַיִן לַעֲבֹד אֶת־הָאֲדָמָה:

> *v'-KHOL SEE-akh ha-sa-DEH TE-rem yih-YEH va-A-retz v'-khol*
> *AY-sev ha-sa-DEH TE-rem yitz-MAKH KEE LO him-TEER a-do-NAI*
> *e-lo-HEEM al ha-A-retz v'-a-DAM A-yin la-a-VOD et ha-a-da-MAH*

6 but a flow would well up from the ground and water
the whole surface of the earth –

ו וְאֵד יַעֲלֶה מִן־הָאָרֶץ וְהִשְׁקָה אֶת־כָּל־
פְּנֵי הָאֲדָמָה:

7 *Hashem* formed man from the dust of the earth. He
blew into his nostrils the breath of life, and man
became a living being.

ז וַיִּיצֶר יְהֹוָה אֱלֹהִים אֶת־הָאָדָם עָפָר
מִן־הָאֲדָמָה וַיִּפַּח בְּאַפָּיו נִשְׁמַת חַיִּים
וַיְהִי הָאָדָם לְנֶפֶשׁ חַיָּה:

8 *Hashem* planted a garden in Eden, in the east, and
placed there the man whom He had formed.

ח וַיִּטַּע יְהֹוָה אֱלֹהִים גַּן־בְּעֵדֶן מִקֶּדֶם
וַיָּשֶׂם שָׁם אֶת־הָאָדָם אֲשֶׁר יָצָר:

9 And from the ground *Hashem* caused to grow
every tree that was pleasing to the sight and good
for food, with the tree of life in the middle of the
garden, and the tree of knowledge of good and bad.

ט וַיַּצְמַח יְהֹוָה אֱלֹהִים מִן־הָאֲדָמָה כָּל־
עֵץ נֶחְמָד לְמַרְאֶה וְטוֹב לְמַאֲכָל וְעֵץ
הַחַיִּים בְּתוֹךְ הַגָּן וְעֵץ הַדַּעַת טוֹב וָרָע:

10 A river issues from Eden to water the garden, and it
then divides and becomes four branches.

י וְנָהָר יֹצֵא מֵעֵדֶן לְהַשְׁקוֹת אֶת־הַגָּן
וּמִשָּׁם יִפָּרֵד וְהָיָה לְאַרְבָּעָה רָאשִׁים:

11 The name of the first is Pishon, the one that winds
through the whole land of Havilah, where the gold
is.

יא שֵׁם הָאֶחָד פִּישׁוֹן הוּא הַסֹּבֵב אֵת כָּל־
אֶרֶץ הַחֲוִילָה אֲשֶׁר־שָׁם הַזָּהָב:

12 The gold of that land is good; bdellium is there, and
lapis lazuli.

יב וּזֲהַב הָאָרֶץ הַהִוא טוֹב שָׁם הַבְּדֹלַח
וְאֶבֶן הַשֹּׁהַם:

13 The name of the second river is Gichon, the one
that winds through the whole land of Cush.

יג וְשֵׁם־הַנָּהָר הַשֵּׁנִי גִּיחוֹן הוּא הַסּוֹבֵב
אֵת כָּל־אֶרֶץ כּוּשׁ:

14 The name of the third river is Tigris, the one that
flows east of Assyria. And the fourth river is the
Euphrates.

יד וְשֵׁם הַנָּהָר הַשְּׁלִישִׁי חִדֶּקֶל הוּא הַהֹלֵךְ
קִדְמַת אַשּׁוּר וְהַנָּהָר הָרְבִיעִי הוּא
פְרָת:

**2:5 Because *Hashem* had not sent rain upon the
earth** The land was poised to allow its seeds to sprout,
but God did not bring forth rain to allow them to grow, because there was no man yet to work the land. *Hashem* did not bring rain until there was a person who could recognize the necessity for rain, and, says *Rashi*, pray for rain. During its short rainy season, *Eretz Yisrael* is dependent on adequate rainfall to produce yearly crops. It is God's design that the Jews living in Israel are to strengthen their relationship with Him through daily prayer requesting adequate rainfall and a successful agricultural season. Since *Hashem* desires a deep relationship with man, He incorporated the need for prayer, the ultimate form of dialogue between man and God, within the natural order.

Droplets on grass near *Beit Shemesh*

15 *Hashem* took the man and placed him in the garden of Eden, to till it and tend it.

טו וַיִּקַּח יְהֹוָה אֱלֹהִים אֶת־הָאָדָם וַיַּנִּחֵהוּ בְגַן־עֵדֶן לְעׇבְדָהּ וּלְשׇׁמְרָהּ׃

16 And *Hashem* commanded the man, saying, "Of every tree of the garden you are free to eat;

טז וַיְצַו יְהֹוָה אֱלֹהִים עַל־הָאָדָם לֵאמֹר מִכֹּל עֵץ־הַגָּן אָכֹל תֹּאכֵל׃

17 but as for the tree of knowledge of good and bad, you must not eat of it; for as soon as you eat of it, you shall die."

יז וּמֵעֵץ הַדַּעַת טוֹב וָרָע לֹא תֹאכַל מִמֶּנּוּ כִּי בְּיוֹם אֲכׇלְךָ מִמֶּנּוּ מוֹת תָּמוּת׃

18 *Hashem* said, "It is not good for man to be alone; I will make a fitting helper for him."

יח וַיֹּאמֶר יְהֹוָה אֱלֹהִים לֹא־טוֹב הֱיוֹת הָאָדָם לְבַדּוֹ אֶעֱשֶׂה־לּוֹ עֵזֶר כְּנֶגְדּוֹ׃

19 And *Hashem* formed out of the earth all the wild beasts and all the birds of the sky, and brought them to the man to see what he would call them; and whatever the man called each living creature, that would be its name.

יט וַיִּצֶר יְהֹוָה אֱלֹהִים מִן־הָאֲדָמָה כׇּל־חַיַּת הַשָּׂדֶה וְאֵת כׇּל־עוֹף הַשָּׁמַיִם וַיָּבֵא אֶל־הָאָדָם לִרְאוֹת מַה־יִּקְרָא־לוֹ וְכֹל אֲשֶׁר יִקְרָא־לוֹ הָאָדָם נֶפֶשׁ חַיָּה הוּא שְׁמוֹ׃

20 And the man gave names to all the cattle and to the birds of the sky and to all the wild beasts; but for *Adam* no fitting helper was found.

כ וַיִּקְרָא הָאָדָם שֵׁמוֹת לְכׇל־הַבְּהֵמָה וּלְעוֹף הַשָּׁמַיִם וּלְכֹל חַיַּת הַשָּׂדֶה וּלְאָדָם לֹא־מָצָא עֵזֶר כְּנֶגְדּוֹ׃

21 So *Hashem* cast a deep sleep upon the man; and, while he slept, He took one of his ribs and closed up the flesh at that spot.

כא וַיַּפֵּל יְהֹוָה אֱלֹהִים תַּרְדֵּמָה עַל־הָאָדָם וַיִּישָׁן וַיִּקַּח אַחַת מִצַּלְעֹתָיו וַיִּסְגֹּר בָּשָׂר תַּחְתֶּנָּה׃

22 And *Hashem* fashioned the rib that He had taken from the man into a woman; and He brought her to the man.

כב וַיִּבֶן יְהֹוָה אֱלֹהִים אֶת־הַצֵּלָע אֲשֶׁר־לָקַח מִן־הָאָדָם לְאִשָּׁה וַיְבִאֶהָ אֶל־הָאָדָם׃

23 Then the man said, "This one at last Is bone of my bones And flesh of my flesh. This one shall be called Woman, For from man was she taken."

כג וַיֹּאמֶר הָאָדָם זֹאת הַפַּעַם עֶצֶם מֵעֲצָמַי וּבָשָׂר מִבְּשָׂרִי לְזֹאת יִקָּרֵא אִשָּׁה כִּי מֵאִישׁ לֻקְחָה־זֹּאת׃

24 Hence a man leaves his father and mother and clings to his wife, so that they become one flesh.

כד עַל־כֵּן יַעֲזׇב־אִישׁ אֶת־אָבִיו וְאֶת־אִמּוֹ וְדָבַק בְּאִשְׁתּוֹ וְהָיוּ לְבָשָׂר אֶחָד׃

25 The two of them were naked, the man and his wife, yet they felt no shame.

כה וַיִּהְיוּ שְׁנֵיהֶם עֲרוּמִּים הָאָדָם וְאִשְׁתּוֹ וְלֹא יִתְבֹּשָׁשׁוּ׃

3 1 Now the serpent was the shrewdest of all the wild beasts that *Hashem* had made. He said to the woman, "Did *Hashem* really say: You shall not eat of any tree of the garden?"

א וְהַנָּחָשׁ הָיָה עָרוּם מִכֹּל חַיַּת הַשָּׂדֶה אֲשֶׁר עָשָׂה יְהֹוָה אֱלֹהִים וַיֹּאמֶר אֶל־הָאִשָּׁה אַף כִּי־אָמַר אֱלֹהִים לֹא תֹאכְלוּ מִכֹּל עֵץ הַגָּן׃

2 The woman replied to the serpent, "We may eat of the fruit of the other trees of the garden.

ב וַתֹּאמֶר הָאִשָּׁה אֶל־הַנָּחָשׁ מִפְּרִי עֵץ־הַגָּן נֹאכֵל׃

3 It is only about fruit of the tree in the middle of the garden that *Hashem* said: 'You shall not eat of it or touch it, lest you die.'"

ג וּמִפְּרִי הָעֵץ אֲשֶׁר בְּתוֹךְ־הַגָּן אָמַר אֱלֹהִים לֹא תֹאכְלוּ מִמֶּנּוּ וְלֹא תִגְּעוּ בּוֹ פֶּן־תְּמֻתוּן׃

4 And the serpent said to the woman, "You are not going to die,

ד וַיֹּאמֶר הַנָּחָשׁ אֶל־הָאִשָּׁה לֹא־מוֹת תְּמֻתוּן׃

5 but *Hashem* knows that as soon as you eat of it your eyes will be opened and you will be like divine beings who know good and bad."

ה כִּי יֹדֵעַ אֱלֹהִים כִּי בְּיוֹם אֲכָלְכֶם מִמֶּנּוּ וְנִפְקְחוּ עֵינֵיכֶם וִהְיִיתֶם כֵּאלֹהִים יֹדְעֵי טוֹב וָרָע:

6 When the woman saw that the tree was good for eating and a delight to the eyes, and that the tree was desirable as a source of wisdom, she took of its fruit and ate. She also gave some to her husband, and he ate.

ו וַתֵּרֶא הָאִשָּׁה כִּי טוֹב הָעֵץ לְמַאֲכָל וְכִי תַאֲוָה־הוּא לָעֵינַיִם וְנֶחְמָד הָעֵץ לְהַשְׂכִּיל וַתִּקַּח מִפִּרְיוֹ וַתֹּאכַל וַתִּתֵּן גַּם־לְאִישָׁהּ עִמָּהּ וַיֹּאכַל:

7 Then the eyes of both of them were opened and they perceived that they were naked; and they sewed together fig leaves and made themselves loincloths.

ז וַתִּפָּקַחְנָה עֵינֵי שְׁנֵיהֶם וַיֵּדְעוּ כִּי עֵירֻמִּם הֵם וַיִּתְפְּרוּ עֲלֵה תְאֵנָה וַיַּעֲשׂוּ לָהֶם חֲגֹרֹת:

8 They heard the sound of *Hashem* moving about in the garden at the breezy time of day; and the man and his wife hid from *Hashem* among the trees of the garden.

ח וַיִּשְׁמְעוּ אֶת־קוֹל יְהוָה אֱלֹהִים מִתְהַלֵּךְ בַּגָּן לְרוּחַ הַיּוֹם וַיִּתְחַבֵּא הָאָדָם וְאִשְׁתּוֹ מִפְּנֵי יְהוָה אֱלֹהִים בְּתוֹךְ עֵץ הַגָּן:

9 *Hashem* called out to the man and said to him, "Where are you?"

ט וַיִּקְרָא יְהוָה אֱלֹהִים אֶל־הָאָדָם וַיֹּאמֶר לוֹ אַיֶּכָּה:

10 He replied, "I heard the sound of You in the garden, and I was afraid because I was naked, so I hid."

י וַיֹּאמֶר אֶת־קֹלְךָ שָׁמַעְתִּי בַּגָּן וָאִירָא כִּי־עֵירֹם אָנֹכִי וָאֵחָבֵא:

11 Then He asked, "Who told you that you were naked? Did you eat of the tree from which I had forbidden you to eat?"

יא וַיֹּאמֶר מִי הִגִּיד לְךָ כִּי עֵירֹם אָתָּה הֲמִן־הָעֵץ אֲשֶׁר צִוִּיתִיךָ לְבִלְתִּי אֲכָל־מִמֶּנּוּ אָכָלְתָּ:

12 The man said, "The woman You put at my side – she gave me of the tree, and I ate."

יב וַיֹּאמֶר הָאָדָם הָאִשָּׁה אֲשֶׁר נָתַתָּה עִמָּדִי הִוא נָתְנָה־לִּי מִן־הָעֵץ וָאֹכֵל:

13 And *Hashem* said to the woman, "What is this you have done!" The woman replied, "The serpent duped me, and I ate."

יג וַיֹּאמֶר יְהוָה אֱלֹהִים לָאִשָּׁה מַה־זֹּאת עָשִׂית וַתֹּאמֶר הָאִשָּׁה הַנָּחָשׁ הִשִּׁיאַנִי וָאֹכֵל:

14 Then *Hashem* said to the serpent, "Because you did this, More cursed shall you be Than all cattle And all the wild beasts: On your belly shall you crawl And dirt shall you eat All the days of your life.

יד וַיֹּאמֶר יְהוָה אֱלֹהִים אֶל־הַנָּחָשׁ כִּי עָשִׂיתָ זֹּאת אָרוּר אַתָּה מִכָּל־הַבְּהֵמָה וּמִכֹּל חַיַּת הַשָּׂדֶה עַל־גְּחֹנְךָ תֵלֵךְ וְעָפָר תֹּאכַל כָּל־יְמֵי חַיֶּיךָ:

15 I will put enmity Between you and the woman, And between your offspring and hers; They shall strike at your head, And you shall strike at their heel."

טו וְאֵיבָה אָשִׁית בֵּינְךָ וּבֵין הָאִשָּׁה וּבֵין זַרְעֲךָ וּבֵין זַרְעָהּ הוּא יְשׁוּפְךָ רֹאשׁ וְאַתָּה תְּשׁוּפֶנּוּ עָקֵב:

16 And to the woman He said, "I will make most severe Your pangs in childbearing; In pain shall you bear children. Yet your urge shall be for your husband, And he shall rule over you."

טז אֶל־הָאִשָּׁה אָמַר הַרְבָּה אַרְבֶּה עִצְּבוֹנֵךְ וְהֵרֹנֵךְ בְּעֶצֶב תֵּלְדִי בָנִים וְאֶל־אִישֵׁךְ תְּשׁוּקָתֵךְ וְהוּא יִמְשָׁל־בָּךְ:

17 To *Adam* He said, "Because you did as your wife said and ate of the tree about which I commanded you, 'You shall not eat of it,' Cursed be the ground because of you; By toil shall you eat of it All the days of your life:

יז וּלְאָדָם אָמַר כִּי־שָׁמַעְתָּ לְקוֹל אִשְׁתֶּךָ וַתֹּאכַל מִן־הָעֵץ אֲשֶׁר צִוִּיתִיךָ לֵאמֹר לֹא תֹאכַל מִמֶּנּוּ אֲרוּרָה הָאֲדָמָה בַּעֲבוּרֶךָ בְּעִצָּבוֹן תֹּאכֲלֶנָּה כֹּל יְמֵי חַיֶּיךָ:

ul-a-DAM a-MAR KEE sha-MA-ta l'-KOL ish-TE-kha va-TO-khal min ha-AYTZ a-SHER tzi-vee-TEE-kha lay-MOR LO to-KHAL mi-ME-nu a-ru-RAH ha-a-da-MAH ba-a-vu-RE-kha b'-i-tza-VON to-kh'-LE-na KOL y'-MAY kha-YE-kha

18 Thorns and thistles shall it sprout for you. But your food shall be the grasses of the field;

יח וְקוֹץ וְדַרְדַּר תַּצְמִיחַ לָךְ וְאָכַלְתָּ אֶת־עֵשֶׂב הַשָּׂדֶה:

19 By the sweat of your brow Shall you get bread to eat, Until you return to the ground – For from it you were taken. For dust you are, And to dust you shall return."

יט בְּזֵעַת אַפֶּיךָ תֹּאכַל לֶחֶם עַד שׁוּבְךָ אֶל־הָאֲדָמָה כִּי מִמֶּנָּה לֻקָּחְתָּ כִּי־עָפָר אַתָּה וְאֶל־עָפָר תָּשׁוּב:

20 The man named his wife *Chava*, because she was the mother of all the living.

כ וַיִּקְרָא הָאָדָם שֵׁם אִשְׁתּוֹ חַוָּה כִּי הִוא הָיְתָה אֵם כָּל־חָי:

21 And *Hashem* made garments of skins for *Adam* and his wife, and clothed them.

כא וַיַּעַשׂ יְהֹוָה אֱלֹהִים לְאָדָם וּלְאִשְׁתּוֹ כָּתְנוֹת עוֹר וַיַּלְבִּשֵׁם:

22 And *Hashem* said, "Now that the man has become like one of us, knowing good and bad, what if he should stretch out his hand and take also from the tree of life and eat, and live forever!"

כב וַיֹּאמֶר יְהֹוָה אֱלֹהִים הֵן הָאָדָם הָיָה כְּאַחַד מִמֶּנּוּ לָדַעַת טוֹב וָרָע וְעַתָּה פֶּן־יִשְׁלַח יָדוֹ וְלָקַח גַּם מֵעֵץ הַחַיִּים וְאָכַל וָחַי לְעֹלָם:

23 So *Hashem* banished him from the garden of Eden, to till the soil from which he was taken.

כג וַיְשַׁלְּחֵהוּ יְהֹוָה אֱלֹהִים מִגַּן־עֵדֶן לַעֲבֹד אֶת־הָאֲדָמָה אֲשֶׁר לֻקַּח מִשָּׁם:

24 He drove the man out, and stationed east of the garden of Eden the cherubim and the fiery ever-turning sword, to guard the way to the tree of life.

כד וַיְגָרֶשׁ אֶת־הָאָדָם וַיַּשְׁכֵּן מִקֶּדֶם לְגַן־עֵדֶן אֶת־הַכְּרֻבִים וְאֵת לַהַט הַחֶרֶב הַמִּתְהַפֶּכֶת לִשְׁמֹר אֶת־דֶּרֶךְ עֵץ הַחַיִּים:

4 1 Now the man knew his wife *Chava*, and she conceived and bore Cain, saying, "I have gained a male child with the help of *Hashem*."

ד א וְהָאָדָם יָדַע אֶת־חַוָּה אִשְׁתּוֹ וַתַּהַר וַתֵּלֶד אֶת־קַיִן וַתֹּאמֶר קָנִיתִי אִישׁ אֶת־יְהֹוָה:

Blooming field in southern Israel

3:17 Cursed be the ground because of you The land is cursed *ba'avurecha* (בעבורך), translated here as 'because of you.' However, according to Rabbi Samson Raphael Hirsch, a prolific writer and leader of Orthodox Jewry in 19th century Germany, *ba'avurecha* means 'for your sake,' in order to rectify man's actions. Following *Adam's* sin, the land's prosperity became a means of measuring man's adherence to *Hashem*; for the Jewish nation, this means following the commandments and keeping God's *Torah*. When they do so, *Hashem* shows His approval through the land's flourishing. This is especially true in *Eretz Yisrael*. Scholars and historians alike note that while the Jews were in exile, the Land of Israel lay fallow and uninhabitable until they returned, and in just a short time the Jews of Israel, following the commandments set out in the *Torah*, have turned a wasteland into a blooming, prosperous country.

2 She then bore his brother Abel. Abel became a keeper of sheep, and Cain became a tiller of the soil.

3 In the course of time, Cain brought an offering to *Hashem* from the fruit of the soil;

4 and Abel, for his part, brought the choicest of the firstlings of his flock. *Hashem* paid heed to Abel and his offering,

5 but to Cain and his offering He paid no heed. Cain was much distressed and his face fell.

6 And *Hashem* said to Cain, "Why are you distressed, And why is your face fallen?

7 Surely, if you do right, There is uplift. But if you do not do right Sin couches at the door; Its urge is toward you, Yet you can be its master."

8 Cain said to his brother Abel and when they were in the field, Cain set upon his brother Abel and killed him.

9 *Hashem* said to Cain, "Where is your brother Abel?" And he said, "I do not know. Am I my brother's keeper?"

10 Then He said, "What have you done? Hark, your brother's blood cries out to Me from the ground!

11 Therefore, you shall be more cursed than the ground, which opened its mouth to receive your brother's blood from your hand.

12 If you till the soil, it shall no longer yield its strength to you. You shall become a ceaseless wanderer on earth."

ב וַתֹּסֶף לָלֶדֶת אֶת־אָחִיו אֶת־הָבֶל וַיְהִי־
הֶבֶל רֹעֵה צֹאן וְקַיִן הָיָה עֹבֵד אֲדָמָה:

ג וַיְהִי מִקֵּץ יָמִים וַיָּבֵא קַיִן מִפְּרִי
הָאֲדָמָה מִנְחָה לַיהוָה:

ד וְהֶבֶל הֵבִיא גַם־הוּא מִבְּכֹרוֹת צֹאנוֹ
וּמֵחֶלְבֵהֶן וַיִּשַׁע יְהוָה אֶל־הֶבֶל וְאֶל־
מִנְחָתוֹ:

ה וְאֶל־קַיִן וְאֶל־מִנְחָתוֹ לֹא שָׁעָה וַיִּחַר
לְקַיִן מְאֹד וַיִּפְּלוּ פָּנָיו:

ו וַיֹּאמֶר יְהוָה אֶל־קָיִן לָמָּה חָרָה לָךְ
וְלָמָּה נָפְלוּ פָנֶיךָ:

ז הֲלוֹא אִם־תֵּיטִיב שְׂאֵת וְאִם לֹא תֵיטִיב
לַפֶּתַח חַטָּאת רֹבֵץ וְאֵלֶיךָ תְּשׁוּקָתוֹ
וְאַתָּה תִּמְשָׁל־בּוֹ:

ח וַיֹּאמֶר קַיִן אֶל־הֶבֶל אָחִיו וַיְהִי בִּהְיוֹתָם
בַּשָּׂדֶה וַיָּקָם קַיִן אֶל־הֶבֶל אָחִיו
וַיַּהַרְגֵהוּ:

ט וַיֹּאמֶר יְהוָה אֶל־קַיִן אֵי הֶבֶל אָחִיךָ
וַיֹּאמֶר לֹא יָדַעְתִּי הֲשֹׁמֵר אָחִי אָנֹכִי:

י וַיֹּאמֶר מֶה עָשִׂיתָ קוֹל דְּמֵי אָחִיךָ
צֹעֲקִים אֵלַי מִן־הָאֲדָמָה:

יא וְעַתָּה אָרוּר אָתָּה מִן־הָאֲדָמָה אֲשֶׁר
פָּצְתָה אֶת־פִּיהָ לָקַחַת אֶת־דְּמֵי אָחִיךָ
מִיָּדֶךָ:

יב כִּי תַעֲבֹד אֶת־הָאֲדָמָה לֹא־תֹסֵף תֵּת־
כֹּחָהּ לָךְ נָע וָנָד תִּהְיֶה בָאָרֶץ:

KEE ta-a-VOD et HA-a-da-MAH lo to-SAYF tayt ko-KHAH
LAKH NA va-NAD tih-YEH va-A-retz

The Israeli parliament building (Knesset) in Yerushalayim

 4:12 You shall become a ceaseless wanderer on earth The Hebrew for 'ceaseless wanderer' in this verse is *na v'nad* (נע ונד). Rabbi Samson Raphael Hirsch distinguishes the word *na* (נע) from *nad* (נד). *Na* refers to a wanderer who can find no physical resting place on Earth, whereas a *nad* is a wanderer whose connection to mankind has been severed. Cain's punishment isolated him from the land as well as from all of mankind; he was cursed with an inability to find a homeland or a society, and subsequently his sin was too much to bear. The privilege of living in a homeland among a society of people who share a common lineage is no small matter. The return of Jewish sovereignty to its biblical homeland in our time, after thousands of years of exile, is truly a mark of God's hand in this world.

נע
נד

8

13 Cain said to *Hashem*, "My punishment is too great to bear!

יג וַיֹּאמֶר קַיִן אֶל־יְהֹוָה גָּדוֹל עֲוֹנִי מִנְּשֹׂא:

14 Since You have banished me this day from the soil, and I must avoid Your presence and become a restless wanderer on earth – anyone who meets me may kill me!"

יד הֵן גֵּרַשְׁתָּ אֹתִי הַיּוֹם מֵעַל פְּנֵי הָאֲדָמָה וּמִפָּנֶיךָ אֶסָּתֵר וְהָיִיתִי נָע וָנָד בָּאָרֶץ וְהָיָה כָל־מֹצְאִי יַהַרְגֵנִי:

15 *Hashem* said to him, "I promise, if anyone kills Cain, sevenfold vengeance shall be taken on him." And *Hashem* put a mark on Cain, lest anyone who met him should kill him.

טו וַיֹּאמֶר לוֹ יְהֹוָה לָכֵן כָּל־הֹרֵג קַיִן שִׁבְעָתַיִם יֻקָּם וַיָּשֶׂם יְהֹוָה לְקַיִן אוֹת לְבִלְתִּי הַכּוֹת־אֹתוֹ כָּל־מֹצְאוֹ:

16 Cain left the presence of *Hashem* and settled in the land of Nod, east of Eden.

טז וַיֵּצֵא קַיִן מִלִּפְנֵי יְהֹוָה וַיֵּשֶׁב בְּאֶרֶץ־נוֹד קִדְמַת־עֵדֶן:

17 Cain knew his wife, and she conceived and bore Enoch. And he then founded a city, and named the city after his son Enoch.

יז וַיֵּדַע קַיִן אֶת־אִשְׁתּוֹ וַתַּהַר וַתֵּלֶד אֶת־חֲנוֹךְ וַיְהִי בֹּנֶה עִיר וַיִּקְרָא שֵׁם הָעִיר כְּשֵׁם בְּנוֹ חֲנוֹךְ:

18 To Enoch was born Irad, and Irad begot Mehujael, and Mehujael begot Methusael, and Methusael begot Lamech.

יח וַיִּוָּלֵד לַחֲנוֹךְ אֶת־עִירָד וְעִירָד יָלַד אֶת־מְחוּיָאֵל וּמְחִיָּיאֵל יָלַד אֶת־מְתוּשָׁאֵל וּמְתוּשָׁאֵל יָלַד אֶת־לָמֶךְ:

19 Lamech took to himself two wives: the name of the one was Adah, and the name of the other was Zillah.

יט וַיִּקַּח־לוֹ לֶמֶךְ שְׁתֵּי נָשִׁים שֵׁם הָאַחַת עָדָה וְשֵׁם הַשֵּׁנִית צִלָּה:

20 Adah bore Jabal; he was the ancestor of those who dwell in tents and amidst herds.

כ וַתֵּלֶד עָדָה אֶת־יָבָל הוּא הָיָה אֲבִי יֹשֵׁב אֹהֶל וּמִקְנֶה:

21 And the name of his brother was Jubal; he was the ancestor of all who play the lyre and the pipe.

כא וְשֵׁם אָחִיו יוּבָל הוּא הָיָה אֲבִי כָּל־תֹּפֵשׂ כִּנּוֹר וְעוּגָב:

22 As for Zillah, she bore Tubal-cain, who forged all implements of copper and iron. And the sister of Tubal-cain was Naamah.

כב וְצִלָּה גַם־הִוא יָלְדָה אֶת־תּוּבַל קַיִן לֹטֵשׁ כָּל־חֹרֵשׁ נְחֹשֶׁת וּבַרְזֶל וַאֲחוֹת תּוּבַל־קַיִן נַעֲמָה:

23 And Lamech said to his wives, "Adah and Zillah, hear my voice; O wives of Lamech, give ear to my speech. I have slain a man for wounding me, a lad for bruising me.

כג וַיֹּאמֶר לֶמֶךְ לְנָשָׁיו עָדָה וְצִלָּה שְׁמַעַן קוֹלִי נְשֵׁי לֶמֶךְ הַאְזֵנָּה אִמְרָתִי כִּי אִישׁ הָרַגְתִּי לְפִצְעִי וְיֶלֶד לְחַבֻּרָתִי:

24 If Cain is avenged sevenfold, Then Lamech seventy-sevenfold."

כד כִּי שִׁבְעָתַיִם יֻקַּם־קָיִן וְלֶמֶךְ שִׁבְעִים וְשִׁבְעָה:

25 *Adam* knew his wife again, and she bore a son and named him *Shet*, meaning, "*Hashem* has provided me with another offspring in place of Abel," for Cain had killed him.

כה וַיֵּדַע אָדָם עוֹד אֶת־אִשְׁתּוֹ וַתֵּלֶד בֵּן וַתִּקְרָא אֶת־שְׁמוֹ שֵׁת כִּי שָׁת־לִי אֱלֹהִים זֶרַע אַחֵר תַּחַת הֶבֶל כִּי הֲרָגוֹ קָיִן:

26 And to *Shet*, in turn, a son was born, and he named him *Enosh*. It was then that men began to invoke *Hashem* by name.

כו וּלְשֵׁת גַּם־הוּא יֻלַּד־בֵּן וַיִּקְרָא אֶת־שְׁמוֹ אֱנוֹשׁ אָז הוּחַל לִקְרֹא בְּשֵׁם יְהֹוָה:

5 ¹ This is the record of *Adam's* line. When *Hashem* created man, He made him in the likeness of *Hashem*;

² male and female He created them. And when they were created, He blessed them and called them Man.

³ When *Adam* had lived 130 years, he begot a son in his likeness after his image, and named him *Shet*.

ה א זֶה סֵפֶר תּוֹלְדֹת אָדָם בְּיוֹם בְּרֹא אֱלֹהִים אָדָם בִּדְמוּת אֱלֹהִים עָשָׂה אֹתוֹ:

ב זָכָר וּנְקֵבָה בְּרָאָם וַיְבָרֶךְ אֹתָם וַיִּקְרָא אֶת־שְׁמָם אָדָם בְּיוֹם הִבָּרְאָם:

ג וַיְחִי אָדָם שְׁלֹשִׁים וּמְאַת שָׁנָה וַיּוֹלֶד בִּדְמוּתוֹ כְּצַלְמוֹ וַיִּקְרָא אֶת־שְׁמוֹ שֵׁת:

vai-KHEE a-DAM sh'-lo-SHEEM um-AT sha-NAH va-YO-led bid-mu-TO k'-tzal-MO va-yik-RA et sh'-MO SHAYT

⁴ After the birth of *Shet*, *Adam* lived 800 years and begot sons and daughters.

ד וַיִּהְיוּ יְמֵי־אָדָם אַחֲרֵי הוֹלִידוֹ אֶת־שֵׁת שְׁמֹנֶה מֵאֹת שָׁנָה וַיּוֹלֶד בָּנִים וּבָנוֹת:

⁵ All the days that *Adam* lived came to 930 years; then he died.

ה וַיִּהְיוּ כָּל־יְמֵי אָדָם אֲשֶׁר־חַי תְּשַׁע מֵאוֹת שָׁנָה וּשְׁלֹשִׁים שָׁנָה וַיָּמֹת:

⁶ When *Shet* had lived 105 years, he begot *Enosh*.

ו וַיְחִי־שֵׁת חָמֵשׁ שָׁנִים וּמְאַת שָׁנָה וַיּוֹלֶד אֶת־אֱנוֹשׁ:

⁷ After the birth of *Enosh*, *Shet* lived 807 years and begot sons and daughters.

ז וַיְחִי־שֵׁת אַחֲרֵי הוֹלִידוֹ אֶת־אֱנוֹשׁ שֶׁבַע שָׁנִים וּשְׁמֹנֶה מֵאוֹת שָׁנָה וַיּוֹלֶד בָּנִים וּבָנוֹת:

⁸ All the days of *Shet* came to 912 years; then he died.

ח וַיִּהְיוּ כָּל־יְמֵי־שֵׁת שְׁתֵּים עֶשְׂרֵה שָׁנָה וּתְשַׁע מֵאוֹת שָׁנָה וַיָּמֹת:

⁹ When *Enosh* had lived 90 years, he begot *Keinan*.

ט וַיְחִי אֱנוֹשׁ תִּשְׁעִים שָׁנָה וַיּוֹלֶד אֶת־קֵינָן:

¹⁰ After the birth of *Keinan*, *Enosh* lived 815 years and begot sons and daughters.

י וַיְחִי אֱנוֹשׁ אַחֲרֵי הוֹלִידוֹ אֶת־קֵינָן חֲמֵשׁ עֶשְׂרֵה שָׁנָה וּשְׁמֹנֶה מֵאוֹת שָׁנָה וַיּוֹלֶד בָּנִים וּבָנוֹת:

¹¹ All the days of *Enosh* came to 905 years; then he died.

יא וַיִּהְיוּ כָּל־יְמֵי אֱנוֹשׁ חָמֵשׁ שָׁנִים וּתְשַׁע מֵאוֹת שָׁנָה וַיָּמֹת:

¹² When *Keinan* had lived 70 years, he begot *Mehalalel*.

יב וַיְחִי קֵינָן שִׁבְעִים שָׁנָה וַיּוֹלֶד אֶת־מַהֲלַלְאֵל:

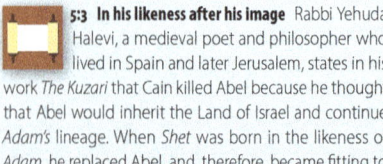

5:3 In his likeness after his image Rabbi Yehuda Halevi, a medieval poet and philosopher who lived in Spain and later Jerusalem, states in his work *The Kuzari* that Cain killed Abel because he thought that Abel would inherit the Land of Israel and continue *Adam's* lineage. When *Shet* was born in the likeness of *Adam*, he replaced Abel, and, therefore, became fitting to inherit the land in *Adam's* stead. From the onset of history,

Eretz Yisrael has been recognized as unique and chosen, and since then, many have sought to inherit it at all costs.

Dramatic sunrise over the Mount of Olives

13 After the birth of *Mehalalel, Keinan* lived 840 years and begot sons and daughters.

יג וַיְחִי קֵינָן אַחֲרֵי הוֹלִידוֹ אֶת־מַהֲלַלְאֵל אַרְבָּעִים שָׁנָה וּשְׁמֹנֶה מֵאוֹת שָׁנָה וַיּוֹלֶד בָּנִים וּבָנוֹת:

14 All the days of *Keinan* came to 910 years; then he died.

יד וַיִּהְיוּ כָּל־יְמֵי קֵינָן עֶשֶׂר שָׁנִים וּתְשַׁע מֵאוֹת שָׁנָה וַיָּמֹת:

15 When *Mehalalel* had lived 65 years, he begot *Yered*.

טו וַיְחִי מַהֲלַלְאֵל חָמֵשׁ שָׁנִים וְשִׁשִּׁים שָׁנָה וַיּוֹלֶד אֶת־יָרֶד:

16 After the birth of *Yered, Mehalalel* lived 830 years and begot sons and daughters.

טז וַיְחִי מַהֲלַלְאֵל אַחֲרֵי הוֹלִידוֹ אֶת־יֶרֶד שְׁלֹשִׁים שָׁנָה וּשְׁמֹנֶה מֵאוֹת שָׁנָה וַיּוֹלֶד בָּנִים וּבָנוֹת:

17 All the days of *Mehalalel* came to 895 years; then he died.

יז וַיִּהְיוּ כָּל־יְמֵי מַהֲלַלְאֵל חָמֵשׁ וְתִשְׁעִים שָׁנָה וּשְׁמֹנֶה מֵאוֹת שָׁנָה וַיָּמֹת:

18 When *Yered* had lived 162 years, he begot Enoch.

יח וַיְחִי־יֶרֶד שְׁתַּיִם וְשִׁשִּׁים שָׁנָה וּמְאַת שָׁנָה וַיּוֹלֶד אֶת־חֲנוֹךְ:

19 After the birth of Enoch, *Yered* lived 800 years and begot sons and daughters.

יט וַיְחִי־יֶרֶד אַחֲרֵי הוֹלִידוֹ אֶת־חֲנוֹךְ שְׁמֹנֶה מֵאוֹת שָׁנָה וַיּוֹלֶד בָּנִים וּבָנוֹת:

20 All the days of *Yered* came to 962 years; then he died.

כ וַיִּהְיוּ כָּל־יְמֵי־יֶרֶד שְׁתַּיִם וְשִׁשִּׁים שָׁנָה וּתְשַׁע מֵאוֹת שָׁנָה וַיָּמֹת:

21 When Enoch had lived 65 years, he begot *Metushelach*.

כא וַיְחִי חֲנוֹךְ חָמֵשׁ וְשִׁשִּׁים שָׁנָה וַיּוֹלֶד אֶת־מְתוּשָׁלַח:

22 After the birth of *Metushelach*, Enoch walked with *Hashem* 300 years; and he begot sons and daughters.

כב וַיִּתְהַלֵּךְ חֲנוֹךְ אֶת־הָאֱלֹהִים אַחֲרֵי הוֹלִידוֹ אֶת־מְתוּשֶׁלַח שְׁלֹשׁ מֵאוֹת שָׁנָה וַיּוֹלֶד בָּנִים וּבָנוֹת:

23 All the days of Enoch came to 365 years.

כג וַיְהִי כָּל־יְמֵי חֲנוֹךְ חָמֵשׁ וְשִׁשִּׁים שָׁנָה וּשְׁלֹשׁ מֵאוֹת שָׁנָה:

24 Enoch walked with *Hashem*; then he was no more, for *Hashem* took him.

כד וַיִּתְהַלֵּךְ חֲנוֹךְ אֶת־הָאֱלֹהִים וְאֵינֶנּוּ כִּי־לָקַח אֹתוֹ אֱלֹהִים:

25 When *Metushelach* had lived 187 years, he begot Lamech.

כה וַיְחִי מְתוּשֶׁלַח שֶׁבַע וּשְׁמֹנִים שָׁנָה וּמְאַת שָׁנָה וַיּוֹלֶד אֶת־לָמֶךְ:

26 After the birth of Lamech, *Metushelach* lived 782 years and begot sons and daughters.

כו וַיְחִי מְתוּשֶׁלַח אַחֲרֵי הוֹלִידוֹ אֶת־לֶמֶךְ שְׁתַּיִם וּשְׁמוֹנִים שָׁנָה וּשְׁבַע מֵאוֹת שָׁנָה וַיּוֹלֶד בָּנִים וּבָנוֹת:

27 All the days of *Metushelach* came to 969 years; then he died.

כז וַיִּהְיוּ כָּל־יְמֵי מְתוּשֶׁלַח תֵּשַׁע וְשִׁשִּׁים שָׁנָה וּתְשַׁע מֵאוֹת שָׁנָה וַיָּמֹת:

28 When Lamech had lived 182 years, he begot a son.

כח וַיְחִי־לֶמֶךְ שְׁתַּיִם וּשְׁמֹנִים שָׁנָה וּמְאַת שָׁנָה וַיּוֹלֶד בֵּן:

29 And he named him *Noach*, saying, "This one will provide us relief from our work and from the toil of our hands, out of the very soil which *Hashem* placed under a curse."

כט וַיִּקְרָא אֶת־שְׁמוֹ נֹחַ לֵאמֹר זֶה יְנַחֲמֵנוּ מִמַּעֲשֵׂנוּ וּמֵעִצְּבוֹן יָדֵינוּ מִן־הָאֲדָמָה אֲשֶׁר אֵרְרָהּ יְהֹוָה:

30 After the birth of *Noach*, Lamech lived 595 years and begot sons and daughters.

ל וַיְחִי־לֶמֶךְ אַחֲרֵי הוֹלִידוֹ אֶת־נֹחַ חָמֵשׁ וְתִשְׁעִים שָׁנָה וַחֲמֵשׁ מֵאֹת שָׁנָה וַיּוֹלֶד בָּנִים וּבָנוֹת:

31 All the days of Lamech came to 777 years; then he died.

לא וַיְהִי כָּל־יְמֵי־לֶמֶךְ שֶׁבַע וְשִׁבְעִים שָׁנָה וּשְׁבַע מֵאוֹת שָׁנָה וַיָּמֹת:

32 When *Noach* had lived 500 years, *Noach* begot *Shem*, Ham, and Japheth.

לב וַיְהִי־נֹחַ בֶּן־חֲמֵשׁ מֵאוֹת שָׁנָה וַיּוֹלֶד נֹחַ אֶת־שֵׁם אֶת־חָם וְאֶת־יָפֶת:

6 1 When men began to increase on earth and daughters were born to them,

א וַיְהִי כִּי־הֵחֵל הָאָדָם לָרֹב עַל־פְּנֵי הָאֲדָמָה וּבָנוֹת יֻלְּדוּ לָהֶם:

2 the divine beings saw how beautiful the daughters of men were and took wives from among those that pleased them.

ב וַיִּרְאוּ בְנֵי־הָאֱלֹהִים אֶת־בְּנוֹת הָאָדָם כִּי טֹבֹת הֵנָּה וַיִּקְחוּ לָהֶם נָשִׁים מִכֹּל אֲשֶׁר בָּחָרוּ:

3 *Hashem* said, "My breath shall not abide in man forever, since he too is flesh; let the days allowed him be one hundred and twenty years."

ג וַיֹּאמֶר יְהֹוָה לֹא־יָדוֹן רוּחִי בָאָדָם לְעֹלָם בְּשַׁגַּם הוּא בָשָׂר וְהָיוּ יָמָיו מֵאָה וְעֶשְׂרִים שָׁנָה:

4 It was then, and later too, that the Nephilim appeared on earth – when the divine beings cohabited with the daughters of men, who bore them offspring. They were the heroes of old, the men of renown.

ד הַנְּפִלִים הָיוּ בָאָרֶץ בַּיָּמִים הָהֵם וְגַם אַחֲרֵי־כֵן אֲשֶׁר יָבֹאוּ בְּנֵי הָאֱלֹהִים אֶל־בְּנוֹת הָאָדָם וְיָלְדוּ לָהֶם הֵמָּה הַגִּבֹּרִים אֲשֶׁר מֵעוֹלָם אַנְשֵׁי הַשֵּׁם:

5 *Hashem* saw how great was man's wickedness on earth, and how every plan devised by his mind was nothing but evil all the time.

ה וַיַּרְא יְהֹוָה כִּי רַבָּה רָעַת הָאָדָם בָּאָרֶץ וְכָל־יֵצֶר מַחְשְׁבֹת לִבּוֹ רַק רַע כָּל־הַיּוֹם:

6 And *Hashem* regretted that He had made man on earth, and His heart was saddened.

ו וַיִּנָּחֶם יְהֹוָה כִּי־עָשָׂה אֶת־הָאָדָם בָּאָרֶץ וַיִּתְעַצֵּב אֶל־לִבּוֹ:

7 *Hashem* said, "I will blot out from the earth the men whom I created – men together with beasts, creeping things, and birds of the sky; for I regret that I made them."

ז וַיֹּאמֶר יְהֹוָה אֶמְחֶה אֶת־הָאָדָם אֲשֶׁר־בָּרָאתִי מֵעַל פְּנֵי הָאֲדָמָה מֵאָדָם עַד־בְּהֵמָה עַד־רֶמֶשׂ וְעַד־עוֹף הַשָּׁמָיִם כִּי נִחַמְתִּי כִּי עֲשִׂיתִם:

8 But *Noach* found favor with *Hashem*.

ח וְנֹחַ מָצָא חֵן בְּעֵינֵי יְהֹוָה:

9 This is the line of *Noach*. – *Noach* was a righteous man; he was blameless in his age; *Noach* walked with *Hashem*. –

ט אֵלֶּה תּוֹלְדֹת נֹחַ נֹחַ אִישׁ צַדִּיק תָּמִים הָיָה בְּדֹרֹתָיו אֶת־הָאֱלֹהִים הִתְהַלֶּךְ־נֹחַ:

10 *Noach* begot three sons: *Shem*, Ham, and Japheth.

י וַיּוֹלֶד נֹחַ שְׁלֹשָׁה בָנִים אֶת־שֵׁם אֶת־חָם וְאֶת־יָפֶת:

11 The earth became corrupt before *Hashem*; the earth was filled with lawlessness.

יא וַתִּשָּׁחֵת הָאָרֶץ לִפְנֵי הָאֱלֹהִים וַתִּמָּלֵא הָאָרֶץ חָמָס:

12 When *Hashem* saw how corrupt the earth was, for all flesh had corrupted its ways on earth,

יב וַיַּרְא אֱלֹהִים אֶת־הָאָרֶץ וְהִנֵּה נִשְׁחָתָה כִּי־הִשְׁחִית כָּל־בָּשָׂר אֶת־דַּרְכּוֹ עַל־הָאָרֶץ:

Genesis

13 *Hashem* said to *Noach*, "I have decided to put an end to all flesh, for the earth is filled with lawlessness because of them: I am about to destroy them with the earth.

וַיֹּאמֶר אֱלֹהִים לְנֹחַ קֵץ כָּל־בָּשָׂר בָּא לְפָנַי כִּי־מָלְאָה הָאָרֶץ חָמָס מִפְּנֵיהֶם וְהִנְנִי מַשְׁחִיתָם אֶת־הָאָרֶץ: יג

va-YO-mer e-lo-HEEM l'-NO-akh KAYTZ kol ba-SAR BA l'-fa-NAI kee ma-l'-AH ha-A-retz kha-MAS mi-p'-nay-HEM v'-hi-n'-NEE mash-khee-TAM et ha-A-retz

14 Make yourself an ark of gopher wood; make it an ark with compartments, and cover it inside and out with pitch.

עֲשֵׂה לְךָ תֵּבַת עֲצֵי־גֹפֶר קִנִּים תַּעֲשֶׂה אֶת־הַתֵּבָה וְכָפַרְתָּ אֹתָהּ מִבַּיִת וּמִחוּץ בַּכֹּפֶר: יד

15 This is how you shall make it: the length of the ark shall be three hundred *amot*, its width fifty *amot*, and its height thirty *amot*.

וְזֶה אֲשֶׁר תַּעֲשֶׂה אֹתָהּ שְׁלֹשׁ מֵאוֹת אַמָּה אֹרֶךְ הַתֵּבָה חֲמִשִּׁים אַמָּה רָחְבָּהּ וּשְׁלֹשִׁים אַמָּה קוֹמָתָהּ: טו

16 Make an opening for daylight in the ark, and terminate it within an *amah* of the top. Put the entrance to the ark in its side; make it with bottom, second, and third decks.

צֹהַר תַּעֲשֶׂה לַתֵּבָה וְאֶל־אַמָּה תְּכַלֶּנָּה מִלְמַעְלָה וּפֶתַח הַתֵּבָה בְּצִדָּהּ תָּשִׂים תַּחְתִּיִּם שְׁנִיִּם וּשְׁלִשִׁים תַּעֲשֶׂהָ: טז

17 "For My part, I am about to bring the Flood – waters upon the earth – to destroy all flesh under the sky in which there is breath of life; everything on earth shall perish.

וַאֲנִי הִנְנִי מֵבִיא אֶת־הַמַּבּוּל מַיִם עַל־הָאָרֶץ לְשַׁחֵת כָּל־בָּשָׂר אֲשֶׁר־בּוֹ רוּחַ חַיִּים מִתַּחַת הַשָּׁמָיִם כֹּל אֲשֶׁר־בָּאָרֶץ יִגְוָע: יז

18 But I will establish My covenant with you, and you shall enter the ark, with your sons, your wife, and your sons' wives.

וַהֲקִמֹתִי אֶת־בְּרִיתִי אִתָּךְ וּבָאתָ אֶל־הַתֵּבָה אַתָּה וּבָנֶיךָ וְאִשְׁתְּךָ וּנְשֵׁי־בָנֶיךָ אִתָּךְ: יח

19 And of all that lives, of all flesh, you shall take two of each into the ark to keep alive with you; they shall be male and female.

וּמִכָּל־הָחַי מִכָּל־בָּשָׂר שְׁנַיִם מִכֹּל תָּבִיא אֶל־הַתֵּבָה לְהַחֲיֹת אִתָּךְ זָכָר וּנְקֵבָה יִהְיוּ: יט

20 From birds of every kind, cattle of every kind, every kind of creeping thing on earth, two of each shall come to you to stay alive.

מֵהָעוֹף לְמִינֵהוּ וּמִן־הַבְּהֵמָה לְמִינָהּ מִכֹּל רֶמֶשׂ הָאֲדָמָה לְמִינֵהוּ שְׁנַיִם מִכֹּל יָבֹאוּ אֵלֶיךָ לְהַחֲיוֹת: כ

21 For your part, take of everything that is eaten and store it away, to serve as food for you and for them."

וְאַתָּה קַח־לְךָ מִכָּל־מַאֲכָל אֲשֶׁר יֵאָכֵל וְאָסַפְתָּ אֵלֶיךָ וְהָיָה לְךָ וְלָהֶם לְאָכְלָה: כא

22 *Noach* did so; just as *Hashem* commanded him, so he did.

וַיַּעַשׂ נֹחַ כְּכֹל אֲשֶׁר צִוָּה אֹתוֹ אֱלֹהִים כֵּן עָשָׂה: כב

6:13 I am about to destroy them with the earth. According to one opinion in the Talmud (*Zevachim* 113b), the effects of the flood were less severe in the Land of Israel. Why did *Hashem* choose to spare this particular land? Rabbi Shneur Zalman of Liadi, the founder of the Chabad Hasidic dynasty in eighteenth century Russia, concludes that the purpose of the flood was to purify the world of its corruption. The flood, then, served as a kind of *mikveh*, a ritual bath, to bring about a process of purification. However, since *Eretz Yisrael* is intrinsically pure, it is impossible to corrupt and, therefore, did not need this type of purification. In fact, whenever the *Torah* discusses sins that can cause exile, it says that the land will purge itself of the sinners. *Eretz Yisrael* cannot be corrupted and does not tolerate impurity on its soil.

An ancient ritual bath in the Golan Heights

7 ¹ Then *Hashem* said to *Noach*, "Go into the ark, with all your household, for you alone have I found righteous before Me in this generation.

² Of every clean animal you shall take seven pairs, males and their mates, and of every animal that is not clean, two, a male and its mate;

³ of the birds of the sky also, seven pairs, male and female, to keep seed alive upon all the earth.

⁴ For in seven days' time I will make it rain upon the earth, forty days and forty nights, and I will blot out from the earth all existence that I created."

⁵ And *Noach* did just as *Hashem* commanded him.

⁶ *Noach* was six hundred years old when the Flood came, waters upon the earth.

⁷ *Noach*, with his sons, his wife, and his sons' wives, went into the ark because of the waters of the Flood.

⁸ Of the clean animals, of the animals that are not clean, of the birds, and of everything that creeps on the ground,

⁹ two of each, male and female, came to *Noach* into the ark, as *Hashem* had commanded *Noach*.

¹⁰ And on the seventh day the waters of the Flood came upon the earth.

¹¹ In the six hundredth year of *Noach*'s life, in the second month, on the seventeenth day of the month, on that day All the fountains of the great deep burst apart, And the floodgates of the sky broke open.

¹² The rain fell on the earth forty days and forty nights.

¹³ That same day *Noach* and *Noach*'s sons, *Shem*, Ham, and Japheth, went into the ark, with *Noach*'s wife and the three wives of his sons

¹⁴ they and all beasts of every kind, all cattle of every kind, all creatures of every kind that creep on the earth, and all birds of every kind, every bird, every winged thing.

¹⁵ They came to *Noach* into the ark, two each of all flesh in which there was breath of life.

ז א וַיֹּ֤אמֶר יְהוָה֙ לְנֹ֔חַ בֹּֽא־אַתָּ֥ה וְכָל־בֵּֽיתְךָ֖ אֶל־הַתֵּבָ֑ה כִּֽי־אֹתְךָ֥ רָאִ֛יתִי צַדִּ֥יק לְפָנַ֖י בַּדּ֥וֹר הַזֶּֽה:

ב מִכֹּ֣ל ׀ הַבְּהֵמָ֣ה הַטְּהוֹרָ֗ה תִּֽקַּח־לְךָ֛ שִׁבְעָ֥ה שִׁבְעָ֖ה אִ֣ישׁ וְאִשְׁתּ֑וֹ וּמִן־הַבְּהֵמָ֡ה אֲ֠שֶׁר לֹ֣א טְהֹרָ֥ה הִ֛וא שְׁנַ֖יִם אִ֥ישׁ וְאִשְׁתּֽוֹ:

ג גַּ֣ם מֵע֧וֹף הַשָּׁמַ֛יִם שִׁבְעָ֥ה שִׁבְעָ֖ה זָכָ֣ר וּנְקֵבָ֑ה לְחַיּ֥וֹת זֶ֖רַע עַל־פְּנֵ֥י כָל־הָאָֽרֶץ:

ד כִּי֩ לְיָמִ֨ים ע֜וֹד שִׁבְעָ֗ה אָֽנֹכִי֙ מַמְטִ֣יר עַל־הָאָ֔רֶץ אַרְבָּעִ֣ים י֔וֹם וְאַרְבָּעִ֖ים לָ֑יְלָה וּמָחִ֗יתִי אֶֽת־כָּל־הַיְקוּם֙ אֲשֶׁ֣ר עָשִׂ֔יתִי מֵעַ֖ל פְּנֵ֥י הָֽאֲדָמָֽה:

ה וַיַּ֖עַשׂ נֹ֑חַ כְּכֹ֥ל אֲשֶׁר־צִוָּ֖הוּ יְהוָֽה:

ו וְנֹ֕חַ בֶּן־שֵׁ֥שׁ מֵא֖וֹת שָׁנָ֑ה וְהַמַּבּ֣וּל הָיָ֔ה מַ֖יִם עַל־הָאָֽרֶץ:

ז וַיָּ֣בֹא נֹ֗חַ וּ֠בָנָיו וְאִשְׁתּ֧וֹ וּנְשֵֽׁי־בָנָ֛יו אִתּ֖וֹ אֶל־הַתֵּבָ֑ה מִפְּנֵ֖י מֵ֥י הַמַּבּֽוּל:

ח מִן־הַבְּהֵמָה֙ הַטְּהוֹרָ֔ה וּמִ֨ן־הַבְּהֵמָ֔ה אֲשֶׁ֥ר אֵינֶ֖נָּה טְהֹרָ֑ה וּמִ֨ן־הָע֔וֹף וְכֹ֥ל אֲשֶׁר־רֹמֵ֖שׂ עַל־הָֽאֲדָמָֽה:

ט שְׁנַ֨יִם שְׁנַ֜יִם בָּ֧אוּ אֶל־נֹ֛חַ אֶל־הַתֵּבָ֖ה זָכָ֣ר וּנְקֵבָ֑ה כַּֽאֲשֶׁ֛ר צִוָּ֥ה אֱלֹהִ֖ים אֶת־נֹֽחַ:

י וַֽיְהִ֖י לְשִׁבְעַ֣ת הַיָּמִ֑ים וּמֵ֣י הַמַּבּ֔וּל הָי֖וּ עַל־הָאָֽרֶץ:

יא בִּשְׁנַ֨ת שֵׁשׁ־מֵא֤וֹת שָׁנָה֙ לְחַיֵּי־נֹ֔חַ בַּחֹ֨דֶשׁ֙ הַשֵּׁנִ֔י בְּשִׁבְעָֽה־עָשָׂ֥ר י֖וֹם לַחֹ֑דֶשׁ בַּיּ֣וֹם הַזֶּ֗ה נִבְקְעוּ֙ כָּל־מַעְיְנֹת֙ תְּה֣וֹם רַבָּ֔ה וַֽאֲרֻבֹּ֥ת הַשָּׁמַ֖יִם נִפְתָּֽחוּ:

יב וַֽיְהִ֥י הַגֶּ֖שֶׁם עַל־הָאָ֑רֶץ אַרְבָּעִ֣ים י֔וֹם וְאַרְבָּעִ֖ים לָֽיְלָה:

יג בְּעֶ֨צֶם הַיּ֤וֹם הַזֶּה֙ בָּ֣א נֹ֔חַ וְשֵׁם־וְחָ֥ם וָיֶ֖פֶת בְּנֵי־נֹ֑חַ וְאֵ֣שֶׁת נֹ֗חַ וּשְׁלֹ֧שֶׁת נְשֵֽׁי־בָנָ֛יו אִתָּ֖ם אֶל־הַתֵּבָֽה:

יד הֵ֜מָּה וְכָל־הַֽחַיָּ֣ה לְמִינָ֗הּ וְכָל־הַבְּהֵמָה֙ לְמִינָ֔הּ וְכָל־הָרֶ֛מֶשׂ הָֽרֹמֵ֥שׂ עַל־הָאָ֖רֶץ לְמִינֵ֑הוּ וְכָל־הָע֣וֹף לְמִינֵ֔הוּ כֹּ֖ל צִפּ֥וֹר כָּל־כָּנָֽף:

טו וַיָּבֹ֥אוּ אֶל־נֹ֖חַ אֶל־הַתֵּבָ֑ה שְׁנַ֤יִם שְׁנַ֨יִם֙ מִכָּל־הַבָּשָׂ֔ר אֲשֶׁר־בּ֖וֹ ר֥וּחַ חַיִּֽים:

16 Thus they that entered comprised male and female of all flesh, as *Hashem* had commanded him. And *Hashem* shut him in.

טז וְהַבָּאִים זָכָר וּנְקֵבָה מִכָּל־בָּשָׂר בָּאוּ כַּאֲשֶׁר צִוָּה אֹתוֹ אֱלֹהִים וַיִּסְגֹּר יְהֹוָה בַּעֲדוֹ:

17 The Flood continued forty days on the earth, and the waters increased and raised the ark so that it rose above the earth.

יז וַיְהִי הַמַּבּוּל אַרְבָּעִים יוֹם עַל־הָאָרֶץ וַיִּרְבּוּ הַמַּיִם וַיִּשְׂאוּ אֶת־הַתֵּבָה וַתָּרָם מֵעַל הָאָרֶץ:

18 The waters swelled and increased greatly upon the earth, and the ark drifted upon the waters.

יח וַיִּגְבְּרוּ הַמַּיִם וַיִּרְבּוּ מְאֹד עַל־הָאָרֶץ וַתֵּלֶךְ הַתֵּבָה עַל־פְּנֵי הַמָּיִם:

19 When the waters had swelled much more upon the earth, all the highest mountains everywhere under the sky were covered.

יט וְהַמַּיִם גָּבְרוּ מְאֹד מְאֹד עַל־הָאָרֶץ וַיְכֻסּוּ כָּל־הֶהָרִים הַגְּבֹהִים אֲשֶׁר־תַּחַת כָּל־הַשָּׁמָיִם:

v'-ha-MA-yim ga-v'-RU m'-OD m'-OD al ha-A-retz vai-khu-SU kol he-ha-REEM ha-g'-vo-HEEM a-sher TA-khat kol ha-sha-MA-yim

20 Fifteen *amot* higher did the waters swell, as the mountains were covered.

כ חֲמֵשׁ עֶשְׂרֵה אַמָּה מִלְמַעְלָה גָּבְרוּ הַמָּיִם וַיְכֻסּוּ הֶהָרִים:

21 And all flesh that stirred on earth perished – birds, cattle, beasts, and all the things that swarmed upon the earth, and all mankind.

כא וַיִּגְוַע כָּל־בָּשָׂר הָרֹמֵשׂ עַל־הָאָרֶץ בָּעוֹף וּבַבְּהֵמָה וּבַחַיָּה וּבְכָל־הַשֶּׁרֶץ הַשֹּׁרֵץ עַל־הָאָרֶץ וְכֹל הָאָדָם:

22 All in whose nostrils was the merest breath of life, all that was on dry land, died.

כב כֹּל אֲשֶׁר נִשְׁמַת־רוּחַ חַיִּים בְּאַפָּיו מִכֹּל אֲשֶׁר בֶּחָרָבָה מֵתוּ:

23 All existence on earth was blotted out – man, cattle, creeping things, and birds of the sky; they were blotted out from the earth. Only *Noach* was left, and those with him in the ark.

כג וַיִּמַח אֶת־כָּל־הַיְקוּם אֲשֶׁר עַל־פְּנֵי הָאֲדָמָה מֵאָדָם עַד־בְּהֵמָה עַד־רֶמֶשׂ וְעַד־עוֹף הַשָּׁמַיִם וַיִּמָּחוּ מִן־הָאָרֶץ וַיִּשָּׁאֶר אַךְ־נֹחַ וַאֲשֶׁר אִתּוֹ בַּתֵּבָה:

24 And when the waters had swelled on the earth one hundred and fifty days,

כד וַיִּגְבְּרוּ הַמַּיִם עַל־הָאָרֶץ חֲמִשִּׁים וּמְאַת יוֹם:

8 ¹ *Hashem* remembered *Noach* and all the beasts and all the cattle that were with him in the ark, and *Hashem* caused a wind to blow across the earth, and the waters subsided.

ח א וַיִּזְכֹּר אֱלֹהִים אֶת־נֹחַ וְאֵת כָּל־הַחַיָּה וְאֶת־כָּל־הַבְּהֵמָה אֲשֶׁר אִתּוֹ בַּתֵּבָה וַיַּעֲבֵר אֱלֹהִים רוּחַ עַל־הָאָרֶץ וַיָּשֹׁכּוּ הַמָּיִם:

7:19 All the highest mountains This verse seems to contradict the assertion that *Eretz Yisrael* was not affected by the flood. The *Ramban*, a leading scholar in medieval Spain, solves this contradiction by stating that rain did not fall over the Land of Israel, but nevertheless, as there was no barrier surrounding the land, the flood waters entered the land from the surrounding lands. Even though the land was flooded, the powerful rain did not fall directly on *Eretz Yisrael*. As a result, the trees were not affected and at the conclusion of the flood, the dove was able to find an olive leaf in bloom. The image of a dove grasping an olive branch has become a symbol of peace. This icon, which emerged at the re-initiation of the world, when God's anger was quenched and *Noach* was commanded to continue mankind anew, emerged from the Land of Israel, the land of peace.

Dove of Peace
President's House, Jerusalem

2 The fountains of the deep and the floodgates of the sky were stopped up, and the rain from the sky was held back;

ב וַיִּסָּֽכְרוּ מַעְיְנֹת תְּהוֹם וַאֲרֻבֹּת הַשָּׁמָיִם וַיִּכָּלֵא הַגֶּשֶׁם מִן־הַשָּׁמָיִם:

3 the waters then receded steadily from the earth. At the end of one hundred and fifty days the waters diminished,

ג וַיָּשֻׁבוּ הַמַּיִם מֵעַל הָאָרֶץ הָלוֹךְ וָשׁוֹב וַיַּחְסְרוּ הַמַּיִם מִקְצֵה חֲמִשִּׁים וּמְאַת יוֹם:

4 so that in the seventh month, on the seventeenth day of the month, the ark came to rest on the mountains of Ararat.

ד וַתָּנַח הַתֵּבָה בַּחֹדֶשׁ הַשְּׁבִיעִי בְּשִׁבְעָה־עָשָׂר יוֹם לַחֹדֶשׁ עַל הָרֵי אֲרָרָט:

5 The waters went on diminishing until the tenth month; in the tenth month, on the first of the month, the tops of the mountains became visible.

ה וְהַמַּיִם הָיוּ הָלוֹךְ וְחָסוֹר עַד הַחֹדֶשׁ הָעֲשִׂירִי בָּעֲשִׂירִי בְּאֶחָד לַחֹדֶשׁ נִרְאוּ רָאשֵׁי הֶהָרִים:

6 At the end of forty days, *Noach* opened the window of the ark that he had made

ו וַיְהִי מִקֵּץ אַרְבָּעִים יוֹם וַיִּפְתַּח נֹחַ אֶת־חַלּוֹן הַתֵּבָה אֲשֶׁר עָשָׂה:

7 and sent out the raven; it went to and fro until the waters had dried up from the earth.

ז וַיְשַׁלַּח אֶת־הָעֹרֵב וַיֵּצֵא יָצוֹא וָשׁוֹב עַד־יְבֹשֶׁת הַמַּיִם מֵעַל הָאָרֶץ:

8 Then he sent out the dove to see whether the waters had decreased from the surface of the ground.

ח וַיְשַׁלַּח אֶת־הַיּוֹנָה מֵאִתּוֹ לִרְאוֹת הֲקַלּוּ הַמַּיִם מֵעַל פְּנֵי הָאֲדָמָה:

9 But the dove could not find a resting place for its foot, and returned to him to the ark, for there was water over all the earth. So putting out his hand, he took it into the ark with him.

ט וְלֹא־מָצְאָה הַיּוֹנָה מָנוֹחַ לְכַף־רַגְלָהּ וַתָּשָׁב אֵלָיו אֶל־הַתֵּבָה כִּי־מַיִם עַל־פְּנֵי כָל־הָאָרֶץ וַיִּשְׁלַח יָדוֹ וַיִּקָּחֶהָ וַיָּבֵא אֹתָהּ אֵלָיו אֶל־הַתֵּבָה:

v'-lo ma-tz'-AH ha-yo-NAH ma-NO-akh l'-khaf rag-LAH va-TA-shov
ay-LAV el ha-tay-VAH kee MA-yim al p'-NAY khol ha-A-retz va-yish-LAKH
ya-DO va-yi-ka-KHE-ha va-ya-VAY o-TAH ay-LAV el ha-tay-VAH

10 He waited another seven days, and again sent out the dove from the ark.

י וַיָּחֶל עוֹד שִׁבְעַת יָמִים אֲחֵרִים וַיֹּסֶף שַׁלַּח אֶת־הַיּוֹנָה מִן־הַתֵּבָה:

11 The dove came back to him toward evening, and there in its bill was a plucked-off olive leaf! Then *Noach* knew that the waters had decreased on the earth.

יא וַתָּבֹא אֵלָיו הַיּוֹנָה לְעֵת עֶרֶב וְהִנֵּה עֲלֵה־זַיִת טָרָף בְּפִיהָ וַיֵּדַע נֹחַ כִּי־קַלּוּ הַמַּיִם מֵעַל הָאָרֶץ:

12 He waited still another seven days and sent the dove forth; and it did not return to him any more.

יב וַיִּיָּחֶל עוֹד שִׁבְעַת יָמִים אֲחֵרִים וַיְשַׁלַּח אֶת־הַיּוֹנָה וְלֹא־יָסְפָה שׁוּב־אֵלָיו עוֹד:

8:9 But the dove could not find a resting place Throughout Talmudic literature, the Jewish people are compared to the dove. Once a dove meets her mate, she never leaves him for another, and a dove, even when her offspring are taken, will never abandon her nest. In a similar fashion, the Children of Israel are faithful to God. The Sages of the *Midrash* comment that the dove that *Noach* sent foreshadows the journey of the Jewish people throughout history. Just as the dove found no rest for the sole of its foot, so the Jews will find no solace in exile. Just as the dove returned to the ark seeking shelter, so the Jews will return from exile to the Land of Israel. Like *Noach*'s dove, the people have remained faithful to *Hashem*, and now, after thousands of years of absence, have returned to His land.

Dove resting at the Western Wall

16

13 In the six hundred and first year, in the first month, on the first of the month, the waters began to dry from the earth; and when *Noach* removed the covering of the ark, he saw that the surface of the ground was drying.

14 And in the second month, on the twenty-seventh day of the month, the earth was dry.

15 *Hashem* spoke to *Noach*, saying,

16 "Come out of the ark, together with your wife, your sons, and your sons' wives.

17 Bring out with you every living thing of all flesh that is with you: birds, animals, and everything that creeps on earth; and let them swarm on the earth and be fertile and increase on earth."

18 So *Noach* came out, together with his sons, his wife, and his sons' wives.

19 Every animal, every creeping thing, and every bird, everything that stirs on earth came out of the ark by families.

20 Then *Noach* built an altar to *Hashem* and, taking of every clean animal and of every clean bird, he offered burnt offerings on the altar.

21 *Hashem* smelled the pleasing odor, and *Hashem* said to Himself: "Never again will I doom the earth because of man, since the devisings of man's mind are evil from his youth; nor will I ever again destroy every living being, as I have done.

22 So long as the earth endures, Seedtime and harvest, Cold and heat, Summer and winter, Day and night Shall not cease."

9 1 *Hashem* blessed *Noach* and his sons, and said to them, "Be fertile and increase, and fill the earth.

2 The fear and the dread of you shall be upon all the beasts of the earth and upon all the birds of the sky – everything with which the earth is astir – and upon all the fish of the sea; they are given into your hand.

3 Every creature that lives shall be yours to eat; as with the green grasses, I give you all these.

4 You must not, however, eat flesh with its life-blood in it.

יג וַיְהִי בְּאַחַת וְשֵׁשׁ־מֵאוֹת שָׁנָה בָּרִאשׁוֹן בְּאֶחָד לַחֹדֶשׁ חָרְבוּ הַמַּיִם מֵעַל הָאָרֶץ וַיָּסַר נֹחַ אֶת־מִכְסֵה הַתֵּבָה וַיַּרְא וְהִנֵּה חָרְבוּ פְּנֵי הָאֲדָמָה:

יד וּבַחֹדֶשׁ הַשֵּׁנִי בְּשִׁבְעָה וְעֶשְׂרִים יוֹם לַחֹדֶשׁ יָבְשָׁה הָאָרֶץ:

טו וַיְדַבֵּר אֱלֹהִים אֶל־נֹחַ לֵאמֹר:

טז צֵא מִן־הַתֵּבָה אַתָּה וְאִשְׁתְּךָ וּבָנֶיךָ וּנְשֵׁי־בָנֶיךָ אִתָּךְ:

יז כָּל־הַחַיָּה אֲשֶׁר־אִתְּךָ מִכָּל־בָּשָׂר בָּעוֹף וּבַבְּהֵמָה וּבְכָל־הָרֶמֶשׂ הָרֹמֵשׂ עַל־הָאָרֶץ הוצא [הַיְצֵא] אִתָּךְ וְשָׁרְצוּ בָאָרֶץ וּפָרוּ וְרָבוּ עַל־הָאָרֶץ:

יח וַיֵּצֵא־נֹחַ וּבָנָיו וְאִשְׁתּוֹ וּנְשֵׁי־בָנָיו אִתּוֹ:

יט כָּל־הַחַיָּה כָּל־הָרֶמֶשׂ וְכָל־הָעוֹף כֹּל רוֹמֵשׂ עַל־הָאָרֶץ לְמִשְׁפְּחֹתֵיהֶם יָצְאוּ מִן־הַתֵּבָה:

כ וַיִּבֶן נֹחַ מִזְבֵּחַ לַיהֹוָה וַיִּקַּח מִכֹּל הַבְּהֵמָה הַטְּהוֹרָה וּמִכֹּל הָעוֹף הַטָּהֹר וַיַּעַל עֹלֹת בַּמִּזְבֵּחַ:

כא וַיָּרַח יְהֹוָה אֶת־רֵיחַ הַנִּיחֹחַ וַיֹּאמֶר יְהֹוָה אֶל־לִבּוֹ לֹא־אֹסִף לְקַלֵּל עוֹד אֶת־הָאֲדָמָה בַּעֲבוּר הָאָדָם כִּי יֵצֶר לֵב הָאָדָם רַע מִנְּעֻרָיו וְלֹא־אֹסִף עוֹד לְהַכּוֹת אֶת־כָּל־חַי כַּאֲשֶׁר עָשִׂיתִי:

כב עֹד כָּל־יְמֵי הָאָרֶץ זֶרַע וְקָצִיר וְקֹר וָחֹם וְקַיִץ וָחֹרֶף וְיוֹם וָלַיְלָה לֹא יִשְׁבֹּתוּ:

ט א וַיְבָרֶךְ אֱלֹהִים אֶת־נֹחַ וְאֶת־בָּנָיו וַיֹּאמֶר לָהֶם פְּרוּ וּרְבוּ וּמִלְאוּ אֶת־הָאָרֶץ:

ב וּמוֹרַאֲכֶם וְחִתְּכֶם יִהְיֶה עַל כָּל־חַיַּת הָאָרֶץ וְעַל כָּל־עוֹף הַשָּׁמָיִם בְּכֹל אֲשֶׁר תִּרְמֹשׂ הָאֲדָמָה וּבְכָל־דְּגֵי הַיָּם בְּיֶדְכֶם נִתָּנוּ:

ג כָּל־רֶמֶשׂ אֲשֶׁר הוּא־חַי לָכֶם יִהְיֶה לְאָכְלָה כְּיֶרֶק עֵשֶׂב נָתַתִּי לָכֶם אֶת־כֹּל:

ד אַךְ־בָּשָׂר בְּנַפְשׁוֹ דָמוֹ לֹא תֹאכֵלוּ:

5 But for your own life-blood I will require a reckoning: I will require it of every beast; of man, too, will I require a reckoning for human life, of every man for that of his fellow man!

6 Whoever sheds the blood of man, By man shall his blood be shed; For in His image Did *Hashem* make man.

7 Be fertile, then, and increase; abound on the earth and increase on it."

8 And *Hashem* said to *Noach* and to his sons with him,

9 "I now establish My covenant with you and your offspring to come,

10 and with every living thing that is with you – birds, cattle, and every wild beast as well – all that have come out of the ark, every living thing on earth.

11 I will maintain My covenant with you: never again shall all flesh be cut off by the waters of a flood, and never again shall there be a flood to destroy the earth."

12 *Hashem* further said, "This is the sign that I set for the covenant between Me and you, and every living creature with you, for all ages to come.

13 I have set My bow in the clouds, and it shall serve as a sign of the covenant between Me and the earth.

14 When I bring clouds over the earth, and the bow appears in the clouds,

15 I will remember My covenant between Me and you and every living creature among all flesh, so that the waters shall never again become a flood to destroy all flesh.

16 When the bow is in the clouds, I will see it and remember the everlasting covenant between *Hashem* and all living creatures, all flesh that is on earth.

17 That," *Hashem* said to *Noach*, "shall be the sign of the covenant that I have established between Me and all flesh that is on earth."

18 The sons of *Noach* who came out of the ark were *Shem*, Ham, and Japheth – Ham being the father of Canaan.

ה וְאַ֨ךְ אֶת־דִּמְכֶ֤ם לְנַפְשֹֽׁתֵיכֶם֙ אֶדְרֹ֔שׁ מִיַּ֤ד כָּל־חַיָּ֣ה אֶדְרְשֶׁ֔נּוּ וּמִיַּ֣ד הָֽאָדָ֗ם מִיַּד֙ אִ֣ישׁ אָחִ֔יו אֶדְרֹ֖שׁ אֶת־נֶ֥פֶשׁ הָֽאָדָֽם׃

ו שֹׁפֵךְ֙ דַּ֣ם הָֽאָדָ֔ם בָּֽאָדָ֖ם דָּמ֣וֹ יִשָּׁפֵ֑ךְ כִּ֚י בְּצֶ֣לֶם אֱלֹהִ֔ים עָשָׂ֖ה אֶת־הָֽאָדָֽם׃

ז וְאַתֶּ֖ם פְּר֣וּ וּרְב֑וּ שִׁרְצ֥וּ בָאָ֖רֶץ וּרְבוּ־בָֽהּ׃

ח וַיֹּ֤אמֶר אֱלֹהִים֙ אֶל־נֹ֔חַ וְאֶל־בָּנָ֥יו אִתּ֖וֹ לֵאמֹֽר׃

ט וַֽאֲנִ֕י הִנְנִ֥י מֵקִ֛ים אֶת־בְּרִיתִ֖י אִתְּכֶ֑ם וְאֶֽת־זַרְעֲכֶ֖ם אַֽחֲרֵיכֶֽם׃

י וְאֵ֣ת כָּל־נֶ֣פֶשׁ הַֽחַיָּ֣ה אֲשֶׁ֣ר אִתְּכֶ֗ם בָּע֧וֹף בַּבְּהֵמָ֛ה וּֽבְכָל־חַיַּ֥ת הָאָ֖רֶץ אִתְּכֶ֑ם מִכֹּל֙ יֹֽצְאֵ֣י הַתֵּבָ֔ה לְכֹ֖ל חַיַּ֥ת הָאָֽרֶץ׃

יא וַֽהֲקִֽמֹתִ֤י אֶת־בְּרִיתִי֙ אִתְּכֶ֔ם וְלֹֽא־יִכָּרֵ֧ת כָּל־בָּשָׂ֛ר ע֖וֹד מִמֵּ֣י הַמַּבּ֑וּל וְלֹֽא־יִֽהְיֶ֥ה ע֛וֹד מַבּ֖וּל לְשַׁחֵ֥ת הָאָֽרֶץ׃

יב וַיֹּ֣אמֶר אֱלֹהִ֗ים זֹ֤את אֽוֹת־הַבְּרִית֙ אֲשֶׁר־אֲנִ֣י נֹתֵ֗ן בֵּינִי֙ וּבֵ֣ינֵיכֶ֔ם וּבֵ֛ין כָּל־נֶ֥פֶשׁ חַיָּ֖ה אֲשֶׁ֣ר אִתְּכֶ֑ם לְדֹרֹ֖ת עוֹלָֽם׃

יג אֶת־קַשְׁתִּ֕י נָתַ֖תִּי בֶּֽעָנָ֑ן וְהָֽיְתָה֙ לְא֣וֹת בְּרִ֔ית בֵּינִ֖י וּבֵ֥ין הָאָֽרֶץ׃

יד וְהָיָ֕ה בְּעַֽנְנִ֥י עָנָ֖ן עַל־הָאָ֑רֶץ וְנִרְאֲתָ֥ה הַקֶּ֖שֶׁת בֶּֽעָנָֽן׃

טו וְזָֽכַרְתִּ֣י אֶת־בְּרִיתִ֗י אֲשֶׁ֤ר בֵּינִי֙ וּבֵ֣ינֵיכֶ֔ם וּבֵ֛ין כָּל־נֶ֥פֶשׁ חַיָּ֖ה בְּכָל־בָּשָׂ֑ר וְלֹֽא־יִֽהְיֶ֨ה ע֤וֹד הַמַּ֨יִם֙ לְמַבּ֔וּל לְשַׁחֵ֖ת כָּל־בָּשָֽׂר׃

טז וְהָֽיְתָ֥ה הַקֶּ֖שֶׁת בֶּֽעָנָ֑ן וּרְאִיתִ֗יהָ לִזְכֹּר֙ בְּרִ֣ית עוֹלָ֔ם בֵּ֣ין אֱלֹהִ֔ים וּבֵין֙ כָּל־נֶ֣פֶשׁ חַיָּ֔ה בְּכָל־בָּשָׂ֖ר אֲשֶׁ֥ר עַל־הָאָֽרֶץ׃

יז וַיֹּ֥אמֶר אֱלֹהִ֖ים אֶל־נֹ֑חַ זֹ֤את אֽוֹת־הַבְּרִית֙ אֲשֶׁ֣ר הֲקִמֹ֔תִי בֵּינִ֕י וּבֵ֥ין כָּל־בָּשָׂ֖ר אֲשֶׁ֥ר עַל־הָאָֽרֶץ׃

יח וַיִּֽהְי֣וּ בְנֵי־נֹ֗חַ הַיֹּֽצְאִים֙ מִן־הַתֵּבָ֔ה שֵׁ֖ם וְחָ֣ם וָיָ֑פֶת וְחָ֕ם ה֖וּא אֲבִ֥י כְנָֽעַן׃

18

19 These three were the sons of *Noach*, and from these the whole world branched out.

יט שְׁלֹשָׁה אֵלֶּה בְּנֵי־נֹחַ וּמֵאֵלֶּה נָפְצָה כָל־הָאָרֶץ:

20 *Noach*, the tiller of the soil, was the first to plant a vineyard.

כ וַיָּחֶל נֹחַ אִישׁ הָאֲדָמָה וַיִּטַּע כָּרֶם:

21 He drank of the wine and became drunk, and he uncovered himself within his tent.

כא וַיֵּשְׁתְּ מִן־הַיַּיִן וַיִּשְׁכָּר וַיִּתְגַּל בְּתוֹךְ אָהֳלֹה:

22 Ham, the father of Canaan, saw his father's nakedness and told his two brothers outside.

כב וַיַּרְא חָם אֲבִי כְנַעַן אֵת עֶרְוַת אָבִיו וַיַּגֵּד לִשְׁנֵי־אֶחָיו בַּחוּץ:

23 But *Shem* and Japheth took a cloth, placed it against both their backs and, walking backward, they covered their father's nakedness; their faces were turned the other way, so that they did not see their father's nakedness.

כג וַיִּקַּח שֵׁם וָיֶפֶת אֶת־הַשִּׂמְלָה וַיָּשִׂימוּ עַל־שְׁכֶם שְׁנֵיהֶם וַיֵּלְכוּ אֲחֹרַנִּית וַיְכַסּוּ אֵת עֶרְוַת אֲבִיהֶם וּפְנֵיהֶם אֲחֹרַנִּית וְעֶרְוַת אֲבִיהֶם לֹא רָאוּ:

24 When *Noach* woke up from his wine and learned what his youngest son had done to him,

כד וַיִּיקֶץ נֹחַ מִיֵּינוֹ וַיֵּדַע אֵת אֲשֶׁר־עָשָׂה־לוֹ בְּנוֹ הַקָּטָן:

25 he said, "Cursed be Canaan; The lowest of slaves Shall he be to his brothers."

כה וַיֹּאמֶר אָרוּר כְּנָעַן עֶבֶד עֲבָדִים יִהְיֶה לְאֶחָיו:

26 And he said, "Blessed be *Hashem*, The God of *Shem*; Let Canaan be a slave to them.

כו וַיֹּאמֶר בָּרוּךְ יְהֹוָה אֱלֹהֵי שֵׁם וִיהִי כְנַעַן עֶבֶד לָמוֹ:

va-YO-mer ba-RUKH a-do-NAI e-LO-hay SHAYM
vee-HEE kh'-NA-an E-ved LA-mo

27 May *Hashem* enlarge Japheth, And let him dwell in the tents of *Shem*; And let Canaan be a slave to them."

כז יַפְתְּ אֱלֹהִים לְיֶפֶת וְיִשְׁכֹּן בְּאָהֳלֵי־שֵׁם וִיהִי כְנַעַן עֶבֶד לָמוֹ:

28 *Noach* lived after the Flood 350 years.

כח וַיְחִי־נֹחַ אַחַר הַמַּבּוּל שְׁלֹשׁ מֵאוֹת שָׁנָה וַחֲמִשִּׁים שָׁנָה:

29 And all the days of *Noach* came to 950 years; then he died.

כט וַיִּהְיוּ כָּל־יְמֵי־נֹחַ תְּשַׁע מֵאוֹת שָׁנָה וַחֲמִשִּׁים שָׁנָה וַיָּמֹת:

10 1 These are the lines of *Shem*, Ham, and Japheth, the sons of *Noach*: sons were born to them after the Flood.

י א וְאֵלֶּה תּוֹלְדֹת בְּנֵי־נֹחַ שֵׁם חָם וָיָפֶת וַיִּוָּלְדוּ לָהֶם בָּנִים אַחַר הַמַּבּוּל:

2 The descendants of Japheth: Gomer, Magog, Media, Javan, Tubal, Meshech, and Tiras.

ב בְּנֵי יֶפֶת גֹּמֶר וּמָגוֹג וּמָדַי וְיָוָן וְתֻבָל וּמֶשֶׁךְ וְתִירָס:

3 The descendants of Gomer: Ashkenaz, Riphath, and Togarmah.

ג וּבְנֵי גֹּמֶר אַשְׁכְּנַז וְרִיפַת וְתֹגַרְמָה:

9:26 Blessed be *Hashem*, The God of *Shem* *Rashi* comments that the God of *Shem* is blessed because He will eventually fulfill His promise to give the Land of Israel to *Shem*'s descendants. While not recorded explicitly in the verse, *Hashem* had revealed this plan to *Noach*, and *Noach*, in his righteousness, accepted it as fact even before the promise had been made. To

bless God means to acknowledge that *Hashem* is the source of blessing. In this verse, *Noach* recognizes that *Eretz Yisrael* is a blessing and a gift, and thanks God for it.

Yerushalayim

⁴ The descendants of Javan: Elishah and Tarshish, the Kittim and the Dodanim.

ד וּבְנֵי יָוָן אֱלִישָׁה וְתַרְשִׁישׁ כִּתִּים וְדֹדָנִים:

⁵ From these the maritime nations branched out. [These are the descendants of Japheth] by their lands – each with its language – their clans and their nations.

ה מֵאֵלֶּה נִפְרְדוּ אִיֵּי הַגּוֹיִם בְּאַרְצֹתָם אִישׁ לִלְשֹׁנוֹ לְמִשְׁפְּחֹתָם בְּגוֹיֵהֶם:

may-AY-leh nif-r'-DU i-iAY ha-go-YIM b'-ar-tzo-TAM EESH
lil-sho-NO l'-mish-p'-kho-TAM b'-go-yay-HEM

⁶ The descendants of Ham: Cush, Mizraim, Put, and Canaan.

ו וּבְנֵי חָם כּוּשׁ וּמִצְרַיִם וּפוּט וּכְנָעַן:

⁷ The descendants of Cush: Seba, Havilah, Sabtah, Raamah, and Sabteca. The descendants of Raamah: Sheba and Dedan.

ז וּבְנֵי כוּשׁ סְבָא וַחֲוִילָה וְסַבְתָּה וְרַעְמָה וְסַבְתְּכָא וּבְנֵי רַעְמָה שְׁבָא וּדְדָן:

⁸ Cush also begot Nimrod, who was the first man of might on earth.

ח וְכוּשׁ יָלַד אֶת־נִמְרֹד הוּא הֵחֵל לִהְיוֹת גִּבֹּר בָּאָרֶץ:

⁹ He was a mighty hunter by the grace of *Hashem*; hence the saying, "Like Nimrod a mighty hunter by the grace of *Hashem*."

ט הוּא הָיָה גִבֹּר־צַיִד לִפְנֵי יְהוָה עַל־כֵּן יֵאָמַר כְּנִמְרֹד גִּבּוֹר צַיִד לִפְנֵי יְהוָה:

¹⁰ The mainstays of his kingdom were Babylon, Erech, Accad, and Calneh in the land of Shinar.

י וַתְּהִי רֵאשִׁית מַמְלַכְתּוֹ בָּבֶל וְאֶרֶךְ וְאַכַּד וְכַלְנֵה בְּאֶרֶץ שִׁנְעָר:

¹¹ From that land Assyria went forth and built Nineveh, Rehoboth-ir, Calah,

יא מִן־הָאָרֶץ הַהִוא יָצָא אַשּׁוּר וַיִּבֶן אֶת־נִינְוֵה וְאֶת־רְחֹבֹת עִיר וְאֶת־כָּלַח:

¹² and Resen between Nineveh and Calah, that is the great city.

יב וְאֶת־רֶסֶן בֵּין נִינְוֵה וּבֵין כָּלַח הִוא הָעִיר הַגְּדֹלָה:

¹³ And Mizraim begot the Ludim, the Anamim, the Lehabim, the Naphtuhim,

יג וּמִצְרַיִם יָלַד אֶת־לוּדִים וְאֶת־עֲנָמִים וְאֶת־לְהָבִים וְאֶת־נַפְתֻּחִים:

¹⁴ the Pathrusim, the Casluhim, and the Caphtorim,* whence the Philistines came forth.

יד וְאֶת־פַּתְרֻסִים וְאֶת־כַּסְלֻחִים אֲשֶׁר יָצְאוּ מִשָּׁם פְּלִשְׁתִּים וְאֶת־כַּפְתֹּרִים:

¹⁵ Canaan begot Sidon, his first-born, and Heth;

טו וּכְנַעַן יָלַד אֶת־צִידֹן בְּכֹרוֹ וְאֶת־חֵת:

---

* "and the Caphtorim" moved up from the end of the verse for clarity

10:5 From these the maritime nations branched out This chapter lists the generations that emerged from *Noach*'s sons after the flood, implying that the nations spread out as a result of natural population growth. Hence, the word *nifridu* (נפרדו), 'divided,' which connotes natural separation, is used here, as opposed to the term *vayafetz* (ויפץ), 'scattered,' used in the

Hebrew prayer book open to Psalms

story of the Tower of Babel (11:8), which connotes forced dispersion. Similarly, the choice of the word *lashon* (לשון), 'tongue,' as opposed to *safa* (שפה), 'language,' which is used in chapter eleven, indicates a natural evolution of dialects as nations moved away from each other. Conceivably, new languages were not yet initiated, only dialects of Hebrew. Rabbi Zalman Sorotzkin, who fled Europe and arrived in Israel during World War II, points out that this verse mentions the three aspects that unite a nation; common ancestry, land and language. Although the Jewish people can be found all over the world, they are united by their common ancestry, their connection to *Eretz Yisrael* and their ability to converse in Hebrew.

נפרדו
ויפץ
שפה
לשון

16 and the Jebusites, the Amorites, the Girgashites,

טז וְאֶת־הַיְבוּסִי וְאֶת־הָאֱמֹרִי וְאֵת הַגִּרְגָּשִׁי:

17 the Hivites, the Arkites, the Sinites,

יז וְאֶת־הַחִוִּי וְאֶת־הָעַרְקִי וְאֶת־הַסִּינִי:

18 the Arvadites, the Zemarites, and the Hamathites. Afterward the clans of the Canaanites spread out.

יח וְאֶת־הָאַרְוָדִי וְאֶת־הַצְּמָרִי וְאֶת־הַחֲמָתִי וְאַחַר נָפֹצוּ מִשְׁפְּחוֹת הַכְּנַעֲנִי:

19 The [original] Canaanite territory extended from Sidon as far as Gerar, near *Azza*, and as far as Sodom, Gomorrah, Admah, and Zeboiim, near Lasha.

יט וַיְהִי גְּבוּל הַכְּנַעֲנִי מִצִּידֹן בֹּאֲכָה גְרָרָה עַד־עַזָּה בֹּאֲכָה סְדֹמָה וַעֲמֹרָה וְאַדְמָה וּצְבֹיִם עַד־לָשַׁע:

20 These are the descendants of Ham, according to their clans and languages, by their lands and nations.

כ אֵלֶּה בְנֵי־חָם לְמִשְׁפְּחֹתָם לִלְשֹׁנֹתָם בְּאַרְצֹתָם בְּגוֹיֵהֶם:

21 Sons were also born to *Shem*, ancestor of all the descendants of *Ever* and older brother of Japheth.

כא וּלְשֵׁם יֻלַּד גַּם־הוּא אֲבִי כָּל־בְּנֵי־עֵבֶר אֲחִי יֶפֶת הַגָּדוֹל:

22 The descendants of *Shem*: Elam, Assyria, *Arpachshad*, Lud, and Aram.

כב בְּנֵי שֵׁם עֵילָם וְאַשּׁוּר וְאַרְפַּכְשַׁד וְלוּד וַאֲרָם:

23 The descendants of Aram: Uz, Hul, Gether, and Mash.

כג וּבְנֵי אֲרָם עוּץ וְחוּל וְגֶתֶר וָמַשׁ:

24 *Arpachshad* begot *Sheila*, and *Sheila* begot *Ever*.

כד וְאַרְפַּכְשַׁד יָלַד אֶת־שָׁלַח וְשֶׁלַח יָלַד אֶת־עֵבֶר:

25 Two sons were born to *Ever*: the name of the first was *Peleg*, for in his days the earth was divided; and the name of his brother was Joktan.

כה וּלְעֵבֶר יֻלַּד שְׁנֵי בָנִים שֵׁם הָאֶחָד פֶּלֶג כִּי בְיָמָיו נִפְלְגָה הָאָרֶץ וְשֵׁם אָחִיו יָקְטָן:

26 Joktan begot Almodad, Sheleph, Hazarmaveth, Jerah,

כו וְיָקְטָן יָלַד אֶת־אַלְמוֹדָד וְאֶת־שָׁלֶף וְאֶת־חֲצַרְמָוֶת וְאֶת־יָרַח:

27 Hadoram, Uzal, Diklah,

כז וְאֶת־הֲדוֹרָם וְאֶת־אוּזָל וְאֶת־דִּקְלָה:

28 Obal, Abimael, Sheba,

כח וְאֶת־עוֹבָל וְאֶת־אֲבִימָאֵל וְאֶת־שְׁבָא:

29 Ophir, Havilah, and Jobab; all these were the descendants of Joktan.

כט וְאֶת־אוֹפִר וְאֶת־חֲוִילָה וְאֶת־יוֹבָב כָּל־אֵלֶּה בְּנֵי יָקְטָן:

30 Their settlements extended from Mesha as far as Sephar, the hill country to the east.

ל וַיְהִי מוֹשָׁבָם מִמֵּשָׁא בֹּאֲכָה סְפָרָה הַר הַקֶּדֶם:

31 These are the descendants of *Shem* according to their clans and languages, by their lands, according to their nations.

לא אֵלֶּה בְנֵי־שֵׁם לְמִשְׁפְּחֹתָם לִלְשֹׁנֹתָם בְּאַרְצֹתָם לְגוֹיֵהֶם:

32 These are the groupings of *Noach*'s descendants, according to their origins, by their nations; and from these the nations branched out over the earth after the Flood.

לב אֵלֶּה מִשְׁפְּחֹת בְּנֵי־נֹחַ לְתוֹלְדֹתָם בְּגוֹיֵהֶם וּמֵאֵלֶּה נִפְרְדוּ הַגּוֹיִם בָּאָרֶץ אַחַר הַמַּבּוּל:

11 **1** Everyone on earth had the same language and the
same words.

יא א וַיְהִי כָל־הָאָרֶץ שָׂפָה אֶחָת וּדְבָרִים
אֲחָדִים:

vai-HEE khol ha-A-retz sa-FAH e-KHAT ud-va-REEM a-kha-DEEM

2 And as they migrated from the east, they came
upon a valley in the land of Shinar and settled there.

ב וַיְהִי בְּנָסְעָם מִקֶּדֶם וַיִּמְצְאוּ בִקְעָה
בְּאֶרֶץ שִׁנְעָר וַיֵּשְׁבוּ שָׁם:

3 They said to one another, "Come, let us make bricks
and burn them hard." – Brick served them as stone,
and bitumen served them as mortar.

ג וַיֹּאמְרוּ אִישׁ אֶל־רֵעֵהוּ הָבָה נִלְבְּנָה
לְבֵנִים וְנִשְׂרְפָה לִשְׂרֵפָה וַתְּהִי לָהֶם
הַלְּבֵנָה לְאָבֶן וְהַחֵמָר הָיָה לָהֶם לַחֹמֶר:

4 And they said, "Come, let us build us a city, and a
tower with its top in the sky, to make a name for
ourselves; else we shall be scattered all over the
world."

ד וַיֹּאמְרוּ הָבָה נִבְנֶה־לָּנוּ עִיר וּמִגְדָּל
וְרֹאשׁוֹ בַשָּׁמַיִם וְנַעֲשֶׂה־לָּנוּ שֵׁם פֶּן־
נָפוּץ עַל־פְּנֵי כָל־הָאָרֶץ:

5 *Hashem* came down to look at the city and tower
that man had built,

ה וַיֵּרֶד יְהֹוָה לִרְאֹת אֶת־הָעִיר וְאֶת־
הַמִּגְדָּל אֲשֶׁר בָּנוּ בְּנֵי הָאָדָם:

6 and *Hashem* said, "If, as one people with one
language for all, this is how they have begun to act,
then nothing that they may propose to do will be
out of their reach.

ו וַיֹּאמֶר יְהֹוָה הֵן עַם אֶחָד וְשָׂפָה אַחַת
לְכֻלָּם וְזֶה הַחִלָּם לַעֲשׂוֹת וְעַתָּה לֹא־
יִבָּצֵר מֵהֶם כֹּל אֲשֶׁר יָזְמוּ לַעֲשׂוֹת:

7 Let us, then, go down and confound their speech
there, so that they shall not understand one
another's speech."

ז הָבָה נֵרְדָה וְנָבְלָה שָׁם שְׂפָתָם אֲשֶׁר
לֹא יִשְׁמְעוּ אִישׁ שְׂפַת רֵעֵהוּ:

8 Thus *Hashem* scattered them from there over the
face of the whole earth; and they stopped building
the city

ח וַיָּפֶץ יְהֹוָה אֹתָם מִשָּׁם עַל־פְּנֵי כָל־
הָאָרֶץ וַיַּחְדְּלוּ לִבְנֹת הָעִיר:

9 That is why it was called Babel, because there
Hashem confounded the speech of the whole earth;
and from there *Hashem* scattered them over the face
of the whole earth.

ט עַל־כֵּן קָרָא שְׁמָהּ בָּבֶל כִּי־שָׁם בָּלַל
יְהֹוָה שְׂפַת כָּל־הָאָרֶץ וּמִשָּׁם הֱפִיצָם
יְהֹוָה עַל־פְּנֵי כָּל־הָאָרֶץ:

10 This is the line of *Shem. Shem* was 100 years old
when he begot *Arpachshad*, two years after the
Flood.

י אֵלֶּה תּוֹלְדֹת שֵׁם שֵׁם בֶּן־מְאַת שָׁנָה
וַיּוֹלֶד אֶת־אַרְפַּכְשָׁד שְׁנָתַיִם אַחַר
הַמַּבּוּל:

11:1 Everyone on earth had the same language
The Hebrew word for 'language,' *safa* (שפה),
also appears in *Sefer Tzefanya* (3:9) when the
prophet describes a *safa b'rurah* (שפה ברורה), 'purity of
speech,' that will be shared by all the nations of the world
in the end of days: "For then I will make the peoples pure
of speech, so that they all invoke *Hashem* by name and
serve Him with one accord." Rabbi Avraham Ibn Ezra
comments that the pure language that *Tzefanya* promises
is the Hebrew language. In future times, the world will
begin to learn Hebrew, the language of Creation. This
promise has begun to come true in our age. Not only has
the Hebrew language been revi-
talized over the past century as
the spoken language in the Jewish homeland, but in more recent
years, thousands of non-Jews
have also begun to study Hebrew
as a way to connect with their
Creator and gain a deeper understanding of the Bible.

שפה ברורה

Reading from the *Torah* at the Western Wall

22

11 After the birth of *Arpachshad, Shem* lived 500 years and begot sons and daughters.

יא וַיְחִי־שֵׁם אַחֲרֵי הוֹלִידוֹ אֶת־אַרְפַּכְשָׁד חֲמֵשׁ מֵאוֹת שָׁנָה וַיּוֹלֶד בָּנִים וּבָנוֹת:

12 When *Arpachshad* had lived 35 years, he begot *Shelach.*

יב וְאַרְפַּכְשַׁד חַי חָמֵשׁ וּשְׁלֹשִׁים שָׁנָה וַיּוֹלֶד אֶת־שָׁלַח:

13 After the birth of *Shelach, Arpachshad* lived 403 years and begot sons and daughters.

יג וַיְחִי אַרְפַּכְשַׁד אַחֲרֵי הוֹלִידוֹ אֶת־שֶׁלַח שָׁלֹשׁ שָׁנִים וְאַרְבַּע מֵאוֹת שָׁנָה וַיּוֹלֶד בָּנִים וּבָנוֹת:

14 When *Shelach* had lived 30 years, he begot *Ever.*

יד וְשֶׁלַח חַי שְׁלֹשִׁים שָׁנָה וַיּוֹלֶד אֶת־עֵבֶר:

15 After the birth of *Ever, Shelach* lived 403 years and begot sons and daughters.

טו וַיְחִי־שֶׁלַח אַחֲרֵי הוֹלִידוֹ אֶת־עֵבֶר שָׁלֹשׁ שָׁנִים וְאַרְבַּע מֵאוֹת שָׁנָה וַיּוֹלֶד בָּנִים וּבָנוֹת:

16 When *Ever* had lived 34 years, he begot *Peleg*

טז וַיְחִי־עֵבֶר אַרְבַּע וּשְׁלֹשִׁים שָׁנָה וַיּוֹלֶד אֶת־פָּלֶג:

17 After the birth of *Peleg, Ever* lived 430 years and begot sons and daughters.

יז וַיְחִי־עֵבֶר אַחֲרֵי הוֹלִידוֹ אֶת־פֶּלֶג שְׁלֹשִׁים שָׁנָה וְאַרְבַּע מֵאוֹת שָׁנָה וַיּוֹלֶד בָּנִים וּבָנוֹת:

18 When *Peleg* had lived 30 years, he begot *Re'u.*

יח וַיְחִי־פֶלֶג שְׁלֹשִׁים שָׁנָה וַיּוֹלֶד אֶת־רְעוּ:

19 After the birth of *Re'u, Peleg* lived 209 years and begot sons and daughters.

יט וַיְחִי־פֶלֶג אַחֲרֵי הוֹלִידוֹ אֶת־רְעוּ תֵּשַׁע שָׁנִים וּמָאתַיִם שָׁנָה וַיּוֹלֶד בָּנִים וּבָנוֹת:

20 When *Re'u* had lived 32 years, he begot *Serug.*

כ וַיְחִי רְעוּ שְׁתַּיִם וּשְׁלֹשִׁים שָׁנָה וַיּוֹלֶד אֶת־שְׂרוּג:

21 After the birth of *Serug, Re'u* lived 207 years and begot sons and daughters.

כא וַיְחִי רְעוּ אַחֲרֵי הוֹלִידוֹ אֶת־שְׂרוּג שֶׁבַע שָׁנִים וּמָאתַיִם שָׁנָה וַיּוֹלֶד בָּנִים וּבָנוֹת:

22 When *Serug* had lived 30 years, he begot *Nachor.*

כב וַיְחִי שְׂרוּג שְׁלֹשִׁים שָׁנָה וַיּוֹלֶד אֶת־נָחוֹר:

23 After the birth of *Nachor, Serug* lived 200 years and begot sons and daughters.

כג וַיְחִי שְׂרוּג אַחֲרֵי הוֹלִידוֹ אֶת־נָחוֹר מָאתַיִם שָׁנָה וַיּוֹלֶד בָּנִים וּבָנוֹת:

24 When *Nachor* had lived 29 years, he begot *Terach.*

כד וַיְחִי נָחוֹר תֵּשַׁע וְעֶשְׂרִים שָׁנָה וַיּוֹלֶד אֶת־תָּרַח:

25 After the birth of *Terach, Nachor* lived 119 years and begot sons and daughters.

כה וַיְחִי נָחוֹר אַחֲרֵי הוֹלִידוֹ אֶת־תֶּרַח תְּשַׁע־עֶשְׂרֵה שָׁנָה וּמְאַת שָׁנָה וַיּוֹלֶד בָּנִים וּבָנוֹת:

26 When *Terach* had lived 70 years, he begot *Avram,* Nahor, and Haran.

כו וַיְחִי־תֶרַח שִׁבְעִים שָׁנָה וַיּוֹלֶד אֶת־אַבְרָם אֶת־נָחוֹר וְאֶת־הָרָן:

27 Now this is the line of *Terach: Terach* begot *Avram,* Nahor, and Haran; and Haran begot Lot.

כז וְאֵלֶּה תּוֹלְדֹת תֶּרַח תֶּרַח הוֹלִיד אֶת־אַבְרָם אֶת־נָחוֹר וְאֶת־הָרָן וְהָרָן הוֹלִיד אֶת־לוֹט:

28 Haran died in the lifetime of his father *Terach,* in his native land, Ur of the Chaldeans.

כח וַיָּמָת הָרָן עַל־פְּנֵי תֶּרַח אָבִיו בְּאֶרֶץ מוֹלַדְתּוֹ בְּאוּר כַּשְׂדִּים:

²⁹ *Avram* and Nahor took to themselves wives, the name of *Avram*'s wife being *Sarai* and that of Nahor's wife Milcah, the daughter of Haran, the father of Milcah and Iscah.

כט וַיִּקַּח אַבְרָם וְנָחוֹר לָהֶם נָשִׁים שֵׁם אֵשֶׁת־אַבְרָם שָׂרָי וְשֵׁם אֵשֶׁת־נָחוֹר מִלְכָּה בַּת־הָרָן אֲבִי־מִלְכָּה וַאֲבִי יִסְכָּה:

³⁰ Now *Sarai* was barren, she had no child.

ל וַתְּהִי שָׂרַי עֲקָרָה אֵין לָהּ וָלָד:

³¹ *Terach* took his son *Avram*, his grandson Lot the son of Haran, and his daughter-in-law *Sarai*, the wife of his son *Avram*, and they set out together from Ur of the Chaldeans for the land of Canaan; but when they had come as far as Haran, they settled there.

לא וַיִּקַּח תֶּרַח אֶת־אַבְרָם בְּנוֹ וְאֶת־לוֹט בֶּן־הָרָן בֶּן־בְּנוֹ וְאֵת שָׂרַי כַּלָּתוֹ אֵשֶׁת אַבְרָם בְּנוֹ וַיֵּצְאוּ אִתָּם מֵאוּר כַּשְׂדִּים לָלֶכֶת אַרְצָה כְּנַעַן וַיָּבֹאוּ עַד־חָרָן וַיֵּשְׁבוּ שָׁם:

³² The days of *Terach* came to 205 years; and *Terach* died in Haran.

לב וַיִּהְיוּ יְמֵי־תֶרַח חָמֵשׁ שָׁנִים וּמָאתַיִם שָׁנָה וַיָּמָת תֶּרַח בְּחָרָן:

12 ¹ *Hashem* said to *Avram*, "Go forth from your native land and from your father's house to the land that I will show you.

יב וַיֹּאמֶר יְהוָה אֶל־אַבְרָם לֶךְ־לְךָ מֵאַרְצְךָ וּמִמּוֹלַדְתְּךָ וּמִבֵּית אָבִיךָ אֶל־הָאָרֶץ אֲשֶׁר אַרְאֶךָּ:

va-YO-mer a-do-NAI el av-RAM lekh l'-KHA may-ar-tz'-KHA u-mi-mo-lad-t'-KHA u-mi-BAYT a-VEE-kha el ha-A-retz a-SHER ar-E-ka

² I will make of you a great nation, And I will bless you; I will make your name great, And you shall be a blessing.

ב וְאֶעֶשְׂךָ לְגוֹי גָּדוֹל וַאֲבָרֶכְךָ וַאֲגַדְּלָה שְׁמֶךָ וֶהְיֵה בְּרָכָה:

³ I will bless those who bless you And curse him that curses you; And all the families of the earth Shall bless themselves by you."

ג וַאֲבָרֲכָה מְבָרְכֶיךָ וּמְקַלֶּלְךָ אָאֹר וְנִבְרְכוּ בְךָ כֹּל מִשְׁפְּחֹת הָאֲדָמָה:

va-a-va-r'-KHA m'-VA-r'-KHE-kha um-ka-lel-KHA a-OR v'-niv-r'-KHU v'-KHA KOL mish-p'-KHOT ha-a-da-MAH

12:1 Go forth from your native land With the words *lech l'cha* (לך לך), literally 'go for yourself,' *Avraham* is commanded to leave everything behind and head to the Holy Land. It would have been enough for God to command him *lech* (לך), 'go'; what is added by the word *l'cha* (לך), 'for yourself'? According to *Rashi*, the word *l'cha* implies that the travel was for *Avraham*'s benefit. Though he is leaving his homeland, family, and father's house, God promises *Avraham* that the journey will be beneficial to him. As a result of his relocation, he will merit the children he has always wanted and will become influential throughout the world, so that he will be able to accomplish his mission to positively influence the world. A journey to *Eretz Yisrael* is not always simple, but the impact it can have is immeasurable.

12:3 I will bless those who bless you and curse him that curses you *Avraham* is commanded to travel to a land unknown to him. To assuage his fears that he would not find friends or supporters in his new home, *Hashem* promises that He will remain on *Avraham*'s side by blessing those who bless him and cursing those who curse him. He concludes with the promise that *Avraham* and his descendants will become a source of blessing to the entire world. This promise has remained in effect through the generations. History has shown that whenever a nation persecutes the Jewish people, curses ultimately befall it. However, wherever the Children of Israel have been welcomed, they have made immeasurable contributions to society, thus earning divine favor for their host nation. On an individual level as well, many non-Jews look to this verse as an important reason to stand with the People of Israel and the Land of Israel.

The Chinese delegation at the Jerusalem March, *Sukkot* 2013

4 *Avram* went forth as *Hashem* had commanded him, and Lot went with him. *Avram* was seventy-five years old when he left Haran.

ד וַיֵּלֶךְ אַבְרָם כַּאֲשֶׁר דִּבֶּר אֵלָיו יְהוָֹה וַיֵּלֶךְ אִתּוֹ לוֹט וְאַבְרָם בֶּן־חָמֵשׁ שָׁנִים וְשִׁבְעִים שָׁנָה בְּצֵאתוֹ מֵחָרָן:

5 *Avram* took his wife *Sarai* and his brother's son Lot, and all the wealth that they had amassed, and the persons that they had acquired in Haran; and they set out for the land of Canaan. When they arrived in the land of Canaan,

ה וַיִּקַּח אַבְרָם אֶת־שָׂרַי אִשְׁתּוֹ וְאֶת־לוֹט בֶּן־אָחִיו וְאֶת־כָּל־רְכוּשָׁם אֲשֶׁר רָכָשׁוּ וְאֶת־הַנֶּפֶשׁ אֲשֶׁר־עָשׂוּ בְחָרָן וַיֵּצְאוּ לָלֶכֶת אַרְצָה כְּנַעַן וַיָּבֹאוּ אַרְצָה כְּנָעַן:

6 *Avram* passed through the land as far as the site of Shechem, at the terebinth of Moreh. The Canaanites were then in the land.

ו וַיַּעֲבֹר אַבְרָם בָּאָרֶץ עַד מְקוֹם שְׁכֶם עַד אֵלוֹן מוֹרֶה וְהַכְּנַעֲנִי אָז בָּאָרֶץ:

7 *Hashem* appeared to *Avram* and said, "I will assign this land to your offspring." And he built a *Mizbayach* there to *Hashem* who had appeared to him.

ז וַיֵּרָא יְהוָֹה אֶל־אַבְרָם וַיֹּאמֶר לְזַרְעֲךָ אֶתֵּן אֶת־הָאָרֶץ הַזֹּאת וַיִּבֶן שָׁם מִזְבֵּחַ לַיהוָֹה הַנִּרְאֶה אֵלָיו:

va-yay-RA a-do-NAI el av-RAM va-YO-mer l'-ZAR-a-KHA e-TAYN et ha-A-retz ha-ZOT va-YI-ven SHAM miz-BAY-akh la-do-NAI ha-nir-EH ay-LAV

8 From there he moved on to the hill country east of *Beit El* and pitched his tent, with *Beit El* on the west and Ai on the east; and he built there a *Mizbayach* to *Hashem* and invoked *Hashem* by name.

ח וַיַּעְתֵּק מִשָּׁם הָהָרָה מִקֶּדֶם לְבֵית־אֵל וַיֵּט אָהֳלֹה בֵּית־אֵל מִיָּם וְהָעַי מִקֶּדֶם וַיִּבֶן־שָׁם מִזְבֵּחַ לַיהוָֹה וַיִּקְרָא בְּשֵׁם יְהוָֹה:

9 Then *Avram* journeyed by stages toward the *Negev*.

ט וַיִּסַּע אַבְרָם הָלוֹךְ וְנָסוֹעַ הַנֶּגְבָּה:

10 There was a famine in the land, and *Avram* went down to Egypt to sojourn there, for the famine was severe in the land.

י וַיְהִי רָעָב בָּאָרֶץ וַיֵּרֶד אַבְרָם מִצְרַיְמָה לָגוּר שָׁם כִּי־כָבֵד הָרָעָב בָּאָרֶץ:

11 As he was about to enter Egypt, he said to his wife *Sarai*, "I know what a beautiful woman you are.

יא וַיְהִי כַּאֲשֶׁר הִקְרִיב לָבוֹא מִצְרָיְמָה וַיֹּאמֶר אֶל־שָׂרַי אִשְׁתּוֹ הִנֵּה־נָא יָדַעְתִּי כִּי אִשָּׁה יְפַת־מַרְאֶה אָתְּ:

12 If the Egyptians see you, and think, 'She is his wife,' they will kill me and let you live.

יב וְהָיָה כִּי־יִרְאוּ אֹתָךְ הַמִּצְרִים וְאָמְרוּ אִשְׁתּוֹ זֹאת וְהָרְגוּ אֹתִי וְאֹתָךְ יְחַיּוּ:

13 Please say that you are my sister, that it may go well with me because of you, and that I may remain alive thanks to you."

יג אִמְרִי־נָא אֲחֹתִי אָתְּ לְמַעַן יִיטַב־לִי בַעֲבוּרֵךְ וְחָיְתָה נַפְשִׁי בִּגְלָלֵךְ:

12:7 *Hashem* appeared to *Avram* This is the first time that the Bible describes God revealing Himself to *Avraham*. Even at the beginning of this chapter when *Hashem* commanded *Avraham* to leave his land, it does not say that *Hashem* appeared to him. The *Kli Yakar*, a biblical commentator who lived in Prague in the early seventeenth century, explains this by reference to the principle that *Hashem* does not reveal Himself prophetically outside the Land of Israel. The command given in Haran at the start of this chapter was heard, but not seen. Only once he arrived in Israel did God actually appear to *Avraham*, which then prompted *Avraham* to build an altar to mark the occasion. God's presence is felt most intensely in *Eretz Yisrael*.

Reconstruction of a four-horned altar at Tel Be'er Sheva

¹⁴ When *Avram* entered Egypt, the Egyptians saw how very beautiful the woman was.

יד וַיְהִי כְּבוֹא אַבְרָם מִצְרָיְמָה וַיִּרְאוּ הַמִּצְרִים אֶת־הָאִשָּׁה כִּי־יָפָה הִוא מְאֹד:

¹⁵ Pharaoh's courtiers saw her and praised her to Pharaoh, and the woman was taken into Pharaoh's palace.

טו וַיִּרְאוּ אֹתָהּ שָׂרֵי פַרְעֹה וַיְהַלְלוּ אֹתָהּ אֶל־פַּרְעֹה וַתֻּקַּח הָאִשָּׁה בֵּית פַּרְעֹה:

¹⁶ And because of her, it went well with *Avram*; he acquired sheep, oxen, asses, male and female slaves, she-asses, and camels.

טז וּלְאַבְרָם הֵיטִיב בַּעֲבוּרָהּ וַיְהִי־לוֹ צֹאן־ וּבָקָר וַחֲמֹרִים וַעֲבָדִים וּשְׁפָחֹת וַאֲתֹנֹת וּגְמַלִּים:

¹⁷ But *Hashem* afflicted Pharaoh and his household with mighty plagues on account of *Sarai*, the wife of *Avram*.

יז וַיְנַגַּע יְהֹוָה אֶת־פַּרְעֹה נְגָעִים גְּדֹלִים וְאֶת־בֵּיתוֹ עַל־דְּבַר שָׂרַי אֵשֶׁת אַבְרָם:

¹⁸ Pharaoh sent for *Avram* and said, "What is this you have done to me! Why did you not tell me that she was your wife?

יח וַיִּקְרָא פַרְעֹה לְאַבְרָם וַיֹּאמֶר מַה־זֹּאת עָשִׂיתָ לִּי לָמָּה לֹא־הִגַּדְתָּ לִּי כִּי אִשְׁתְּךָ הִוא:

¹⁹ Why did you say, 'She is my sister,' so that I took her as my wife? Now, here is your wife; take her and begone!"

יט לָמָה אָמַרְתָּ אֲחֹתִי הִוא וָאֶקַּח אֹתָהּ לִי לְאִשָּׁה וְעַתָּה הִנֵּה אִשְׁתְּךָ קַח וָלֵךְ:

²⁰ And Pharaoh put men in charge of him, and they sent him off with his wife and all that he possessed.

כ וַיְצַו עָלָיו פַּרְעֹה אֲנָשִׁים וַיְשַׁלְּחוּ אֹתוֹ וְאֶת־אִשְׁתּוֹ וְאֶת־כָּל־אֲשֶׁר־לוֹ:

13 ¹ From Egypt, *Avram* went up into the *Negev*, with his wife and all that he possessed, together with Lot.

יג א וַיַּעַל אַבְרָם מִמִּצְרַיִם הוּא וְאִשְׁתּוֹ וְכָל־ אֲשֶׁר־לוֹ וְלוֹט עִמּוֹ הַנֶּגְבָּה:

² Now *Avram* was very rich in cattle, silver, and gold.

ב וְאַבְרָם כָּבֵד מְאֹד בַּמִּקְנֶה בַּכֶּסֶף וּבַזָּהָב:

³ And he proceeded by stages from the *Negev* as far as *Beit El*, to the place where his tent had been formerly, between *Beit El* and Ai,

ג וַיֵּלֶךְ לְמַסָּעָיו מִנֶּגֶב וְעַד־בֵּית־אֵל עַד־ הַמָּקוֹם אֲשֶׁר־הָיָה שָׁם אֹהֳלֹה [אָהֳלוֹ] בַּתְּחִלָּה בֵּין בֵּית־אֵל וּבֵין הָעָי:

⁴ the site of the *Mizbayach* that he had built there at first; and there *Avram* invoked *Hashem* by name.

ד אֶל־מְקוֹם הַמִּזְבֵּחַ אֲשֶׁר־עָשָׂה שָׁם בָּרִאשֹׁנָה וַיִּקְרָא שָׁם אַבְרָם בְּשֵׁם יְהֹוָה:

⁵ Lot, who went with *Avram*, also had flocks and herds and tents,

ה וְגַם־לְלוֹט הַהֹלֵךְ אֶת־אַבְרָם הָיָה צֹאן־ וּבָקָר וְאֹהָלִים:

⁶ so that the land could not support them staying together; for their possessions were so great that they could not remain together.

ו וְלֹא־נָשָׂא אֹתָם הָאָרֶץ לָשֶׁבֶת יַחְדָּו כִּי־ הָיָה רְכוּשָׁם רָב וְלֹא יָכְלוּ לָשֶׁבֶת יַחְדָּו:

⁷ And there was quarreling between the herdsmen of *Avram*'s cattle and those of Lot's cattle. – The Canaanites and Perizzites were then dwelling in the land.

ז וַיְהִי־רִיב בֵּין רֹעֵי מִקְנֵה־אַבְרָם וּבֵין רֹעֵי מִקְנֵה־לוֹט וְהַכְּנַעֲנִי וְהַפְּרִזִּי אָז יֹשֵׁב בָּאָרֶץ:

8 *Avram* said to Lot, "Let there be no strife between you and me, between my herdsmen and yours, for we are kinsmen.

ח וַיֹּאמֶר אַבְרָם אֶל־לוֹט אַל־נָא תְהִי מְרִיבָה בֵּינִי וּבֵינֶיךָ וּבֵין רֹעַי וּבֵין רֹעֶיךָ כִּי־אֲנָשִׁים אַחִים אֲנָחְנוּ:

9 Is not the whole land before you? Let us separate: if you go north, I will go south; and if you go south, I will go north."

ט הֲלֹא כָל־הָאָרֶץ לְפָנֶיךָ הִפָּרֶד נָא מֵעָלָי אִם־הַשְּׂמֹאל וְאֵימִנָה וְאִם־הַיָּמִין וְאַשְׂמְאִילָה:

10 Lot looked about him and saw how well watered was the whole plain of the *Yarden*, all of it – this was before *Hashem* had destroyed Sodom and Gomorrah – all the way to Zoar, like the garden of *Hashem*, like the land of Egypt.

י וַיִּשָּׂא־לוֹט אֶת־עֵינָיו וַיַּרְא אֶת־כָּל־כִּכַּר הַיַּרְדֵּן כִּי כֻלָּהּ מַשְׁקֶה לִפְנֵי שַׁחֵת יְהוָֹה אֶת־סְדֹם וְאֶת־עֲמֹרָה כְּגַן־יְהוָֹה כְּאֶרֶץ מִצְרַיִם בֹּאֲכָה צֹעַר:

va-yi-sa LOT et ay-NAV va-YAR et kol ki-KAR ha-yar-DAYN KEE khu-LAH mash-KEH lif-NAY sha-KHAYT a-do-NAI et s'-DOM v'-et a-mo-RAH k'-gan a-do-NAI k'-E-retz mitz-RA-yim bo-a-KHA TZO-ar

11 So Lot chose for himself the whole plain of the *Yarden*, and Lot journeyed eastward. Thus they parted from each other;

יא וַיִּבְחַר־לוֹ לוֹט אֵת כָּל־כִּכַּר הַיַּרְדֵּן וַיִּסַּע לוֹט מִקֶּדֶם וַיִּפָּרְדוּ אִישׁ מֵעַל אָחִיו:

12 *Avram* remained in the land of Canaan, while Lot settled in the cities of the Plain, pitching his tents near Sodom.

יב אַבְרָם יָשַׁב בְּאֶרֶץ־כְּנָעַן וְלוֹט יָשַׁב בְּעָרֵי הַכִּכָּר וַיֶּאֱהַל עַד־סְדֹם:

13 Now the inhabitants of Sodom were very wicked sinners against *Hashem*.

יג וְאַנְשֵׁי סְדֹם רָעִים וְחַטָּאִים לַיהוָֹה מְאֹד:

14 And *Hashem* said to *Avram*, after Lot had parted from him, "Raise your eyes and look out from where you are, to the north and south, to the east and west,

יד וַיהוָֹה אָמַר אֶל־אַבְרָם אַחֲרֵי הִפָּרֶד־לוֹט מֵעִמּוֹ שָׂא נָא עֵינֶיךָ וּרְאֵה מִן־הַמָּקוֹם אֲשֶׁר־אַתָּה שָׁם צָפֹנָה וָנֶגְבָּה וָקֵדְמָה וָיָמָּה:

15 for I give all the land that you see to you and your offspring forever.

טו כִּי אֶת־כָּל־הָאָרֶץ אֲשֶׁר־אַתָּה רֹאֶה לְךָ אֶתְּנֶנָּה וּלְזַרְעֲךָ עַד־עוֹלָם:

16 I will make your offspring as the dust of the earth, so that if one can count the dust of the earth, then your offspring too can be counted.

טז וְשַׂמְתִּי אֶת־זַרְעֲךָ כַּעֲפַר הָאָרֶץ אֲשֶׁר אִם־יוּכַל אִישׁ לִמְנוֹת אֶת־עֲפַר הָאָרֶץ גַּם־זַרְעֲךָ יִמָּנֶה:

17 Up, walk about the land, through its length and its breadth, for I give it to you."

יז קוּם הִתְהַלֵּךְ בָּאָרֶץ לְאָרְכָּהּ וּלְרָחְבָּהּ כִּי לְךָ אֶתְּנֶנָּה:

13:10 How well watered was the whole plain of the *Yarden* After conflict arises between their shepherds, it becomes clear that *Avraham* and Lot must separate. Lot chooses the fertile, well-watered plain of the *Yarden*, leaving Canaan, a land with meager water sources of its own, to *Avraham*. The area that Lot chooses, though lush and bountiful, was filled with cruel and corrupt inhabitants who are ultimately destroyed in Sodom and Gomorrah. *Avraham*, on the other hand, settles in the holy Land of Israel, where he begins to fulfill his spiritual calling. Though other places can be attractive, when it comes to sanctity and Godliness there is no better place on earth than *Eretz Yisrael*.

Jordan River

18 And *Avram* moved his tent, and came to dwell at the terebinths of Mamre, which are in *Chevron*; and he built a *Mizbayach* there to *Hashem*.

14 1 Now, when King Amraphel of Shinar, King Arioch of Ellasar, King Chedorlaomer of Elam, and King Tidal of Goiim

2 made war on King Bera of Sodom, King Birsha of Gomorrah, King Shinab of Admah, King Shemeber of Zeboiim, and the king of Bela, which is Zoar,

3 all the latter joined forces at the Valley of Siddim, now the Dead Sea.

4 Twelve years they served Chedorlaomer, and in the thirteenth year they rebelled.

5 In the fourteenth year Chedorlaomer and the kings who were with him came and defeated the Rephaim at Ashteroth-karnaim, the Zuzim at Ham, the Emim at Shaveh-kiriathaim,

6 and the Horites in their hill country of Seir as far as *El-paran*, which is by the wilderness.

7 On their way back they came to En-mishpat, which is Kadesh, and subdued all the territory of the Amalekites, and also the Amorites who dwelt in Hazazon-tamar.

8 Then the king of Sodom, the king of Gomorrah, the king of Admah, the king of Zeboiim, and the king of Bela, which is Zoar, went forth and engaged them in battle in the Valley of Siddim:

9 King Chedorlaomer of Elam, King Tidal of Goiim, King Amraphel of Shinar, and King Arioch of Ellasar – four kings against those five.

10 Now the Valley of Siddim was dotted with bitumen pits; and the kings of Sodom and Gomorrah, in their flight, threw themselves into them, while the rest escaped to the hill country.

11 [The invaders] seized all the wealth of Sodom and Gomorrah and all their provisions, and went their way.

12 They also took Lot, the son of *Avram*'s brother, and his possessions, and departed; for he had settled in Sodom.

יח וַיֶּאֱהַל אַבְרָם וַיָּבֹא וַיֵּשֶׁב בְּאֵלֹנֵי מַמְרֵא אֲשֶׁר בְּחֶבְרוֹן וַיִּבֶן־שָׁם מִזְבֵּחַ לַיהוָה׃

יד א וַיְהִי בִּימֵי אַמְרָפֶל מֶלֶךְ־שִׁנְעָר אַרְיוֹךְ מֶלֶךְ אֶלָּסָר כְּדָרְלָעֹמֶר מֶלֶךְ עֵילָם וְתִדְעָל מֶלֶךְ גּוֹיִם׃

ב עָשׂוּ מִלְחָמָה אֶת־בֶּרַע מֶלֶךְ סְדֹם וְאֶת־בִּרְשַׁע מֶלֶךְ עֲמֹרָה שִׁנְאָב ׀ מֶלֶךְ אַדְמָה וְשֶׁמְאֵבֶר מֶלֶךְ צביים [צְבוֹיִם] וּמֶלֶךְ בֶּלַע הִיא־צֹעַר׃

ג כָּל־אֵלֶּה חָבְרוּ אֶל־עֵמֶק הַשִּׂדִּים הוּא יָם הַמֶּלַח׃

ד שְׁתֵּים עֶשְׂרֵה שָׁנָה עָבְדוּ אֶת־כְּדָרְלָעֹמֶר וּשְׁלֹשׁ־עֶשְׂרֵה שָׁנָה מָרָדוּ׃

ה וּבְאַרְבַּע עֶשְׂרֵה שָׁנָה בָּא כְדָרְלָעֹמֶר וְהַמְּלָכִים אֲשֶׁר אִתּוֹ וַיַּכּוּ אֶת־רְפָאִים בְּעַשְׁתְּרֹת קַרְנַיִם וְאֶת־הַזּוּזִים בְּהָם וְאֵת הָאֵימִים בְּשָׁוֵה קִרְיָתָיִם׃

ו וְאֶת־הַחֹרִי בְּהַרְרָם שֵׂעִיר עַד אֵיל פָּארָן אֲשֶׁר עַל־הַמִּדְבָּר׃

ז וַיָּשֻׁבוּ וַיָּבֹאוּ אֶל־עֵין מִשְׁפָּט הִוא קָדֵשׁ וַיַּכּוּ אֶת־כָּל־שְׂדֵה הָעֲמָלֵקִי וְגַם אֶת־הָאֱמֹרִי הַיֹּשֵׁב בְּחַצְצֹן תָּמָר׃

ח וַיֵּצֵא מֶלֶךְ־סְדֹם וּמֶלֶךְ עֲמֹרָה וּמֶלֶךְ אַדְמָה וּמֶלֶךְ צביים [צְבוֹיִם] וּמֶלֶךְ בֶּלַע הִוא־צֹעַר וַיַּעַרְכוּ אִתָּם מִלְחָמָה בְּעֵמֶק הַשִּׂדִּים׃

ט אֵת כְּדָרְלָעֹמֶר מֶלֶךְ עֵילָם וְתִדְעָל מֶלֶךְ גּוֹיִם וְאַמְרָפֶל מֶלֶךְ שִׁנְעָר וְאַרְיוֹךְ מֶלֶךְ אֶלָּסָר אַרְבָּעָה מְלָכִים אֶת־הַחֲמִשָּׁה׃

י וְעֵמֶק הַשִּׂדִּים בֶּאֱרֹת בֶּאֱרֹת חֵמָר וַיָּנֻסוּ מֶלֶךְ־סְדֹם וַעֲמֹרָה וַיִּפְּלוּ־שָׁמָּה וְהַנִּשְׁאָרִים הֶרָה נָּסוּ׃

יא וַיִּקְחוּ אֶת־כָּל־רְכֻשׁ סְדֹם וַעֲמֹרָה וְאֶת־כָּל־אָכְלָם וַיֵּלֵכוּ׃

יב וַיִּקְחוּ אֶת־לוֹט וְאֶת־רְכֻשׁוֹ בֶּן־אֲחִי אַבְרָם וַיֵּלֵכוּ וְהוּא יֹשֵׁב בִּסְדֹם׃

13 A fugitive brought the news to *Avram* the Hebrew, who was dwelling at the terebinths of Mamre the Amorite, kinsman of Eshkol and Aner, these being *Avram*'s allies.

יג וַיָּבֹא הַפָּלִיט וַיַּגֵּד לְאַבְרָם הָעִבְרִי וְהוּא שֹׁכֵן בְּאֵלֹנֵי מַמְרֵא הָאֱמֹרִי אֲחִי אֶשְׁכֹּל וַאֲחִי עָנֵר וְהֵם בַּעֲלֵי בְרִית־אַבְרָם:

14 When *Avram* heard that his kinsman had been taken captive, he mustered his retainers, born into his household, numbering three hundred and eighteen, and went in pursuit as far as *Dan*.

יד וַיִּשְׁמַע אַבְרָם כִּי נִשְׁבָּה אָחִיו וַיָּרֶק אֶת־חֲנִיכָיו יְלִידֵי בֵיתוֹ שְׁמֹנָה עָשָׂר וּשְׁלֹשׁ מֵאוֹת וַיִּרְדֹּף עַד־דָּן:

15 At night, he and his servants deployed against them and defeated them; and he pursued them as far as Hobah, which is north of Damascus.

טו וַיֵּחָלֵק עֲלֵיהֶם לַיְלָה הוּא וַעֲבָדָיו וַיַּכֵּם וַיִּרְדְּפֵם עַד־חוֹבָה אֲשֶׁר מִשְּׂמֹאל לְדַמָּשֶׂק:

16 He brought back all the possessions; he also brought back his kinsman Lot and his possessions, and the women and the rest of the people.

טז וַיָּשֶׁב אֵת כָּל־הָרְכֻשׁ וְגַם אֶת־לוֹט אָחִיו וּרְכֻשׁוֹ הֵשִׁיב וְגַם אֶת־הַנָּשִׁים וְאֶת־הָעָם:

17 When he returned from defeating Chedorlaomer and the kings with him, the king of Sodom came out to meet him in the Valley of Shaveh, which is the Valley of the King.

יז וַיֵּצֵא מֶלֶךְ־סְדֹם לִקְרָאתוֹ אַחֲרֵי שׁוּבוֹ מֵהַכּוֹת אֶת־כְּדָרְלָעֹמֶר וְאֶת־הַמְּלָכִים אֲשֶׁר אִתּוֹ אֶל־עֵמֶק שָׁוֵה הוּא עֵמֶק הַמֶּלֶךְ:

18 And King Melchizedek of *Shalem* brought out bread and wine; he was a priest of *Hashem* Most High.

יח וּמַלְכִּי־צֶדֶק מֶלֶךְ שָׁלֵם הוֹצִיא לֶחֶם וָיָיִן וְהוּא כֹהֵן לְאֵל עֶלְיוֹן:

u-mal-kee TZE-dek ME-lekh sha-LAYM ho-TZEE LE-khem va-ya-YIN v'-HU
kho-HAYN l'-AYL el-YON

19 He blessed him, saying, "Blessed be *Avram* of *Hashem* Most High, Creator of heaven and earth.

יט וַיְבָרְכֵהוּ וַיֹּאמַר בָּרוּךְ אַבְרָם לְאֵל עֶלְיוֹן קֹנֵה שָׁמַיִם וָאָרֶץ:

20 And blessed be *Hashem* Most High, Who has delivered your foes into your hand." And [*Avram*] gave him a tenth of everything.

כ וּבָרוּךְ אֵל עֶלְיוֹן אֲשֶׁר־מִגֵּן צָרֶיךָ בְּיָדֶךָ וַיִּתֶּן־לוֹ מַעֲשֵׂר מִכֹּל:

21 Then the king of Sodom said to *Avram*, "Give me the persons, and take the possessions for yourself."

כא וַיֹּאמֶר מֶלֶךְ־סְדֹם אֶל־אַבְרָם תֶּן־לִי הַנֶּפֶשׁ וְהָרְכֻשׁ קַח־לָךְ:

22 But *Avram* said to the king of Sodom, "I swear to *Hashem*, *Hashem* Most High, Creator of heaven and earth:

כב וַיֹּאמֶר אַבְרָם אֶל־מֶלֶךְ סְדֹם הֲרִימֹתִי יָדִי אֶל־יְהֹוָה אֵל עֶלְיוֹן קֹנֵה שָׁמַיִם וָאָרֶץ:

23 I will not take so much as a thread or a sandal strap of what is yours; you shall not say, 'It is I who made *Avram* rich.'

כג אִם־מִחוּט וְעַד שְׂרוֹךְ־נַעַל וְאִם־אֶקַּח מִכָּל־אֲשֶׁר־לָךְ וְלֹא תֹאמַר אֲנִי הֶעֱשַׁרְתִּי אֶת־אַבְרָם:

Old City of Yerushalayim

14:18 And King Melchizedek of *Shalem* The Sages explain that Melchizedek, King of *Shalem*, is actually *Shem*, the son of *Noach*, and that *Shalem* is an early name for *Yerushalayim*. After *Avraham* emerges victorious from war, Melchizedek greets him with bread and wine and blesses him and the God who delivered him, thereby attributing *Avraham*'s success to divine justice. Even before knowledge of one God and His righteous ways had spread throughout the world, the concept of divine justice was present in *Shalem*, Israel's future capital.

²⁴ For me, nothing but what my servants have used up; as for the share of the men who went with me – Aner, Eshkol, and Mamre – let them take their share."

כד בִּלְעָדַי רַק אֲשֶׁר אָכְלוּ הַנְּעָרִים וְחֵלֶק הָאֲנָשִׁים אֲשֶׁר הָלְכוּ אִתִּי עָנֵר אֶשְׁכֹּל וּמַמְרֵא הֵם יִקְחוּ חֶלְקָם:

15 ¹ Some time later, the word of *Hashem* came to *Avram* in a vision. He said, "Fear not, *Avram*, I am a shield to you; Your reward shall be very great."

טו א אַחַר הַדְּבָרִים הָאֵלֶּה הָיָה דְבַר־יְהֹוָה אֶל־אַבְרָם בַּמַּחֲזֶה לֵאמֹר אַל־תִּירָא אַבְרָם אָנֹכִי מָגֵן לָךְ שְׂכָרְךָ הַרְבֵּה מְאֹד:

² But *Avram* said, "O *Hashem*, what can You give me, seeing that I shall die childless, and the one in charge of my household is Dammesek *Eliezer*!"

ב וַיֹּאמֶר אַבְרָם אֲדֹנָי יֱהֹוִה מַה־תִּתֶּן־לִי וְאָנֹכִי הוֹלֵךְ עֲרִירִי וּבֶן־מֶשֶׁק בֵּיתִי הוּא דַּמֶּשֶׂק אֱלִיעֶזֶר:

³ *Avram* said further, "Since You have granted me no offspring, my steward will be my heir."

ג וַיֹּאמֶר אַבְרָם הֵן לִי לֹא נָתַתָּה זָרַע וְהִנֵּה בֶן־בֵּיתִי יוֹרֵשׁ אֹתִי:

⁴ The word of *Hashem* came to him in reply, "That one shall not be your heir; none but your very own issue shall be your heir."

ד וְהִנֵּה דְבַר־יְהֹוָה אֵלָיו לֵאמֹר לֹא יִירָשְׁךָ זֶה כִּי־אִם אֲשֶׁר יֵצֵא מִמֵּעֶיךָ הוּא יִירָשֶׁךָ:

⁵ He took him outside and said, "Look toward heaven and count the stars, if you are able to count them." And He added, "So shall your offspring be."

ה וַיּוֹצֵא אֹתוֹ הַחוּצָה וַיֹּאמֶר הַבֶּט־נָא הַשָּׁמַיְמָה וּסְפֹר הַכּוֹכָבִים אִם־תּוּכַל לִסְפֹּר אֹתָם וַיֹּאמֶר לוֹ כֹּה יִהְיֶה זַרְעֶךָ:

⁶ And because he put his trust in *Hashem*, He reckoned it to his merit.

ו וְהֶאֱמִן בַּיהֹוָה וַיַּחְשְׁבֶהָ לּוֹ צְדָקָה:

⁷ Then He said to him, "I am *Hashem* who brought you out from Ur of the Chaldeans to assign this land to you as a possession."

ז וַיֹּאמֶר אֵלָיו אֲנִי יְהֹוָה אֲשֶׁר הוֹצֵאתִיךָ מֵאוּר כַּשְׂדִּים לָתֶת לְךָ אֶת־הָאָרֶץ הַזֹּאת לְרִשְׁתָּהּ:

⁸ And he said, "O *Hashem*, how shall I know that I am to possess it?"

ח וַיֹּאמַר אֲדֹנָי יֱהֹוִה בַּמָּה אֵדַע כִּי אִירָשֶׁנָּה:

⁹ He answered, "Bring Me a three-year-old heifer, a three-year-old she-goat, a three-year-old ram, a turtledove, and a young bird."

ט וַיֹּאמֶר אֵלָיו קְחָה לִי עֶגְלָה מְשֻׁלֶּשֶׁת וְעֵז מְשֻׁלֶּשֶׁת וְאַיִל מְשֻׁלָּשׁ וְתֹר וְגוֹזָל:

¹⁰ He brought Him all these and cut them in two, placing each half opposite the other; but he did not cut up the bird.

י וַיִּקַּח־לוֹ אֶת־כָּל־אֵלֶּה וַיְבַתֵּר אֹתָם בַּתָּוֶךְ וַיִּתֵּן אִישׁ־בִּתְרוֹ לִקְרַאת רֵעֵהוּ וְאֶת־הַצִּפֹּר לֹא בָתָר:

¹¹ Birds of prey came down upon the carcasses, and *Avram* drove them away.

יא וַיֵּרֶד הָעַיִט עַל־הַפְּגָרִים וַיַּשֵּׁב אֹתָם אַבְרָם:

¹² As the sun was about to set, a deep sleep fell upon *Avram*, and a great dark dread descended upon him.

יב וַיְהִי הַשֶּׁמֶשׁ לָבוֹא וְתַרְדֵּמָה נָפְלָה עַל־אַבְרָם וְהִנֵּה אֵימָה חֲשֵׁכָה גְדֹלָה נֹפֶלֶת עָלָיו:

¹³ And He said to *Avram*, "Know well that your offspring shall be strangers in a land not theirs, and they shall be enslaved and oppressed four hundred years;

יג וַיֹּאמֶר לְאַבְרָם יָדֹעַ תֵּדַע כִּי־גֵר יִהְיֶה זַרְעֲךָ בְּאֶרֶץ לֹא לָהֶם וַעֲבָדוּם וְעִנּוּ אֹתָם אַרְבַּע מֵאוֹת שָׁנָה:

14 but I will execute judgment on the nation they shall
serve, and in the end they shall go free with great
wealth.

יד וְגַם אֶת־הַגּוֹי אֲשֶׁר יַעֲבֹדוּ דָּן אָנֹכִי
וְאַחֲרֵי־כֵן יֵצְאוּ בִּרְכֻשׁ גָּדוֹל:

15 As for you, You shall go to your fathers in peace;
You shall be buried at a ripe old age.

טו וְאַתָּה תָּבוֹא אֶל־אֲבֹתֶיךָ בְּשָׁלוֹם תִּקָּבֵר
בְּשֵׂיבָה טוֹבָה:

16 And they shall return here in the fourth generation,
for the iniquity of the Amorites is not yet complete."

טז וְדוֹר רְבִיעִי יָשׁוּבוּ הֵנָּה כִּי לֹא־שָׁלֵם
עֲוֹן הָאֱמֹרִי עַד־הֵנָּה:

17 When the sun set and it was very dark, there
appeared a smoking oven, and a flaming torch
which passed between those pieces.

יז וַיְהִי הַשֶּׁמֶשׁ בָּאָה וַעֲלָטָה הָיָה וְהִנֵּה
תַנּוּר עָשָׁן וְלַפִּיד אֵשׁ אֲשֶׁר עָבַר בֵּין
הַגְּזָרִים הָאֵלֶּה:

18 On that day *Hashem* made a covenant with *Avram*,
saying, "To your offspring I assign this land, from
the river of Egypt to the great river, the river
Euphrates:

יח בַּיּוֹם הַהוּא כָּרַת יְהוָֹה אֶת־אַבְרָם
בְּרִית לֵאמֹר לְזַרְעֲךָ נָתַתִּי אֶת־הָאָרֶץ
הַזֹּאת מִנְּהַר מִצְרַיִם עַד־הַנָּהָר הַגָּדֹל
נְהַר־פְּרָת:

ba-YOM ha-HU ka-RAT a-do-NAI et av-RAM b'-REET lay-MOR
l'-zar-a-KHA na-TA-tee et ha-A-retz ha-ZOT mi-n'-HAR
mitz-RA-yim ad ha-na-HAR ha-ga-DOL n'-har p'-RAT

19 the Kenites, the Kenizzites, the Kadmonites,

יט אֶת־הַקֵּינִי וְאֶת־הַקְּנִזִּי וְאֵת הַקַּדְמֹנִי:

20 the Hittites, the Perizzites, the Rephaim,

כ וְאֶת־הַחִתִּי וְאֶת־הַפְּרִזִּי וְאֶת־הָרְפָאִים:

21 the Amorites, the Canaanites, the Girgashites, and
the Jebusites."

כא וְאֶת־הָאֱמֹרִי וְאֶת־הַכְּנַעֲנִי וְאֶת־הַגִּרְגָּשִׁי
וְאֶת־הַיְבוּסִי:

16 1 *Sarai*, *Avram*'s wife, had borne him no children.
She had an Egyptian maidservant whose name was
Hagar.

טז א וְשָׂרַי אֵשֶׁת אַבְרָם לֹא יָלְדָה לוֹ וְלָהּ
שִׁפְחָה מִצְרִית וּשְׁמָהּ הָגָר:

2 And *Sarai* said to *Avram*, "Look, *Hashem* has kept
me from bearing. Consort with my maid; perhaps
I shall have a son through her." And *Avram* heeded
Sarai's request.

ב וַתֹּאמֶר שָׂרַי אֶל־אַבְרָם הִנֵּה־נָא עֲצָרַנִי
יְהוָֹה מִלֶּדֶת בֹּא־נָא אֶל־שִׁפְחָתִי אוּלַי
אִבָּנֶה מִמֶּנָּה וַיִּשְׁמַע אַבְרָם לְקוֹל שָׂרָי:

3 So *Sarai*, *Avram*'s wife, took her maid, Hagar the
Egyptian – after *Avram* had dwelt in the land of
Canaan ten years – and gave her to her husband
Avram as concubine.

ג וַתִּקַּח שָׂרַי אֵשֶׁת־אַבְרָם אֶת־הָגָר
הַמִּצְרִית שִׁפְחָתָהּ מִקֵּץ עֶשֶׂר שָׁנִים
לְשֶׁבֶת אַבְרָם בְּאֶרֶץ כְּנַעַן וַתִּתֵּן אֹתָהּ
לְאַבְרָם אִישָׁהּ לוֹ לְאִשָּׁה:

 **15:18 To your offspring I
assign this land** In this
monumental covenant
between *Hashem* and *Avraham*,
God states that on this day He has
given the Land of Israel to *Avraham's* descendants. While *Hashem*
uses the term *natatee* (נתתי), 'I have
given,' in the past tense, in refer-
ence to generations that have not yet been born, *Rashi*
explains that this is not a grammatical error. Since God's

Woman wrapped in the Israeli flag at sunrise

word is the ultimate truth, it is as if
it has already been done. Though
it took more than four hundred
years until this promise was fulfilled, the children of *Avraham*
waited with faith. This patient wait-
ing served as good practice for the
nearly two thousand years of wait-
ing that preceded our present re-
turn to Zion. With the birth of the State of Israel, another
promise to *Avraham* has been fulfilled.

4 He cohabited with Hagar and she conceived; and when she saw that she had conceived, her mistress was lowered in her esteem.

ד וַיָּבֹא אֶל־הָגָר וַתַּהַר וַתֵּרֶא כִּי הָרָתָה וַתֵּקַל גְּבִרְתָּהּ בְּעֵינֶיהָ:

5 And *Sarai* said to *Avram*, "The wrong done me is your fault! I myself put my maid in your bosom; now that she sees that she is pregnant, I am lowered in her esteem. *Hashem* decide between you and me!"

ה וַתֹּאמֶר שָׂרַי אֶל־אַבְרָם חֲמָסִי עָלֶיךָ אָנֹכִי נָתַתִּי שִׁפְחָתִי בְּחֵיקֶךָ וַתֵּרֶא כִּי הָרָתָה וָאֵקַל בְּעֵינֶיהָ יִשְׁפֹּט יְהוָה בֵּינִי וּבֵינֶיךָ:

6 *Avram* said to *Sarai*, "Your maid is in your hands. Deal with her as you think right." Then *Sarai* treated her harshly, and she ran away from her.

ו וַיֹּאמֶר אַבְרָם אֶל־שָׂרַי הִנֵּה שִׁפְחָתֵךְ בְּיָדֵךְ עֲשִׂי־לָהּ הַטּוֹב בְּעֵינָיִךְ וַתְּעַנֶּהָ שָׂרַי וַתִּבְרַח מִפָּנֶיהָ:

7 An angel of *Hashem* found her by a spring of water in the wilderness, the spring on the road to Shur,

ז וַיִּמְצָאָהּ מַלְאַךְ יְהוָה עַל־עֵין הַמַּיִם בַּמִּדְבָּר עַל־הָעַיִן בְּדֶרֶךְ שׁוּר:

8 and said, "Hagar, slave of *Sarai*, where have you come from, and where are you going?" And she said, "I am running away from my mistress *Sarai*."

ח וַיֹּאמַר הָגָר שִׁפְחַת שָׂרַי אֵי־מִזֶּה בָאת וְאָנָה תֵלֵכִי וַתֹּאמֶר מִפְּנֵי שָׂרַי גְּבִרְתִּי אָנֹכִי בֹּרַחַת:

9 And the angel of *Hashem* said to her, "Go back to your mistress, and submit to her harsh treatment."

ט וַיֹּאמֶר לָהּ מַלְאַךְ יְהוָה שׁוּבִי אֶל־גְּבִרְתֵּךְ וְהִתְעַנִּי תַּחַת יָדֶיהָ:

10 And the angel of *Hashem* said to her, "I will greatly increase your offspring, And they shall be too many to count."

י וַיֹּאמֶר לָהּ מַלְאַךְ יְהוָה הַרְבָּה אַרְבֶּה אֶת־זַרְעֵךְ וְלֹא יִסָּפֵר מֵרֹב:

11 The angel of *Hashem* said to her further, "Behold, you are with child And shall bear a son; You shall call him Ishmael, For *Hashem* has paid heed to your suffering.

יא וַיֹּאמֶר לָהּ מַלְאַךְ יְהוָה הִנָּךְ הָרָה וְיֹלַדְתְּ בֵּן וְקָרָאת שְׁמוֹ יִשְׁמָעֵאל כִּי־שָׁמַע יְהוָה אֶל־עָנְיֵךְ:

12 He shall be a wild ass of a man; His hand against everyone, And everyone's hand against him; He shall dwell alongside of all his kinsmen."

יב וְהוּא יִהְיֶה פֶּרֶא אָדָם יָדוֹ בַכֹּל וְיַד כֹּל בּוֹ וְעַל־פְּנֵי כָל־אֶחָיו יִשְׁכֹּן:

13 And she called *Hashem* who spoke to her, "You Are El-roi," by which she meant, "Have I not gone on seeing after He saw me!"

יג וַתִּקְרָא שֵׁם־יְהוָה הַדֹּבֵר אֵלֶיהָ אַתָּה אֵל רֳאִי כִּי אָמְרָה הֲגַם הֲלֹם רָאִיתִי אַחֲרֵי רֹאִי:

14 Therefore the well was called Beer-lahai-roi; it is between Kadesh and Bered.

יד עַל־כֵּן קָרָא לַבְּאֵר בְּאֵר לַחַי רֹאִי הִנֵּה בֵין־קָדֵשׁ וּבֵין בָּרֶד:

*al KAYN ka-RA la-b'-AYR b'-AYR la-KHAI ro-EE
hi-NAY vayn ka-DAYSH u-VAYN BA-red*

16:14 Therefore the well was called Beer-lahai-roi No longer able to bear her suffering in the home of her mistress *Sara*, Hagar runs to the desert in search of relief and solitude. According to Rabbi Samson Raphael Hirsch, when Hagar subsequently encounters the angel she realizes that one is never alone or out of God's sight. The well where this encounter takes place is therefore named *be'er lachai ro-ee* (באר לחי ראי), the 'well of the Living One who sees me.' Specifically in *Eretz Yisrael*, God's presence and watchful eye is felt strongly, as it says in *Devarim* (11:12) "on which *Hashem* your God always keeps His eye."

Sunburst over the Old City of *Yerushalayim*

¹⁵ Hagar bore a son to *Avram*, and *Avram* gave the son that Hagar bore him the name Ishmael.

טו וַתֵּלֶד הָגָר לְאַבְרָם בֵּן וַיִּקְרָא אַבְרָם שֶׁם־בְּנוֹ אֲשֶׁר־יָלְדָה הָגָר יִשְׁמָעֵאל:

¹⁶ *Avram* was eighty-six years old when Hagar bore Ishmael to *Avram*.

טז וְאַבְרָם בֶּן־שְׁמֹנִים שָׁנָה וְשֵׁשׁ שָׁנִים בְּלֶדֶת־הָגָר אֶת־יִשְׁמָעֵאל לְאַבְרָם:

17 ¹ When *Avram* was ninety-nine years old, *Hashem* appeared to *Avram* and said to him, "I am *El Shaddai*. Walk in My ways and be blameless.

יז א וַיְהִי אַבְרָם בֶּן־תִּשְׁעִים שָׁנָה וְתֵשַׁע שָׁנִים וַיֵּרָא יְהוָה אֶל־אַבְרָם וַיֹּאמֶר אֵלָיו אֲנִי־אֵל שַׁדַּי הִתְהַלֵּךְ לְפָנַי וֶהְיֵה תָמִים:

² I will establish My covenant between Me and you, and I will make you exceedingly numerous."

ב וְאֶתְּנָה בְרִיתִי בֵּינִי וּבֵינֶךָ וְאַרְבֶּה אוֹתְךָ בִּמְאֹד מְאֹד:

³ *Avram* threw himself on his face; and *Hashem* spoke to him further,

ג וַיִּפֹּל אַבְרָם עַל־פָּנָיו וַיְדַבֵּר אִתּוֹ אֱלֹהִים לֵאמֹר:

⁴ "As for Me, this is My covenant with you: You shall be the father of a multitude of nations.

ד אֲנִי הִנֵּה בְרִיתִי אִתָּךְ וְהָיִיתָ לְאַב הֲמוֹן גּוֹיִם:

⁵ And you shall no longer be called *Avram*, but your name shall be *Avraham*, for I make you the father of a multitude of nations.

ה וְלֹא־יִקָּרֵא עוֹד אֶת־שִׁמְךָ אַבְרָם וְהָיָה שִׁמְךָ אַבְרָהָם כִּי אַב־הֲמוֹן גּוֹיִם נְתַתִּיךָ:

⁶ I will make you exceedingly fertile, and make nations of you; and kings shall come forth from you.

ו וְהִפְרֵתִי אֹתְךָ בִּמְאֹד מְאֹד וּנְתַתִּיךָ לְגוֹיִם וּמְלָכִים מִמְּךָ יֵצֵאוּ:

⁷ I will maintain My covenant between Me and you, and your offspring to come, as an everlasting covenant throughout the ages, to be *Hashem* to you and to your offspring to come.

ז וַהֲקִמֹתִי אֶת־בְּרִיתִי בֵּינִי וּבֵינֶךָ וּבֵין זַרְעֲךָ אַחֲרֶיךָ לְדֹרֹתָם לִבְרִית עוֹלָם לִהְיוֹת לְךָ לֵאלֹהִים וּלְזַרְעֲךָ אַחֲרֶיךָ:

⁸ I assign the land you sojourn in to you and your offspring to come, all the land of Canaan, as an everlasting holding. I will be their God."

ח וְנָתַתִּי לְךָ וּלְזַרְעֲךָ אַחֲרֶיךָ אֵת אֶרֶץ מְגֻרֶיךָ אֵת כָּל־אֶרֶץ כְּנַעַן לַאֲחֻזַּת עוֹלָם וְהָיִיתִי לָהֶם לֵאלֹהִים:

v'-na-ta-TEE l'-KHA ul-zar-a-KHA a-kha-RE-kha AYT E-retz m'-gu-RE-kha AYT kol E-retz k'-NA-an la-a-khu-ZAT o-LAM v'-ha-YEE-tee la-HEM LAay-lo-HEEM

⁹ *Hashem* further said to *Avraham*, "As for you, you and your offspring to come throughout the ages shall keep My covenant.

ט וַיֹּאמֶר אֱלֹהִים אֶל־אַבְרָהָם וְאַתָּה אֶת־בְּרִיתִי תִשְׁמֹר אַתָּה וְזַרְעֲךָ אַחֲרֶיךָ לְדֹרֹתָם:

¹⁰ Such shall be the covenant between Me and you and your offspring to follow which you shall keep: every male among you shall be circumcised.

י זֹאת בְּרִיתִי אֲשֶׁר תִּשְׁמְרוּ בֵּינִי וּבֵינֵיכֶם וּבֵין זַרְעֲךָ אַחֲרֶיךָ הִמּוֹל לָכֶם כָּל־זָכָר:

¹¹ You shall circumcise the flesh of your foreskin, and that shall be the sign of the covenant between Me and you.

יא וּנְמַלְתֶּם אֵת בְּשַׂר עָרְלַתְכֶם וְהָיָה לְאוֹת בְּרִית בֵּינִי וּבֵינֵיכֶם:

¹² And throughout the generations, every male among you shall be circumcised at the age of eight days. As for the homeborn slave and the one bought from an outsider who is not of your offspring,

יב וּבֶן־שְׁמֹנַת יָמִים יִמּוֹל לָכֶם כָּל־זָכָר לְדֹרֹתֵיכֶם יְלִיד בָּיִת וּמִקְנַת־כֶּסֶף מִכֹּל בֶּן־נֵכָר אֲשֶׁר לֹא מִזַּרְעֲךָ הוּא:

13 they must be circumcised, homeborn, and purchased alike. Thus shall My covenant be marked in your flesh as an everlasting pact.

14 And if any male who is uncircumcised fails to circumcise the flesh of his foreskin, that person shall be cut off from his kin; he has broken My covenant."

15 And *Hashem* said to *Avraham*, "As for your wife *Sarai*, you shall not call her *Sarai*, but her name shall be *Sara*.

16 I will bless her; indeed, I will give you a son by her. I will bless her so that she shall give rise to nations; rulers of peoples shall issue from her."

17 *Avraham* threw himself on his face and laughed, as he said to himself, "Can a child be born to a man a hundred years old, or can *Sara* bear a child at ninety?"

18 And *Avraham* said to *Hashem*, "O that Ishmael might live by Your favor!"

19 *Hashem* said, "Nevertheless, *Sara* your wife shall bear you a son, and you shall name him *Yitzchak*; and I will maintain My covenant with him as an everlasting covenant for his offspring to come.

20 As for Ishmael, I have heeded you. I hereby bless him. I will make him fertile and exceedingly numerous. He shall be the father of twelve chieftains, and I will make of him a great nation.

21 But My covenant I will maintain with *Yitzchak*, whom *Sara* shall bear to you at this season next year."

יג הַמּוֹל יִמּוֹל יְלִיד בֵּיתְךָ וּמִקְנַת כַּסְפֶּךָ וְהָיְתָה בְרִיתִי בִּבְשַׂרְכֶם לִבְרִית עוֹלָם:

יד וְעָרֵל זָכָר אֲשֶׁר לֹא־יִמּוֹל אֶת־בְּשַׂר עָרְלָתוֹ וְנִכְרְתָה הַנֶּפֶשׁ הַהִוא מֵעַמֶּיהָ אֶת־בְּרִיתִי הֵפַר:

טו וַיֹּאמֶר אֱלֹהִים אֶל־אַבְרָהָם שָׂרַי אִשְׁתְּךָ לֹא־תִקְרָא אֶת־שְׁמָהּ שָׂרָי כִּי שָׂרָה שְׁמָהּ:

טז וּבֵרַכְתִּי אֹתָהּ וְגַם נָתַתִּי מִמֶּנָּה לְךָ בֵּן וּבֵרַכְתִּיהָ וְהָיְתָה לְגוֹיִם מַלְכֵי עַמִּים מִמֶּנָּה יִהְיוּ:

יז וַיִּפֹּל אַבְרָהָם עַל־פָּנָיו וַיִּצְחָק וַיֹּאמֶר בְּלִבּוֹ הַלְּבֶן מֵאָה־שָׁנָה יִוָּלֵד וְאִם־שָׂרָה הֲבַת־תִּשְׁעִים שָׁנָה תֵּלֵד:

יח וַיֹּאמֶר אַבְרָהָם אֶל־הָאֱלֹהִים לוּ יִשְׁמָעֵאל יִחְיֶה לְפָנֶיךָ:

יט וַיֹּאמֶר אֱלֹהִים אֲבָל שָׂרָה אִשְׁתְּךָ יֹלֶדֶת לְךָ בֵּן וְקָרָאתָ אֶת־שְׁמוֹ יִצְחָק וַהֲקִמֹתִי אֶת־בְּרִיתִי אִתּוֹ לִבְרִית עוֹלָם לְזַרְעוֹ אַחֲרָיו:

כ וּלְיִשְׁמָעֵאל שְׁמַעְתִּיךָ הִנֵּה בֵּרַכְתִּי אֹתוֹ וְהִפְרֵיתִי אֹתוֹ וְהִרְבֵּיתִי אֹתוֹ בִּמְאֹד מְאֹד שְׁנֵים־עָשָׂר נְשִׂיאִם יוֹלִיד וּנְתַתִּיו לְגוֹי גָּדוֹל:

כא וְאֶת־בְּרִיתִי אָקִים אֶת־יִצְחָק אֲשֶׁר תֵּלֵד לְךָ שָׂרָה לַמּוֹעֵד הַזֶּה בַּשָּׁנָה הָאַחֶרֶת:

v'-et b'-ree-TEE a-KEEM et yitz-KHAK a-SHER tay-LAYD l'-KHA sa-RAH la-mo-AYD ha-ZEH ba-sha-NAH ha-a-KHE-ret

22 And when He was done speaking with him, *Hashem* was gone from *Avraham*.

כב וַיְכַל לְדַבֵּר אִתּוֹ וַיַּעַל אֱלֹהִים מֵעַל אַבְרָהָם:

Father and son in the Negev desert

17:21 But My covenant I will maintain with *Yitzchak* *Avraham* was chosen to be God's emissary in this world, to live in the Land of Israel, and to establish a nation with a unique mission. But who would be *Avraham*'s heir, Ishmael or *Yitzchak*? This ambiguity is eliminated when *Hashem* declares that, although a great nation will emerge from Ishmael's lineage, *Yitzchak* is the chosen heir to *Avraham*'s legacy and *Eretz Yisrael*.

23 Then *Avraham* took his son Ishmael, and all his homeborn slaves and all those he had bought, every male in *Avraham*'s household, and he circumcised the flesh of their foreskins on that very day, as *Hashem* had spoken to him.

כג וַיִּקַּח אַבְרָהָם אֶת־יִשְׁמָעֵאל בְּנוֹ וְאֵת כָּל־יְלִידֵי בֵיתוֹ וְאֵת כָּל־מִקְנַת כַּסְפּוֹ כָּל־זָכָר בְּאַנְשֵׁי בֵּית אַבְרָהָם וַיָּמָל אֶת־ בְּשַׂר עָרְלָתָם בְּעֶצֶם הַיּוֹם הַזֶּה כַּאֲשֶׁר דִּבֶּר אִתּוֹ אֱלֹהִים:

24 *Avraham* was ninety-nine years old when he circumcised the flesh of his foreskin,

כד וְאַבְרָהָם בֶּן־תִּשְׁעִים וָתֵשַׁע שָׁנָה בְּהִמֹּלוֹ בְּשַׂר עָרְלָתוֹ:

25 and his son Ishmael was thirteen years old when he was circumcised in the flesh of his foreskin.

כה וְיִשְׁמָעֵאל בְּנוֹ בֶּן־שְׁלֹשׁ עֶשְׂרֵה שָׁנָה בְּהִמֹּלוֹ אֵת בְּשַׂר עָרְלָתוֹ:

26 Thus *Avraham* and his son Ishmael were circumcised on that very day;

כו בְּעֶצֶם הַיּוֹם הַזֶּה נִמּוֹל אַבְרָהָם וְיִשְׁמָעֵאל בְּנוֹ:

27 and all his household, his homeborn slaves and those that had been bought from outsiders, were circumcised with him.

כז וְכָל־אַנְשֵׁי בֵיתוֹ יְלִיד בָּיִת וּמִקְנַת־כֶּסֶף מֵאֵת בֶּן־נֵכָר נִמֹּלוּ אִתּוֹ:

18 1 *Hashem* appeared to him by the terebinths of Mamre; he was sitting at the entrance of the tent as the day grew hot.

יח א  וַיֵּרָא אֵלָיו יְהֹוָה בְּאֵלֹנֵי מַמְרֵא וְהוּא יֹשֵׁב פֶּתַח־הָאֹהֶל כְּחֹם הַיּוֹם:

*va-yay-RA ay-LAV a-do-NAI b'-ay-lo-NAY mam-RAY v'-HU
yo-SHAYV pe-takh ha-O-hel k'-KHOM ha-YOM*

2 Looking up, he saw three men standing near him. As soon as he saw them, he ran from the entrance of the tent to greet them and, bowing to the ground,

ב וַיִּשָּׂא עֵינָיו וַיַּרְא וְהִנֵּה שְׁלֹשָׁה אֲנָשִׁים נִצָּבִים עָלָיו וַיַּרְא וַיָּרָץ לִקְרָאתָם מִפֶּתַח הָאֹהֶל וַיִּשְׁתַּחוּ אָרְצָה:

3 he said, "My lords, if it please you, do not go on past your servant.

ג וַיֹּאמַר אֲדֹנָי אִם־נָא מָצָאתִי חֵן בְּעֵינֶיךָ אַל־נָא תַעֲבֹר מֵעַל עַבְדֶּךָ:

4 Let a little water be brought; bathe your feet and recline under the tree.

ד יֻקַּח־נָא מְעַט־מַיִם וְרַחֲצוּ רַגְלֵיכֶם וְהִשָּׁעֲנוּ תַּחַת הָעֵץ:

5 And let me fetch a morsel of bread that you may refresh yourselves; then go on – seeing that you have come your servant's way." They replied, "Do as you have said."

ה וְאֶקְחָה פַת־לֶחֶם וְסַעֲדוּ לִבְּכֶם אַחַר תַּעֲבֹרוּ כִּי־עַל־כֵּן עֲבַרְתֶּם עַל־עַבְדְּכֶם וַיֹּאמְרוּ כֵּן תַּעֲשֶׂה כַּאֲשֶׁר דִּבַּרְתָּ:

6 *Avraham* hastened into the tent to *Sara*, and said, "Quick, three *se'eem* of choice flour! Knead and make cakes!"

ו וַיְמַהֵר אַבְרָהָם הָאֹהֱלָה אֶל־שָׂרָה וַיֹּאמֶר מַהֲרִי שְׁלֹשׁ סְאִים קֶמַח סֹלֶת לוּשִׁי וַעֲשִׂי עֻגוֹת:

18:1 By the terebinths of Mamre Mamre was the name of *Avraham*'s ally (Genesis 14:13). *Rashi* explains that of his three allies, Mamre was the only one who supported the idea of circumcision, and it was for this reason that *Hashem* reveals himself to *Avraham* in his

Terebinth tree at Nachal Sanin

territory. This teaches us an important lesson: A person should choose to live in a place conducive to spiritual growth. Choosing to live in the Land of Israel means choosing an environment that can foster a person's spiritual development and relationship with God.

7 Then *Avraham* ran to the herd, took a calf, tender and choice, and gave it to a servant-boy, who hastened to prepare it.

ז וְאֶל־הַבָּקָר רָץ אַבְרָהָם וַיִּקַּח בֶּן־בָּקָר רַךְ וָטוֹב וַיִּתֵּן אֶל־הַנַּעַר וַיְמַהֵר לַעֲשׂוֹת אֹתוֹ:

8 He took curds and milk and the calf that had been prepared and set these before them; and he waited on them under the tree as they ate.

ח וַיִּקַּח חֶמְאָה וְחָלָב וּבֶן־הַבָּקָר אֲשֶׁר עָשָׂה וַיִּתֵּן לִפְנֵיהֶם וְהוּא־עֹמֵד עֲלֵיהֶם תַּחַת הָעֵץ וַיֹּאכֵלוּ:

9 They said to him, "Where is your wife *Sara*?" And he replied, "There, in the tent."

ט וַיֹּאמְרוּ אֵלָיו אַיֵּה שָׂרָה אִשְׁתֶּךָ וַיֹּאמֶר הִנֵּה בָאֹהֶל:

10 Then one said, "I will return to you next year, and your wife *Sara* shall have a son!" *Sara* was listening at the entrance of the tent, which was behind him.

י וַיֹּאמֶר שׁוֹב אָשׁוּב אֵלֶיךָ כָּעֵת חַיָּה וְהִנֵּה־בֵן לְשָׂרָה אִשְׁתֶּךָ וְשָׂרָה שֹׁמַעַת פֶּתַח הָאֹהֶל וְהוּא אַחֲרָיו:

11 Now *Avraham* and *Sara* were old, advanced in years; *Sara* had stopped having the periods of women.

יא וְאַבְרָהָם וְשָׂרָה זְקֵנִים בָּאִים בַּיָּמִים חָדַל לִהְיוֹת לְשָׂרָה אֹרַח כַּנָּשִׁים:

12 And *Sara* laughed to herself, saying, "Now that I am withered, am I to have enjoyment – with my husband so old?"

יב וַתִּצְחַק שָׂרָה בְּקִרְבָּהּ לֵאמֹר אַחֲרֵי בְלֹתִי הָיְתָה־לִּי עֶדְנָה וַאדֹנִי זָקֵן:

13 Then *Hashem* said to *Avraham*, "Why did *Sara* laugh, saying, 'Shall I in truth bear a child, old as I am?'

יג וַיֹּאמֶר יְהוָה אֶל־אַבְרָהָם לָמָּה זֶּה צָחֲקָה שָׂרָה לֵאמֹר הַאַף אֻמְנָם אֵלֵד וַאֲנִי זָקַנְתִּי:

14 Is anything too wondrous for *Hashem*? I will return to you at the same season next year, and *Sara* shall have a son."

יד הֲיִפָּלֵא מֵיְהוָה דָּבָר לַמּוֹעֵד אָשׁוּב אֵלֶיךָ כָּעֵת חַיָּה וּלְשָׂרָה בֵן:

15 *Sara* lied, saying, "I did not laugh," for she was frightened. But He replied, "You did laugh."

טו וַתְּכַחֵשׁ שָׂרָה לֵאמֹר לֹא צָחַקְתִּי כִּי יָרֵאָה וַיֹּאמֶר לֹא כִּי צָחָקְתְּ:

16 The men set out from there and looked down toward Sodom, *Avraham* walking with them to see them off.

טז וַיָּקֻמוּ מִשָּׁם הָאֲנָשִׁים וַיַּשְׁקִפוּ עַל־פְּנֵי סְדֹם וְאַבְרָהָם הֹלֵךְ עִמָּם לְשַׁלְּחָם:

17 Now *Hashem* had said, "Shall I hide from *Avraham* what I am about to do,

יז וַיהוָה אָמָר הַמְכַסֶּה אֲנִי מֵאַבְרָהָם אֲשֶׁר אֲנִי עֹשֶׂה:

18 since *Avraham* is to become a great and populous nation and all the nations of the earth are to bless themselves by him?

יח וְאַבְרָהָם הָיוֹ יִהְיֶה לְגוֹי גָּדוֹל וְעָצוּם וְנִבְרְכוּ בוֹ כֹּל גּוֹיֵי הָאָרֶץ:

19 For I have singled him out, that he may instruct his children and his posterity to keep the way of *Hashem* by doing what is just and right, in order that *Hashem* may bring about for *Avraham* what He has promised him."

יט כִּי יְדַעְתִּיו לְמַעַן אֲשֶׁר יְצַוֶּה אֶת־בָּנָיו וְאֶת־בֵּיתוֹ אַחֲרָיו וְשָׁמְרוּ דֶּרֶךְ יְהוָה לַעֲשׂוֹת צְדָקָה וּמִשְׁפָּט לְמַעַן הָבִיא יְהוָה עַל־אַבְרָהָם אֵת אֲשֶׁר־דִּבֶּר עָלָיו:

20 Then *Hashem* said, "The outrage of Sodom and Gomorrah is so great, and their sin so grave!

כ וַיֹּאמֶר יְהוָה זַעֲקַת סְדֹם וַעֲמֹרָה כִּי־רָבָּה וְחַטָּאתָם כִּי כָבְדָה מְאֹד:

36

²¹ I will go down to see whether they have acted altogether according to the outcry that has reached Me; if not, I will take note."

כא אֵרֲדָה־נָּא וְאֶרְאֶה הַכְּצַעֲקָתָהּ הַבָּאָה אֵלַי עָשׂוּ כָּלָה וְאִם־לֹא אֵדָעָה:

²² The men went on from there to Sodom, while *Avraham* remained standing before *Hashem*.

כב וַיִּפְנוּ מִשָּׁם הָאֲנָשִׁים וַיֵּלְכוּ סְדֹמָה וְאַבְרָהָם עוֹדֶנּוּ עֹמֵד לִפְנֵי יְהוָה:

²³ *Avraham* came forward and said, "Will You sweep away the innocent along with the guilty?

כג וַיִּגַּשׁ אַבְרָהָם וַיֹּאמַר הַאַף תִּסְפֶּה צַדִּיק עִם־רָשָׁע:

²⁴ What if there should be fifty innocent within the city; will You then wipe out the place and not forgive it for the sake of the innocent fifty who are in it?

כד אוּלַי יֵשׁ חֲמִשִּׁים צַדִּיקִם בְּתוֹךְ הָעִיר הַאַף תִּסְפֶּה וְלֹא־תִשָּׂא לַמָּקוֹם לְמַעַן חֲמִשִּׁים הַצַּדִּיקִם אֲשֶׁר בְּקִרְבָּהּ:

²⁵ Far be it from You to do such a thing, to bring death upon the innocent as well as the guilty, so that innocent and guilty fare alike. Far be it from You! Shall not the Judge of all the earth deal justly?"

כה חָלִלָה לְּךָ מֵעֲשֹׂת כַּדָּבָר הַזֶּה לְהָמִית צַדִּיק עִם־רָשָׁע וְהָיָה כַצַּדִּיק כָּרָשָׁע חָלִלָה לָּךְ הֲשֹׁפֵט כָּל־הָאָרֶץ לֹא יַעֲשֶׂה מִשְׁפָּט:

²⁶ And *Hashem* answered, "If I find within the city of Sodom fifty innocent ones, I will forgive the whole place for their sake."

כו וַיֹּאמֶר יְהוָה אִם־אֶמְצָא בִסְדֹם חֲמִשִּׁים צַדִּיקִם בְּתוֹךְ הָעִיר וְנָשָׂאתִי לְכָל־הַמָּקוֹם בַּעֲבוּרָם:

²⁷ *Avraham* spoke up, saying, "Here I venture to speak to my Lord, I who am but dust and ashes:

כז וַיַּעַן אַבְרָהָם וַיֹּאמַר הִנֵּה־נָא הוֹאַלְתִּי לְדַבֵּר אֶל־אֲדֹנָי וְאָנֹכִי עָפָר וָאֵפֶר:

²⁸ What if the fifty innocent should lack five? Will You destroy the whole city for want of the five?" And He answered, "I will not destroy if I find forty-five there."

כח אוּלַי יַחְסְרוּן חֲמִשִּׁים הַצַּדִּיקִם חֲמִשָּׁה הֲתַשְׁחִית בַּחֲמִשָּׁה אֶת־כָּל־הָעִיר וַיֹּאמֶר לֹא אַשְׁחִית אִם־אֶמְצָא שָׁם אַרְבָּעִים וַחֲמִשָּׁה:

²⁹ But he spoke to Him again, and said, "What if forty should be found there?" And He answered, "I will not do it, for the sake of the forty."

כט וַיֹּסֶף עוֹד לְדַבֵּר אֵלָיו וַיֹּאמַר אוּלַי יִמָּצְאוּן שָׁם אַרְבָּעִים וַיֹּאמֶר לֹא אֶעֱשֶׂה בַּעֲבוּר הָאַרְבָּעִים:

³⁰ And he said, "Let not my Lord be angry if I go on: What if thirty should be found there?" And He answered, "I will not do it if I find thirty there."

ל וַיֹּאמֶר אַל־נָא יִחַר לַאדֹנָי וַאֲדַבֵּרָה אוּלַי יִמָּצְאוּן שָׁם שְׁלֹשִׁים וַיֹּאמֶר לֹא אֶעֱשֶׂה אִם־אֶמְצָא שָׁם שְׁלֹשִׁים:

³¹ And he said, "I venture again to speak to my Lord: What if twenty should be found there?" And He answered, "I will not destroy, for the sake of the twenty."

לא וַיֹּאמֶר הִנֵּה־נָא הוֹאַלְתִּי לְדַבֵּר אֶל־אֲדֹנָי אוּלַי יִמָּצְאוּן שָׁם עֶשְׂרִים וַיֹּאמֶר לֹא אַשְׁחִית בַּעֲבוּר הָעֶשְׂרִים:

³² And he said, "Let not my Lord be angry if I speak but this last time: What if ten should be found there?" And He answered, "I will not destroy, for the sake of the ten."

לב וַיֹּאמֶר אַל־נָא יִחַר לַאדֹנָי וַאֲדַבְּרָה אַךְ־הַפַּעַם אוּלַי יִמָּצְאוּן שָׁם עֲשָׂרָה וַיֹּאמֶר לֹא אַשְׁחִית בַּעֲבוּר הָעֲשָׂרָה:

³³ When *Hashem* had finished speaking to *Avraham*, He departed; and *Avraham* returned to his place.

לג וַיֵּלֶךְ יְהוָה כַּאֲשֶׁר כִּלָּה לְדַבֵּר אֶל־אַבְרָהָם וְאַבְרָהָם שָׁב לִמְקֹמוֹ:

9 ¹ The two angels arrived in Sodom in the evening, as Lot was sitting in the gate of Sodom. When Lot saw them, he rose to greet them and, bowing low with his face to the ground,

² he said, "Please, my lords, turn aside to your servant's house to spend the night, and bathe your feet; then you may be on your way early." But they said, "No, we will spend the night in the square."

³ But he urged them strongly, so they turned his way and entered his house. He prepared a feast for them and baked unleavened bread, and they ate.

⁴ They had not yet lain down, when the townspeople, the men of Sodom, young and old – all the people to the last man – gathered about the house.

⁵ And they shouted to Lot and said to him, "Where are the men who came to you tonight? Bring them out to us, that we may be intimate with them."

⁶ So Lot went out to them to the entrance, shut the door behind him,

⁷ and said, "I beg you, my friends, do not commit such a wrong.

⁸ Look, I have two daughters who have not known a man. Let me bring them out to you, and you may do to them as you please; but do not do anything to these men, since they have come under the shelter of my roof."

⁹ But they said, "Stand back! The fellow," they said, "came here as an alien, and already he acts the ruler! Now we will deal worse with you than with them." And they pressed hard against the person of Lot, and moved forward to break the door.

¹⁰ But the men stretched out their hands and pulled Lot into the house with them, and shut the door.

¹¹ And the people who were at the entrance of the house, young and old, they struck with blinding light, so that they were helpless to find the entrance.

¹² Then the men said to Lot, "Whom else have you here? Sons-in-law, your sons and daughters, or anyone else that you have in the city – bring them out of the place.

יט א וַיָּבֹאוּ שְׁנֵי הַמַּלְאָכִים סְדֹמָה בָּעֶרֶב וְלוֹט יֹשֵׁב בְּשַׁעַר־סְדֹם וַיַּרְא־לוֹט וַיָּקָם לִקְרָאתָם וַיִּשְׁתַּחוּ אַפַּיִם אָרְצָה:

ב וַיֹּאמֶר הִנֶּה נָּא־אֲדֹנַי סוּרוּ נָא אֶל־ בֵּית עַבְדְּכֶם וְלִינוּ וְרַחֲצוּ רַגְלֵיכֶם וְהִשְׁכַּמְתֶּם וַהֲלַכְתֶּם לְדַרְכְּכֶם וַיֹּאמְרוּ לֹא כִּי בָרְחוֹב נָלִין:

ג וַיִּפְצַר־בָּם מְאֹד וַיָּסֻרוּ אֵלָיו וַיָּבֹאוּ אֶל־ בֵּיתוֹ וַיַּעַשׂ לָהֶם מִשְׁתֶּה וּמַצּוֹת אָפָה וַיֹּאכֵלוּ:

ד טֶרֶם יִשְׁכָּבוּ וְאַנְשֵׁי הָעִיר אַנְשֵׁי סְדֹם נָסַבּוּ עַל־הַבַּיִת מִנַּעַר וְעַד־זָקֵן כָּל־ הָעָם מִקָּצֶה:

ה וַיִּקְרְאוּ אֶל־לוֹט וַיֹּאמְרוּ לוֹ אַיֵּה הָאֲנָשִׁים אֲשֶׁר־בָּאוּ אֵלֶיךָ הַלָּיְלָה הוֹצִיאֵם אֵלֵינוּ וְנֵדְעָה אֹתָם:

ו וַיֵּצֵא אֲלֵהֶם לוֹט הַפֶּתְחָה וְהַדֶּלֶת סָגַר אַחֲרָיו:

ז וַיֹּאמַר אַל־נָא אַחַי תָּרֵעוּ:

ח הִנֵּה־נָא לִי שְׁתֵּי בָנוֹת אֲשֶׁר לֹא־יָדְעוּ אִישׁ אוֹצִיאָה־נָּא אֶתְהֶן אֲלֵיכֶם וַעֲשׂוּ לָהֶן כַּטּוֹב בְּעֵינֵיכֶם רַק לָאֲנָשִׁים הָאֵל אַל־תַּעֲשׂוּ דָבָר כִּי־עַל־כֵּן בָּאוּ בְּצֵל קֹרָתִי:

ט וַיֹּאמְרוּ גֶּשׁ־הָלְאָה וַיֹּאמְרוּ הָאֶחָד בָּא־ לָגוּר וַיִּשְׁפֹּט שָׁפוֹט עַתָּה נָרַע לְךָ מֵהֶם וַיִּפְצְרוּ בָאִישׁ בְּלוֹט מְאֹד וַיִּגְּשׁוּ לִשְׁבֹּר הַדָּלֶת:

י וַיִּשְׁלְחוּ הָאֲנָשִׁים אֶת־יָדָם וַיָּבִיאוּ אֶת־ לוֹט אֲלֵיהֶם הַבָּיְתָה וְאֶת־הַדֶּלֶת סָגָרוּ:

יא וְאֶת־הָאֲנָשִׁים אֲשֶׁר־פֶּתַח הַבַּיִת הִכּוּ בַּסַּנְוֵרִים מִקָּטֹן וְעַד־גָּדוֹל וַיִּלְאוּ לִמְצֹא הַפָּתַח:

יב וַיֹּאמְרוּ הָאֲנָשִׁים אֶל־לוֹט עֹד מִי־לְךָ פֹה חָתָן וּבָנֶיךָ וּבְנֹתֶיךָ וְכֹל אֲשֶׁר־לְךָ בָּעִיר הוֹצֵא מִן־הַמָּקוֹם:

13 For we are about to destroy this place; because the outcry against them before *Hashem* has become so great that *Hashem* has sent us to destroy it."

יג כִּי־מַשְׁחִתִים אֲנַחְנוּ אֶת־הַמָּקוֹם הַזֶּה כִּי־גָדְלָה צַעֲקָתָם אֶת־פְּנֵי יְהוָֹה וַיְשַׁלְּחֵנוּ יְהוָֹה לְשַׁחֲתָהּ:

14 So Lot went out and spoke to his sons-in-law, who had married his daughters, and said, "Up, get out of this place, for *Hashem* is about to destroy the city." But he seemed to his sons-in-law as one who jests.

יד וַיֵּצֵא לוֹט וַיְדַבֵּר אֶל־חֲתָנָיו לֹקְחֵי בְנֹתָיו וַיֹּאמֶר קוּמוּ צְּאוּ מִן־הַמָּקוֹם הַזֶּה כִּי־מַשְׁחִית יְהוָֹה אֶת־הָעִיר וַיְהִי כִמְצַחֵק בְּעֵינֵי חֲתָנָיו:

15 As dawn broke, the angels urged Lot on, saying, "Up, take your wife and your two remaining daughters, lest you be swept away because of the iniquity of the city."

טו וּכְמוֹ הַשַּׁחַר עָלָה וַיָּאִיצוּ הַמַּלְאָכִים בְּלוֹט לֵאמֹר קוּם קַח אֶת־אִשְׁתְּךָ וְאֶת־שְׁתֵּי בְנֹתֶיךָ הַנִּמְצָאֹת פֶּן־תִּסָּפֶה בַּעֲוֹן הָעִיר:

16 Still he delayed. So the men seized his hand, and the hands of his wife and his two daughters – in *Hashem*'s mercy on him – and brought him out and left him outside the city.

טז וַיִּתְמַהְמָהּ וַיַּחֲזִיקוּ הָאֲנָשִׁים בְּיָדוֹ וּבְיַד־אִשְׁתּוֹ וּבְיַד שְׁתֵּי בְנֹתָיו בְּחֶמְלַת יְהוָֹה עָלָיו וַיֹּצִאֻהוּ וַיַּנִּחֻהוּ מִחוּץ לָעִיר:

17 When they had brought them outside, one said, "Flee for your life! Do not look behind you, nor stop anywhere in the Plain; flee to the hills, lest you be swept away."

יז וַיְהִי כְהוֹצִיאָם אֹתָם הַחוּצָה וַיֹּאמֶר הִמָּלֵט עַל־נַפְשֶׁךָ אַל־תַּבִּיט אַחֲרֶיךָ וְאַל־תַּעֲמֹד בְּכָל־הַכִּכָּר הָהָרָה הִמָּלֵט פֶּן־תִּסָּפֶה:

18 But Lot said to them, "Oh no, my lord!

יח וַיֹּאמֶר לוֹט אֲלֵהֶם אַל־נָא אֲדֹנָי:

19 You have been so gracious to your servant, and have already shown me so much kindness in order to save my life; but I cannot flee to the hills, lest the disaster overtake me and I die.

יט הִנֵּה־נָא מָצָא עַבְדְּךָ חֵן בְּעֵינֶיךָ וַתַּגְדֵּל חַסְדְּךָ אֲשֶׁר עָשִׂיתָ עִמָּדִי לְהַחֲיוֹת אֶת־נַפְשִׁי וְאָנֹכִי לֹא אוּכַל לְהִמָּלֵט הָהָרָה פֶּן־תִּדְבָּקַנִי הָרָעָה וָמַתִּי:

20 Look, that town there is near enough to flee to; it is such a little place! Let me flee there – it is such a little place – and let my life be saved."

כ הִנֵּה־נָא הָעִיר הַזֹּאת קְרֹבָה לָנוּס שָׁמָּה וְהִיא מִצְעָר אִמָּלְטָה נָּא שָׁמָּה הֲלֹא מִצְעָר הִוא וּתְחִי נַפְשִׁי:

21 He replied, "Very well, I will grant you this favor too, and I will not annihilate the town of which you have spoken.

כא וַיֹּאמֶר אֵלָיו הִנֵּה נָשָׂאתִי פָנֶיךָ גַּם לַדָּבָר הַזֶּה לְבִלְתִּי הָפְכִּי אֶת־הָעִיר אֲשֶׁר דִּבַּרְתָּ:

22 Hurry, flee there, for I cannot do anything until you arrive there." Hence the town came to be called Zoar.

כב מַהֵר הִמָּלֵט שָׁמָּה כִּי לֹא אוּכַל לַעֲשׂוֹת דָּבָר עַד־בֹּאֲךָ שָׁמָּה עַל־כֵּן קָרָא שֵׁם־הָעִיר צוֹעַר:

23 As the sun rose upon the earth and Lot entered Zoar,

כג הַשֶּׁמֶשׁ יָצָא עַל־הָאָרֶץ וְלוֹט בָּא צֹעֲרָה:

24 *Hashem* rained upon Sodom and Gomorrah sulfurous fire from *Hashem* out of heaven.

כד וַיהוָֹה הִמְטִיר עַל־סְדֹם וְעַל־עֲמֹרָה גָּפְרִית וָאֵשׁ מֵאֵת יְהוָֹה מִן־הַשָּׁמָיִם:

25 He annihilated those cities and the entire Plain, and all the inhabitants of the cities and the vegetation of the ground.

כה וַיַּהֲפֹךְ אֶת־הֶעָרִים הָאֵל וְאֵת כָּל־הַכִּכָּר וְאֵת כָּל־יֹשְׁבֵי הֶעָרִים וְצֶמַח הָאֲדָמָה:

va-ya-ha-FOKH et he-a-REEM ha-AYL v'-AYT kol ha-ki-KAR v'-AYT kol yo-sh'-VAY he-a-REEM v'-TZE-makh ha-a-da-MAH

26 Lot's wife looked back, and she thereupon turned into a pillar of salt.

כו וַתַּבֵּט אִשְׁתּוֹ מֵאַחֲרָיו וַתְּהִי נְצִיב מֶלַח:

27 Next morning, *Avraham* hurried to the place where he had stood before *Hashem*,

כז וַיַּשְׁכֵּם אַבְרָהָם בַּבֹּקֶר אֶל־הַמָּקוֹם אֲשֶׁר־עָמַד שָׁם אֶת־פְּנֵי יְהוָה:

28 and, looking down toward Sodom and Gomorrah and all the land of the Plain, he saw the smoke of the land rising like the smoke of a kiln.

כח וַיַּשְׁקֵף עַל־פְּנֵי סְדֹם וַעֲמֹרָה וְעַל־כָּל־פְּנֵי אֶרֶץ הַכִּכָּר וַיַּרְא וְהִנֵּה עָלָה קִיטֹר הָאָרֶץ כְּקִיטֹר הַכִּבְשָׁן:

29 Thus it was that, when *Hashem* destroyed the cities of the Plain and annihilated the cities where Lot dwelt, *Hashem* was mindful of *Avraham* and removed Lot from the midst of the upheaval.

כט וַיְהִי בְּשַׁחֵת אֱלֹהִים אֶת־עָרֵי הַכִּכָּר וַיִּזְכֹּר אֱלֹהִים אֶת־אַבְרָהָם וַיְשַׁלַּח אֶת־לוֹט מִתּוֹךְ הַהֲפֵכָה בַּהֲפֹךְ אֶת־הֶעָרִים אֲשֶׁר־יָשַׁב בָּהֵן לוֹט:

30 Lot went up from Zoar and settled in the hill country with his two daughters, for he was afraid to dwell in Zoar; and he and his two daughters lived in a cave.

ל וַיַּעַל לוֹט מִצּוֹעַר וַיֵּשֶׁב בָּהָר וּשְׁתֵּי בְנֹתָיו עִמּוֹ כִּי יָרֵא לָשֶׁבֶת בְּצוֹעַר וַיֵּשֶׁב בַּמְּעָרָה הוּא וּשְׁתֵּי בְנֹתָיו:

31 And the older one said to the younger, "Our father is old, and there is not a man on earth to consort with us in the way of all the world.

לא וַתֹּאמֶר הַבְּכִירָה אֶל־הַצְּעִירָה אָבִינוּ זָקֵן וְאִישׁ אֵין בָּאָרֶץ לָבוֹא עָלֵינוּ כְּדֶרֶךְ כָּל־הָאָרֶץ:

32 Come, let us make our father drink wine, and let us lie with him, that we may maintain life through our father."

לב לְכָה נַשְׁקֶה אֶת־אָבִינוּ יַיִן וְנִשְׁכְּבָה עִמּוֹ וּנְחַיֶּה מֵאָבִינוּ זָרַע:

33 That night they made their father drink wine, and the older one went in and lay with her father; he did not know when she lay down or when she rose.

לג וַתַּשְׁקֶיןָ אֶת־אֲבִיהֶן יַיִן בַּלַּיְלָה הוּא וַתָּבֹא הַבְּכִירָה וַתִּשְׁכַּב אֶת־אָבִיהָ וְלֹא־יָדַע בְּשִׁכְבָהּ וּבְקוּמָהּ:

34 The next day the older one said to the younger, "See, I lay with Father last night; let us make him drink wine tonight also, and you go and lie with him, that we may maintain life through our father."

לד וַיְהִי מִמָּחֳרָת וַתֹּאמֶר הַבְּכִירָה אֶל־הַצְּעִירָה הֵן־שָׁכַבְתִּי אֶמֶשׁ אֶת־אָבִי נַשְׁקֶנּוּ יַיִן גַּם־הַלַּיְלָה וּבֹאִי שִׁכְבִי עִמּוֹ וּנְחַיֶּה מֵאָבִינוּ זָרַע:

19:25 And the vegetation of the ground The destruction of Sodom is complete, total annihilation. The obliteration includes not just the people, but also the overturning of the city and the very earth that they resided on. The *Ramban* comments that here, God set a precedent that the Land of Israel, which includes Sodom, does not tolerate corruption. This serves as a warning for future inhabitants of this holy place to guard their behavior. As it says in *Sefer Devarim* (29:22,24) "all its soil devastated by sulfur and salt, beyond sowing and producing, no grass growing in it, just like the upheaval of Sodom and Gomorrah… Because they forsook the covenant that the Lᴏʀᴅ, God of their fathers, made with them when He freed them from the land of Egypt… because they forsook the covenant of *Hashem*."

"Vegetation of the ground" on an Israeli farm

³⁵ That night also they made their father drink wine, and the younger one went and lay with him; he did not know when she lay down or when she rose.

לה וַתַּשְׁקֶ֨יןָ גַּ֜ם בַּלַּ֤יְלָה הַהוּא֙ אֶת־אֲבִיהֶ֔ן יָ֑יִן וַתָּקָ֤ם הַצְּעִירָה֙ וַתִּשְׁכַּ֣ב עִמּ֔וֹ וְלֹֽא־יָדַ֥ע בְּשִׁכְבָ֖הּ וּבְקֻמָֽהּ׃

³⁶ Thus the two daughters of Lot came to be with child by their father.

לו וַתַּהֲרֶ֛יןָ שְׁתֵּ֥י בְנֽוֹת־ל֖וֹט מֵאֲבִיהֶֽן׃

³⁷ The older one bore a son and named him Moab; he is the father of the Moabites of today.

לז וַתֵּ֤לֶד הַבְּכִירָה֙ בֵּ֔ן וַתִּקְרָ֥א שְׁמ֖וֹ מוֹאָ֑ב ה֥וּא אֲבִֽי־מוֹאָ֖ב עַד־הַיּֽוֹם׃

³⁸ And the younger also bore a son, and she called him Ben-ammi; he is the father of the Ammonites of today.

לח וְהַצְּעִירָ֤ה גַם־הִוא֙ יָ֣לְדָה בֵּ֔ן וַתִּקְרָ֥א שְׁמ֖וֹ בֶּן־עַמִּ֑י ה֛וּא אֲבִ֥י בְנֵֽי־עַמּ֖וֹן עַד־הַיּֽוֹם׃

20 ¹ *Avraham* journeyed from there to the region of the *Negev* and settled between Kadesh and Shur. While he was sojourning in Gerar,

א וַיִּסַּ֨ע מִשָּׁ֜ם אַבְרָהָ֗ם אַ֚רְצָה הַנֶּ֔גֶב וַיֵּ֥שֶׁב בֵּין־קָדֵ֖שׁ וּבֵ֣ין שׁ֑וּר וַיָּ֖גׇר בִּגְרָֽר׃

*va-yi-SA mi-SHAM av-ra-HAM AR-tzah ha-NE-gev va-YAY-shev
bayn ka-DAYSH u-VAYN SHUR va-YA-gor big-RAR*

² *Avraham* said of *Sara* his wife, "She is my sister." So King Abimelech of Gerar had *Sara* brought to him.

ב וַיֹּ֧אמֶר אַבְרָהָ֛ם אֶל־שָׂרָ֥ה אִשְׁתּ֖וֹ אֲחֹ֣תִי הִ֑וא וַיִּשְׁלַ֗ח אֲבִימֶ֙לֶךְ֙ מֶ֣לֶךְ גְּרָ֔ר וַיִּקַּ֖ח אֶת־שָׂרָֽה׃

*va-YO-mer av-ra-HAM el sa-RAH ish-TO a-KHO-tee HEE va-yish-LAKH
a-vee-ME-lekh ME-lekh g'-RAR va-yi-KAKH et sa-RAH*

³ But *Hashem* came to Abimelech in a dream by night and said to him, "You are to die because of the woman that you have taken, for she is a married woman."

ג וַיָּבֹ֧א אֱלֹהִ֛ים אֶל־אֲבִימֶ֖לֶךְ בַּחֲל֣וֹם הַלָּ֑יְלָה וַיֹּ֣אמֶר ל֗וֹ הִנְּךָ֥ מֵת֙ עַל־הָאִשָּׁ֣ה אֲשֶׁר־לָקַ֔חְתָּ וְהִ֖וא בְּעֻ֥לַת בָּֽעַל׃

20:1 *Avraham* journeyed from there Scripture does not provide any reason for *Avraham's* travels. Consequently, Rabbi David Kimchi, a medieval commentator and grammarian known as the *Radak*, posits that *Avraham* travels in order to dwell in the different parts of the land that *Hashem* gave to him. By residing in various places, even for short periods of time, *Avraham* thereby adds his own effort to acquire the breadth and width of the land promised to him. In this way, *Avraham* is fulfilling God's command "walk about the land" (Genesis 13:17). Saddened by the loss of the cities of Sodom and Gomorrah, *Avraham* wonders if the destruction could have been prevented by his presence there. He resolves to reach further areas in *Eretz Yisrael*.

20:2 So King Abimelech of Gerar had *Sara* brought to him Although *Sara* was taken captive by both Pharoah (Genesis 12:19) and Abimelech, her courage and bravery inspired many Jewish women over the centuries, especially those who carried her name. Sarah Braverman, the "first lady of the IDF," was born in Romania in 1918, and arrived in Israel when she was 20 years old. Upon her arrival, she immediately joined the Jewish liberation movement. Braverman was one of the first women to join "*Palmach*," the special fighting forces of the Haganah and one of the forerunners of the Israeli army. Braverman was chosen to be one of three women in a group of 37 Palmach fighters to take part in the 1943 parachuting mission behind enemy lines into Nazi Europe. After the creation of the State of Israel, Braverman helped establish the IDF Women's Corps. Sarah Braverman truly lived up to her namesake, the original *Sara*. She was a brave and devoted Jewish heroine, who put her life on the line time and again to protect and defend her people.

Sarah Braverman (1918–2013)

4 Now Abimelech had not approached her. He said, "O *Hashem*, will You slay people even though innocent?

ד וַאֲבִימֶלֶךְ לֹא קָרַב אֵלֶיהָ וַיֹּאמַר אֲדֹנָי הֲגוֹי גַּם־צַדִּיק תַּהֲרֹג:

5 He himself said to me, 'She is my sister!' And she also said, 'He is my brother.' When I did this, my heart was blameless and my hands were clean."

ה הֲלֹא הוּא אָמַר־לִי אֲחֹתִי הִוא וְהִיא־גַם־הִוא אָמְרָה אָחִי הוּא בְּתָם־לְבָבִי וּבְנִקְיֹן כַּפַּי עָשִׂיתִי זֹאת:

6 And *Hashem* said to him in the dream, "I knew that you did this with a blameless heart, and so I kept you from sinning against Me. That was why I did not let you touch her.

ו וַיֹּאמֶר אֵלָיו הָאֱלֹהִים בַּחֲלֹם גַּם אָנֹכִי יָדַעְתִּי כִּי בְתָם־לְבָבְךָ עָשִׂיתָ זֹּאת וָאֶחְשֹׂךְ גַּם־אָנֹכִי אוֹתְךָ מֵחֲטוֹ־לִי עַל־כֵּן לֹא־נְתַתִּיךָ לִנְגֹּעַ אֵלֶיהָ:

7 Therefore, restore the man's wife – since he is a *navi*, he will intercede for you – to save your life. If you fail to restore her, know that you shall die, you and all that are yours."

ז וְעַתָּה הָשֵׁב אֵשֶׁת־הָאִישׁ כִּי־נָבִיא הוּא וְיִתְפַּלֵּל בַּעַדְךָ וֶחְיֵה וְאִם־אֵינְךָ מֵשִׁיב דַּע כִּי־מוֹת תָּמוּת אַתָּה וְכָל־אֲשֶׁר־לָךְ:

8 Early next morning, Abimelech called his servants and told them all that had happened; and the men were greatly frightened.

ח וַיַּשְׁכֵּם אֲבִימֶלֶךְ בַּבֹּקֶר וַיִּקְרָא לְכָל־עֲבָדָיו וַיְדַבֵּר אֶת־כָּל־הַדְּבָרִים הָאֵלֶּה בְּאָזְנֵיהֶם וַיִּירְאוּ הָאֲנָשִׁים מְאֹד:

9 Then Abimelech summoned *Avraham* and said to him, "What have you done to us? What wrong have I done that you should bring so great a guilt upon me and my kingdom? You have done to me things that ought not to be done.

ט וַיִּקְרָא אֲבִימֶלֶךְ לְאַבְרָהָם וַיֹּאמֶר לוֹ מֶה־עָשִׂיתָ לָּנוּ וּמֶה־חָטָאתִי לָךְ כִּי־הֵבֵאתָ עָלַי וְעַל־מַמְלַכְתִּי חֲטָאָה גְדֹלָה מַעֲשִׂים אֲשֶׁר לֹא־יֵעָשׂוּ עָשִׂיתָ עִמָּדִי:

10 What, then," Abimelech demanded of *Avraham*, "was your purpose in doing this thing?"

י וַיֹּאמֶר אֲבִימֶלֶךְ אֶל־אַבְרָהָם מָה רָאִיתָ כִּי עָשִׂיתָ אֶת־הַדָּבָר הַזֶּה:

11 "I thought," said *Avraham*, "surely there is no fear of *Hashem* in this place, and they will kill me because of my wife.

יא וַיֹּאמֶר אַבְרָהָם כִּי אָמַרְתִּי רַק אֵין־יִרְאַת אֱלֹהִים בַּמָּקוֹם הַזֶּה וַהֲרָגוּנִי עַל־דְּבַר אִשְׁתִּי:

12 And besides, she is in truth my sister, my father's daughter though not my mother's; and she became my wife.

יב וְגַם־אָמְנָה אֲחֹתִי בַת־אָבִי הִוא אַךְ לֹא בַת־אִמִּי וַתְּהִי־לִי לְאִשָּׁה:

13 So when *Hashem* made me wander from my father's house, I said to her, 'Let this be the kindness that you shall do me: whatever place we come to, say there of me: He is my brother.'"

יג וַיְהִי כַּאֲשֶׁר הִתְעוּ אֹתִי אֱלֹהִים מִבֵּית אָבִי וָאֹמַר לָהּ זֶה חַסְדֵּךְ אֲשֶׁר תַּעֲשִׂי עִמָּדִי אֶל כָּל־הַמָּקוֹם אֲשֶׁר נָבוֹא שָׁמָּה אִמְרִי־לִי אָחִי הוּא:

14 Abimelech took sheep and oxen, and male and female slaves, and gave them to *Avraham*; and he restored his wife *Sara* to him.

יד וַיִּקַּח אֲבִימֶלֶךְ צֹאן וּבָקָר וַעֲבָדִים וּשְׁפָחֹת וַיִּתֵּן לְאַבְרָהָם וַיָּשֶׁב לוֹ אֵת שָׂרָה אִשְׁתּוֹ:

15 And Abimelech said, "Here, my land is before you; settle wherever you please."

טו וַיֹּאמֶר אֲבִימֶלֶךְ הִנֵּה אַרְצִי לְפָנֶיךָ בַּטּוֹב בְּעֵינֶיךָ שֵׁב:

16 And to *Sara* he said, "I herewith give your brother a thousand pieces of silver; this will serve you as vindication before all who are with you, and you are cleared before everyone."

טז וּלְשָׂרָה אָמַר הִנֵּה נָתַתִּי אֶלֶף כֶּסֶף לְאָחִיךְ הִנֵּה הוּא־לָךְ כְּסוּת עֵינַיִם לְכֹל אֲשֶׁר אִתָּךְ וְאֵת כֹּל וְנֹכָחַת:

17 *Avraham* then prayed to *Hashem*, and *Hashem* healed Abimelech and his wife and his slave girls, so that they bore children;

יז וַיִּתְפַּלֵּל אַבְרָהָם אֶל־הָאֱלֹהִים וַיִּרְפָּא אֱלֹהִים אֶת־אֲבִימֶלֶךְ וְאֶת־אִשְׁתּוֹ וְאַמְהֹתָיו וַיֵּלֵדוּ:

18 for *Hashem* had closed fast every womb of the household of Abimelech because of *Sara*, the wife of *Avraham*.

יח כִּי־עָצֹר עָצַר יְהוָה בְּעַד כָּל־רֶחֶם לְבֵית אֲבִימֶלֶךְ עַל־דְּבַר שָׂרָה אֵשֶׁת אַבְרָהָם:

21 1 *Hashem* took note of *Sara* as He had promised, and *Hashem* did for *Sara* as He had spoken.

א וַיהוָה פָּקַד אֶת־שָׂרָה כַּאֲשֶׁר אָמָר וַיַּעַשׂ יְהוָה לְשָׂרָה כַּאֲשֶׁר דִּבֵּר:

2 *Sara* conceived and bore a son to *Avraham* in his old age, at the set time of which *Hashem* had spoken.

ב וַתַּהַר וַתֵּלֶד שָׂרָה לְאַבְרָהָם בֵּן לִזְקֻנָיו לַמּוֹעֵד אֲשֶׁר־דִּבֶּר אֹתוֹ אֱלֹהִים:

3 *Avraham* gave his newborn son, whom *Sara* had borne him, the name of *Yitzchak*.

ג וַיִּקְרָא אַבְרָהָם אֶת־שֶׁם־בְּנוֹ הַנּוֹלַד־לוֹ אֲשֶׁר־יָלְדָה־לּוֹ שָׂרָה יִצְחָק:

4 And when his son *Yitzchak* was eight days old, *Avraham* circumcised him, as *Hashem* had commanded him.

ד וַיָּמָל אַבְרָהָם אֶת־יִצְחָק בְּנוֹ בֶּן־שְׁמֹנַת יָמִים כַּאֲשֶׁר צִוָּה אֹתוֹ אֱלֹהִים:

5 Now *Avraham* was a hundred years old when his son *Yitzchak* was born to him.

ה וְאַבְרָהָם בֶּן־מְאַת שָׁנָה בְּהִוָּלֶד לוֹ אֵת יִצְחָק בְּנוֹ:

6 *Sara* said, "*Hashem* has brought me laughter; everyone who hears will laugh with me."

ו וַתֹּאמֶר שָׂרָה צְחֹק עָשָׂה לִי אֱלֹהִים כָּל־הַשֹּׁמֵעַ יִצְחַק־לִי:

7 And she added, "Who would have said to *Avraham* That *Sara* would suckle children! Yet I have borne a son in his old age."

ז וַתֹּאמֶר מִי מִלֵּל לְאַבְרָהָם הֵינִיקָה בָנִים שָׂרָה כִּי־יָלַדְתִּי בֵן לִזְקֻנָיו:

8 The child grew up and was weaned, and *Avraham* held a great feast on the day that *Yitzchak* was weaned.

ח וַיִּגְדַּל הַיֶּלֶד וַיִּגָּמַל וַיַּעַשׂ אַבְרָהָם מִשְׁתֶּה גָדוֹל בְּיוֹם הִגָּמֵל אֶת־יִצְחָק:

9 *Sara* saw the son whom Hagar the Egyptian had borne to *Avraham* playing.

ט וַתֵּרֶא שָׂרָה אֶת־בֶּן־הָגָר הַמִּצְרִית אֲשֶׁר־יָלְדָה לְאַבְרָהָם מְצַחֵק:

10 She said to *Avraham*, "Cast out that slave-woman and her son, for the son of that slave shall not share in the inheritance with my son *Yitzchak*."

י וַתֹּאמֶר לְאַבְרָהָם גָּרֵשׁ הָאָמָה הַזֹּאת וְאֶת־בְּנָהּ כִּי לֹא יִירַשׁ בֶּן־הָאָמָה הַזֹּאת עִם־בְּנִי עִם־יִצְחָק:

11 The matter distressed *Avraham* greatly, for it concerned a son of his.

יא וַיֵּרַע הַדָּבָר מְאֹד בְּעֵינֵי אַבְרָהָם עַל אוֹדֹת בְּנוֹ:

12 But *Hashem* said to *Avraham*, "Do not be distressed over the boy or your slave; whatever *Sara* tells you, do as she says, for it is through *Yitzchak* that offspring shall be continued for you.

יב וַיֹּאמֶר אֱלֹהִים אֶל־אַבְרָהָם אַל־יֵרַע בְּעֵינֶיךָ עַל־הַנַּעַר וְעַל־אֲמָתֶךָ כֹּל אֲשֶׁר תֹּאמַר אֵלֶיךָ שָׂרָה שְׁמַע בְּקֹלָהּ כִּי בְיִצְחָק יִקָּרֵא לְךָ זָרַע:

13 As for the son of the slave-woman, I will make a nation of him, too, for he is your seed."

יג וְגַם אֶת־בֶּן־הָאָמָה לְגוֹי אֲשִׂימֶנּוּ כִּי זַרְעֲךָ הוּא:

¹⁴ Early next morning *Avraham* took some bread and a skin of water, and gave them to Hagar. He placed them over her shoulder, together with the child, and sent her away. And she wandered about in the wilderness of *Be'er Sheva*.

יד וַיַּשְׁכֵּם אַבְרָהָם ׀ בַּבֹּקֶר וַיִּקַּח־לֶחֶם וְחֵמַת מַיִם וַיִּתֵּן אֶל־הָגָר שָׂם עַל־שִׁכְמָהּ וְאֶת־הַיֶּלֶד וַיְשַׁלְּחֶהָ וַתֵּלֶךְ וַתֵּתַע בְּמִדְבַּר בְּאֵר שָׁבַע:

¹⁵ When the water was gone from the skin, she left the child under one of the bushes,

טו וַיִּכְלוּ הַמַּיִם מִן־הַחֵמֶת וַתַּשְׁלֵךְ אֶת־הַיֶּלֶד תַּחַת אַחַד הַשִּׂיחִם:

¹⁶ and went and sat down at a distance, a bowshot away; for she thought, "Let me not look on as the child dies." And sitting thus afar, she burst into tears.

טז וַתֵּלֶךְ וַתֵּשֶׁב לָהּ מִנֶּגֶד הַרְחֵק כִּמְטַחֲוֵי קֶשֶׁת כִּי אָמְרָה אַל־אֶרְאֶה בְּמוֹת הַיָּלֶד וַתֵּשֶׁב מִנֶּגֶד וַתִּשָּׂא אֶת־קֹלָהּ וַתֵּבְךְּ:

¹⁷ *Hashem* heard the cry of the boy, and an angel of *Hashem* called to Hagar from heaven and said to her, "What troubles you, Hagar? Fear not, for *Hashem* has heeded the cry of the boy where he is.

יז וַיִּשְׁמַע אֱלֹהִים אֶת־קוֹל הַנַּעַר וַיִּקְרָא מַלְאַךְ אֱלֹהִים ׀ אֶל־הָגָר מִן־הַשָּׁמַיִם וַיֹּאמֶר לָהּ מַה־לָּךְ הָגָר אַל־תִּירְאִי כִּי־שָׁמַע אֱלֹהִים אֶל־קוֹל הַנַּעַר בַּאֲשֶׁר הוּא־שָׁם:

¹⁸ Come, lift up the boy and hold him by the hand, for I will make a great nation of him."

יח קוּמִי שְׂאִי אֶת־הַנַּעַר וְהַחֲזִיקִי אֶת־יָדֵךְ בּוֹ כִּי־לְגוֹי גָּדוֹל אֲשִׂימֶנּוּ:

¹⁹ Then *Hashem* opened her eyes and she saw a well of water. She went and filled the skin with water, and let the boy drink.

יט וַיִּפְקַח אֱלֹהִים אֶת־עֵינֶיהָ וַתֵּרֶא בְּאֵר מָיִם וַתֵּלֶךְ וַתְּמַלֵּא אֶת־הַחֵמֶת מַיִם וַתַּשְׁקְ אֶת־הַנָּעַר:

²⁰ *Hashem* was with the boy and he grew up; he dwelt in the wilderness and became a bowman.

כ וַיְהִי אֱלֹהִים אֶת־הַנַּעַר וַיִּגְדָּל וַיֵּשֶׁב בַּמִּדְבָּר וַיְהִי רֹבֶה קַשָּׁת:

²¹ He lived in the wilderness of Paran; and his mother got a wife for him from the land of Egypt.

כא וַיֵּשֶׁב בְּמִדְבַּר פָּארָן וַתִּקַּח־לוֹ אִמּוֹ אִשָּׁה מֵאֶרֶץ מִצְרָיִם:

²² At that time Abimelech and Phicol, chief of his troops, said to *Avraham*, "Hashem is with you in everything that you do.

כב וַיְהִי בָּעֵת הַהִוא וַיֹּאמֶר אֲבִימֶלֶךְ וּפִיכֹל שַׂר־צְבָאוֹ אֶל־אַבְרָהָם לֵאמֹר אֱלֹהִים עִמְּךָ בְּכֹל אֲשֶׁר־אַתָּה עֹשֶׂה:

²³ Therefore swear to me here by *Hashem* that you will not deal falsely with me or with my kith and kin, but will deal with me and with the land in which you have sojourned as loyally as I have dealt with you."

כג וְעַתָּה הִשָּׁבְעָה לִּי בֵאלֹהִים הֵנָּה אִם־תִּשְׁקֹר לִי וּלְנִינִי וּלְנֶכְדִּי כַּחֶסֶד אֲשֶׁר־עָשִׂיתִי עִמְּךָ תַּעֲשֶׂה עִמָּדִי וְעִם־הָאָרֶץ אֲשֶׁר־גַּרְתָּה בָּהּ:

²⁴ And *Avraham* said, "I swear it."

כד וַיֹּאמֶר אַבְרָהָם אָנֹכִי אִשָּׁבֵעַ:

²⁵ Then *Avraham* reproached Abimelech for the well of water which the servants of Abimelech had seized.

כה וְהוֹכִחַ אַבְרָהָם אֶת־אֲבִימֶלֶךְ עַל־אֹדוֹת בְּאֵר הַמַּיִם אֲשֶׁר גָּזְלוּ עַבְדֵי אֲבִימֶלֶךְ:

²⁶ But Abimelech said, "I do not know who did this; you did not tell me, nor have I heard of it until today."

כו וַיֹּאמֶר אֲבִימֶלֶךְ לֹא יָדַעְתִּי מִי עָשָׂה אֶת־הַדָּבָר הַזֶּה וְגַם־אַתָּה לֹא־הִגַּדְתָּ לִּי וְגַם אָנֹכִי לֹא שָׁמַעְתִּי בִּלְתִּי הַיּוֹם:

²⁷ *Avraham* took sheep and oxen and gave them to Abimelech, and the two of them made a pact.

כז וַיִּקַּח אַבְרָהָם צֹאן וּבָקָר וַיִּתֵּן לַאֲבִימֶלֶךְ וַיִּכְרְתוּ שְׁנֵיהֶם בְּרִית:

²⁸ *Avraham* then set seven ewes of the flock by themselves,

כח וַיַּצֵּב אַבְרָהָם אֶת־שֶׁבַע כִּבְשֹׂת הַצֹּאן לְבַדְּהֶן:

²⁹ and Abimelech said to *Avraham*, "What mean these seven ewes which you have set apart?"

כט וַיֹּאמֶר אֲבִימֶלֶךְ אֶל־אַבְרָהָם מָה הֵנָּה שֶׁבַע כְּבָשֹׂת הָאֵלֶּה אֲשֶׁר הִצַּבְתָּ לְבַדָּנָה:

³⁰ He replied, "You are to accept these seven ewes from me as proof that I dug this well."

ל וַיֹּאמֶר כִּי אֶת־שֶׁבַע כְּבָשֹׂת תִּקַּח מִיָּדִי בַּעֲבוּר תִּהְיֶה־לִּי לְעֵדָה כִּי חָפַרְתִּי אֶת־הַבְּאֵר הַזֹּאת:

³¹ Hence that place was called *Be'er Sheva*, for there the two of them swore an oath.

לא עַל־כֵּן קָרָא לַמָּקוֹם הַהוּא בְּאֵר שָׁבַע כִּי שָׁם נִשְׁבְּעוּ שְׁנֵיהֶם:

al KAYN ka-RA la-ma-KOM ha-HU b'-AYR SHA-va KEE SHAM nish-b'-U sh'-nay-HEM

³² When they had concluded the pact at *Be'er Sheva*, Abimelech and Phicol, chief of his troops, departed and returned to the land of the Philistines.

לב וַיִּכְרְתוּ בְרִית בִּבְאֵר שָׁבַע וַיָּקָם אֲבִימֶלֶךְ וּפִיכֹל שַׂר־צְבָאוֹ וַיָּשֻׁבוּ אֶל־אֶרֶץ פְּלִשְׁתִּים:

³³ [*Avraham*] planted a tamarisk at *Be'er Sheva*, and invoked there the name of *Hashem*, the Everlasting God.

לג וַיִּטַּע אֶשֶׁל בִּבְאֵר שָׁבַע וַיִּקְרָא־שָׁם בְּשֵׁם יְהוָה אֵל עוֹלָם:

va-yi-TA E-shel biv-AYR SHA-va va-YIK-ra SHAM b'-SHAYM a-do-NAI AYL o-LAM

³⁴ And *Avraham* resided in the land of the Philistines a long time.

לד וַיָּגָר אַבְרָהָם בְּאֶרֶץ פְּלִשְׁתִּים יָמִים רַבִּים:

22 ¹ Some time afterward, *Hashem* put *Avraham* to the test. He said to him, "*Avraham*," and he answered, "Here I am."

כב א וַיְהִי אַחַר הַדְּבָרִים הָאֵלֶּה וְהָאֱלֹהִים נִסָּה אֶת־אַבְרָהָם וַיֹּאמֶר אֵלָיו אַבְרָהָם וַיֹּאמֶר הִנֵּנִי:

באר שבע

21:31 Hence that place was called *Be'er Sheva* *Avraham* names the place where he entered the covenant with Abimelech *Be'er Sheva*. The name *Be'er Sheva* (באר שבע), is made up of two Hebrew words. *Be'er* (באר) means 'well,' hinting to the fact that this covenant acknowledged *Avraham*'s right to the water well. The second part of the word is made up of the root ש-ב-ע, which means both 'seven' and 'oath.' Thus, *Be'er Sheva* can mean either 'well of the seven' or 'well of the oath.' This double meaning hints both to the seven female sheep set aside by *Avraham* as verification of the oath, and to the oath taken with regard to the well itself.

Avraham's well in Be'er Sheva

עולם

21:33 The name of *Hashem*, the Everlasting God The Hebrew word used in this verse for everlasting is *olam* (עולם), which also means 'world' or 'universe.' The word *olam* is closely related to the word *ne'elam* (נעלם), meaning 'hidden.' The phrase "*El Olam*" (אל עולם), 'Everlasting God,' alludes to the fact that *Hashem* is also King over that which is hidden from us. God has specifically designed a world that is ruled by the laws of nature and hides His presence. It is up to man to see past His mask and reveal the Godliness that is hidden throughout the universe.

2 And He said, "Take your son, your favored one, *Yitzchak*, whom you love, and go to the land of *Moriah*, and offer him there as a burnt offering on one of the heights that I will point out to you."

ב וַיֹּאמֶר קַח־נָא אֶת־בִּנְךָ אֶת־יְחִידְךָ אֲשֶׁר־אָהַבְתָּ אֶת־יִצְחָק וְלֶךְ־לְךָ אֶל־אֶרֶץ הַמֹּרִיָּה וְהַעֲלֵהוּ שָׁם לְעֹלָה עַל אַחַד הֶהָרִים אֲשֶׁר אֹמַר אֵלֶיךָ:

va-YO-mer kakh NA et bin-KHA et y'-khee-d'-KHA a-sher a-HAV-ta et yitz-KHAK v'-LEKH l'-KHA el E-retz ha-mo-ri-YAH v'-ha-a-LAY-hu SHAM l'-o-LAH AL a-KHAD he-ha-REEM a-SHER o-MAR ay-LE-kha

3 So early next morning, *Avraham* saddled his ass and took with him two of his servants and his son *Yitzchak*. He split the wood for the burnt offering, and he set out for the place of which *Hashem* had told him.

ג וַיַּשְׁכֵּם אַבְרָהָם בַּבֹּקֶר וַיַּחֲבֹשׁ אֶת־חֲמֹרוֹ וַיִּקַּח אֶת־שְׁנֵי נְעָרָיו אִתּוֹ וְאֵת יִצְחָק בְּנוֹ וַיְבַקַּע עֲצֵי עֹלָה וַיָּקָם וַיֵּלֶךְ אֶל־הַמָּקוֹם אֲשֶׁר־אָמַר־לוֹ הָאֱלֹהִים:

4 On the third day *Avraham* looked up and saw the place from afar.

ד בַּיּוֹם הַשְּׁלִישִׁי וַיִּשָּׂא אַבְרָהָם אֶת־עֵינָיו וַיַּרְא אֶת־הַמָּקוֹם מֵרָחֹק:

5 Then *Avraham* said to his servants, "You stay here with the ass. The boy and I will go up there; we will worship and we will return to you."

ה וַיֹּאמֶר אַבְרָהָם אֶל־נְעָרָיו שְׁבוּ־לָכֶם פֹּה עִם־הַחֲמוֹר וַאֲנִי וְהַנַּעַר נֵלְכָה עַד־כֹּה וְנִשְׁתַּחֲוֶה וְנָשׁוּבָה אֲלֵיכֶם:

6 *Avraham* took the wood for the burnt offering and put it on his son *Yitzchak*. He himself took the firestone and the knife; and the two walked off together.

ו וַיִּקַּח אַבְרָהָם אֶת־עֲצֵי הָעֹלָה וַיָּשֶׂם עַל־יִצְחָק בְּנוֹ וַיִּקַּח בְּיָדוֹ אֶת־הָאֵשׁ וְאֶת־הַמַּאֲכֶלֶת וַיֵּלְכוּ שְׁנֵיהֶם יַחְדָּו:

7 Then *Yitzchak* said to his father *Avraham*, "Father!" And he answered, "Yes, my son." And he said, "Here are the firestone and the wood; but where is the sheep for the burnt offering?"

ז וַיֹּאמֶר יִצְחָק אֶל־אַבְרָהָם אָבִיו וַיֹּאמֶר אָבִי וַיֹּאמֶר הִנֶּנִּי בְנִי וַיֹּאמֶר הִנֵּה הָאֵשׁ וְהָעֵצִים וְאַיֵּה הַשֶּׂה לְעֹלָה:

8 And *Avraham* said, "*Hashem* will see to the sheep for His burnt offering, my son." And the two of them walked on together.

ח וַיֹּאמֶר אַבְרָהָם אֱלֹהִים יִרְאֶה־לּוֹ הַשֶּׂה לְעֹלָה בְּנִי וַיֵּלְכוּ שְׁנֵיהֶם יַחְדָּו:

9 They arrived at the place of which *Hashem* had told him. *Avraham* built a *Mizbayach* there; he laid out the wood; he bound his son *Yitzchak*; he laid him on the *Mizbayach*, on top of the wood.

ט וַיָּבֹאוּ אֶל־הַמָּקוֹם אֲשֶׁר אָמַר־לוֹ הָאֱלֹהִים וַיִּבֶן שָׁם אַבְרָהָם אֶת־הַמִּזְבֵּחַ וַיַּעֲרֹךְ אֶת־הָעֵצִים וַיַּעֲקֹד אֶת־יִצְחָק בְּנוֹ וַיָּשֶׂם אֹתוֹ עַל־הַמִּזְבֵּחַ מִמַּעַל לָעֵצִים:

10 And *Avraham* picked up the knife to slay his son.

י וַיִּשְׁלַח אַבְרָהָם אֶת־יָדוֹ וַיִּקַּח אֶת־הַמַּאֲכֶלֶת לִשְׁחֹט אֶת־בְּנוֹ:

11 Then an angel of *Hashem* called to him from heaven: "*Avraham! Avraham!*" And he answered, "Here I am."

יא וַיִּקְרָא אֵלָיו מַלְאַךְ יְהֹוָה מִן־הַשָּׁמַיִם וַיֹּאמֶר אַבְרָהָם אַבְרָהָם וַיֹּאמֶר הִנֵּנִי:

12 And he said, "Do not raise your hand against the boy, or do anything to him. For now I know that you fear *Hashem*, since you have not withheld your son, your favored one, from Me."

יב וַיֹּאמֶר אַל־תִּשְׁלַח יָדְךָ אֶל־הַנַּעַר וְאַל־תַּעַשׂ לוֹ מְאוּמָה כִּי עַתָּה יָדַעְתִּי כִּי־יְרֵא אֱלֹהִים אַתָּה וְלֹא חָשַׂכְתָּ אֶת־בִּנְךָ אֶת־יְחִידְךָ מִמֶּנִּי:

13 When *Avraham* looked up, his eye fell upon a ram, caught in the thicket by its horns. So *Avraham* went and took the ram and offered it up as a burnt offering in place of his son.

יג וַיִּשָּׂא אַבְרָהָם אֶת־עֵינָיו וַיַּרְא וְהִנֵּה־אַיִל אַחַר נֶאֱחַז בַּסְּבַךְ בְּקַרְנָיו וַיֵּלֶךְ אַבְרָהָם וַיִּקַּח אֶת־הָאַיִל וַיַּעֲלֵהוּ לְעֹלָה תַּחַת בְּנוֹ:

14 And *Avraham* named that site Adonai-yireh, whence the present saying, "On the mount of *Hashem* there is vision."

יד וַיִּקְרָא אַבְרָהָם שֵׁם־הַמָּקוֹם הַהוּא יְהֹוָה יִרְאֶה אֲשֶׁר יֵאָמֵר הַיּוֹם בְּהַר יְהֹוָה יֵרָאֶה:

15 The angel of *Hashem* called to *Avraham* a second time from heaven,

טו וַיִּקְרָא מַלְאַךְ יְהֹוָה אֶל־אַבְרָהָם שֵׁנִית מִן־הַשָּׁמָיִם:

16 and said, "By Myself I swear, *Hashem* declares: Because you have done this and have not withheld your son, your favored one,

טז וַיֹּאמֶר בִּי נִשְׁבַּעְתִּי נְאֻם־יְהֹוָה כִּי יַעַן אֲשֶׁר עָשִׂיתָ אֶת־הַדָּבָר הַזֶּה וְלֹא חָשַׂכְתָּ אֶת־בִּנְךָ אֶת־יְחִידֶךָ:

17 I will bestow My blessing upon you and make your descendants as numerous as the stars of heaven and the sands on the seashore; and your descendants shall seize the gates of their foes.

יז כִּי־בָרֵךְ אֲבָרֶכְךָ וְהַרְבָּה אַרְבֶּה אֶת־זַרְעֲךָ כְּכוֹכְבֵי הַשָּׁמַיִם וְכַחוֹל אֲשֶׁר עַל־שְׂפַת הַיָּם וְיִרַשׁ זַרְעֲךָ אֵת שַׁעַר אֹיְבָיו:

18 All the nations of the earth shall bless themselves by your descendants, because you have obeyed My command."

יח וְהִתְבָּרֲכוּ בְזַרְעֲךָ כֹּל גּוֹיֵי הָאָרֶץ עֵקֶב אֲשֶׁר שָׁמַעְתָּ בְּקֹלִי:

v'-hit-ba-r'-KHU v'-zar-a-KHA KOL go-YAY ha-A-retz
AY-kev a-SHER sha-MA-ta b'-ko-LEE

19 *Avraham* then returned to his servants, and they departed together for *Be'er Sheva*; and *Avraham* stayed in *Be'er Sheva*.

יט וַיָּשָׁב אַבְרָהָם אֶל־נְעָרָיו וַיָּקֻמוּ וַיֵּלְכוּ יַחְדָּו אֶל־בְּאֵר שָׁבַע וַיֵּשֶׁב אַבְרָהָם בִּבְאֵר שָׁבַע:

20 Some time later, *Avraham* was told, "Milcah too has borne children to your brother Nahor:

כ וַיְהִי אַחֲרֵי הַדְּבָרִים הָאֵלֶּה וַיֻּגַּד לְאַבְרָהָם לֵאמֹר הִנֵּה יָלְדָה מִלְכָּה גַם־הִוא בָּנִים לְנָחוֹר אָחִיךָ:

21 Uz the first-born, and Buz his brother, and Kemuel the father of Aram;

כא אֶת־עוּץ בְּכֹרוֹ וְאֶת־בּוּז אָחִיו וְאֶת־קְמוּאֵל אֲבִי אֲרָם:

22 and Chesed, Hazo, Pildash, Jidlaph, and Bethuel"

כב וְאֶת־כֶּשֶׂד וְאֶת־חֲזוֹ וְאֶת־פִּלְדָּשׁ וְאֶת־יִדְלָף וְאֵת בְּתוּאֵל:

22:18 All the nations of the earth shall bless themselves by your descendants After *Avraham* demonstrates his unwavering faith in *Hashem* with the binding of *Yitzchak*, the Lord repeats His original promise found in *Sefer Bereishit* (12:3), and assures *Avraham* that all the nations of the world will be blessed through him. When we look at the many contributions that the State of Israel makes to the entire world even beyond its spiritual message – such as its technological, agricultural and humanitarian innovations – we see that the State of Israel is a fulfillment of this biblical promise.

Contemporary Israel has come to be known as the "Start-up Nation," and there are actually more Israeli companies on the NASDAQ stock exchange than any foreign country besides China. Israel plays an outsized role in the global economy, proving this blessing's efficacy.

PM Ehud Barak visiting the NASDAQ

23 Bethuel being the father of *Rivka*. These eight Milcah bore to Nahor, *Avraham*'s brother.

24 And his concubine, whose name was Reumah, also bore children: Tebah, Gaham, Tahash, and Maacah.

23 1 *Sara*'s lifetime – the span of *Sara*'s life – came to one hundred and twenty-seven years.

2 *Sara* died in *Kiryat Arba* – now *Chevron* – in the land of Canaan; and *Avraham* proceeded to mourn for *Sara* and to bewail her.

3 Then *Avraham* rose from beside his dead, and spoke to the Hittites, saying,

4 "I am a resident alien among you; sell me a burial site among you, that I may remove my dead for burial."

5 And the Hittites replied to *Avraham*, saying to him,

6 "Hear us, my lord: you are the elect of *Hashem* among us. Bury your dead in the choicest of our burial places; none of us will withhold his burial place from you for burying your dead."

7 Thereupon *Avraham* bowed low to the people of the land, the Hittites,

8 and he said to them, "If it is your wish that I remove my dead for burial, you must agree to intercede for me with Ephron son of Zohar.

9 Let him sell me the cave of Machpelah that he owns, which is at the edge of his land. Let him sell it to me, at the full price, for a burial site in your midst."

10 Ephron was present among the Hittites; so Ephron the Hittite answered *Avraham* in the hearing of the Hittites, all who entered the gate of his town, saying,

11 "No, my lord, hear me: I give you the field and I give you the cave that is in it; I give it to you in the presence of my people. Bury your dead."

12 Then *Avraham* bowed low before the people of the land,

13 and spoke to Ephron in the hearing of the people of the land, saying, "If only you would hear me out! Let me pay the price of the land; accept it from me, that I may bury my dead there."

כג וּבְתוּאֵל יָלַד אֶת־רִבְקָה שְׁמֹנָה אֵלֶּה יָלְדָה מִלְכָּה לְנָחוֹר אֲחִי אַבְרָהָם:

כד וּפִילַגְשׁוֹ וּשְׁמָהּ רְאוּמָה וַתֵּלֶד גַּם־הִוא אֶת־טֶבַח וְאֶת־גַּחַם וְאֶת־תַּחַשׁ וְאֶת־מַעֲכָה:

כג א וַיִּהְיוּ חַיֵּי שָׂרָה מֵאָה שָׁנָה וְעֶשְׂרִים שָׁנָה וְשֶׁבַע שָׁנִים שְׁנֵי חַיֵּי שָׂרָה:

ב וַתָּמָת שָׂרָה בְּקִרְיַת אַרְבַּע הִוא חֶבְרוֹן בְּאֶרֶץ כְּנָעַן וַיָּבֹא אַבְרָהָם לִסְפֹּד לְשָׂרָה וְלִבְכֹּתָהּ:

ג וַיָּקָם אַבְרָהָם מֵעַל פְּנֵי מֵתוֹ וַיְדַבֵּר אֶל־בְּנֵי־חֵת לֵאמֹר:

ד גֵּר־וְתוֹשָׁב אָנֹכִי עִמָּכֶם תְּנוּ לִי אֲחֻזַּת־קֶבֶר עִמָּכֶם וְאֶקְבְּרָה מֵתִי מִלְּפָנָי:

ה וַיַּעֲנוּ בְנֵי־חֵת אֶת־אַבְרָהָם לֵאמֹר לוֹ:

ו שְׁמָעֵנוּ אֲדֹנִי נְשִׂיא אֱלֹהִים אַתָּה בְּתוֹכֵנוּ בְּמִבְחַר קְבָרֵינוּ קְבֹר אֶת־מֵתֶךָ אִישׁ מִמֶּנּוּ אֶת־קִבְרוֹ לֹא־יִכְלֶה מִמְּךָ מִקְּבֹר מֵתֶךָ:

ז וַיָּקָם אַבְרָהָם וַיִּשְׁתַּחוּ לְעַם־הָאָרֶץ לִבְנֵי־חֵת:

ח וַיְדַבֵּר אִתָּם לֵאמֹר אִם־יֵשׁ אֶת־נַפְשְׁכֶם לִקְבֹּר אֶת־מֵתִי מִלְּפָנַי שְׁמָעוּנִי וּפִגְעוּ־לִי בְּעֶפְרוֹן בֶּן־צֹחַר:

ט וְיִתֶּן־לִי אֶת־מְעָרַת הַמַּכְפֵּלָה אֲשֶׁר־לוֹ אֲשֶׁר בִּקְצֵה שָׂדֵהוּ בְּכֶסֶף מָלֵא יִתְּנֶנָּה לִי בְּתוֹכְכֶם לַאֲחֻזַּת־קָבֶר:

י וְעֶפְרוֹן יֹשֵׁב בְּתוֹךְ בְּנֵי־חֵת וַיַּעַן עֶפְרוֹן הַחִתִּי אֶת־אַבְרָהָם בְּאָזְנֵי בְנֵי־חֵת לְכֹל בָּאֵי שַׁעַר־עִירוֹ לֵאמֹר:

יא לֹא־אֲדֹנִי שְׁמָעֵנִי הַשָּׂדֶה נָתַתִּי לָךְ וְהַמְּעָרָה אֲשֶׁר־בּוֹ לְךָ נְתַתִּיהָ לְעֵינֵי בְנֵי־עַמִּי נְתַתִּיהָ לָּךְ קְבֹר מֵתֶךָ:

יב וַיִּשְׁתַּחוּ אַבְרָהָם לִפְנֵי עַם הָאָרֶץ:

יג וַיְדַבֵּר אֶל־עֶפְרוֹן בְּאָזְנֵי עַם־הָאָרֶץ לֵאמֹר אַךְ אִם־אַתָּה לוּ שְׁמָעֵנִי נָתַתִּי כֶּסֶף הַשָּׂדֶה קַח מִמֶּנִּי וְאֶקְבְּרָה אֶת־מֵתִי שָׁמָּה:

¹⁴ And Ephron replied to *Avraham*, saying to him,

וַיַּעַן עֶפְרוֹן אֶת־אַבְרָהָם לֵאמֹר לוֹ: יד

¹⁵ "My lord, do hear me! A piece of land worth four hundred *shekalim* of silver – what is that between you and me? Go and bury your dead."

אֲדֹנִי שְׁמָעֵנִי אֶרֶץ אַרְבַּע מֵאֹת שֶׁקֶל־ טו
כֶּסֶף בֵּינִי וּבֵינְךָ מַה־הִוא וְאֶת־מֵתְךָ
קְבֹר:

¹⁶ *Avraham* accepted Ephron's terms. *Avraham* paid out to Ephron the money that he had named in the hearing of the Hittites – four hundred *shekalim* of silver at the going merchants' rate.

וַיִּשְׁמַע אַבְרָהָם אֶל־עֶפְרוֹן וַיִּשְׁקֹל טז
אַבְרָהָם לְעֶפְרֹן אֶת־הַכֶּסֶף אֲשֶׁר דִּבֶּר
בְּאָזְנֵי בְנֵי־חֵת אַרְבַּע מֵאוֹת שֶׁקֶל כֶּסֶף
עֹבֵר לַסֹּחֵר:

¹⁷ So Ephron's land in Machpelah, near Mamre – the field with its cave and all the trees anywhere within the confines of that field – passed

וַיָּקָם שְׂדֵה עֶפְרוֹן אֲשֶׁר בַּמַּכְפֵּלָה אֲשֶׁר יז
לִפְנֵי מַמְרֵא הַשָּׂדֶה וְהַמְּעָרָה אֲשֶׁר־בּוֹ
וְכָל־הָעֵץ אֲשֶׁר בַּשָּׂדֶה אֲשֶׁר בְּכָל־גְּבֻלוֹ
סָבִיב:

¹⁸ to *Avraham* as his possession, in the presence of the Hittites, of all who entered the gate of his town.

לְאַבְרָהָם לְמִקְנָה לְעֵינֵי בְנֵי־חֵת בְּכֹל יח
בָּאֵי שַׁעַר־עִירוֹ:

¹⁹ And then *Avraham* buried his wife *Sara* in the cave of the field of Machpelah, facing Mamre – now *Chevron* – in the land of Canaan.

וְאַחֲרֵי־כֵן קָבַר אַבְרָהָם אֶת־שָׂרָה יט
אִשְׁתּוֹ אֶל־מְעָרַת שְׂדֵה הַמַּכְפֵּלָה עַל־
פְּנֵי מַמְרֵא הוּא חֶבְרוֹן בְּאֶרֶץ כְּנָעַן:

*v'-a-kha-ray KHAYN ka-VAR av-ra-HAM et sa-RAH ish-TO el m'-a-RAT s'-DAY
ha-makh-pay-LAH al p'-NAY mam-RAY HEE khev-RON b'-E-retz k'-NA-an*

²⁰ Thus the field with its cave passed from the Hittites to *Avraham*, as a burial site.

וַיָּקָם הַשָּׂדֶה וְהַמְּעָרָה אֲשֶׁר־בּוֹ כ
לְאַבְרָהָם לַאֲחֻזַּת־קָבֶר מֵאֵת בְּנֵי־חֵת:

*va-YA-kom ha-sa-DEH v'-ha-m'-a-RAH a-sher BO l'-av-ra-HAM
la-a-khu-zat KA-ver may-AYT b'-nay KHAYT*

24 ¹ *Avraham* was now old, advanced in years, and *Hashem* had blessed *Avraham* in all things.

וְאַבְרָהָם זָקֵן בָּא בַּיָּמִים וַיהוָה בֵּרַךְ א **כד**
אֶת־אַבְרָהָם בַּכֹּל:

² And *Avraham* said to the senior servant of his household, who had charge of all that he owned, "Put your hand under my thigh

וַיֹּאמֶר אַבְרָהָם אֶל־עַבְדּוֹ זְקַן בֵּיתוֹ ב
הַמֹּשֵׁל בְּכָל־אֲשֶׁר־לוֹ שִׂים־נָא יָדְךָ
תַּחַת יְרֵכִי:

חברון

23:19 Now *Chevron* The names of many Israeli cities have profound sigificance. According to a Midrash quoted by the *Ramban*, the Hebrew name for Hebron, '*Chevron*' (חברון), is a contraction of the word *chaver* (חבר), 'friend,' and the word *na-eh* (נאה) 'beloved.' Thus, the very name of the city of *Chevron* alludes to its most famous resident *Avraham*, who was the first beloved friend of the Lord, as *Hashem* says in *Sefer Yeshayahu* (41:8), "Seed of *Avraham* My friend."

Kiryat Arba with Chevron in the background

23:20 Passed from the Hittites to *Avraham*, as a burial site At the time of *Sara's* death, *Avraham* had been living in the Land of Israel for over sixty years, yet this is the first mention of him actually purchasing land. Rabbi Moshe Lichtman, in his book *Eretz Yisrael in the Parasha*, notes that purchasing the land for *Sara's* burial highlights the fundamental truth that one must sacrifice for *Eretz Yisrael*. It was only after *Avraham* experienced the hardship of the loss of his wife that he acquired his first piece of property. Lest this be discouraging, Jewish tradition teaches that "the reward is proportionate to the effort" (*Ethics of the Fathers*, 5:26). Because of the great sacrifice and effort the Jewish people have made in reclaiming *Eretz Yisrael*, we can be assured that the reward will likewise be great.

³ and I will make you swear by *Hashem*, the God of heaven and the God of the earth, that you will not take a wife for my son from the daughters of the Canaanites among whom I dwell,

ג וְאַשְׁבִּיעֲךָ בַּיהוָה אֱלֹהֵי הַשָּׁמַיִם וֵאלֹהֵי הָאָרֶץ אֲשֶׁר לֹא־תִקַּח אִשָּׁה לִבְנִי מִבְּנוֹת הַכְּנַעֲנִי אֲשֶׁר אָנֹכִי יוֹשֵׁב בְּקִרְבּוֹ:

⁴ but will go to the land of my birth and get a wife for my son *Yitzchak*."

ד כִּי אֶל־אַרְצִי וְאֶל־מוֹלַדְתִּי תֵּלֵךְ וְלָקַחְתָּ אִשָּׁה לִבְנִי לְיִצְחָק:

⁵ And the servant said to him, "What if the woman does not consent to follow me to this land, shall I then take your son back to the land from which you came?"

ה וַיֹּאמֶר אֵלָיו הָעֶבֶד אוּלַי לֹא־תֹאבֶה הָאִשָּׁה לָלֶכֶת אַחֲרַי אֶל־הָאָרֶץ הַזֹּאת הֶהָשֵׁב אָשִׁיב אֶת־בִּנְךָ אֶל־הָאָרֶץ אֲשֶׁר־יָצָאתָ מִשָּׁם:

⁶ *Avraham* answered him, "On no account must you take my son back there!

ו וַיֹּאמֶר אֵלָיו אַבְרָהָם הִשָּׁמֶר לְךָ פֶּן־תָּשִׁיב אֶת־בְּנִי שָׁמָּה:

⁷ *Hashem*, the God of heaven, who took me from my father's house and from my native land, who promised me on oath, saying, 'I will assign this land to your offspring' – He will send His angel before you, and you will get a wife for my son from there.

ז יְהוָה אֱלֹהֵי הַשָּׁמַיִם אֲשֶׁר לְקָחַנִי מִבֵּית אָבִי וּמֵאֶרֶץ מוֹלַדְתִּי וַאֲשֶׁר דִּבֶּר־לִי וַאֲשֶׁר נִשְׁבַּע־לִי לֵאמֹר לְזַרְעֲךָ אֶתֵּן אֶת־הָאָרֶץ הַזֹּאת הוּא יִשְׁלַח מַלְאָכוֹ לְפָנֶיךָ וְלָקַחְתָּ אִשָּׁה לִבְנִי מִשָּׁם:

⁸ And if the woman does not consent to follow you, you shall then be clear of this oath to me; but do not take my son back there."

ח וְאִם־לֹא תֹאבֶה הָאִשָּׁה לָלֶכֶת אַחֲרֶיךָ וְנִקִּיתָ מִשְּׁבֻעָתִי זֹאת רַק אֶת־בְּנִי לֹא תָשֵׁב שָׁמָּה:

⁹ So the servant put his hand under the thigh of his master *Avraham* and swore to him as bidden.

ט וַיָּשֶׂם הָעֶבֶד אֶת־יָדוֹ תַּחַת יֶרֶךְ אַבְרָהָם אֲדֹנָיו וַיִּשָּׁבַע לוֹ עַל־הַדָּבָר הַזֶּה:

¹⁰ Then the servant took ten of his master's camels and set out, taking with him all the bounty of his master; and he made his way to Aram-Naharaim, to the city of Nahor.

י וַיִּקַּח הָעֶבֶד עֲשָׂרָה גְמַלִּים מִגְּמַלֵּי אֲדֹנָיו וַיֵּלֶךְ וְכָל־טוּב אֲדֹנָיו בְּיָדוֹ וַיָּקָם וַיֵּלֶךְ אֶל־אֲרַם נַהֲרַיִם אֶל־עִיר נָחוֹר:

> *va-yi-KAKH ha-E-ved a-sa-RAH g'-ma-LEEM mi-g'-ma-LAY*
> *a-do-NAV va-YAY-lekh v'-khol TUV a-do-NAV b'-ya-DO va-YA-kom*
> *va-YAY-lekh el a-RAM na-ha-RA-yim el EER na-KHOR*

¹¹ He made the camels kneel down by the well outside the city, at evening time, the time when women come out to draw water.

יא וַיַּבְרֵךְ הַגְּמַלִּים מִחוּץ לָעִיר אֶל־בְּאֵר הַמָּיִם לְעֵת עֶרֶב לְעֵת צֵאת הַשֹּׁאֲבֹת:

¹² And he said, "*Hashem*, God of my master *Avraham*, grant me good fortune this day, and deal graciously with my master *Avraham*:

יב וַיֹּאמַר יְהוָה אֱלֹהֵי אֲדֹנִי אַבְרָהָם הַקְרֵה־נָא לְפָנַי הַיּוֹם וַעֲשֵׂה־חֶסֶד עִם אֲדֹנִי אַבְרָהָם:

 24:10 Then the servant took ten of his master's camels The Hebrew word for 'camel' is *gamal* (גמל), which also means 'to be independent.' We find the usage of this word in a variety of contexts: "The child grew up, and was 'weaned' (*vayigamal*)" (Genesis 21:8); "and borne almonds" (*vayigmol* – i.e. 'became independent of the stalk'; Numbers 17:23). According to

Rabbi Natan Slifkin, popularly known as the "Zoo Rabbi," the Hebrew name for camel refers to the animal's ability to survive without water for up to seven months. It is fitting that the independent camel was the method of transportation used by *Avraham*'s servant to bring back a wife for *Yitzchak*, as *Rivka* made the independent choice to leave her family in order to join *Yitzchak* in *Eretz Yisrael*.

A camel on the Mount of Olives

13 Here I stand by the spring as the daughters of the townsmen come out to draw water;

יג הִנֵּה אָנֹכִי נִצָּב עַל־עֵין הַמָּיִם וּבְנוֹת אַנְשֵׁי הָעִיר יֹצְאֹת לִשְׁאֹב מָיִם:

14 let the maiden to whom I say, 'Please, lower your jar that I may drink,' and who replies, 'Drink, and I will also water your camels' – let her be the one whom You have decreed for Your servant *Yitzchak*. Thereby shall I know that You have dealt graciously with my master."

יד וְהָיָה הַנַּעֲרָ אֲשֶׁר אֹמַר אֵלֶיהָ הַטִּי־נָא כַדֵּךְ וְאֶשְׁתֶּה וְאָמְרָה שְׁתֵה וְגַם־גְּמַלֶּיךָ אַשְׁקֶה אֹתָהּ הֹכַחְתָּ לְעַבְדְּךָ לְיִצְחָק וּבָהּ אֵדַע כִּי־עָשִׂיתָ חֶסֶד עִם־אֲדֹנִי:

15 He had scarcely finished speaking, when *Rivka*, who was born to Bethuel, the son of Milcah the wife of *Avraham*'s brother Nahor, came out with her jar on her shoulder.

טו וַיְהִי־הוּא טֶרֶם כִּלָּה לְדַבֵּר וְהִנֵּה רִבְקָה יֹצֵאת אֲשֶׁר יֻלְּדָה לִבְתוּאֵל בֶּן־מִלְכָּה אֵשֶׁת נָחוֹר אֲחִי אַבְרָהָם וְכַדָּהּ עַל־שִׁכְמָהּ:

16 The maiden was very beautiful, a virgin whom no man had known. She went down to the spring, filled her jar, and came up.

טז וְהַנַּעֲרָ טֹבַת מַרְאֶה מְאֹד בְּתוּלָה וְאִישׁ לֹא יְדָעָהּ וַתֵּרֶד הָעַיְנָה וַתְּמַלֵּא כַדָּהּ וַתָּעַל:

17 The servant ran toward her and said, "Please, let me sip a little water from your jar."

יז וַיָּרָץ הָעֶבֶד לִקְרָאתָהּ וַיֹּאמֶר הַגְמִיאִינִי נָא מְעַט־מַיִם מִכַּדֵּךְ:

18 "Drink, my lord," she said, and she quickly lowered her jar upon her hand and let him drink.

יח וַתֹּאמֶר שְׁתֵה אֲדֹנִי וַתְּמַהֵר וַתֹּרֶד כַּדָּהּ עַל־יָדָהּ וַתַּשְׁקֵהוּ:

19 When she had let him drink his fill, she said, "I will also draw for your camels, until they finish drinking."

יט וַתְּכַל לְהַשְׁקֹתוֹ וַתֹּאמֶר גַּם לִגְמַלֶּיךָ אֶשְׁאָב עַד אִם־כִּלּוּ לִשְׁתֹּת:

20 Quickly emptying her jar into the trough, she ran back to the well to draw, and she drew for all his camels.

כ וַתְּמַהֵר וַתְּעַר כַּדָּהּ אֶל־הַשֹּׁקֶת וַתָּרָץ עוֹד אֶל־הַבְּאֵר לִשְׁאֹב וַתִּשְׁאַב לְכָל־גְּמַלָּיו:

21 The man, meanwhile, stood gazing at her, silently wondering whether *Hashem* had made his errand successful or not.

כא וְהָאִישׁ מִשְׁתָּאֵה לָהּ מַחֲרִישׁ לָדַעַת הַהִצְלִיחַ יְהוָֹה דַּרְכּוֹ אִם־לֹא:

22 When the camels had finished drinking, the man took a gold nose-ring weighing a *beka*, and two gold bands for her arms, ten *shekalim* in weight.

כב וַיְהִי כַּאֲשֶׁר כִּלּוּ הַגְּמַלִּים לִשְׁתּוֹת וַיִּקַּח הָאִישׁ נֶזֶם זָהָב בֶּקַע מִשְׁקָלוֹ וּשְׁנֵי צְמִידִים עַל־יָדֶיהָ עֲשָׂרָה זָהָב מִשְׁקָלָם:

23 "Pray tell me," he said, "whose daughter are you? Is there room in your father's house for us to spend the night?"

כג וַיֹּאמֶר בַּת־מִי אַתְּ הַגִּידִי נָא לִי הֲיֵשׁ בֵּית־אָבִיךְ מָקוֹם לָנוּ לָלִין:

24 She replied, "I am the daughter of Bethuel the son of Milcah, whom she bore to Nahor."

כד וַתֹּאמֶר אֵלָיו בַּת־בְּתוּאֵל אָנֹכִי בֶּן־מִלְכָּה אֲשֶׁר יָלְדָה לְנָחוֹר:

25 And she went on, "There is plenty of straw and feed at home, and also room to spend the night."

כה וַתֹּאמֶר אֵלָיו גַּם־תֶּבֶן גַּם־מִסְפּוֹא רַב עִמָּנוּ גַּם־מָקוֹם לָלוּן:

26 The man bowed low in homage to *Hashem*

כו וַיִּקֹּד הָאִישׁ וַיִּשְׁתַּחוּ לַיהוָֹה:

27 and said, "Blessed be *Hashem*, the God of my master *Avraham*, who has not withheld His steadfast faithfulness from my master. For I have been guided on my errand by *Hashem*, to the house of my master's kinsmen."

כז וַיֹּאמֶר בָּרוּךְ יְהוָה אֱלֹהֵי אֲדֹנִי אַבְרָהָם אֲשֶׁר לֹא־עָזַב חַסְדּוֹ וַאֲמִתּוֹ מֵעִם אֲדֹנִי אָנֹכִי בַּדֶּרֶךְ נָחַנִי יְהוָה בֵּית אֲחֵי אֲדֹנִי:

28 The maiden ran and told all this to her mother's household.

כח וַתָּרָץ הַנַּעֲרָ וַתַּגֵּד לְבֵית אִמָּהּ כַּדְּבָרִים הָאֵלֶּה:

29 Now *Rivka* had a brother whose name was Laban. Laban ran out to the man at the spring

כט וּלְרִבְקָה אָח וּשְׁמוֹ לָבָן וַיָּרָץ לָבָן אֶל־הָאִישׁ הַחוּצָה אֶל־הָעָיִן:

30 when he saw the nose-ring and the bands on his sister's arms, and when he heard his sister *Rivka* say, "Thus the man spoke to me." He went up to the man, who was still standing beside the camels at the spring.

ל וַיְהִי כִּרְאֹת אֶת־הַנֶּזֶם וְאֶת־הַצְּמִדִים עַל־יְדֵי אֲחֹתוֹ וּכְשָׁמְעוֹ אֶת־דִּבְרֵי רִבְקָה אֲחֹתוֹ לֵאמֹר כֹּה־דִבֶּר אֵלַי הָאִישׁ וַיָּבֹא אֶל־הָאִישׁ וְהִנֵּה עֹמֵד עַל־הַגְּמַלִּים עַל־הָעָיִן:

31 "Come in, O blessed of *Hashem*," he said, "why do you remain outside, when I have made ready the house and a place for the camels?"

לא וַיֹּאמֶר בּוֹא בְּרוּךְ יְהוָה לָמָּה תַעֲמֹד בַּחוּץ וְאָנֹכִי פִּנִּיתִי הַבַּיִת וּמָקוֹם לַגְּמַלִּים:

32 So the man entered the house, and the camels were unloaded. The camels were given straw and feed, and water was brought to bathe his feet and the feet of the men with him.

לב וַיָּבֹא הָאִישׁ הַבַּיְתָה וַיְפַתַּח הַגְּמַלִּים וַיִּתֵּן תֶּבֶן וּמִסְפּוֹא לַגְּמַלִּים וּמַיִם לִרְחֹץ רַגְלָיו וְרַגְלֵי הָאֲנָשִׁים אֲשֶׁר אִתּוֹ:

33 But when food was set before him, he said, "I will not eat until I have told my tale." He said, "Speak, then."

לג וַיּוּשַׂם [וַיּוּשֶׂם] לְפָנָיו לֶאֱכֹל וַיֹּאמֶר לֹא אֹכַל עַד אִם־דִּבַּרְתִּי דְּבָרָי וַיֹּאמֶר דַּבֵּר:

34 "I am *Avraham*'s servant," he began.

לד וַיֹּאמַר עֶבֶד אַבְרָהָם אָנֹכִי:

35 "*Hashem* has greatly blessed my master, and he has become rich: He has given him sheep and cattle, silver and gold, male and female slaves, camels and asses.

לה וַיהוָה בֵּרַךְ אֶת־אֲדֹנִי מְאֹד וַיִּגְדָּל וַיִּתֶּן־לוֹ צֹאן וּבָקָר וְכֶסֶף וְזָהָב וַעֲבָדִם וּשְׁפָחֹת וּגְמַלִּים וַחֲמֹרִים:

36 And *Sara*, my master's wife, bore my master a son in her old age, and he has assigned to him everything he owns.

לו וַתֵּלֶד שָׂרָה אֵשֶׁת אֲדֹנִי בֵן לַאדֹנִי אַחֲרֵי זִקְנָתָהּ וַיִּתֶּן־לוֹ אֶת־כָּל־אֲשֶׁר־לוֹ:

37 Now my master made me swear, saying, 'You shall not get a wife for my son from the daughters of the Canaanites in whose land I dwell;

לז וַיַּשְׁבִּעֵנִי אֲדֹנִי לֵאמֹר לֹא־תִקַּח אִשָּׁה לִבְנִי מִבְּנוֹת הַכְּנַעֲנִי אֲשֶׁר אָנֹכִי יֹשֵׁב בְּאַרְצוֹ:

38 but you shall go to my father's house, to my kindred, and get a wife for my son.'

לח אִם־לֹא אֶל־בֵּית־אָבִי תֵּלֵךְ וְאֶל־מִשְׁפַּחְתִּי וְלָקַחְתָּ אִשָּׁה לִבְנִי:

39 And I said to my master, 'What if the woman does not follow me?'

לט וָאֹמַר אֶל־אֲדֹנִי אֻלַי לֹא־תֵלֵךְ הָאִשָּׁה אַחֲרָי:

40 He replied to me, '*Hashem*, whose ways I have followed, will send His angel with you and make your errand successful; and you will get a wife for my son from my kindred, from my father's house.

41 Thus only shall you be freed from my adjuration: if, when you come to my kindred, they refuse you – only then shall you be freed from my adjuration.'

42 "I came today to the spring, and I said: *Hashem*, God of my master *Avraham*, if You would indeed grant success to the errand on which I am engaged!

43 As I stand by the spring of water, let the young woman who comes out to draw and to whom I say, 'Please, let me drink a little water from your jar,'

44 and who answers, 'You may drink, and I will also draw for your camels' – let her be the wife whom *Hashem* has decreed for my master's son.'

45 I had scarcely finished praying in my heart, when *Rivka* came out with her jar on her shoulder, and went down to the spring and drew. And I said to her, 'Please give me a drink.'

46 She quickly lowered her jar and said, 'Drink, and I will also water your camels.' So I drank, and she also watered the camels.

47 I inquired of her, 'Whose daughter are you?' And she said, 'The daughter of Bethuel, son of Nahor, whom Milcah bore to him.' And I put the ring on her nose and the bands on her arms.

48 Then I bowed low in homage to *Hashem* and blessed *Hashem*, the God of my master *Avraham*, who led me on the right way to get the daughter of my master's brother for his son.

49 And now, if you mean to treat my master with true kindness, tell me; and if not, tell me also, that I may turn right or left."

50 Then Laban and Bethuel answered, "The matter was decreed by *Hashem*; we cannot speak to you bad or good.

51 Here is *Rivka* before you; take her and go, and let her be a wife to your master's son, as *Hashem* has spoken."

52 When *Avraham*'s servant heard their words, he bowed low to the ground before *Hashem*.

מ וַיֹּ֖אמֶר אֵלָ֑י יְהֹוָ֞ה אֲשֶׁר־הִתְהַלַּ֣כְתִּי לְפָנָ֗יו יִשְׁלַ֨ח מַלְאָכ֤וֹ אִתָּךְ֙ וְהִצְלִ֣יחַ דַּרְכֶּ֔ךָ וְלָקַחְתָּ֤ אִשָּׁה֙ לִבְנִ֔י מִמִּשְׁפַּחְתִּ֖י וּמִבֵּ֥ית אָבִֽי:

מא אָ֤ז תִּנָּקֶה֙ מֵאָ֣לָתִ֔י כִּ֥י תָב֖וֹא אֶל־מִשְׁפַּחְתִּ֑י וְאִם־לֹ֤א יִתְּנוּ֙ לָ֔ךְ וְהָיִ֥יתָ נָקִ֖י מֵאָלָתִֽי:

מב וָאָבֹ֥א הַיּ֖וֹם אֶל־הָעָ֑יִן וָאֹמַ֗ר יְהֹוָה֙ אֱלֹהֵי֙ אֲדֹנִ֣י אַבְרָהָ֔ם אִם־יֶשְׁךָ־נָּ֗א מַצְלִ֣יחַ דַּרְכִּ֔י אֲשֶׁ֥ר אָנֹכִ֖י הֹלֵ֥ךְ עָלֶֽיהָ:

מג הִנֵּ֛ה אָנֹכִ֥י נִצָּ֖ב עַל־עֵ֣ין הַמָּ֑יִם וְהָיָ֤ה הָעַלְמָה֙ הַיֹּצֵ֣את לִשְׁאֹ֔ב וְאָמַרְתִּ֣י אֵלֶ֔יהָ הַשְׁקִינִי־נָ֥א מְעַט־מַ֖יִם מִכַּדֵּֽךְ:

מד וְאָמְרָ֤ה אֵלַי֙ גַּם־אַתָּ֣ה שְׁתֵ֔ה וְגַ֥ם לִגְמַלֶּ֖יךָ אֶשְׁאָ֑ב הִ֣וא הָֽאִשָּׁ֔ה אֲשֶׁר־הֹכִ֥יחַ יְהֹוָ֖ה לְבֶן־אֲדֹנִֽי:

מה אֲנִי֩ טֶ֨רֶם אֲכַלֶּ֜ה לְדַבֵּ֣ר אֶל־לִבִּ֗י וְהִנֵּ֨ה רִבְקָ֜ה יֹצֵ֗את וְכַדָּ֣הּ עַל־שִׁכְמָ֔הּ וַתֵּ֥רֶד הָעַ֖יְנָה וַתִּשְׁאָ֑ב וָאֹמַ֥ר אֵלֶ֖יהָ הַשְׁקִ֥ינִי נָֽא:

מו וַתְּמַהֵ֗ר וַתּ֤וֹרֶד כַּדָּהּ֙ מֵֽעָלֶ֔יהָ וַתֹּ֣אמֶר שְׁתֵ֔ה וְגַם־גְּמַלֶּ֖יךָ אַשְׁקֶ֑ה וָאֵ֕שְׁתְּ וְגַ֥ם הַגְּמַלִּ֖ים הִשְׁקָֽתָה:

מז וָאֶשְׁאַ֣ל אֹתָ֗הּ וָאֹמַר֮ בַּת־מִ֣י אַתְּ֒ וַתֹּ֗אמֶר בַּת־בְּתוּאֵל֙ בֶּן־נָח֔וֹר אֲשֶׁ֥ר יָֽלְדָה־לּ֖וֹ מִלְכָּ֑ה וָאָשִׂ֤ם הַנֶּ֨זֶם֙ עַל־אַפָּ֔הּ וְהַצְּמִידִ֖ים עַל־יָדֶֽיהָ:

מח וָאֶקֹּ֥ד וָֽאֶשְׁתַּחֲוֶ֖ה לַֽיהֹוָ֑ה וָֽאֲבָרֵ֗ךְ אֶת־יְהֹוָה֙ אֱלֹהֵי֙ אֲדֹנִ֣י אַבְרָהָ֔ם אֲשֶׁ֤ר הִנְחַ֨נִי֙ בְּדֶ֣רֶךְ אֱמֶ֔ת לָקַ֛חַת אֶת־בַּת־אֲחִ֥י אֲדֹנִ֖י לִבְנֽוֹ:

מט וְ֠עַתָּ֠ה אִם־יֶשְׁכֶ֨ם עֹשִׂ֜ים חֶ֤סֶד וֶֽאֱמֶת֙ אֶת־אֲדֹנִ֔י הַגִּ֣ידוּ לִ֑י וְאִם־לֹ֕א הַגִּ֣ידוּ לִ֔י וְאֶפְנֶ֥ה עַל־יָמִ֖ין א֥וֹ עַל־שְׂמֹֽאל:

נ וַיַּ֨עַן לָבָ֤ן וּבְתוּאֵל֙ וַיֹּ֣אמְר֔וּ מֵיְהֹוָ֖ה יָצָ֣א הַדָּבָ֑ר לֹ֥א נוּכַ֛ל דַּבֵּ֥ר אֵלֶ֖יךָ רַ֥ע אוֹ־טֽוֹב:

נא הִנֵּֽה־רִבְקָ֥ה לְפָנֶ֖יךָ קַ֣ח וָלֵ֑ךְ וּתְהִ֤י אִשָּׁה֙ לְבֶן־אֲדֹנֶ֔יךָ כַּֽאֲשֶׁ֖ר דִּבֶּ֥ר יְהֹוָֽה:

נב וַיְהִ֕י כַּֽאֲשֶׁ֥ר שָׁמַ֛ע עֶ֥בֶד אַבְרָהָ֖ם אֶת־דִּבְרֵיהֶ֑ם וַיִּשְׁתַּ֥חוּ אַ֖רְצָה לַֽיהֹוָֽה:

53 The servant brought out objects of silver and gold, and garments, and gave them to *Rivka*; and he gave presents to her brother and her mother.

נג וַיּוֹצֵא הָעֶבֶד כְּלֵי־כֶסֶף וּכְלֵי זָהָב וּבְגָדִים וַיִּתֵּן לְרִבְקָה וּמִגְדָּנֹת נָתַן לְאָחִיהָ וּלְאִמָּהּ:

54 Then he and the men with him ate and drank, and they spent the night. When they arose next morning, he said, "Give me leave to go to my master."

נד וַיֹּאכְלוּ וַיִּשְׁתּוּ הוּא וְהָאֲנָשִׁים אֲשֶׁר־עִמּוֹ וַיָּלִינוּ וַיָּקוּמוּ בַבֹּקֶר וַיֹּאמֶר שַׁלְּחֻנִי לַאדֹנִי:

55 But her brother and her mother said, "Let the maiden remain with us some ten days; then you may go."

נה וַיֹּאמֶר אָחִיהָ וְאִמָּהּ תֵּשֵׁב הַנַּעֲרָ אִתָּנוּ יָמִים אוֹ עָשׂוֹר אַחַר תֵּלֵךְ:

56 He said to them, "Do not delay me, now that *Hashem* has made my errand successful. Give me leave that I may go to my master."

נו וַיֹּאמֶר אֲלֵהֶם אַל־תְּאַחֲרוּ אֹתִי וַיהֹוָה הִצְלִיחַ דַּרְכִּי שַׁלְּחוּנִי וְאֵלְכָה לַאדֹנִי:

57 And they said, "Let us call the girl and ask for her reply."

נז וַיֹּאמְרוּ נִקְרָא לַנַּעֲרָ וְנִשְׁאֲלָה אֶת־פִּיהָ:

58 They called *Rivka* and said to her, "Will you go with this man?" And she said, "I will."

נח וַיִּקְרְאוּ לְרִבְקָה וַיֹּאמְרוּ אֵלֶיהָ הֲתֵלְכִי עִם־הָאִישׁ הַזֶּה וַתֹּאמֶר אֵלֵךְ:

59 So they sent off their sister *Rivka* and her nurse along with *Avraham*'s servant and his men.

נט וַיְשַׁלְּחוּ אֶת־רִבְקָה אֲחֹתָם וְאֶת־מֵנִקְתָּהּ וְאֶת־עֶבֶד אַבְרָהָם וְאֶת־אֲנָשָׁיו:

60 And they blessed *Rivka* and said to her, "O sister! May you grow Into thousands of myriads; May your offspring seize he gates of their foes."

ס וַיְבָרֲכוּ אֶת־רִבְקָה וַיֹּאמְרוּ לָהּ אֲחֹתֵנוּ אַתְּ הֲיִי לְאַלְפֵי רְבָבָה וְיִירַשׁ זַרְעֵךְ אֵת שַׁעַר שֹׂנְאָיו:

61 Then *Rivka* and her maids arose, mounted the camels, and followed the man. So the servant took *Rivka* and went his way.

סא וַתָּקָם רִבְקָה וְנַעֲרֹתֶיהָ וַתִּרְכַּבְנָה עַל־הַגְּמַלִּים וַתֵּלַכְנָה אַחֲרֵי הָאִישׁ וַיִּקַּח הָעֶבֶד אֶת־רִבְקָה וַיֵּלַךְ:

62 *Yitzchak* had just come back from the vicinity of Beer-lahai-roi, for he was settled in the region of the *Negev*.

סב וְיִצְחָק בָּא מִבּוֹא בְּאֵר לַחַי רֹאִי וְהוּא יוֹשֵׁב בְּאֶרֶץ הַנֶּגֶב:

63 And *Yitzchak* went out walking in the field toward evening and, looking up, he saw camels approaching.

סג וַיֵּצֵא יִצְחָק לָשׂוּחַ בַּשָּׂדֶה לִפְנוֹת עָרֶב וַיִּשָּׂא עֵינָיו וַיַּרְא וְהִנֵּה גְמַלִּים בָּאִים:

64 Raising her eyes, *Rivka* saw *Yitzchak*. She alighted from the camel

סד וַתִּשָּׂא רִבְקָה אֶת־עֵינֶיהָ וַתֵּרֶא אֶת־יִצְחָק וַתִּפֹּל מֵעַל הַגָּמָל:

65 and said to the servant, "Who is that man walking in the field toward us?" And the servant said, "That is my master." So she took her veil and covered herself.

סה וַתֹּאמֶר אֶל־הָעֶבֶד מִי־הָאִישׁ הַלָּזֶה הַהֹלֵךְ בַּשָּׂדֶה לִקְרָאתֵנוּ וַיֹּאמֶר הָעֶבֶד הוּא אֲדֹנִי וַתִּקַּח הַצָּעִיף וַתִּתְכָּס:

66 The servant told *Yitzchak* all the things that he had done.

סו וַיְסַפֵּר הָעֶבֶד לְיִצְחָק אֵת כָּל־הַדְּבָרִים אֲשֶׁר עָשָׂה:

67 *Yitzchak* then brought her into the tent of his mother *Sara*, and he took *Rivka* as his wife. *Yitzchak* loved her, and thus found comfort after his mother's death.

סז וַיְבִאֶהָ יִצְחָק הָאֹהֱלָה שָׂרָה אִמּוֹ וַיִּקַּח אֶת־רִבְקָה וַתְּהִי־לוֹ לְאִשָּׁה וַיֶּאֱהָבֶהָ וַיִּנָּחֵם יִצְחָק אַחֲרֵי אִמּוֹ:

25 **1** *Avraham* took another wife, whose name was Keturah.

א וַיֹּסֶף אַבְרָהָם וַיִּקַּח אִשָּׁה וּשְׁמָהּ קְטוּרָה:

2 She bore him Zimran, Jokshan, Medan, Midian, Ishbak, and Shuah.

ב וַתֵּלֶד לוֹ אֶת־זִמְרָן וְאֶת־יָקְשָׁן וְאֶת־מְדָן וְאֶת־מִדְיָן וְאֶת־יִשְׁבָּק וְאֶת־שׁוּחַ:

3 Jokshan begot Sheba and Dedan. The descendants of Dedan were the Assyrians, the Letushim, and the Leummim.

ג וְיָקְשָׁן יָלַד אֶת־שְׁבָא וְאֶת־דְּדָן וּבְנֵי דְדָן הָיוּ אַשּׁוּרִם וּלְטוּשִׁים וּלְאֻמִּים:

4 The descendants of Midian were Ephah, Epher, Enoch, Abida, and Eldaah. All these were descendants of Keturah.

ד וּבְנֵי מִדְיָן עֵיפָה וָעֵפֶר וַחֲנֹךְ וַאֲבִידָע וְאֶלְדָּעָה כָּל־אֵלֶּה בְּנֵי קְטוּרָה:

5 *Avraham* willed all that he owned to *Yitzchak*;

ה וַיִּתֵּן אַבְרָהָם אֶת־כָּל־אֲשֶׁר־לוֹ לְיִצְחָק:

6 but to *Avraham*'s sons by concubines *Avraham* gave gifts while he was still living, and he sent them away from his son *Yitzchak* eastward, to the land of the East.

ו וְלִבְנֵי הַפִּילַגְשִׁים אֲשֶׁר לְאַבְרָהָם נָתַן אַבְרָהָם מַתָּנֹת וַיְשַׁלְּחֵם מֵעַל יִצְחָק בְּנוֹ בְּעוֹדֶנּוּ חַי קֵדְמָה אֶל־אֶרֶץ קֶדֶם:

7 This was the total span of *Avraham*'s life: one hundred and seventy-five years.

ז וְאֵלֶּה יְמֵי שְׁנֵי־חַיֵּי אַבְרָהָם אֲשֶׁר־חָי מְאַת שָׁנָה וְשִׁבְעִים שָׁנָה וְחָמֵשׁ שָׁנִים:

8 And *Avraham* breathed his last, dying at a good ripe age, old and contented; and he was gathered to his kin.

ח וַיִּגְוַע וַיָּמָת אַבְרָהָם בְּשֵׂיבָה טוֹבָה זָקֵן וְשָׂבֵעַ וַיֵּאָסֶף אֶל־עַמָּיו:

9 His sons *Yitzchak* and Ishmael buried him in the cave of Machpelah, in the field of Ephron son of Zohar the Hittite, facing Mamre,

ט וַיִּקְבְּרוּ אֹתוֹ יִצְחָק וְיִשְׁמָעֵאל בָּנָיו אֶל־מְעָרַת הַמַּכְפֵּלָה אֶל־שְׂדֵה עֶפְרֹן בֶּן־צֹחַר הַחִתִּי אֲשֶׁר עַל־פְּנֵי מַמְרֵא:

va-yik-b'-RU o-TO yitz-KHAK v'-yish-ma-AYL ba-NAV
el m'-a-RAT ha-makh-pay-LAH el s'-DAY ef-RON ben
TZO-khar ha-khi-TEE a-SHER al p'-NAY mam-RAY

10 the field that *Avraham* had bought from the Hittites; there *Avraham* was buried, and *Sara* his wife.

י הַשָּׂדֶה אֲשֶׁר־קָנָה אַבְרָהָם מֵאֵת בְּנֵי־חֵת שָׁמָּה קֻבַּר אַבְרָהָם וְשָׂרָה אִשְׁתּוֹ:

25:9 His sons *Yitzchak* and Ishmael buried him in the cave of *Machpelah* The *Torah* states that *Avraham*, *Sara*, *Yitzchak*, *Rivka*, *Yaakov* and *Leah* are all buried in *Machpelah* Cave. According to tradition, *Adam* and *Chava* were buried there as well. *Avraham*'s purchase of this property to bury *Sara* was the first concrete action that established a Jewish connection with a particular site in *Eretz Yisrael*, and upon his death he is also buried in this place. Although the entire Land of Israel was promised to the Children of Israel, there are three key places that were actually purchased, in order that they could never be accused of having taken possession of them inappropriately. *Avraham* purchased the Cave of *Machpelah*, *Yaakov* bought *Yosef*'s burial plot in *Shechem* (Genesis 33:19) and King *David* paid for the site of the *Beit Hamikdash* (II Samuel 24:24). While we are fortunate that we can actually visit the Cave of *Machpelah* today, sadly, Jewish authority over *Chevron*, *Shechem* and *Har Habayit*, is disputed by much of the world. We pray for the time when the biblical record will be recognized and respected by the nations.

Cave of the Machpelah in Chevron

¹¹ After the death of *Avraham*, *Hashem* blessed his son *Yitzchak*. And *Yitzchak* settled near Beer-lahai-roi.

יא וַיְהִי אַחֲרֵי מוֹת אַבְרָהָם וַיְבָרֶךְ אֱלֹהִים אֶת־יִצְחָק בְּנוֹ וַיֵּשֶׁב יִצְחָק עִם־בְּאֵר לַחַי רֹאִי׃

¹² This is the line of Ishmael, *Avraham*'s son, whom Hagar the Egyptian, *Sara*'s slave, bore to *Avraham*.

יב וְאֵלֶּה תֹּלְדֹת יִשְׁמָעֵאל בֶּן־אַבְרָהָם אֲשֶׁר יָלְדָה הָגָר הַמִּצְרִית שִׁפְחַת שָׂרָה לְאַבְרָהָם׃

¹³ These are the names of the sons of Ishmael, by their names, in the order of their birth: Nebaioth, the first-born of Ishmael, Kedar, Adbeel, Mibsam,

יג וְאֵלֶּה שְׁמוֹת בְּנֵי יִשְׁמָעֵאל בִּשְׁמֹתָם לְתוֹלְדֹתָם בְּכֹר יִשְׁמָעֵאל נְבָיֹת וְקֵדָר וְאַדְבְּאֵל וּמִבְשָׂם׃

¹⁴ Mishma, Dumah, Massa,

יד וּמִשְׁמָע וְדוּמָה וּמַשָּׂא׃

¹⁵ Hadad, Tema, Jetur, Naphish, and Kedmah.

טו חֲדַד וְתֵימָא יְטוּר נָפִישׁ וָקֵדְמָה׃

¹⁶ These are the sons of Ishmael and these are their names by their villages and by their encampments: twelve chieftains of as many tribes.

טז אֵלֶּה הֵם בְּנֵי יִשְׁמָעֵאל וְאֵלֶּה שְׁמֹתָם בְּחַצְרֵיהֶם וּבְטִירֹתָם שְׁנֵים־עָשָׂר נְשִׂיאִם לְאֻמֹּתָם׃

¹⁷ These were the years of the life of Ishmael: one hundred and thirty-seven years; then he breathed his last and died, and was gathered to his kin.

יז וְאֵלֶּה שְׁנֵי חַיֵּי יִשְׁמָעֵאל מְאַת שָׁנָה וּשְׁלֹשִׁים שָׁנָה וְשֶׁבַע שָׁנִים וַיִּגְוַע וַיָּמָת וַיֵּאָסֶף אֶל־עַמָּיו׃

¹⁸ They dwelt from Havilah, by Shur, which is close to Egypt, all the way to Assyria; they camped alongside all their kinsmen.

יח וַיִּשְׁכְּנוּ מֵחֲוִילָה עַד־שׁוּר אֲשֶׁר עַל־פְּנֵי מִצְרַיִם בֹּאֲכָה אַשּׁוּרָה עַל־פְּנֵי כָל־אֶחָיו נָפָל׃

¹⁹ This is the story of *Yitzchak*, son of *Avraham*. *Avraham* begot *Yitzchak*.

יט וְאֵלֶּה תּוֹלְדֹת יִצְחָק בֶּן־אַבְרָהָם אַבְרָהָם הוֹלִיד אֶת־יִצְחָק׃

²⁰ *Yitzchak* was forty years old when he took to wife *Rivka*, daughter of Bethuel the Aramean of Paddan-aram, sister of Laban the Aramean.

כ וַיְהִי יִצְחָק בֶּן־אַרְבָּעִים שָׁנָה בְּקַחְתּוֹ אֶת־רִבְקָה בַּת־בְּתוּאֵל הָאֲרַמִּי מִפַּדַּן אֲרָם אֲחוֹת לָבָן הָאֲרַמִּי לוֹ לְאִשָּׁה׃

²¹ *Yitzchak* pleaded with *Hashem* on behalf of his wife, because she was barren; and *Hashem* responded to his plea, and his wife *Rivka* conceived.

כא וַיֶּעְתַּר יִצְחָק לַיהוָה לְנֹכַח אִשְׁתּוֹ כִּי עֲקָרָה הִוא וַיֵּעָתֶר לוֹ יְהוָה וַתַּהַר רִבְקָה אִשְׁתּוֹ׃

²² But the children struggled in her womb, and she said, "If so, why do I exist?" She went to inquire of *Hashem*,

כב וַיִּתְרֹצֲצוּ הַבָּנִים בְּקִרְבָּהּ וַתֹּאמֶר אִם־כֵּן לָמָּה זֶּה אָנֹכִי וַתֵּלֶךְ לִדְרֹשׁ אֶת־יְהוָה׃

²³ and *Hashem* answered her, "Two nations are in your womb, Two separate peoples shall issue from your body; One people shall be mightier than the other, And the older shall serve the younger."

כג וַיֹּאמֶר יְהוָה לָהּ שְׁנֵי גיים [גוֹיִם] בְּבִטְנֵךְ וּשְׁנֵי לְאֻמִּים מִמֵּעַיִךְ יִפָּרֵדוּ וּלְאֹם מִלְאֹם יֶאֱמָץ וְרַב יַעֲבֹד צָעִיר׃

²⁴ When her time to give birth was at hand, there were twins in her womb.

כד וַיִּמְלְאוּ יָמֶיהָ לָלֶדֶת וְהִנֵּה תוֹמִם בְּבִטְנָהּ׃

²⁵ The first one emerged red, like a hairy mantle all over; so they named him Esau.

כה וַיֵּצֵא הָרִאשׁוֹן אַדְמוֹנִי כֻּלּוֹ כְּאַדֶּרֶת שֵׂעָר וַיִּקְרְאוּ שְׁמוֹ עֵשָׂו׃

26 Then his brother emerged, holding on to the heel of Esau; so they named him *Yaakov*. *Yitzchak* was sixty years old when they were born.

27 When the boys grew up, Esau became a skillful hunter, a man of the outdoors; but *Yaakov* was a mild man who stayed in camp.

28 *Yitzchak* favored Esau because he had a taste for game; but *Rivka* favored *Yaakov*.

29 Once when *Yaakov* was cooking a stew, Esau came in from the open, famished.

30 And Esau said to *Yaakov*, "Give me some of that red stuff to gulp down, for I am famished" – which is why he was named Edom.

31 *Yaakov* said, "First sell me your birthright."

32 And Esau said, "I am at the point of death, so of what use is my birthright to me?"

33 But *Yaakov* said, "Swear to me first." So he swore to him, and sold his birthright to *Yaakov*.

34 *Yaakov* then gave Esau bread and lentil stew; he ate and drank, and he rose and went away. Thus did Esau spurn the birthright.

26 1 There was a famine in the land – aside from the previous famine that had occurred in the days of *Avraham* – and *Yitzchak* went to Abimelech, king of the Philistines, in Gerar.

2 *Hashem* had appeared to him and said, "Do not go down to Egypt; stay in the land which I point out to you.

3 Reside in this land, and I will be with you and bless you; I will assign all these lands to you and to your heirs, fulfilling the oath that I swore to your father *Avraham*.

כו וְאַחֲרֵי־כֵן יָצָא אָחִיו וְיָדוֹ אֹחֶזֶת בַּעֲקֵב עֵשָׂו וַיִּקְרָא שְׁמוֹ יַעֲקֹב וְיִצְחָק בֶּן־שִׁשִּׁים שָׁנָה בְּלֶדֶת אֹתָם:

כז וַיִּגְדְּלוּ הַנְּעָרִים וַיְהִי עֵשָׂו אִישׁ יֹדֵעַ צַיִד אִישׁ שָׂדֶה וְיַעֲקֹב אִישׁ תָּם יֹשֵׁב אֹהָלִים:

כח וַיֶּאֱהַב יִצְחָק אֶת־עֵשָׂו כִּי־צַיִד בְּפִיו וְרִבְקָה אֹהֶבֶת אֶת־יַעֲקֹב:

כט וַיָּזֶד יַעֲקֹב נָזִיד וַיָּבֹא עֵשָׂו מִן־הַשָּׂדֶה וְהוּא עָיֵף:

ל וַיֹּאמֶר עֵשָׂו אֶל־יַעֲקֹב הַלְעִיטֵנִי נָא מִן־הָאָדֹם הָאָדֹם הַזֶּה כִּי עָיֵף אָנֹכִי עַל־כֵּן קָרָא־שְׁמוֹ אֱדוֹם:

לא וַיֹּאמֶר יַעֲקֹב מִכְרָה כַיּוֹם אֶת־בְּכֹרָתְךָ לִי:

לב וַיֹּאמֶר עֵשָׂו הִנֵּה אָנֹכִי הוֹלֵךְ לָמוּת וְלָמָּה־זֶּה לִי בְּכֹרָה:

לג וַיֹּאמֶר יַעֲקֹב הִשָּׁבְעָה לִּי כַּיּוֹם וַיִּשָּׁבַע לוֹ וַיִּמְכֹּר אֶת־בְּכֹרָתוֹ לְיַעֲקֹב:

לד וְיַעֲקֹב נָתַן לְעֵשָׂו לֶחֶם וּנְזִיד עֲדָשִׁים וַיֹּאכַל וַיֵּשְׁתְּ וַיָּקָם וַיֵּלַךְ וַיִּבֶז עֵשָׂו אֶת־הַבְּכֹרָה:

א וַיְהִי רָעָב בָּאָרֶץ מִלְּבַד הָרָעָב הָרִאשׁוֹן אֲשֶׁר הָיָה בִּימֵי אַבְרָהָם וַיֵּלֶךְ יִצְחָק אֶל־אֲבִימֶלֶךְ מֶלֶךְ־פְּלִשְׁתִּים גְּרָרָה:

ב וַיֵּרָא אֵלָיו יְהוָה וַיֹּאמֶר אַל־תֵּרֵד מִצְרָיְמָה שְׁכֹן בָּאָרֶץ אֲשֶׁר אֹמַר אֵלֶיךָ:

ג גּוּר בָּאָרֶץ הַזֹּאת וְאֶהְיֶה עִמְּךָ וַאֲבָרְכֶךָּ כִּי־לְךָ וּלְזַרְעֲךָ אֶתֵּן אֶת־כָּל־הָאֲרָצֹת הָאֵל וַהֲקִמֹתִי אֶת־הַשְּׁבֻעָה אֲשֶׁר נִשְׁבַּעְתִּי לְאַבְרָהָם אָבִיךָ:

GUR ba-A-retz ha-ZOT v'-eh-YEH i-m'-KHA va-a-va-r'-KHE-ka kee l'-KHA
ul-zar-a-KHA e-TAYN et kol ha-a-ra-TZOT ha-AYL va-ha-ki-mo-TEE
et ha-sh'-vu-AH a-SHER nish-BA-tee l'-av-ra-HAM a-VEE-kha

26:3 Reside in this land, and I will be with you and bless you
Yitzchak is warned that despite the famine in *Eretz Yisrael*, he is not to escape the hardship by fleeing to Egypt. Though *Avraham* went down to Egypt when there was a plague in Israel, and *Yaakov* likewise descended to Egypt towards the end of his life, God told *Yitzchak* not to leave the Land of Israel. Due to the unique spiritual status he acquired after being offered on the altar, *Yitzchak* was the only one of the three forefathers to never step foot outside of the Holy Land.

A valley in the Galilee

4 I will make your heirs as numerous as the stars of
heaven, and assign to your heirs all these lands,
so that all the nations of the earth shall bless
themselves by your heirs

ד וְהִרְבֵּיתִי אֶת־זַרְעֲךָ כְּכוֹכְבֵי הַשָּׁמַיִם
וְנָתַתִּי לְזַרְעֲךָ אֵת כָּל־הָאֲרָצֹת הָאֵל
וְהִתְבָּרֲכוּ בְזַרְעֲךָ כֹּל גּוֹיֵי הָאָרֶץ:

v'-hir-bay-TEE et zar-a-KHA k'-kho-kh'-VAY ha-sha-MA-yim
v'-na-ta-TEE l'-zar-a-KHA AYT kol ha-a-ra-TZOT ha-AYL
v'-hit-ba-r'-KHU v'-zar-a-KHA KOL go-YAY ha-A-retz

5 inasmuch as *Avraham* obeyed Me and kept My
charge: My commandments, My laws, and My
teachings."

ה עֵקֶב אֲשֶׁר־שָׁמַע אַבְרָהָם בְּקֹלִי וַיִּשְׁמֹר
מִשְׁמַרְתִּי מִצְוֹתַי חֻקּוֹתַי וְתוֹרֹתָי:

6 So *Yitzchak* stayed in Gerar.

ו וַיֵּשֶׁב יִצְחָק בִּגְרָר:

7 When the men of the place asked him about his
wife, he said, "She is my sister," for he was afraid
to say "my wife," thinking, "The men of the place
might kill me on account of *Rivka*, for she is
beautiful."

ז וַיִּשְׁאֲלוּ אַנְשֵׁי הַמָּקוֹם לְאִשְׁתּוֹ וַיֹּאמֶר
אֲחֹתִי הִוא כִּי יָרֵא לֵאמֹר אִשְׁתִּי פֶּן־
יַהַרְגֻנִי אַנְשֵׁי הַמָּקוֹם עַל־רִבְקָה כִּי־
טוֹבַת מַרְאֶה הִיא:

8 When some time had passed, Abimelech king of the
Philistines, looking out of the window, saw *Yitzchak*
fondling his wife *Rivka*.

ח וַיְהִי כִּי אָרְכוּ־לוֹ שָׁם הַיָּמִים וַיַּשְׁקֵף
אֲבִימֶלֶךְ מֶלֶךְ פְּלִשְׁתִּים בְּעַד הַחַלּוֹן
וַיַּרְא וְהִנֵּה יִצְחָק מְצַחֵק אֵת רִבְקָה
אִשְׁתּוֹ:

9 Abimelech sent for *Yitzchak* and said, "So she
is your wife! Why then did you say: 'She is my
sister?'" *Yitzchak* said to him, "Because I thought I
might lose my life on account of her."

ט וַיִּקְרָא אֲבִימֶלֶךְ לְיִצְחָק וַיֹּאמֶר אַךְ הִנֵּה
אִשְׁתְּךָ הִוא וְאֵיךְ אָמַרְתָּ אֲחֹתִי הִוא
וַיֹּאמֶר אֵלָיו יִצְחָק כִּי אָמַרְתִּי פֶּן־אָמוּת
עָלֶיהָ:

10 Abimelech said, "What have you done to us! One
of the people might have lain with your wife, and
you would have brought guilt upon us."

י וַיֹּאמֶר אֲבִימֶלֶךְ מַה־זֹּאת עָשִׂיתָ לָּנוּ
כִּמְעַט שָׁכַב אַחַד הָעָם אֶת־אִשְׁתֶּךָ
וְהֵבֵאתָ עָלֵינוּ אָשָׁם:

11 Abimelech then charged all the people, saying,
"Anyone who molests this man or his wife shall be
put to death."

יא וַיְצַו אֲבִימֶלֶךְ אֶת־כָּל־הָעָם לֵאמֹר
הַנֹּגֵעַ בָּאִישׁ הַזֶּה וּבְאִשְׁתּוֹ מוֹת יוּמָת:

12 *Yitzchak* sowed in that land and reaped a
hundredfold the same year. *Hashem* blessed him,

יב וַיִּזְרַע יִצְחָק בָּאָרֶץ הַהִוא וַיִּמְצָא בַּשָּׁנָה
הַהִוא מֵאָה שְׁעָרִים וַיְבָרֲכֵהוּ יְהוָה:

**26:4 I will make your heirs as numerous as the
stars of heaven** Why are the children of *Avraham* compared to the stars? The poetess Chana
Senesh was born in Hungary in 1921 and in 1939 she
emigrated to what was then the British Mandate of Palestine. Senesh was a brave heroine who volunteered to
leave her beloved Palestine in 1944 in order to fight with
the partisans against the Nazis. Unfortunately, she was
caught, tried for treason and eventually executed. In one
of her beautiful poems she wrote, "There are stars whose
radiance is visible on earth though they have long been
extinct. There are people whose brilliance continues to
light the world though
they are no longer among
the living. These lights are
particularly bright when
the night is dark. They
light the way for mankind."
Like the stars in Senesh's
poem, the Jew's role in
this world is to light the
way for mankind, despite
the darkness we have
encountered throughout our history.

View of the Milky Way from the Negev desert

13 and the man grew richer and richer until he was very wealthy:

יג וַיִּגְדַּל הָאִישׁ וַיֵּלֶךְ הָלוֹךְ וְגָדֵל עַד כִּי־גָדַל מְאֹד׃

14 he acquired flocks and herds, and a large household, so that the Philistines envied him.

יד וַיְהִי־לוֹ מִקְנֵה־צֹאן וּמִקְנֵה בָקָר וַעֲבֻדָּה רַבָּה וַיְקַנְאוּ אֹתוֹ פְּלִשְׁתִּים׃

15 And the Philistines stopped up all the wells which his father's servants had dug in the days of his father *Avraham*, filling them with earth.

טו וְכָל־הַבְּאֵרֹת אֲשֶׁר חָפְרוּ עַבְדֵי אָבִיו בִּימֵי אַבְרָהָם אָבִיו סִתְּמוּם פְּלִשְׁתִּים וַיְמַלְאוּם עָפָר׃

16 And Abimelech said to *Yitzchak*, "Go away from us, for you have become far too big for us."

טז וַיֹּאמֶר אֲבִימֶלֶךְ אֶל־יִצְחָק לֵךְ מֵעִמָּנוּ כִּי־עָצַמְתָּ־מִמֶּנּוּ מְאֹד׃

va-YO-mer a-vee-ME-lekh el yitz-KHAK LAYKH
may-i-MA-nu kee a-TZAM-ta mi-ME-nu m'-OD

17 So *Yitzchak* departed from there and encamped in the wadi of Gerar, where he settled.

יז וַיֵּלֶךְ מִשָּׁם יִצְחָק וַיִּחַן בְּנַחַל־גְּרָר וַיֵּשֶׁב שָׁם׃

18 *Yitzchak* dug anew the wells which had been dug in the days of his father *Avraham* and which the Philistines had stopped up after *Avraham*'s death; and he gave them the same names that his father had given them.

יח וַיָּשָׁב יִצְחָק וַיַּחְפֹּר אֶת־בְּאֵרֹת הַמַּיִם אֲשֶׁר חָפְרוּ בִּימֵי אַבְרָהָם אָבִיו וַיְסַתְּמוּם פְּלִשְׁתִּים אַחֲרֵי מוֹת אַבְרָהָם וַיִּקְרָא לָהֶן שֵׁמוֹת כַּשֵּׁמֹת אֲשֶׁר־קָרָא לָהֶן אָבִיו׃

19 But when *Yitzchak*'s servants, digging in the wadi, found there a well of spring water,

יט וַיַּחְפְּרוּ עַבְדֵי־יִצְחָק בַּנָּחַל וַיִּמְצְאוּ־שָׁם בְּאֵר מַיִם חַיִּים׃

20 the herdsmen of Gerar quarreled with *Yitzchak*'s herdsmen, saying, "The water is ours." He named that well Esek, because they contended with him.

כ וַיָּרִיבוּ רֹעֵי גְרָר עִם־רֹעֵי יִצְחָק לֵאמֹר לָנוּ הַמָּיִם וַיִּקְרָא שֵׁם־הַבְּאֵר עֵשֶׂק כִּי הִתְעַשְּׂקוּ עִמּוֹ׃

21 And when they dug another well, they disputed over that one also; so he named it Sitnah.

כא וַיַּחְפְּרוּ בְּאֵר אַחֶרֶת וַיָּרִיבוּ גַּם־עָלֶיהָ וַיִּקְרָא שְׁמָהּ שִׂטְנָה׃

22 He moved from there and dug yet another well, and they did not quarrel over it; so he called it Rehoboth, saying, "Now at last *Hashem* has granted us ample space to increase in the land."

כב וַיַּעְתֵּק מִשָּׁם וַיַּחְפֹּר בְּאֵר אַחֶרֶת וְלֹא רָבוּ עָלֶיהָ וַיִּקְרָא שְׁמָהּ רְחֹבוֹת וַיֹּאמֶר כִּי־עַתָּה הִרְחִיב יְהֹוָה לָנוּ וּפָרִינוּ בָאָרֶץ׃

va-ya-TAYK mi-SHAM va-yakh-POR b'-AYR a-KHE-ret v'-LO
ra-VU a-LE-ha va-yik-RA sh'-MAH r'-kho-VOT va-YO-mer kee
a-TAH hir-KHEEV a-do-NAI LA-nu u-fa-REE-nu va-A-retz

23 From there he went up to *Be'er Sheva*.

כג וַיַּעַל מִשָּׁם בְּאֵר שָׁבַע׃

26:16 Go away from us, for you have become far too big for us The story of *Yitzchak* among the Philistines alludes to the history of the Jewish people during their lengthy exile, hosted by various foreign nations. Rabbi Zalman Sorotzkin points out that *Yitzchak* is one Jew in an entire country, yet the Philistines claim that there is no room for him. As a successful farmer, *Yitzchak* is not an economic burden on his hosts, and yet the Philistines banish him. They could have learned agricultural techniques and benefitted from his water, but they instead choose to ignore the valuable contributions he could make, and they clog the wells he has dug. Similarly, many Jewish inventors and innovators have been expelled from their host nations throughout history. The only safe place where the Children of Israel can flourish is in the Land of Israel.

Law building at the Hebrew University in *Yerushalayim*

²⁴ That night *Hashem* appeared to him and said, "I am the God of your father *Avraham*. Fear not, for I am with you, and I will bless you and increase your offspring for the sake of My servant *Avraham*."

כד וַיֵּרָ֨א אֵלָ֤יו יְהֹוָה֙ בַּלַּ֣יְלָה הַה֔וּא וַיֹּ֕אמֶר אָנֹכִ֕י אֱלֹהֵ֖י אַבְרָהָ֣ם אָבִ֑יךָ אַל־תִּירָא֙ כִּֽי־אִתְּךָ֣ אָנֹ֔כִי וּבֵֽרַכְתִּ֙יךָ֙ וְהִרְבֵּיתִ֣י אֶת־ זַרְעֲךָ֔ בַּעֲב֖וּר אַבְרָהָ֥ם עַבְדִּֽי:

²⁵ So he built a *Mizbayach* there and invoked *Hashem* by name. *Yitzchak* pitched his tent there and his servants started digging a well.

כה וַיִּ֧בֶן שָׁ֣ם מִזְבֵּ֗חַ וַיִּקְרָא֙ בְּשֵׁ֣ם יְהֹוָ֔ה וַיֶּט־ שָׁ֖ם אָֽהֳל֑וֹ וַיִּכְרוּ־שָׁ֥ם עַבְדֵֽי־יִצְחָ֖ק בְּאֵֽר:

²⁶ And Abimelech came to him from Gerar, with Ahuzzath his councilor and Phicol chief of his troops.

כו וַאֲבִימֶ֕לֶךְ הָלַ֥ךְ אֵלָ֖יו מִגְּרָ֑ר וַאֲחֻזַּת֙ מֵֽרֵעֵ֔הוּ וּפִיכֹ֖ל שַׂר־צְבָאֽוֹ:

²⁷ *Yitzchak* said to them, "Why have you come to me, seeing that you have been hostile to me and have driven me away from you?"

כז וַיֹּ֤אמֶר אֲלֵהֶם֙ יִצְחָ֔ק מַדּ֖וּעַ בָּאתֶ֣ם אֵלָ֑י וְאַתֶּם֙ שְׂנֵאתֶ֣ם אֹתִ֔י וַתְּשַׁלְּח֖וּנִי מֵאִתְּכֶֽם:

²⁸ And they said, "We now see plainly that *Hashem* has been with you, and we thought: Let there be a sworn treaty between our two parties, between you and us. Let us make a pact with you

כח וַיֹּאמְר֗וּ רָא֣וֹ רָאִ֘ינוּ֮ כִּֽי־הָיָ֣ה יְהֹוָ֣ה ׀ עִמָּךְ֒ וַנֹּ֗אמֶר תְּהִ֨י נָ֥א אָלָ֛ה בֵּינוֹתֵ֖ינוּ בֵּינֵ֣ינוּ וּבֵינֶ֑ךָ וְנִכְרְתָ֥ה בְרִ֖ית עִמָּֽךְ:

²⁹ that you will not do us harm, just as we have not molested you but have always dealt kindly with you and sent you away in peace. From now on, be you blessed of *Hashem*!"

כט אִם־תַּעֲשֵׂ֨ה עִמָּ֜נוּ רָעָ֗ה כַּאֲשֶׁר֙ לֹ֣א נְגַֽעֲנ֔וּךָ וְכַאֲשֶׁ֨ר עָשִׂ֤ינוּ עִמְּךָ֙ רַק־ט֔וֹב וַנְּשַׁלֵּחֲךָ֖ בְּשָׁל֑וֹם אַתָּ֥ה עַתָּ֖ה בְּר֥וּךְ יְהֹוָֽה:

³⁰ Then he made for them a feast, and they ate and drank.

ל וַיַּ֤עַשׂ לָהֶם֙ מִשְׁתֶּ֔ה וַיֹּאכְל֖וּ וַיִּשְׁתּֽוּ:

³¹ Early in the morning, they exchanged oaths. *Yitzchak* then bade them farewell, and they departed from him in peace.

לא וַיַּשְׁכִּ֣ימוּ בַבֹּ֔קֶר וַיִּשָּׁבְע֖וּ אִ֣ישׁ לְאָחִ֑יו וַיְשַׁלְּחֵ֣ם יִצְחָ֔ק וַיֵּלְכ֥וּ מֵאִתּ֖וֹ בְּשָׁלֽוֹם:

³² That same day *Yitzchak*'s servants came and told him about the well they had dug, and said to him, "We have found water!"

לב וַיְהִ֣י ׀ בַּיּ֣וֹם הַה֗וּא וַיָּבֹ֙אוּ֙ עַבְדֵ֣י יִצְחָ֔ק וַיַּגִּ֣דוּ ל֔וֹ עַל־אֹד֥וֹת הַבְּאֵ֖ר אֲשֶׁ֣ר חָפָ֑רוּ וַיֹּ֥אמְרוּ ל֖וֹ מָצָ֥אנוּ מָֽיִם:

³³ He named it Shibah; therefore the name of the city is *Be'er Sheva* to this day.

לג וַיִּקְרָ֥א אֹתָ֖הּ שִׁבְעָ֑ה עַל־כֵּ֤ן שֵׁם־הָעִיר֙ בְּאֵ֣ר שֶׁ֔בַע עַ֖ד הַיּ֥וֹם הַזֶּֽה:

³⁴ When Esau was forty years old, he took to wife Judith daughter of *Be'eri* the Hittite, and Basemath daughter of Elon the Hittite;

לד וַיְהִ֤י עֵשָׂו֙ בֶּן־אַרְבָּעִ֣ים שָׁנָ֔ה וַיִּקַּ֤ח אִשָּׁה֙ אֶת־יְהוּדִ֔ית בַּת־בְּאֵרִ֖י הַֽחִתִּ֑י וְאֶת־ בָּשְׂמַ֔ת בַּת־אֵילֹ֖ן הַֽחִתִּֽי:

³⁵ and they were a source of bitterness to *Yitzchak* and *Rivka*.

לה וַתִּהְיֶ֖יןָ מֹ֣רַת ר֑וּחַ לְיִצְחָ֖ק וּלְרִבְקָֽה:

7 ¹ When *Yitzchak* was old and his eyes were too dim to see, he called his older son Esau and said to him, "My son." He answered, "Here I am."

כז א וַיְהִי֙ כִּֽי־זָקֵ֣ן יִצְחָ֔ק וַתִּכְהֶ֥יןָ עֵינָ֖יו מֵרְאֹ֑ת וַיִּקְרָ֞א אֶת־עֵשָׂ֣ו ׀ בְּנ֣וֹ הַגָּדֹ֗ל וַיֹּ֤אמֶר אֵלָיו֙ בְּנִ֔י וַיֹּ֥אמֶר אֵלָ֖יו הִנֵּֽנִי:

² And he said, "I am old now, and I do not know how soon I may die.

ב וַיֹּ֕אמֶר הִנֵּה־נָ֖א זָקַ֑נְתִּי לֹ֥א יָדַ֖עְתִּי י֥וֹם מוֹתִֽי:

3 Take your gear, your quiver and bow, and go out into the open and hunt me some game.

ג וְעַתָּה שָׂא־נָא כֵלֶיךָ תֶּלְיְךָ וְקַשְׁתֶּךָ וְצֵא הַשָּׂדֶה וְצוּדָה לִּי צידה [צָיִד:]

4 Then prepare a dish for me such as I like, and bring it to me to eat, so that I may give you my innermost blessing before I die."

ד וַעֲשֵׂה־לִי מַטְעַמִּים כַּאֲשֶׁר אָהַבְתִּי וְהָבִיאָה לִּי וְאֹכֵלָה בַּעֲבוּר תְּבָרֶכְךָ נַפְשִׁי בְּטֶרֶם אָמוּת:

5 *Rivka* had been listening as *Yitzchak* spoke to his son Esau. When Esau had gone out into the open to hunt game to bring home,

ה וְרִבְקָה שֹׁמַעַת בְּדַבֵּר יִצְחָק אֶל־עֵשָׂו בְּנוֹ וַיֵּלֶךְ עֵשָׂו הַשָּׂדֶה לָצוּד צַיִד לְהָבִיא:

6 *Rivka* said to her son *Yaakov*, "I overheard your father speaking to your brother Esau, saying,

ו וְרִבְקָה אָמְרָה אֶל־יַעֲקֹב בְּנָהּ לֵאמֹר הִנֵּה שָׁמַעְתִּי אֶת־אָבִיךָ מְדַבֵּר אֶל־עֵשָׂו אָחִיךָ לֵאמֹר:

7 'Bring me some game and prepare a dish for me to eat, that I may bless you, with *Hashem's* approval, before I die.'

ז הָבִיאָה לִּי צַיִד וַעֲשֵׂה־לִי מַטְעַמִּים וְאֹכֵלָה וַאֲבָרֶכְכָה לִפְנֵי יְהֹוָה לִפְנֵי מוֹתִי:

8 Now, my son, listen carefully as I instruct you.

ח וְעַתָּה בְנִי שְׁמַע בְּקֹלִי לַאֲשֶׁר אֲנִי מְצַוָּה אֹתָךְ:

9 Go to the flock and fetch me two choice kids, and I will make of them a dish for your father, such as he likes.

ט לֶךְ־נָא אֶל־הַצֹּאן וְקַח־לִי מִשָּׁם שְׁנֵי גְּדָיֵי עִזִּים טֹבִים וְאֶעֱשֶׂה אֹתָם מַטְעַמִּים לְאָבִיךָ כַּאֲשֶׁר אָהֵב:

10 Then take it to your father to eat, in order that he may bless you before he dies."

י וְהֵבֵאתָ לְאָבִיךָ וְאָכָל בַּעֲבֻר אֲשֶׁר יְבָרֶכְךָ לִפְנֵי מוֹתוֹ:

11 *Yaakov* answered his mother *Rivka*, "But my brother Esau is a hairy man and I am smooth-skinned.

יא וַיֹּאמֶר יַעֲקֹב אֶל־רִבְקָה אִמּוֹ הֵן עֵשָׂו אָחִי אִישׁ שָׂעִר וְאָנֹכִי אִישׁ חָלָק:

12 If my father touches me, I shall appear to him as a trickster and bring upon myself a curse, not a blessing."

יב אוּלַי יְמֻשֵּׁנִי אָבִי וְהָיִיתִי בְעֵינָיו כִּמְתַעְתֵּעַ וְהֵבֵאתִי עָלַי קְלָלָה וְלֹא בְרָכָה:

13 But his mother said to him, "Your curse, my son, be upon me! Just do as I say and go fetch them for me."

יג וַתֹּאמֶר לוֹ אִמּוֹ עָלַי קִלְלָתְךָ בְּנִי אַךְ שְׁמַע בְּקֹלִי וְלֵךְ קַח־לִי:

14 He got them and brought them to his mother, and his mother prepared a dish such as his father liked.

יד וַיֵּלֶךְ וַיִּקַּח וַיָּבֵא לְאִמּוֹ וַתַּעַשׂ אִמּוֹ מַטְעַמִּים כַּאֲשֶׁר אָהֵב אָבִיו:

15 *Rivka* then took the best clothes of her older son Esau, which were there in the house, and had her younger son *Yaakov* put them on;

טו וַתִּקַּח רִבְקָה אֶת־בִּגְדֵי עֵשָׂו בְּנָהּ הַגָּדֹל הַחֲמֻדֹת אֲשֶׁר אִתָּהּ בַּבָּיִת וַתַּלְבֵּשׁ אֶת־יַעֲקֹב בְּנָהּ הַקָּטָן:

16 and she covered his hands and the hairless part of his neck with the skins of the kids.

טז וְאֵת עֹרֹת גְּדָיֵי הָעִזִּים הִלְבִּישָׁה עַל־יָדָיו וְעַל חֶלְקַת צַוָּארָיו:

17 Then she put in the hands of her son *Yaakov* the dish and the bread that she had prepared.

יז וַתִּתֵּן אֶת־הַמַּטְעַמִּים וְאֶת־הַלֶּחֶם אֲשֶׁר עָשָׂתָה בְּיַד יַעֲקֹב בְּנָהּ:

18 He went to his father and said, "Father." And he said, "Yes, which of my sons are you?"

יח וַיָּבֹא אֶל־אָבִיו וַיֹּאמֶר אָבִי וַיֹּאמֶר הִנֶּנִּי מִי אַתָּה בְּנִי:

19 Yaakov said to his father, "I am Esau, your first-born; I have done as you told me. Pray sit up and eat of my game, that you may give me your innermost blessing."

יט וַיֹּאמֶר יַעֲקֹב אֶל־אָבִיו אָנֹכִי עֵשָׂו בְּכֹרֶךָ עָשִׂיתִי כַּאֲשֶׁר דִּבַּרְתָּ אֵלָי קוּם־נָא שְׁבָה וְאָכְלָה מִצֵּידִי בַּעֲבוּר תְּבָרְכַנִּי נַפְשֶׁךָ:

20 Yitzchak said to his son, "How did you succeed so quickly, my son?" And he said, "Because Hashem your God granted me good fortune."

כ וַיֹּאמֶר יִצְחָק אֶל־בְּנוֹ מַה־זֶּה מִהַרְתָּ לִמְצֹא בְּנִי וַיֹּאמֶר כִּי הִקְרָה יְהוָה אֱלֹהֶיךָ לְפָנָי:

21 Yitzchak said to Yaakov, "Come closer that I may feel you, my son – whether you are really my son Esau or not."

כא וַיֹּאמֶר יִצְחָק אֶל־יַעֲקֹב גְּשָׁה־נָּא וַאֲמֻשְׁךָ בְּנִי הַאַתָּה זֶה בְּנִי עֵשָׂו אִם־לֹא:

22 So Yaakov drew close to his father Yitzchak, who felt him and wondered. "The voice is the voice of Yaakov, yet the hands are the hands of Esau."

כב וַיִּגַּשׁ יַעֲקֹב אֶל־יִצְחָק אָבִיו וַיְמֻשֵּׁהוּ וַיֹּאמֶר הַקֹּל קוֹל יַעֲקֹב וְהַיָּדַיִם יְדֵי עֵשָׂו:

23 He did not recognize him, because his hands were hairy like those of his brother Esau; and so he blessed him.

כג וְלֹא הִכִּירוֹ כִּי־הָיוּ יָדָיו כִּידֵי עֵשָׂו אָחִיו שְׂעִרֹת וַיְבָרְכֵהוּ:

24 He asked, "Are you really my son Esau?" And when he said, "I am,"

כד וַיֹּאמֶר אַתָּה זֶה בְּנִי עֵשָׂו וַיֹּאמֶר אָנִי:

25 he said, "Serve me and let me eat of my son's game that I may give you my innermost blessing." So he served him and he ate, and he brought him wine and he drank.

כה וַיֹּאמֶר הַגִּשָׁה לִּי וְאֹכְלָה מִצֵּיד בְּנִי לְמַעַן תְּבָרֶכְךָ נַפְשִׁי וַיַּגֶּשׁ־לוֹ וַיֹּאכַל וַיָּבֵא לוֹ יַיִן וַיֵּשְׁתְּ:

26 Then his father Yitzchak said to him, "Come close and kiss me, my son";

כו וַיֹּאמֶר אֵלָיו יִצְחָק אָבִיו גְּשָׁה־נָּא וּשְׁקָה־לִּי בְּנִי:

27 and he went up and kissed him. And he smelled his clothes and he blessed him, saying, "Ah, the smell of my son is like the smell of the fields that Hashem has blessed.

כז וַיִּגַּשׁ וַיִּשַּׁק־לוֹ וַיָּרַח אֶת־רֵיחַ בְּגָדָיו וַיְבָרְכֵהוּ וַיֹּאמֶר רְאֵה רֵיחַ בְּנִי כְּרֵיחַ שָׂדֶה אֲשֶׁר בֵּרֲכוֹ יְהוָה:

28 "May Hashem give you Of the dew of heaven and the fat of the earth, Abundance of new grain and wine.

כח וְיִתֶּן־לְךָ הָאֱלֹהִים מִטַּל הַשָּׁמַיִם וּמִשְׁמַנֵּי הָאָרֶץ וְרֹב דָּגָן וְתִירֹשׁ:

*v'-yi-ten l'-KHA ha-e-lo-HEEM mi-TAL ha-sha-MA-yim
u-mish-ma-NAY ha-A-retz v'-ROV da-GAN v'-ti-ROSH*

27:28 May Hashem give you of the dew of heaven and the fat of the earth The Zohar, our primary mystical text, says that this blessing is what has sustained the People of Israel throughout the millennia. If so, why was Yitzchak the one who gave the blessing and not Avraham or Yaakov? Rabbi Shlomo Carlebach, the influential Hebrew songwriter of the 20th century, ex-plained that both Avraham and Yaakov spent part of their lives outside Israel. Therefore it was only Yitzchak, who never once left the Holy Land, who was worthy of bestow-ing this powerful blessing.

Almond blossom in Yerushalayim wet with dew

29 Let peoples serve you, And nations bow to you; Be master over your brothers, And let your mother's sons bow to you. Cursed be they who curse you, Blessed they who bless you."

כט יַעַבְדוּךָ עַמִּים וישתחו [וְיִשְׁתַּחֲווּ] לְךָ לְאֻמִּים הֱוֵה גְבִיר לְאַחֶיךָ וְיִשְׁתַּחֲווּ לְךָ בְּנֵי אִמֶּךָ אֹרְרֶיךָ אָרוּר וּמְבָרֲכֶיךָ בָּרוּךְ:

30 No sooner had *Yaakov* left the presence of his father *Yitzchak* – after *Yitzchak* had finished blessing *Yaakov* – than his brother Esau came back from his hunt.

ל וַיְהִי כַּאֲשֶׁר כִּלָּה יִצְחָק לְבָרֵךְ אֶת־יַעֲקֹב וַיְהִי אַךְ יָצֹא יָצָא יַעֲקֹב מֵאֵת פְּנֵי יִצְחָק אָבִיו וְעֵשָׂו אָחִיו בָּא מִצֵּידוֹ:

31 He too prepared a dish and brought it to his father. And he said to his father, "Let my father sit up and eat of his son's game, so that you may give me your innermost blessing."

לא וַיַּעַשׂ גַּם־הוּא מַטְעַמִּים וַיָּבֵא לְאָבִיו וַיֹּאמֶר לְאָבִיו יָקֻם אָבִי וְיֹאכַל מִצֵּיד בְּנוֹ בַּעֲבוּר תְּבָרֲכַנִּי נַפְשֶׁךָ:

32 His father *Yitzchak* said to him, "Who are you?" And he said, "I am your son, Esau, your first-born!"

לב וַיֹּאמֶר לוֹ יִצְחָק אָבִיו מִי־אָתָּה וַיֹּאמֶר אֲנִי בִּנְךָ בְכֹרְךָ עֵשָׂו:

33 *Yitzchak* was seized with very violent trembling. "Who was it then," he demanded, "that hunted game and brought it to me? Moreover, I ate of it before you came, and I blessed him; now he must remain blessed!"

לג וַיֶּחֱרַד יִצְחָק חֲרָדָה גְּדֹלָה עַד־מְאֹד וַיֹּאמֶר מִי־אֵפוֹא הוּא הַצָּד־צַיִד וַיָּבֵא לִי וָאֹכַל מִכֹּל בְּטֶרֶם תָּבוֹא וָאֲבָרֲכֵהוּ גַּם־בָּרוּךְ יִהְיֶה:

34 When Esau heard his father's words, he burst into wild and bitter sobbing, and said to his father, "Bless me too, Father!"

לד כִּשְׁמֹעַ עֵשָׂו אֶת־דִּבְרֵי אָבִיו וַיִּצְעַק צְעָקָה גְּדֹלָה וּמָרָה עַד־מְאֹד וַיֹּאמֶר לְאָבִיו בָּרֲכֵנִי גַם־אָנִי אָבִי:

35 But he answered, "Your brother came with guile and took away your blessing."

לה וַיֹּאמֶר בָּא אָחִיךָ בְּמִרְמָה וַיִּקַּח בִּרְכָתֶךָ:

36 [Esau] said, "Was he, then, named *Yaakov* that he might supplant me these two times? First he took away my birthright and now he has taken away my blessing!" And he added, "Have you not reserved a blessing for me?"

לו וַיֹּאמֶר הֲכִי קָרָא שְׁמוֹ יַעֲקֹב וַיַּעְקְבֵנִי זֶה פַעֲמַיִם אֶת־בְּכֹרָתִי לָקָח וְהִנֵּה עַתָּה לָקַח בִּרְכָתִי וַיֹּאמַר הֲלֹא־אָצַלְתָּ לִּי בְּרָכָה:

37 *Yitzchak* answered, saying to Esau, "But I have made him master over you: I have given him all his brothers for servants, and sustained him with grain and wine. What, then, can I still do for you, my son?"

לז וַיַּעַן יִצְחָק וַיֹּאמֶר לְעֵשָׂו הֵן גְּבִיר שַׂמְתִּיו לָךְ וְאֶת־כָּל־אֶחָיו נָתַתִּי לוֹ לַעֲבָדִים וְדָגָן וְתִירֹשׁ סְמַכְתִּיו וּלְכָה אֵפוֹא מָה אֶעֱשֶׂה בְּנִי:

38 And Esau said to his father, "Have you but one blessing, Father? Bless me too, Father!" And Esau wept aloud.

לח וַיֹּאמֶר עֵשָׂו אֶל־אָבִיו הַבְרָכָה אַחַת הִוא־לְךָ אָבִי בָּרֲכֵנִי גַם־אָנִי אָבִי וַיִּשָּׂא עֵשָׂו קֹלוֹ וַיֵּבְךְּ:

39 And his father *Yitzchak* answered, saying to him, "See, your abode shall enjoy the fat of the earth And the dew of heaven above.

לט וַיַּעַן יִצְחָק אָבִיו וַיֹּאמֶר אֵלָיו הִנֵּה מִשְׁמַנֵּי הָאָרֶץ יִהְיֶה מוֹשָׁבֶךָ וּמִטַּל הַשָּׁמַיִם מֵעָל:

40 Yet by your sword you shall live, And you shall serve your brother; But when you grow restive, You shall break his yoke from your neck."

מ וְעַל־חַרְבְּךָ תִחְיֶה וְאֶת־אָחִיךָ תַּעֲבֹד וְהָיָה כַּאֲשֶׁר תָּרִיד וּפָרַקְתָּ עֻלּוֹ מֵעַל צַוָּארֶךָ:

⁴¹ Now Esau harbored a grudge against *Yaakov* because of the blessing which his father had given him, and Esau said to himself, "Let but the mourning period of my father come, and I will kill my brother *Yaakov*."

מא וַיִּשְׂטֹם עֵשָׂו אֶת־יַעֲקֹב עַל־הַבְּרָכָה אֲשֶׁר בֵּרְכוֹ אָבִיו וַיֹּאמֶר עֵשָׂו בְּלִבּוֹ יִקְרְבוּ יְמֵי אֵבֶל אָבִי וְאַהַרְגָה אֶת־ יַעֲקֹב אָחִי׃

⁴² When the words of her older son Esau were reported to *Rivka*, she sent for her younger son *Yaakov* and said to him, "Your brother Esau is consoling himself by planning to kill you.

מב וַיֻּגַּד לְרִבְקָה אֶת־דִּבְרֵי עֵשָׂו בְּנָהּ הַגָּדֹל וַתִּשְׁלַח וַתִּקְרָא לְיַעֲקֹב בְּנָהּ הַקָּטָן וַתֹּאמֶר אֵלָיו הִנֵּה עֵשָׂו אָחִיךָ מִתְנַחֵם לְךָ לְהָרְגֶךָ׃

⁴³ Now, my son, listen to me. Flee at once to Haran, to my brother Laban.

מג וְעַתָּה בְנִי שְׁמַע בְּקֹלִי וְקוּם בְּרַח־לְךָ אֶל־לָבָן אָחִי חָרָנָה׃

⁴⁴ Stay with him a while, until your brother's fury subsides

מד וְיָשַׁבְתָּ עִמּוֹ יָמִים אֲחָדִים עַד אֲשֶׁר־ תָּשׁוּב חֲמַת אָחִיךָ׃

⁴⁵ until your brother's anger against you subsides – and he forgets what you have done to him. Then I will fetch you from there. Let me not lose you both in one day!"

מה עַד־שׁוּב אַף־אָחִיךָ מִמְּךָ וְשָׁכַח אֵת אֲשֶׁר־עָשִׂיתָ לּוֹ וְשָׁלַחְתִּי וּלְקַחְתִּיךָ מִשָּׁם לָמָה אֶשְׁכַּל גַּם־שְׁנֵיכֶם יוֹם אֶחָד׃

⁴⁶ *Rivka* said to *Yitzchak*, "I am disgusted with my life because of the Hittite women. If *Yaakov* marries a Hittite woman like these, from among the native women, what good will life be to me?"

מו וַתֹּאמֶר רִבְקָה אֶל־יִצְחָק קַצְתִּי בְחַיַּי מִפְּנֵי בְּנוֹת חֵת אִם־לֹקֵחַ יַעֲקֹב אִשָּׁה מִבְּנוֹת־חֵת כָּאֵלֶּה מִבְּנוֹת הָאָרֶץ לָמָה לִּי חַיִּים׃

כח ¹ So *Yitzchak* sent for *Yaakov* and blessed him. He instructed him, saying, "You shall not take a wife from among the Canaanite women.

כח א וַיִּקְרָא יִצְחָק אֶל־יַעֲקֹב וַיְבָרֶךְ אֹתוֹ וַיְצַוֵּהוּ וַיֹּאמֶר לוֹ לֹא־תִקַּח אִשָּׁה מִבְּנוֹת כְּנָעַן׃

² Up, go to Paddan-aram, to the house of Bethuel, your mother's father, and take a wife there from among the daughters of Laban, your mother's brother,

ב קוּם לֵךְ פַּדֶּנָה אֲרָם בֵּיתָה בְתוּאֵל אֲבִי אִמֶּךָ וְקַח־לְךָ מִשָּׁם אִשָּׁה מִבְּנוֹת לָבָן אֲחִי אִמֶּךָ׃

³ May *El Shaddai* bless you, make you fertile and numerous, so that you become an assembly of peoples.

ג וְאֵל שַׁדַּי יְבָרֵךְ אֹתְךָ וְיַפְרְךָ וְיַרְבֶּךָ וְהָיִיתָ לִקְהַל עַמִּים׃

⁴ May He grant the blessing of *Avraham* to you and your offspring, that you may possess the land where you are sojourning, which *Hashem* assigned to *Avraham*."

ד וְיִתֶּן־לְךָ אֶת־בִּרְכַּת אַבְרָהָם לְךָ וּלְזַרְעֲךָ אִתָּךְ לְרִשְׁתְּךָ אֶת־אֶרֶץ מְגֻרֶיךָ אֲשֶׁר־נָתַן אֱלֹהִים לְאַבְרָהָם׃

v'-yi-ten l'-KHA et bir-KAT av-ra-HAM l'-KHA ul-zar-a-KHA i-TAKH
l'-rish-t'-KHA et E-retz m'-gu-RE-kha a-sher na-TAN e-lo-HEEM l'-av-ra-HAM

⁵ Then *Yitzchak* sent *Yaakov* off, and he went to Paddan-aram, to Laban the son of Bethuel the Aramean, the brother of *Rivka*, mother of *Yaakov* and Esau.

ה וַיִּשְׁלַח יִצְחָק אֶת־יַעֲקֹב וַיֵּלֶךְ פַּדֶּנָה אֲרָם אֶל־לָבָן בֶּן־בְּתוּאֵל הָאֲרַמִּי אֲחִי רִבְקָה אֵם יַעֲקֹב וְעֵשָׂו׃

6 When Esau saw that *Yitzchak* had blessed *Yaakov* and sent him off to Paddan-aram to take a wife from there, charging him, as he blessed him, "You shall not take a wife from among the Canaanite women,"

ו וַיַּ֣רְא עֵשָׂ֗ו כִּֽי־בֵרַ֣ךְ יִצְחָק֮ אֶֽת־יַעֲקֹב֒ וְשִׁלַּ֤ח אֹתוֹ֙ פַּדֶּ֣נָֽה אֲרָ֔ם לָקַֽחַת־ל֥וֹ מִשָּׁ֖ם אִשָּׁ֑ה בְּבָרְכ֣וֹ אֹת֔וֹ וַיְצַ֤ו עָלָיו֙ לֵאמֹ֔ר לֹֽא־תִקַּ֥ח אִשָּׁ֖ה מִבְּנ֥וֹת כְּנָֽעַן׃

7 and that *Yaakov* had obeyed his father and mother and gone to Paddan-aram,

ז וַיִּשְׁמַ֣ע יַעֲקֹ֔ב אֶל־אָבִ֖יו וְאֶל־אִמּ֑וֹ וַיֵּ֖לֶךְ פַּדֶּ֥נָֽה אֲרָֽם׃

8 Esau realized that the Canaanite women displeased his father *Yitzchak*.

ח וַיַּ֣רְא עֵשָׂ֔ו כִּ֥י רָע֖וֹת בְּנ֣וֹת כְּנָ֑עַן בְּעֵינֵ֖י יִצְחָ֥ק אָבִֽיו׃

9 So Esau went to Ishmael and took to wife, in addition to the wives he had, Mahalath the daughter of Ishmael son of *Avraham*, sister of Nebaioth.

ט וַיֵּ֥לֶךְ עֵשָׂ֖ו אֶל־יִשְׁמָעֵ֑אל וַיִּקַּ֡ח אֶֽת־מָֽחֲלַ֣ת ׀ בַּת־יִשְׁמָעֵ֣אל בֶּן־אַבְרָהָ֠ם אֲח֨וֹת נְבָי֜וֹת עַל־נָשָׁ֖יו ל֥וֹ לְאִשָּֽׁה׃

10 *Yaakov* left *Be'er Sheva*, and set out for Haran.

י 🔲 וַיֵּצֵ֥א יַעֲקֹ֖ב מִבְּאֵ֣ר שָׁ֑בַע וַיֵּ֖לֶךְ חָרָֽנָה׃

11 He came upon a certain place and stopped there for the night, for the sun had set. Taking one of the stones of that place, he put it under his head and lay down in that place.

יא וַיִּפְגַּ֨ע בַּמָּק֜וֹם וַיָּ֤לֶן שָׁם֙ כִּי־בָ֣א הַשֶּׁ֔מֶשׁ וַיִּקַּח֙ מֵֽאַבְנֵ֣י הַמָּק֔וֹם וַיָּ֖שֶׂם מְרַֽאֲשֹׁתָ֑יו וַיִּשְׁכַּ֖ב בַּמָּק֥וֹם הַהֽוּא׃

va-yif-GA ba-ma-KOHM va-ya-LAYN shahm ki va ha-SHE-mesh
va-yi-KAKH me-ahv-NAY ha-ma-KOME va-ya-SAYM
m'-ra-sho-TAV va-yish-KAHV ba-ma-KOHM ha-HU

12 He had a dream; a stairway was set on the ground and its top reached to the sky, and angels of *Hashem* were going up and down on it.

יב וַֽיַּחֲלֹ֗ם וְהִנֵּ֤ה סֻלָּם֙ מֻצָּ֣ב אַ֔רְצָה וְרֹאשׁ֖וֹ מַגִּ֣יעַ הַשָּׁמָ֑יְמָה וְהִנֵּה֙ מַלְאֲכֵ֣י אֱלֹהִ֔ים עֹלִ֥ים וְיֹרְדִ֖ים בּֽוֹ׃

13 And *Hashem* was standing beside him and He said, "I am *Hashem*, the God of your father *Avraham* and the God of *Yitzchak*: the ground on which you are lying I will assign to you and to your offspring.

יג וְהִנֵּ֨ה יְהוָ֜ה נִצָּ֣ב עָלָיו֮ וַיֹּאמַר֒ אֲנִ֣י יְהוָ֗ה אֱלֹהֵי֙ אַבְרָהָ֣ם אָבִ֔יךָ וֵאלֹהֵ֖י יִצְחָ֑ק הָאָ֗רֶץ אֲשֶׁ֤ר אַתָּה֙ שֹׁכֵ֣ב עָלֶ֔יהָ לְךָ֥ אֶתְּנֶ֖נָּה וּלְזַרְעֶֽךָ׃

14 Your descendants shall be as the dust of the earth; you shall spread out to the west and to the east, to the north and to the south. All the families of the earth shall bless themselves by you and your descendants.

יד וְהָיָ֤ה זַרְעֲךָ֙ כַּעֲפַ֣ר הָאָ֔רֶץ וּפָרַצְתָּ֛ יָ֥מָּה וָקֵ֖דְמָה וְצָפֹ֣נָה וָנֶ֑גְבָּה וְנִבְרֲכ֥וּ בְךָ֛ כָּל־מִשְׁפְּחֹ֥ת הָאֲדָמָ֖ה וּבְזַרְעֶֽךָ׃

28:11 He came upon a certain place Where is the place that *Yaakov* slept? American congregational Rabbi David Stavsky explained in one of his High Holy Day sermons that the Hebrew word used in this verse is *ba-makom* (בְּמָקוֹם), 'upon *the* place,' and not *bi-makom* (בְּמָקוֹם), 'upon *a* place.' The use of the definite article means this refers to the most important spot in the entire world. As Rabbi Stavsky said, *Yaakov* came upon "the place where Jacob's father Isaac, and his grandfather Abraham, had built an altar. The place where Isaac was bound to the altar. The place which, for centuries, has tied us to *Hashem. Hamakom*, 'the place,' was Mount *Moriah*, eventually to become the heart and soul of Jerusalem, and it was as if a magnet had drawn young Jacob to wander the hot Mesopotamian desert that night, to that particular place. And dear friends, I dare say that whatever force pulled Jacob to that place that night, pulls you and me to that place. It is a deep mystical pull. It is holiness."

Sunset over Mount *Moriah*, the Temple Mount in *Yerushalayim*

15 Remember, I am with you: I will protect you wherever you go and will bring you back to this land. I will not leave you until I have done what I have promised you."

טו וְהִנֵּה אָנֹכִי עִמָּךְ וּשְׁמַרְתִּיךָ בְּכֹל אֲשֶׁר־תֵּלֵךְ וַהֲשִׁבֹתִיךָ אֶל־הָאֲדָמָה הַזֹּאת כִּי לֹא אֶעֱזָבְךָ עַד אֲשֶׁר אִם־עָשִׂיתִי אֵת אֲשֶׁר־דִּבַּרְתִּי לָךְ:

16 Yaakov awoke from his sleep and said, "Surely *Hashem* is present in this place, and I did not know it!"

טז וַיִּיקַץ יַעֲקֹב מִשְּׁנָתוֹ וַיֹּאמֶר אָכֵן יֵשׁ יְהוָה בַּמָּקוֹם הַזֶּה וְאָנֹכִי לֹא יָדָעְתִּי:

17 Shaken, he said, "How awesome is this place! This is none other than the abode of *Hashem*, and that is the gateway to heaven."

יז וַיִּירָא וַיֹּאמַר מַה־נּוֹרָא הַמָּקוֹם הַזֶּה אֵין זֶה כִּי אִם־בֵּית אֱלֹהִים וְזֶה שַׁעַר הַשָּׁמָיִם:

va-yee-RA va-yo-MAR mah no-RA ha-ma-KOM ha-ZEH AYN ZEH KEE im BAYT e-lo-HEEM v'-ZEH SHA-ar ha-sha-MA-yim

18 Early in the morning, *Yaakov* took the stone that he had put under his head and set it up as a pillar and poured oil on the top of it.

יח וַיַּשְׁכֵּם יַעֲקֹב בַּבֹּקֶר וַיִּקַּח אֶת־הָאֶבֶן אֲשֶׁר־שָׂם מְרַאֲשֹׁתָיו וַיָּשֶׂם אֹתָהּ מַצֵּבָה וַיִּצֹק שֶׁמֶן עַל־רֹאשָׁהּ:

19 He named that site *Beit El*; but previously the name of the city had been Luz.

יט וַיִּקְרָא אֶת־שֵׁם־הַמָּקוֹם הַהוּא בֵּית־אֵל וְאוּלָם לוּז שֵׁם־הָעִיר לָרִאשֹׁנָה:

va-yik-RA et shaym ha-ma-KOM ha-HU bayt EL v'-u-LAM LUZ shaym ha-EER la-ri-sho-NAH

20 *Yaakov* then made a vow, saying, "If *Hashem* remains with me, if He protects me on this journey that I am making, and gives me bread to eat and clothing to wear,

כ וַיִּדַּר יַעֲקֹב נֶדֶר לֵאמֹר אִם־יִהְיֶה אֱלֹהִים עִמָּדִי וּשְׁמָרַנִי בַּדֶּרֶךְ הַזֶּה אֲשֶׁר אָנֹכִי הוֹלֵךְ וְנָתַן־לִי לֶחֶם לֶאֱכֹל וּבֶגֶד לִלְבֹּשׁ:

21 and if I return safe to my father's house – *Hashem* shall be my God.

כא וְשַׁבְתִּי בְשָׁלוֹם אֶל־בֵּית אָבִי וְהָיָה יְהוָה לִי לֵאלֹהִים:

22 And this stone, which I have set up as a pillar, shall be *Hashem*'s abode; and of all that You give me, I will set aside a tithe for You."

כב וְהָאֶבֶן הַזֹּאת אֲשֶׁר־שַׂמְתִּי מַצֵּבָה יִהְיֶה בֵּית אֱלֹהִים וְכֹל אֲשֶׁר תִּתֶּן־לִי עַשֵּׂר אֲעַשְּׂרֶנּוּ לָךְ:

28:17 This is none other than the abode of *Hashem* According to *Rashi*, these words refer to the Temple Mount in *Yerushalayim*. He explains that the foot of the ladder in *Yaakov*'s dream was in *Be'er Sheva*, and its head was in *Beit El*. Therefore the middle of the ladder hung over Mount *Moriah* and the intensity of the encounter with *Hashem* occurred in that spot. When *Yaakov* awakens, he realizes that he has seen no ordinary place, but "the abode of *Hashem*," the most intimate spot for prayers to ascend heavenward and the site where the *Beit Hamik-dash* would later stand. The *Beit Hamikdash* is referred to here as 'abode' or 'house' because in the Temple, *Hashem*'s revealed presence – the *shechina* (שכינה) – dwells with His people, just as a husband dwells intimately with his wife in their home.

28:19 He named that site *Beit El* When *Yaakov* arrives in *Beit El*, the city near which his grandfather *Avraham* called to *Hashem* for the first time in the Land of Israel (Genesis 12:8), he recognizes its unique spiritual character. From that moment on, *Beit El* appears throughout the Bible as a special location for prayer. The Hebrew name *Beit El* means "The House of the Lord," and signifies its powerful purpose. Rabbi Zalman Sorotzkin explains that a home protects a person from the elements, extreme temperatures and rain. Similarly, we are meant to view "The House of the Lord" as a safe haven, protecting us from danger and therefore an ideal location for coming close to God.

Ariel view of the Temple Mount

Ariel view of *Beit El*

29 **1** *Yaakov* resumed his journey and came to the land of the Easterners.

א וַיִּשָּׂא יַעֲקֹב רַגְלָיו וַיֵּלֶךְ אַרְצָה בְנֵי־קֶדֶם:

va-yi-SA ya-a-KOV rag-LAV va-YAY-lekh AR-tzah v'-nay KE-dem

2 There before his eyes was a well in the open. Three flocks of sheep were lying there beside it, for the flocks were watered from that well. The stone on the mouth of the well was large.

ב וַיַּרְא וְהִנֵּה בְאֵר בַּשָּׂדֶה וְהִנֵּה־שָׁם שְׁלֹשָׁה עֶדְרֵי־צֹאן רֹבְצִים עָלֶיהָ כִּי מִן־הַבְּאֵר הַהִוא יַשְׁקוּ הָעֲדָרִים וְהָאֶבֶן גְּדֹלָה עַל־פִּי הַבְּאֵר:

3 When all the flocks were gathered there, the stone would be rolled from the mouth of the well and the sheep watered; then the stone would be put back in its place on the mouth of the well.

ג וְנֶאֶסְפוּ־שָׁמָּה כָל־הָעֲדָרִים וְגָלֲלוּ אֶת־הָאֶבֶן מֵעַל פִּי הַבְּאֵר וְהִשְׁקוּ אֶת־הַצֹּאן וְהֵשִׁיבוּ אֶת־הָאֶבֶן עַל־פִּי הַבְּאֵר לִמְקֹמָהּ:

4 *Yaakov* said to them, "My friends, where are you from?" And they said, "We are from Haran."

ד וַיֹּאמֶר לָהֶם יַעֲקֹב אַחַי מֵאַיִן אַתֶּם וַיֹּאמְרוּ מֵחָרָן אֲנָחְנוּ:

5 He said to them, "Do you know Laban the son of Nahor?" And they said, "Yes, we do."

ה וַיֹּאמֶר לָהֶם הַיְדַעְתֶּם אֶת־לָבָן בֶּן־נָחוֹר וַיֹּאמְרוּ יָדָעְנוּ:

6 He continued, "Is he well?" They answered, "Yes, he is; and there is his daughter *Rachel*, coming with the flock."

ו וַיֹּאמֶר לָהֶם הֲשָׁלוֹם לוֹ וַיֹּאמְרוּ שָׁלוֹם וְהִנֵּה רָחֵל בִּתּוֹ בָּאָה עִם־הַצֹּאן:

7 He said, "It is still broad daylight, too early to round up the animals; water the flock and take them to pasture."

ז וַיֹּאמֶר הֵן עוֹד הַיּוֹם גָּדוֹל לֹא־עֵת הֵאָסֵף הַמִּקְנֶה הַשְׁקוּ הַצֹּאן וּלְכוּ רְעוּ:

8 But they said, "We cannot, until all the flocks are rounded up; then the stone is rolled off the mouth of the well and we water the sheep."

ח וַיֹּאמְרוּ לֹא נוּכַל עַד אֲשֶׁר יֵאָסְפוּ כָּל־הָעֲדָרִים וְגָלֲלוּ אֶת־הָאֶבֶן מֵעַל פִּי הַבְּאֵר וְהִשְׁקִינוּ הַצֹּאן:

9 While he was still speaking with them, *Rachel* came with her father's flock; for she was a shepherdess.

ט עוֹדֶנּוּ מְדַבֵּר עִמָּם וְרָחֵל בָּאָה עִם־הַצֹּאן אֲשֶׁר לְאָבִיהָ כִּי רֹעָה הִוא:

10 And when *Yaakov* saw *Rachel*, the daughter of his uncle Laban, and the flock of his uncle Laban, *Yaakov* went up and rolled the stone off the mouth of the well, and watered the flock of his uncle Laban.

י וַיְהִי כַּאֲשֶׁר רָאָה יַעֲקֹב אֶת־רָחֵל בַּת־לָבָן אֲחִי אִמּוֹ וְאֶת־צֹאן לָבָן אֲחִי אִמּוֹ וַיִּגַּשׁ יַעֲקֹב וַיָּגֶל אֶת־הָאֶבֶן מֵעַל פִּי הַבְּאֵר וַיַּשְׁקְ אֶת־צֹאן לָבָן אֲחִי אִמּוֹ:

11 Then *Yaakov* kissed *Rachel*, and broke into tears.

יא וַיִּשַּׁק יַעֲקֹב לְרָחֵל וַיִּשָּׂא אֶת־קֹלוֹ וַיֵּבְךְּ:

12 *Yaakov* told *Rachel* that he was her father's kinsman, that he was *Rivka*'s son; and she ran and told her father.

יב וַיַּגֵּד יַעֲקֹב לְרָחֵל כִּי אֲחִי אָבִיהָ הוּא וְכִי בֶן־רִבְקָה הוּא וַתָּרָץ וַתַּגֵּד לְאָבִיהָ:

29:1 To the land of the Easterners The distinction between *Eretz Yisrael* and other lands becomes clear to *Yaakov* as he enters the "land of the Easterners," where he immediately encounters jealous shepherds

Tel Be'er Sheva, the biblical city which *Yaakov* left to run to Haran

and later the crooked Lavan. This new land stands in stark contrast to the Land of Israel where *Yaakov*'s grandfather *Avraham* had sought to bring righteousness and Godliness to the world.

13 On hearing the news of his sister's son *Yaakov*, Laban ran to greet him; he embraced him and kissed him, and took him into his house. He told Laban all that had happened,

יג וַיְהִי כִשְׁמֹעַ לָבָן אֶת־שֵׁמַע יַעֲקֹב בֶּן־אֲחֹתוֹ וַיָּרָץ לִקְרָאתוֹ וַיְחַבֶּק־לוֹ וַיְנַשֶּׁק־לוֹ וַיְבִיאֵהוּ אֶל־בֵּיתוֹ וַיְסַפֵּר לְלָבָן אֵת כָּל־הַדְּבָרִים הָאֵלֶּה:

14 and Laban said to him, "You are truly my bone and flesh." When he had stayed with him a month's time,

יד וַיֹּאמֶר לוֹ לָבָן אַךְ עַצְמִי וּבְשָׂרִי אָתָּה וַיֵּשֶׁב עִמּוֹ חֹדֶשׁ יָמִים:

15 Laban said to *Yaakov*, "Just because you are a kinsman, should you serve me for nothing? Tell me, what shall your wages be?"

טו וַיֹּאמֶר לָבָן לְיַעֲקֹב הֲכִי־אָחִי אַתָּה וַעֲבַדְתַּנִי חִנָּם הַגִּידָה לִּי מַה־מַּשְׂכֻּרְתֶּךָ:

16 Now Laban had two daughters; the name of the older one was *Leah*, and the name of the younger was *Rachel*.

טז וּלְלָבָן שְׁתֵּי בָנוֹת שֵׁם הַגְּדֹלָה לֵאָה וְשֵׁם הַקְּטַנָּה רָחֵל:

17 *Leah* had weak eyes; *Rachel* was shapely and beautiful.

יז וְעֵינֵי לֵאָה רַכּוֹת וְרָחֵל הָיְתָה יְפַת־תֹּאַר וִיפַת מַרְאֶה:

18 *Yaakov* loved *Rachel*; so he answered, "I will serve you seven years for your younger daughter *Rachel*."

יח וַיֶּאֱהַב יַעֲקֹב אֶת־רָחֵל וַיֹּאמֶר אֶעֱבָדְךָ שֶׁבַע שָׁנִים בְּרָחֵל בִּתְּךָ הַקְּטַנָּה:

19 Laban said, "Better that I give her to you than that I should give her to an outsider. Stay with me."

יט וַיֹּאמֶר לָבָן טוֹב תִּתִּי אֹתָהּ לָךְ מִתִּתִּי אֹתָהּ לְאִישׁ אַחֵר שְׁבָה עִמָּדִי:

20 So *Yaakov* served seven years for *Rachel* and they seemed to him but a few days because of his love for her.

כ וַיַּעֲבֹד יַעֲקֹב בְּרָחֵל שֶׁבַע שָׁנִים וַיִּהְיוּ בְעֵינָיו כְּיָמִים אֲחָדִים בְּאַהֲבָתוֹ אֹתָהּ:

21 Then *Yaakov* said to Laban, "Give me my wife, for my time is fulfilled, that I may cohabit with her."

כא וַיֹּאמֶר יַעֲקֹב אֶל־לָבָן הָבָה אֶת־אִשְׁתִּי כִּי מָלְאוּ יָמָי וְאָבוֹאָה אֵלֶיהָ:

22 And Laban gathered all the people of the place and made a feast.

כב וַיֶּאֱסֹף לָבָן אֶת־כָּל־אַנְשֵׁי הַמָּקוֹם וַיַּעַשׂ מִשְׁתֶּה:

23 When evening came, he took his daughter *Leah* and brought her to him; and he cohabited with her.

כג וַיְהִי בָעֶרֶב וַיִּקַּח אֶת־לֵאָה בִתּוֹ וַיָּבֵא אֹתָהּ אֵלָיו וַיָּבֹא אֵלֶיהָ:

24 Laban had given his maidservant *Zilpa* to his daughter *Leah* as her maid.

כד וַיִּתֵּן לָבָן לָהּ אֶת־זִלְפָּה שִׁפְחָתוֹ לְלֵאָה בִתּוֹ שִׁפְחָה:

25 When morning came, there was *Leah*! So he said to Laban, "What is this you have done to me? I was in your service for *Rachel*! Why did you deceive me?"

כה וַיְהִי בַבֹּקֶר וְהִנֵּה־הִוא לֵאָה וַיֹּאמֶר אֶל־לָבָן מַה־זֹּאת עָשִׂיתָ לִּי הֲלֹא בְרָחֵל עָבַדְתִּי עִמָּךְ וְלָמָּה רִמִּיתָנִי:

26 Laban said, "It is not the practice in our place to marry off the younger before the older.

כו וַיֹּאמֶר לָבָן לֹא־יֵעָשֶׂה כֵן בִּמְקוֹמֵנוּ לָתֵת הַצְּעִירָה לִפְנֵי הַבְּכִירָה:

27 Wait until the bridal week of this one is over and we will give you that one too, provided you serve me another seven years."

כז מַלֵּא שְׁבֻעַ זֹאת וְנִתְּנָה לְךָ גַּם־אֶת־זֹאת בַּעֲבֹדָה אֲשֶׁר תַּעֲבֹד עִמָּדִי עוֹד שֶׁבַע־שָׁנִים אֲחֵרוֹת:

28 *Yaakov* did so; he waited out the bridal week of the one, and then he gave him his daughter *Rachel* as wife. –

כח וַיַּעַשׂ יַעֲקֹב כֵּן וַיְמַלֵּא שְׁבֻעַ זֹאת וַיִּתֶּן־לוֹ אֶת־רָחֵל בִּתּוֹ לוֹ לְאִשָּׁה:

²⁹ Laban had given his maidservant *Bilha* to his daughter *Rachel* as her maid.

כט וַיִּתֵּן לָבָן לְרָחֵל בִּתּוֹ אֶת־בִּלְהָה שִׁפְחָתוֹ לָהּ לְשִׁפְחָה:

³⁰ And *Yaakov* cohabited with *Rachel* also; indeed, he loved *Rachel* more than *Leah*. And he served him another seven years.

ל וַיָּבֹא גַּם אֶל־רָחֵל וַיֶּאֱהַב גַּם־אֶת־רָחֵל מִלֵּאָה וַיַּעֲבֹד עִמּוֹ עוֹד שֶׁבַע־שָׁנִים אֲחֵרוֹת:

³¹ *Hashem* saw that *Leah* was unloved and he opened her womb; but *Rachel* was barren.

לא וַיַּרְא יְהוָה כִּי־שְׂנוּאָה לֵאָה וַיִּפְתַּח אֶת־רַחְמָהּ וְרָחֵל עֲקָרָה:

³² *Leah* conceived and bore a son, and named him *Reuven*; for she declared, "It means: 'Hashem has seen my affliction'; it also means: 'Now my husband will love me.'"

לב וַתַּהַר לֵאָה וַתֵּלֶד בֵּן וַתִּקְרָא שְׁמוֹ רְאוּבֵן כִּי אָמְרָה כִּי־רָאָה יְהוָה בְּעָנְיִי כִּי עַתָּה יֶאֱהָבַנִי אִישִׁי:

³³ She conceived again and bore a son, and declared, "This is because *Hashem* heard that I was unloved and has given me this one also"; so she named him *Shimon*.

לג וַתַּהַר עוֹד וַתֵּלֶד בֵּן וַתֹּאמֶר כִּי־שָׁמַע יְהוָה כִּי־שְׂנוּאָה אָנֹכִי וַיִּתֶּן־לִי גַּם־אֶת־זֶה וַתִּקְרָא שְׁמוֹ שִׁמְעוֹן:

³⁴ Again she conceived and bore a son and declared, "This time my husband will become attached to me, for I have borne him three sons." Therefore he was named *Levi*.

לד וַתַּהַר עוֹד וַתֵּלֶד בֵּן וַתֹּאמֶר עַתָּה הַפַּעַם יִלָּוֶה אִישִׁי אֵלַי כִּי־יָלַדְתִּי לוֹ שְׁלֹשָׁה בָנִים עַל־כֵּן קָרָא־שְׁמוֹ לֵוִי:

³⁵ She conceived again and bore a son, and declared, "This time I will praise *Hashem*." Therefore she named him *Yehuda*. Then she stopped bearing.

לה וַתַּהַר עוֹד וַתֵּלֶד בֵּן וַתֹּאמֶר הַפַּעַם אוֹדֶה אֶת־יְהוָה עַל־כֵּן קָרְאָה שְׁמוֹ יְהוּדָה וַתַּעֲמֹד מִלֶּדֶת:

30 ¹ When *Rachel* saw that she had borne *Yaakov* no children, she became envious of her sister; and *Rachel* said to *Yaakov*, "Give me children, or I shall die."

ל א וַתֵּרֶא רָחֵל כִּי לֹא יָלְדָה לְיַעֲקֹב וַתְּקַנֵּא רָחֵל בַּאֲחֹתָהּ וַתֹּאמֶר אֶל־יַעֲקֹב הָבָה־לִּי בָנִים וְאִם־אַיִן מֵתָה אָנֹכִי:

² *Yaakov* was incensed at *Rachel*, and said, "Can I take the place of *Hashem*, who has denied you fruit of the womb?"

ב וַיִּחַר־אַף יַעֲקֹב בְּרָחֵל וַיֹּאמֶר הֲתַחַת אֱלֹהִים אָנֹכִי אֲשֶׁר־מָנַע מִמֵּךְ פְּרִי־בָטֶן:

³ She said, "Here is my maid *Bilha*. Consort with her, that she may bear on my knees and that through her I too may have children."

ג וַתֹּאמֶר הִנֵּה אֲמָתִי בִלְהָה בֹּא אֵלֶיהָ וְתֵלֵד עַל־בִּרְכַּי וְאִבָּנֶה גַם־אָנֹכִי מִמֶּנָּה:

⁴ So she gave him her maid *Bilha* as concubine, and *Yaakov* cohabited with her.

ד וַתִּתֶּן־לוֹ אֶת־בִּלְהָה שִׁפְחָתָהּ לְאִשָּׁה וַיָּבֹא אֵלֶיהָ יַעֲקֹב:

⁵ *Bilha* conceived and bore *Yaakov* a son.

ה וַתַּהַר בִּלְהָה וַתֵּלֶד לְיַעֲקֹב בֵּן:

⁶ And *Rachel* said, "Hashem has vindicated me; indeed, He has heeded my plea and given me a son." Therefore she named him *Dan*.

ו וַתֹּאמֶר רָחֵל דָּנַנִּי אֱלֹהִים וְגַם שָׁמַע בְּקֹלִי וַיִּתֶּן־לִי בֵּן עַל־כֵּן קָרְאָה שְׁמוֹ דָּן:

⁷ *Rachel's* maid *Bilha* conceived again and bore *Yaakov* a second son.

ז וַתַּהַר עוֹד וַתֵּלֶד בִּלְהָה שִׁפְחַת רָחֵל בֵּן שֵׁנִי לְיַעֲקֹב:

8 And *Rachel* said, "A fateful contest I waged with my sister; yes, and I have prevailed." So she named him *Naftali.*

ח וַתֹּאמֶר רָחֵל נַפְתּוּלֵי אֱלֹהִים נִפְתַּלְתִּי עִם־אֲחֹתִי גַּם־יָכֹלְתִּי וַתִּקְרָא שְׁמוֹ נַפְתָּלִי:

9 When *Leah* saw that she had stopped bearing, she took her maid *Zilpa* and gave her to *Yaakov* as concubine.

ט וַתֵּרֶא לֵאָה כִּי עָמְדָה מִלֶּדֶת וַתִּקַּח אֶת־זִלְפָּה שִׁפְחָתָהּ וַתִּתֵּן אֹתָהּ לְיַעֲקֹב לְאִשָּׁה:

10 And when *Leah*'s maid *Zilpa* bore *Yaakov* a son,

י וַתֵּלֶד זִלְפָּה שִׁפְחַת לֵאָה לְיַעֲקֹב בֵּן:

11 *Leah* said, "What luck!" So she named him *Gad.*

יא וַתֹּאמֶר לֵאָה בגד [בָּא] [גָּד] וַתִּקְרָא אֶת־שְׁמוֹ גָּד:

12 When *Leah*'s maid *Zilpa* bore *Yaakov* a second son,

יב וַתֵּלֶד זִלְפָּה שִׁפְחַת לֵאָה בֵּן שֵׁנִי לְיַעֲקֹב:

13 *Leah* declared, "What fortune!" meaning, "Women will deem me fortunate." So she named him *Asher.*

יג וַתֹּאמֶר לֵאָה בְּאָשְׁרִי כִּי אִשְּׁרוּנִי בָּנוֹת וַתִּקְרָא אֶת־שְׁמוֹ אָשֵׁר:

14 Once, at the time of the wheat harvest, *Reuven* came upon some mandrakes in the field and brought them to his mother *Leah.* *Rachel* said to *Leah,* "Please give me some of your son's mandrakes."

יד וַיֵּלֶךְ רְאוּבֵן בִּימֵי קְצִיר־חִטִּים וַיִּמְצָא דוּדָאִים בַּשָּׂדֶה וַיָּבֵא אֹתָם אֶל־לֵאָה אִמּוֹ וַתֹּאמֶר רָחֵל אֶל־לֵאָה תְּנִי־נָא לִי מִדּוּדָאֵי בְּנֵךְ:

15 But she said to her, "Was it not enough for you to take away my husband, that you would also take my son's mandrakes?" *Rachel* replied, "I promise, he shall lie with you tonight, in return for your son's mandrakes."

טו וַתֹּאמֶר לָהּ הַמְעַט קַחְתֵּךְ אֶת־אִישִׁי וְלָקַחַת גַּם אֶת־דּוּדָאֵי בְּנִי וַתֹּאמֶר רָחֵל לָכֵן יִשְׁכַּב עִמָּךְ הַלַּיְלָה תַּחַת דּוּדָאֵי בְנֵךְ:

16 When *Yaakov* came home from the field in the evening, *Leah* went out to meet him and said, "You are to sleep with me, for I have hired you with my son's mandrakes." And he lay with her that night.

טז וַיָּבֹא יַעֲקֹב מִן־הַשָּׂדֶה בָּעֶרֶב וַתֵּצֵא לֵאָה לִקְרָאתוֹ וַתֹּאמֶר אֵלַי תָּבוֹא כִּי שָׂכֹר שְׂכַרְתִּיךָ בְּדוּדָאֵי בְּנִי וַיִּשְׁכַּב עִמָּהּ בַּלַּיְלָה הוּא:

17 *Hashem* heeded *Leah,* and she conceived and bore him a fifth son.

יז וַיִּשְׁמַע אֱלֹהִים אֶל־לֵאָה וַתַּהַר וַתֵּלֶד לְיַעֲקֹב בֵּן חֲמִישִׁי:

18 And *Leah* said, "*Hashem* has given me my reward for having given my maid to my husband." So she named him *Yissachar.*

יח וַתֹּאמֶר לֵאָה נָתַן אֱלֹהִים שְׂכָרִי אֲשֶׁר־נָתַתִּי שִׁפְחָתִי לְאִישִׁי וַתִּקְרָא שְׁמוֹ יִשָּׂשכָר:

19 When *Leah* conceived again and bore *Yaakov* a sixth son,

יט וַתַּהַר עוֹד לֵאָה וַתֵּלֶד בֵּן־שִׁשִּׁי לְיַעֲקֹב:

20 *Leah* said, "*Hashem* has given me a choice gift; this time my husband will exalt me, for I have borne him six sons." So she named him *Zevulun.*

כ וַתֹּאמֶר לֵאָה זְבָדַנִי אֱלֹהִים אֹתִי זֵבֶד טוֹב הַפַּעַם יִזְבְּלֵנִי אִישִׁי כִּי־יָלַדְתִּי לוֹ שִׁשָּׁה בָנִים וַתִּקְרָא אֶת־שְׁמוֹ זְבֻלוּן:

21 Last, she bore a daughter, and named her *Dina.*

כא וְאַחַר יָלְדָה בַּת וַתִּקְרָא אֶת־שְׁמָהּ דִּינָה:

22 Now *Hashem* remembered *Rachel; Hashem* heeded her and opened her womb.

כב וַיִּזְכֹּר אֱלֹהִים אֶת־רָחֵל וַיִּשְׁמַע אֵלֶיהָ אֱלֹהִים וַיִּפְתַּח אֶת־רַחְמָהּ:

²³ She conceived and bore a son, and said, "*Hashem* has taken away my disgrace."

כג וַתַּהַר וַתֵּלֶד בֵּן וַתֹּאמֶר אָסַף אֱלֹהִים אֶת־חֶרְפָּתִי:

²⁴ So she named him *Yosef*, which is to say, "May *Hashem* add another son for me."

כד וַתִּקְרָא אֶת־שְׁמוֹ יוֹסֵף לֵאמֹר יֹסֵף יְהוָֹה לִי בֵּן אַחֵר:

²⁵ After *Rachel* had borne *Yosef*, *Yaakov* said to Laban, "Give me leave to go back to my own homeland.

כה וַיְהִי כַּאֲשֶׁר יָלְדָה רָחֵל אֶת־יוֹסֵף וַיֹּאמֶר יַעֲקֹב אֶל־לָבָן שַׁלְּחֵנִי וְאֵלְכָה אֶל־מְקוֹמִי וּלְאַרְצִי:

vai-HEE ka-a-SHER ya-l'-DAH ra-KHAYL et yo-SAYF va-YO-mer ya-a-KOV
el la-VAN sha-l'-KHAY-nee v'-AY-l'-KHAH el m'-ko-MEE ul-ar-TZEE

²⁶ Give me my wives and my children, for whom I have served you, that I may go; for well you know what services I have rendered you."

כו תְּנָה אֶת־נָשַׁי וְאֶת־יְלָדַי אֲשֶׁר עָבַדְתִּי אֹתְךָ בָּהֵן וְאֵלֵכָה כִּי אַתָּה יָדַעְתָּ אֶת־עֲבֹדָתִי אֲשֶׁר עֲבַדְתִּיךָ:

²⁷ But Laban said to him, "If you will indulge me, I have learned by divination that *Hashem* has blessed me on your account."

כז וַיֹּאמֶר אֵלָיו לָבָן אִם־נָא מָצָאתִי חֵן בְּעֵינֶיךָ נִחַשְׁתִּי וַיְבָרֲכֵנִי יְהוָֹה בִּגְלָלֶךָ:

²⁸ And he continued, "Name the wages due from me, and I will pay you."

כח וַיֹּאמַר נָקְבָה שְׂכָרְךָ עָלַי וְאֶתֵּנָה:

²⁹ But he said, "You know well how I have served you and how your livestock has fared with me.

כט וַיֹּאמֶר אֵלָיו אַתָּה יָדַעְתָּ אֵת אֲשֶׁר עֲבַדְתִּיךָ וְאֵת אֲשֶׁר־הָיָה מִקְנְךָ אִתִּי:

³⁰ For the little you had before I came has grown to much, since *Hashem* has blessed you wherever I turned. And now, when shall I make provision for my own household?"

ל כִּי מְעַט אֲשֶׁר־הָיָה לְךָ לְפָנַי וַיִּפְרֹץ לָרֹב וַיְבָרֶךְ יְהוָֹה אֹתְךָ לְרַגְלִי וְעַתָּה מָתַי אֶעֱשֶׂה גַם־אָנֹכִי לְבֵיתִי:

³¹ He said, "What shall I pay you?" And *Yaakov* said, "Pay me nothing! If you will do this thing for me, I will again pasture and keep your flocks:

לא וַיֹּאמֶר מָה אֶתֶּן־לָךְ וַיֹּאמֶר יַעֲקֹב לֹא־תִתֶּן־לִי מְאוּמָה אִם־תַּעֲשֶׂה־לִּי הַדָּבָר הַזֶּה אָשׁוּבָה אֶרְעֶה צֹאנְךָ אֶשְׁמֹר:

³² let me pass through your whole flock today, removing from there every speckled and spotted animal – every dark-colored sheep and every spotted and speckled goat. Such shall be my wages.

לב אֶעֱבֹר בְּכָל־צֹאנְךָ הַיּוֹם הָסֵר מִשָּׁם כָּל־שֶׂה נָקֹד וְטָלוּא וְכָל־שֶׂה־חוּם בַּכְּשָׂבִים וְטָלוּא וְנָקֹד בָּעִזִּים וְהָיָה שְׂכָרִי:

³³ In the future when you go over my wages, let my honesty toward you testify for me: if there are among my goats any that are not speckled or spotted or any sheep that are not dark-colored, they got there by theft."

לג וְעָנְתָה־בִּי צִדְקָתִי בְּיוֹם מָחָר כִּי־תָבוֹא עַל־שְׂכָרִי לְפָנֶיךָ כֹּל אֲשֶׁר־אֵינֶנּוּ נָקֹד וְטָלוּא בָּעִזִּים וְחוּם בַּכְּשָׂבִים גָּנוּב הוּא אִתִּי:

 30:25 To go back to my own homeland Once *Rachel* has finally been blessed with a son, *Yosef*, *Yaakov* concludes that his time in exile has ended and he begins to prepare to return to the Land of Israel. Later in the Bible, *Rashi* explains that *Yosef* is referred to as a "flame" who will extinguish Esau who "shall be straw" (Obadiah 1:18). Once Esau's defeater is born, *Yaakov* is free to return to the Land of Israel, from which he fled out of fear of Esau. The birth of *Yosef* reinforces *Yaakov*'s faith in *Hashem* and urges him to return home. *Yaakov* understands that his "own homeland" is only in *Eretz Yisrael*.

Child planting an Israeli flag on the beach in Haifa

³⁴ And Laban said, "Very well, let it be as you say."

לד וַיֹּאמֶר לָבָן הֵן לוּ יְהִי כִדְבָרֶךָ:

³⁵ But that same day he removed the streaked and spotted he-goats and all the speckled and spotted she-goats – every one that had white on it – and all the dark-colored sheep, and left them in the charge of his sons.

לה וַיָּסַר בַּיּוֹם הַהוּא אֶת־הַתְּיָשִׁים הָעֲקֻדִּים וְהַטְּלֻאִים וְאֵת כָּל־הָעִזִּים הַנְּקֻדּוֹת וְהַטְּלֻאֹת כֹּל אֲשֶׁר־לָבָן בּוֹ וְכָל־חוּם בַּכְּשָׂבִים וַיִּתֵּן בְּיַד־בָּנָיו:

³⁶ And he put a distance of three days' journey between himself and *Yaakov*, while *Yaakov* was pasturing the rest of Laban's flock.

לו וַיָּשֶׂם דֶּרֶךְ שְׁלֹשֶׁת יָמִים בֵּינוֹ וּבֵין יַעֲקֹב וְיַעֲקֹב רֹעֶה אֶת־צֹאן לָבָן הַנּוֹתָרֹת:

³⁷ *Yaakov* then got fresh shoots of poplar, and of almond and plane, and peeled white stripes in them, laying bare the white of the shoots.

לז וַיִּקַּח־לוֹ יַעֲקֹב מַקַּל לִבְנֶה לַח וְלוּז וְעַרְמוֹן וַיְפַצֵּל בָּהֵן פְּצָלוֹת לְבָנוֹת מַחְשֹׂף הַלָּבָן אֲשֶׁר עַל־הַמַּקְלוֹת:

³⁸ The rods that he had peeled he set up in front of the goats in the troughs, the water receptacles, that the goats came to drink from. Their mating occurred when they came to drink,

לח וַיַּצֵּג אֶת־הַמַּקְלוֹת אֲשֶׁר פִּצֵּל בָּרֳהָטִים בְּשִׁקֲתוֹת הַמָּיִם אֲשֶׁר תָּבֹאןָ הַצֹּאן לִשְׁתּוֹת לְנֹכַח הַצֹּאן וַיֵּחַמְנָה בְּבֹאָן לִשְׁתּוֹת:

³⁹ and since the goats mated by the rods, the goats brought forth streaked, speckled, and spotted young.

לט וַיֶּחֱמוּ הַצֹּאן אֶל־הַמַּקְלוֹת וַתֵּלַדְןָ הַצֹּאן עֲקֻדִּים נְקֻדִּים וּטְלֻאִים:

⁴⁰ But *Yaakov* dealt separately with the sheep; he made these animals face the streaked or wholly dark-colored animals in Laban's flock. And so he produced special flocks for himself, which he did not put with Laban's flocks.

מ וְהַכְּשָׂבִים הִפְרִיד יַעֲקֹב וַיִּתֵּן פְּנֵי הַצֹּאן אֶל־עָקֹד וְכָל־חוּם בְּצֹאן לָבָן וַיָּשֶׁת־לוֹ עֲדָרִים לְבַדּוֹ וְלֹא שָׁתָם עַל־צֹאן לָבָן:

⁴¹ Moreover, when the sturdier animals were mating, *Yaakov* would place the rods in the troughs, in full view of the animals, so that they mated by the rods;

מא וְהָיָה בְּכָל־יַחֵם הַצֹּאן הַמְקֻשָּׁרוֹת וְשָׂם יַעֲקֹב אֶת־הַמַּקְלוֹת לְעֵינֵי הַצֹּאן בָּרֳהָטִים לְיַחְמֵנָּה בַּמַּקְלוֹת:

⁴² but with the feebler animals he would not place them there. Thus the feeble ones went to Laban and the sturdy to *Yaakov*.

מב וּבְהַעֲטִיף הַצֹּאן לֹא יָשִׂים וְהָיָה הָעֲטֻפִים לְלָבָן וְהַקְּשֻׁרִים לְיַעֲקֹב:

⁴³ So the man grew exceedingly prosperous, and came to own large flocks, maidservants and menservants, camels and asses.

מג וַיִּפְרֹץ הָאִישׁ מְאֹד מְאֹד וַיְהִי־לוֹ צֹאן רַבּוֹת וּשְׁפָחוֹת וַעֲבָדִים וּגְמַלִּים וַחֲמֹרִים:

1 ¹ Now he heard the things that Laban's sons were saying: "*Yaakov* has taken all that was our father's, and from that which was our father's he has built up all this wealth."

לא א וַיִּשְׁמַע אֶת־דִּבְרֵי בְנֵי־לָבָן לֵאמֹר לָקַח יַעֲקֹב אֵת כָּל־אֲשֶׁר לְאָבִינוּ וּמֵאֲשֶׁר לְאָבִינוּ עָשָׂה אֵת כָּל־הַכָּבֹד הַזֶּה:

² *Yaakov* also saw that Laban's manner toward him was not as it had been in the past.

ב וַיַּרְא יַעֲקֹב אֶת־פְּנֵי לָבָן וְהִנֵּה אֵינֶנּוּ עִמּוֹ כִּתְמוֹל שִׁלְשׁוֹם:

³ Then *Hashem* said to *Yaakov*, "Return to the land of your fathers where you were born, and I will be with you."

ג וַיֹּאמֶר יְהֹוָה אֶל־יַעֲקֹב שׁוּב אֶל־אֶרֶץ אֲבוֹתֶיךָ וּלְמוֹלַדְתֶּךָ וְאֶהְיֶה עִמָּךְ:

va-YO-mer a-do-NAI el ya-a-KOV SHUV el E-retz
a-vo-TE-kha ul-mo-lad-TE-kha v'-eh-YEH i-MAKH

⁴ *Yaakov* had *Rachel* and *Leah* called to the field, where his flock was,

ד וַיִּשְׁלַח יַעֲקֹב וַיִּקְרָא לְרָחֵל וּלְלֵאָה הַשָּׂדֶה אֶל־צֹאנוֹ:

⁵ and said to them, "I see that your father's manner toward me is not as it has been in the past. But the God of my father has been with me.

ה וַיֹּאמֶר לָהֶן רֹאֶה אָנֹכִי אֶת־פְּנֵי אֲבִיכֶן כִּי־אֵינֶנּוּ אֵלַי כִּתְמֹל שִׁלְשֹׁם וֵאלֹהֵי אָבִי הָיָה עִמָּדִי:

⁶ As you know, I have served your father with all my might;

ו וְאַתֵּנָה יְדַעְתֶּן כִּי בְּכָל־כֹּחִי עָבַדְתִּי אֶת־אֲבִיכֶן:

⁷ but your father has cheated me, changing my wages time and again. *Hashem*, however, would not let him do me harm.

ז וַאֲבִיכֶן הֵתֶל בִּי וְהֶחֱלִף אֶת־מַשְׂכֻּרְתִּי עֲשֶׂרֶת מֹנִים וְלֹא־נְתָנוֹ אֱלֹהִים לְהָרַע עִמָּדִי:

⁸ If he said thus, 'The speckled shall be your wages,' then all the flocks would drop speckled young; and if he said thus, 'The streaked shall be your wages,' then all the flocks would drop streaked young.

ח אִם־כֹּה יֹאמַר נְקֻדִּים יִהְיֶה שְׂכָרֶךָ וְיָלְדוּ כָל־הַצֹּאן נְקֻדִּים וְאִם־כֹּה יֹאמַר עֲקֻדִּים יִהְיֶה שְׂכָרֶךָ וְיָלְדוּ כָל־הַצֹּאן עֲקֻדִּים:

⁹ *Hashem* has taken away your father's livestock and given it to me.

ט וַיַּצֵּל אֱלֹהִים אֶת־מִקְנֵה אֲבִיכֶם וַיִּתֶּן־לִי:

¹⁰ "Once, at the mating time of the flocks, I had a dream in which I saw that the he-goats mating with the flock were streaked, speckled, and mottled.

י וַיְהִי בְּעֵת יַחֵם הַצֹּאן וָאֶשָּׂא עֵינַי וָאֵרֶא בַּחֲלוֹם וְהִנֵּה הָעַתֻּדִים הָעֹלִים עַל־הַצֹּאן עֲקֻדִּים נְקֻדִּים וּבְרֻדִּים:

¹¹ And in the dream an angel of *Hashem* said to me, '*Yaakov*!' 'Here,' I answered.

יא וַיֹּאמֶר אֵלַי מַלְאַךְ הָאֱלֹהִים בַּחֲלוֹם יַעֲקֹב וָאֹמַר הִנֵּנִי:

¹² And he said, 'Note well that all the he-goats which are mating with the flock are streaked, speckled, and mottled; for I have noted all that Laban has been doing to you.

יב וַיֹּאמֶר שָׂא־נָא עֵינֶיךָ וּרְאֵה כָּל־הָעַתֻּדִים הָעֹלִים עַל־הַצֹּאן עֲקֻדִּים נְקֻדִּים וּבְרֻדִּים כִּי רָאִיתִי אֵת כָּל־אֲשֶׁר לָבָן עֹשֶׂה לָּךְ:

¹³ I am the God of *Beit El*, where you anointed a pillar and where you made a vow to Me. Now, arise and leave this land and return to your native land.'"

יג אָנֹכִי הָאֵל בֵּית־אֵל אֲשֶׁר מָשַׁחְתָּ שָּׁם מַצֵּבָה אֲשֶׁר נָדַרְתָּ לִּי שָׁם נֶדֶר עַתָּה קוּם צֵא מִן־הָאָרֶץ הַזֹּאת וְשׁוּב אֶל־אֶרֶץ מוֹלַדְתֶּךָ:

31:3 Return to the land of your fathers With these words, *Hashem* implies that He will be with *Yaakov* only if he returns to the land of his fathers, the Land of Israel, but not if he stays with *Lavan* in Haran. Rabbi Meir Leibush Weiser, a Bible commentator and

Rays of sun over the Sea of Galilee

Hebrew grammarian commonly known by the acronym *Malbim*, explains that *Hashem* intentionally removed His protection from *Yaakov* in order to motivate him to return to *Eretz Yisrael*. After spending so much time outside the Holy Land, it is time for *Yaakov* to go home.

14 Then *Rachel* and *Leah* answered him, saying, "Have we still a share in the inheritance of our father's house?

יד וַתַּעַן רָחֵל וְלֵאָה וַתֹּאמַרְנָה לּוֹ הַעוֹד לָנוּ חֵלֶק וְנַחֲלָה בְּבֵית אָבִינוּ:

15 Surely, he regards us as outsiders, now that he has sold us and has used up our purchase price.

טו הֲלוֹא נָכְרִיּוֹת נֶחְשַׁבְנוּ לוֹ כִּי מְכָרָנוּ וַיֹּאכַל גַּם־אָכוֹל אֶת־כַּסְפֵּנוּ:

16 Truly, all the wealth that *Hashem* has taken away from our father belongs to us and to our children. Now then, do just as *Hashem* has told you."

טז כִּי כָל־הָעֹשֶׁר אֲשֶׁר הִצִּיל אֱלֹהִים מֵאָבִינוּ לָנוּ הוּא וּלְבָנֵינוּ וְעַתָּה כֹּל אֲשֶׁר אָמַר אֱלֹהִים אֵלֶיךָ עֲשֵׂה:

17 Thereupon *Yaakov* put his children and wives on camels;

יז וַיָּקָם יַעֲקֹב וַיִּשָּׂא אֶת־בָּנָיו וְאֶת־נָשָׁיו עַל־הַגְּמַלִּים:

18 and he drove off all his livestock and all the wealth that he had amassed, the livestock in his possession that he had acquired in Paddan-aram, to go to his father *Yitzchak* in the land of Canaan.

יח וַיִּנְהַג אֶת־כָּל־מִקְנֵהוּ וְאֶת־כָּל־רְכֻשׁוֹ אֲשֶׁר רָכָשׁ מִקְנֵה קִנְיָנוֹ אֲשֶׁר רָכַשׁ בְּפַדַּן אֲרָם לָבוֹא אֶל־יִצְחָק אָבִיו אַרְצָה כְּנָעַן:

19 Meanwhile Laban had gone to shear his sheep, and *Rachel* stole her father's household idols.

יט וְלָבָן הָלַךְ לִגְזֹז אֶת־צֹאנוֹ וַתִּגְנֹב רָחֵל אֶת־הַתְּרָפִים אֲשֶׁר לְאָבִיהָ:

20 *Yaakov* kept Laban the Aramean in the dark, not telling him that he was fleeing,

כ וַיִּגְנֹב יַעֲקֹב אֶת־לֵב לָבָן הָאֲרַמִּי עַל־ בְּלִי הִגִּיד לוֹ כִּי בֹרֵחַ הוּא:

21 and fled with all that he had. Soon he was across the Euphrates and heading toward the hill country of *Gilad*.

כא וַיִּבְרַח הוּא וְכָל־אֲשֶׁר־לוֹ וַיָּקָם וַיַּעֲבֹר אֶת־הַנָּהָר וַיָּשֶׂם אֶת־פָּנָיו הַר הַגִּלְעָד:

22 On the third day, Laban was told that *Yaakov* had fled.

כב וַיֻּגַּד לְלָבָן בַּיּוֹם הַשְּׁלִישִׁי כִּי בָרַח יַעֲקֹב:

23 So he took his kinsmen with him and pursued him a distance of seven days, catching up with him in the hill country of *Gilad*.

כג וַיִּקַּח אֶת־אֶחָיו עִמּוֹ וַיִּרְדֹּף אַחֲרָיו דֶּרֶךְ שִׁבְעַת יָמִים וַיַּדְבֵּק אֹתוֹ בְּהַר הַגִּלְעָד:

24 But *Hashem* appeared to Laban the Aramean in a dream by night and said to him, "Beware of attempting anything with *Yaakov*, good or bad."

כד וַיָּבֹא אֱלֹהִים אֶל־לָבָן הָאֲרַמִּי בַּחֲלֹם הַלָּיְלָה וַיֹּאמֶר לוֹ הִשָּׁמֶר לְךָ פֶּן־תְּדַבֵּר עִם־יַעֲקֹב מִטּוֹב עַד־רָע:

25 Laban overtook *Yaakov*. *Yaakov* had pitched his tent on the Height, and Laban with his kinsmen encamped in the hill country of *Gilad*.

כה וַיַּשֵּׂג לָבָן אֶת־יַעֲקֹב וְיַעֲקֹב תָּקַע אֶת־ אָהֳלוֹ בָּהָר וְלָבָן תָּקַע אֶת־אֶחָיו בְּהַר הַגִּלְעָד:

26 And Laban said to *Yaakov*, "What did you mean by keeping me in the dark and carrying off my daughters like captives of the sword?

כו וַיֹּאמֶר לָבָן לְיַעֲקֹב מֶה עָשִׂיתָ וַתִּגְנֹב אֶת־לְבָבִי וַתְּנַהֵג אֶת־בְּנֹתַי כִּשְׁבֻיוֹת חָרֶב:

27 Why did you flee in secrecy and mislead me and not tell me? I would have sent you off with festive music, with timbrel and lyre.

כז לָמָּה נַחְבֵּאתָ לִבְרֹחַ וַתִּגְנֹב אֹתִי וְלֹא־ הִגַּדְתָּ לִּי וָאֲשַׁלֵּחֲךָ בְּשִׂמְחָה וּבְשִׁרִים בְּתֹף וּבְכִנּוֹר:

28 You did not even let me kiss my sons and daughters good-by! It was a foolish thing for you to do.

כח וְלֹא נְטַשְׁתַּנִי לְנַשֵּׁק לְבָנַי וְלִבְנֹתָי עַתָּה הִסְכַּלְתָּ עֲשׂוֹ:

29 I have it in my power to do you harm; but the God of your father said to me last night, 'Beware of attempting anything with *Yaakov*, good or bad.'

כט יֶשׁ־לְאֵל יָדִי לַעֲשׂוֹת עִמָּכֶם רָע וֵאלֹהֵי אֲבִיכֶם אֶמֶשׁ אָמַר אֵלַי לֵאמֹר הִשָּׁמֶר לְךָ מִדַּבֵּר עִם־יַעֲקֹב מִטּוֹב עַד־רָע:

30 Very well, you had to leave because you were longing for your father's house; but why did you steal my gods?"

ל וְעַתָּה הָלֹךְ הָלַכְתָּ כִּי־נִכְסֹף נִכְסַפְתָּה לְבֵית אָבִיךָ לָמָּה גָנַבְתָּ אֶת־אֱלֹהָי:

31 *Yaakov* answered Laban, saying, "I was afraid because I thought you would take your daughters from me by force.

לא וַיַּעַן יַעֲקֹב וַיֹּאמֶר לְלָבָן כִּי יָרֵאתִי כִּי אָמַרְתִּי פֶּן־תִּגְזֹל אֶת־בְּנוֹתֶיךָ מֵעִמִּי:

32 But anyone with whom you find your gods shall not remain alive! In the presence of our kinsmen, point out what I have of yours and take it." *Yaakov*, of course, did not know that *Rachel* had stolen them.

לב עִם אֲשֶׁר תִּמְצָא אֶת־אֱלֹהֶיךָ לֹא יִחְיֶה נֶגֶד אַחֵינוּ הַכֶּר־לְךָ מָה עִמָּדִי וְקַח־לָךְ וְלֹא־יָדַע יַעֲקֹב כִּי רָחֵל גְּנָבָתַם:

33 So Laban went into *Yaakov*'s tent and *Leah*'s tent and the tents of the two maidservants; but he did not find them. Leaving *Leah*'s tent, he entered *Rachel*'s tent.

לג וַיָּבֹא לָבָן בְּאֹהֶל יַעֲקֹב וּבְאֹהֶל לֵאָה וּבְאֹהֶל שְׁתֵּי הָאֲמָהֹת וְלֹא מָצָא וַיֵּצֵא מֵאֹהֶל לֵאָה וַיָּבֹא בְּאֹהֶל רָחֵל:

34 *Rachel*, meanwhile, had taken the idols and placed them in the camel cushion and sat on them; and Laban rummaged through the tent without finding them.

לד וְרָחֵל לָקְחָה אֶת־הַתְּרָפִים וַתְּשִׂמֵם בְּכַר הַגָּמָל וַתֵּשֶׁב עֲלֵיהֶם וַיְמַשֵּׁשׁ לָבָן אֶת־כָּל־הָאֹהֶל וְלֹא מָצָא:

35 For she said to her father, "Let not my lord take it amiss that I cannot rise before you, for the period of women is upon me." Thus he searched, but could not find the household idols.

לה וַתֹּאמֶר אֶל־אָבִיהָ אַל־יִחַר בְּעֵינֵי אֲדֹנִי כִּי לוֹא אוּכַל לָקוּם מִפָּנֶיךָ כִּי־דֶרֶךְ נָשִׁים לִי וַיְחַפֵּשׂ וְלֹא מָצָא אֶת־הַתְּרָפִים:

36 Now *Yaakov* became incensed and took up his grievance with Laban. *Yaakov* spoke up and said to Laban, "What is my crime, what is my guilt that you should pursue me?

לו וַיִּחַר לְיַעֲקֹב וַיָּרֶב בְּלָבָן וַיַּעַן יַעֲקֹב וַיֹּאמֶר לְלָבָן מַה־פִּשְׁעִי מַה חַטָּאתִי כִּי דָלַקְתָּ אַחֲרָי:

37 You rummaged through all my things; what have you found of all your household objects? Set it here, before my kinsmen and yours, and let them decide between us two.

לז כִּי־מִשַּׁשְׁתָּ אֶת־כָּל־כֵּלַי מַה־מָּצָאתָ מִכֹּל כְּלֵי־בֵיתֶךָ שִׂים כֹּה נֶגֶד אַחַי וְאַחֶיךָ וְיוֹכִיחוּ בֵּין שְׁנֵינוּ:

38 "These twenty years I have spent in your service, your ewes and she-goats never miscarried, nor did I feast on rams from your flock.

לח זֶה עֶשְׂרִים שָׁנָה אָנֹכִי עִמָּךְ רְחֵלֶיךָ וְעִזֶּיךָ לֹא שִׁכֵּלוּ וְאֵילֵי צֹאנְךָ לֹא אָכָלְתִּי:

39 That which was torn by beasts I never brought to you; I myself made good the loss; you exacted it of me, whether snatched by day or snatched by night.

לט טְרֵפָה לֹא־הֵבֵאתִי אֵלֶיךָ אָנֹכִי אֲחַטֶּנָּה מִיָּדִי תְּבַקְשֶׁנָּה גְּנֻבְתִי יוֹם וּגְנֻבְתִי לָיְלָה:

40 Often, scorching heat ravaged me by day and frost by night; and sleep fled from my eyes.

מ הָיִיתִי בַיּוֹם אֲכָלַנִי חֹרֶב וְקֶרַח בַּלָּיְלָה וַתִּדַּד שְׁנָתִי מֵעֵינָי:

⁴¹ Of the twenty years that I spent in your household, I served you fourteen years for your two daughters, and six years for your flocks; and you changed my wages time and again.

מא זֶה־לִּי עֶשְׂרִים שָׁנָה בְּבֵיתֶךָ עֲבַדְתִּיךָ אַרְבַּע־עֶשְׂרֵה שָׁנָה בִּשְׁתֵּי בְנֹתֶיךָ וְשֵׁשׁ שָׁנִים בְּצֹאנֶךָ וַתַּחֲלֵף אֶת־מַשְׂכֻּרְתִּי עֲשֶׂרֶת מֹנִים:

⁴² Had not the God of my father, the God of *Avraham* and the Fear of *Yitzchak*, been with me, you would have sent me away empty-handed. But *Hashem* took notice of my plight and the toil of my hands, and He gave judgment last night."

מב לוּלֵי אֱלֹהֵי אָבִי אֱלֹהֵי אַבְרָהָם וּפַחַד יִצְחָק הָיָה לִי כִּי עַתָּה רֵיקָם שִׁלַּחְתָּנִי אֶת־עָנְיִי וְאֶת־יְגִיעַ כַּפַּי רָאָה אֱלֹהִים וַיּוֹכַח אָמֶשׁ:

⁴³ Then Laban spoke up and said to *Yaakov*, "The daughters are my daughters, the children are my children, and the flocks are my flocks; all that you see is mine. Yet what can I do now about my daughters or the children they have borne?

מג וַיַּעַן לָבָן וַיֹּאמֶר אֶל־יַעֲקֹב הַבָּנוֹת בְּנֹתַי וְהַבָּנִים בָּנַי וְהַצֹּאן צֹאנִי וְכֹל אֲשֶׁר־אַתָּה רֹאֶה לִי־הוּא וְלִבְנֹתַי מָה־אֶעֱשֶׂה לָאֵלֶּה הַיּוֹם אוֹ לִבְנֵיהֶן אֲשֶׁר יָלָדוּ:

⁴⁴ Come, then, let us make a pact, you and I, that there may be a witness between you and me."

מד וְעַתָּה לְכָה נִכְרְתָה בְרִית אֲנִי וָאָתָּה וְהָיָה לְעֵד בֵּינִי וּבֵינֶךָ:

⁴⁵ Thereupon *Yaakov* took a stone and set it up as a pillar.

מה וַיִּקַּח יַעֲקֹב אָבֶן וַיְרִימֶהָ מַצֵּבָה:

⁴⁶ And *Yaakov* said to his kinsmen, "Gather stones." So they took stones and made a mound; and they partook of a meal there by the mound.

מו וַיֹּאמֶר יַעֲקֹב לְאֶחָיו לִקְטוּ אֲבָנִים וַיִּקְחוּ אֲבָנִים וַיַּעֲשׂוּ־גָל וַיֹּאכְלוּ שָׁם עַל־הַגָּל:

⁴⁷ Laban named it Yegar-sahadutha, but *Yaakov* named it Gal-ed.

מז וַיִּקְרָא־לוֹ לָבָן יְגַר שָׂהֲדוּתָא וְיַעֲקֹב קָרָא לוֹ גַּלְעֵד:

⁴⁸ And Laban declared, "This mound is a witness between you and me this day." That is why it was named Gal-ed;

מח וַיֹּאמֶר לָבָן הַגַּל הַזֶּה עֵד בֵּינִי וּבֵינְךָ הַיּוֹם עַל־כֵּן קָרָא־שְׁמוֹ גַּלְעֵד:

⁴⁹ and [it was called] *Mitzpa*, because he said, "May *Hashem* watch between you and me, when we are out of sight of each other.

מט וְהַמִּצְפָּה אֲשֶׁר אָמַר יִצֶף יְהֹוָה בֵּינִי וּבֵינֶךָ כִּי נִסָּתֵר אִישׁ מֵרֵעֵהוּ:

⁵⁰ If you ill-treat my daughters or take other wives besides my daughters – though no one else be about, remember, *Hashem* Himself will be witness between you and me."

נ אִם־תְּעַנֶּה אֶת־בְּנֹתַי וְאִם־תִּקַּח נָשִׁים עַל־בְּנֹתַי אֵין אִישׁ עִמָּנוּ רְאֵה אֱלֹהִים עֵד בֵּינִי וּבֵינֶךָ:

⁵¹ And Laban said to *Yaakov*, "Here is this mound and here the pillar which I have set up between you and me:

נא וַיֹּאמֶר לָבָן לְיַעֲקֹב הִנֵּה הַגַּל הַזֶּה וְהִנֵּה הַמַּצֵּבָה אֲשֶׁר יָרִיתִי בֵּינִי וּבֵינֶךָ:

⁵² this mound shall be witness and this pillar shall be witness that I am not to cross to you past this mound, and that you are not to cross to me past this mound and this pillar, with hostile intent.

נב עֵד הַגַּל הַזֶּה וְעֵדָה הַמַּצֵּבָה אִם־אָנִי לֹא־אֶעֱבֹר אֵלֶיךָ אֶת־הַגַּל הַזֶּה וְאִם־אַתָּה לֹא־תַעֲבֹר אֵלַי אֶת־הַגַּל הַזֶּה וְאֶת־הַמַּצֵּבָה הַזֹּאת לְרָעָה:

⁵³ May the God of *Avraham* and the god of Nahor" – their ancestral deities – "judge between us." And *Yaakov* swore by the Fear of his father *Yitzchak*.

נג אֱלֹהֵי אַבְרָהָם וֵאלֹהֵי נָחוֹר יִשְׁפְּטוּ בֵינֵינוּ אֱלֹהֵי אֲבִיהֶם וַיִּשָּׁבַע יַעֲקֹב בְּפַחַד אָבִיו יִצְחָק:

Genesis

54 *Yaakov* then offered up a sacrifice on the Height, and invited his kinsmen to partake of the meal. After the meal, they spent the night on the Height.

נד וַיִּזְבַּח יַעֲקֹב זֶבַח בָּהָר וַיִּקְרָא לְאֶחָיו לֶאֱכָל־לָחֶם וַיֹּאכְלוּ לֶחֶם וַיָּלִינוּ בָּהָר:

32 ¹ Early in the morning, Laban kissed his sons and daughters and bade them good-by; then Laban left on his journey homeward.

ב א וַיַּשְׁכֵּם לָבָן בַּבֹּקֶר וַיְנַשֵּׁק לְבָנָיו וְלִבְנוֹתָיו וַיְבָרֶךְ אֶתְהֶם וַיֵּלֶךְ וַיָּשָׁב לָבָן לִמְקֹמוֹ:

² *Yaakov* went on his way, and angels of *Hashem* encountered him.

ב וְיַעֲקֹב הָלַךְ לְדַרְכּוֹ וַיִּפְגְּעוּ־בוֹ מַלְאֲכֵי אֱלֹהִים:

³ When he saw them, *Yaakov* said, "This is *Hashem*'s camp." So he named that place Mahanaim.

ג וַיֹּאמֶר יַעֲקֹב כַּאֲשֶׁר רָאָם מַחֲנֵה אֱלֹהִים זֶה וַיִּקְרָא שֵׁם־הַמָּקוֹם הַהוּא מַחֲנָיִם:

⁴ *Yaakov* sent messengers ahead to his brother Esau in the land of Seir, the country of Edom,

ד וַיִּשְׁלַח יַעֲקֹב מַלְאָכִים לְפָנָיו אֶל־עֵשָׂו אָחִיו אַרְצָה שֵׂעִיר שְׂדֵה אֱדוֹם:

⁵ and instructed them as follows, "Thus shall you say, 'To my lord Esau, thus says your servant *Yaakov*: I stayed with Laban and remained until now;

ה וַיְצַו אֹתָם לֵאמֹר כֹּה תֹאמְרוּן לַאדֹנִי לְעֵשָׂו כֹּה אָמַר עַבְדְּךָ יַעֲקֹב עִם־לָבָן גַּרְתִּי וָאֵחַר עַד־עָתָּה:

⁶ I have acquired cattle, asses, sheep, and male and female slaves; and I send this message to my lord in the hope of gaining your favor.'"

ו וַיְהִי־לִי שׁוֹר וַחֲמוֹר צֹאן וְעֶבֶד וְשִׁפְחָה וָאֶשְׁלְחָה לְהַגִּיד לַאדֹנִי לִמְצֹא־חֵן בְּעֵינֶיךָ:

⁷ The messengers returned to *Yaakov*, saying, "We came to your brother Esau; he himself is coming to meet you, and there are four hundred men with him."

ז וַיָּשֻׁבוּ הַמַּלְאָכִים אֶל־יַעֲקֹב לֵאמֹר בָּאנוּ אֶל־אָחִיךָ אֶל־עֵשָׂו וְגַם הֹלֵךְ לִקְרָאתְךָ וְאַרְבַּע־מֵאוֹת אִישׁ עִמּוֹ:

⁸ *Yaakov* was greatly frightened; in his anxiety, he divided the people with him, and the flocks and herds and camels, into two camps,

ח וַיִּירָא יַעֲקֹב מְאֹד וַיֵּצֶר לוֹ וַיַּחַץ אֶת־הָעָם אֲשֶׁר־אִתּוֹ וְאֶת־הַצֹּאן וְאֶת־הַבָּקָר וְהַגְּמַלִּים לִשְׁנֵי מַחֲנוֹת:

⁹ thinking, "If Esau comes to the one camp and attacks it, the other camp may yet escape."

ט וַיֹּאמֶר אִם־יָבוֹא עֵשָׂו אֶל־הַמַּחֲנֶה הָאַחַת וְהִכָּהוּ וְהָיָה הַמַּחֲנֶה הַנִּשְׁאָר לִפְלֵיטָה:

va-YO-mer im ya-VO ay-SAV el ha-ma-kha-NEH ha-a-KHAT v'-hi-KA-hu v'-ha-YAH ha-ma-kha-NEH ha-nish-AR lif-lay-TAH

פליטה

32:9 The other camp may yet escape Whenever the same Hebrew word is used to describe unrelated events, the Bible is drawing a deep connection between the two events. The word for 'escape' in this verse is *playta* (פליטה), the same word used by the Prophet *Ovadya* (1:17) "But on Mount Zion a remnant (*playta*) shall survive, and it shall be holy. The house of *Yaakov* shall dispossess those who had dispossessed them. The house of *Yaakov* shall be fire, and the house of *Yosef* a flame, and the house of Esau shall be straw." As he prepares for war with his brother Esau, *Yaakov* alludes to the fact that Zion is the only real refuge for the Jewish people from all future battles with the descendants of Esau.

Mount Zion, *Yerushalayim*

10 Then *Yaakov* said, "O God of my father *Avraham* and God of my father *Yitzchak*, *Hashem*, who said to me, 'Return to your native land and I will deal bountifully with you'!

11 I am unworthy of all the kindness that You have so steadfastly shown Your servant: with my staff alone I crossed this *Yarden*, and now I have become two camps.

12 Deliver me, I pray, from the hand of my brother, from the hand of Esau; else, I fear, he may come and strike me down, mothers and children alike.

13 Yet You have said, 'I will deal bountifully with you and make your offspring as the sands of the sea, which are too numerous to count.'"

14 After spending the night there, he selected from what was at hand these presents for his brother Esau:

15 200 she-goats and 20 he-goats; 200 ewes and 20 rams;

16 30 milch camels with their colts; 40 cows and 10 bulls; 20 she-asses and 10 he-asses.

17 These he put in the charge of his servants, drove by drove, and he told his servants, "Go on ahead, and keep a distance between droves."

18 He instructed the one in front as follows, "When my brother Esau meets you and asks you, 'Whose man are you? Where are you going? And whose [animals] are these ahead of you?'

19 you shall answer, 'Your servant *Yaakov*'s; they are a gift sent to my lord Esau; and [*Yaakov*] himself is right behind us.'"

20 He gave similar instructions to the second one, and the third, and all the others who followed the droves, namely, "Thus and so shall you say to Esau when you reach him.

21 And you shall add, 'And your servant *Yaakov* himself is right behind us.'" For he reasoned, "If I propitiate him with presents in advance, and then face him, perhaps he will show me favor."

22 And so the gift went on ahead, while he remained in camp that night.

י וַיֹּאמֶר יַעֲקֹב אֱלֹהֵי אָבִי אַבְרָהָם וֵאלֹהֵי אָבִי יִצְחָק יְהֹוָה הָאֹמֵר אֵלַי שׁוּב לְאַרְצְךָ וּלְמוֹלַדְתְּךָ וְאֵיטִיבָה עִמָּךְ:

יא קָטֹנְתִּי מִכֹּל הַחֲסָדִים וּמִכָּל־הָאֱמֶת אֲשֶׁר עָשִׂיתָ אֶת־עַבְדֶּךָ כִּי בְמַקְלִי עָבַרְתִּי אֶת־הַיַּרְדֵּן הַזֶּה וְעַתָּה הָיִיתִי לִשְׁנֵי מַחֲנוֹת:

יב הַצִּילֵנִי נָא מִיַּד אָחִי מִיַּד עֵשָׂו כִּי־יָרֵא אָנֹכִי אֹתוֹ פֶּן־יָבוֹא וְהִכַּנִי אֵם עַל־בָּנִים:

יג וְאַתָּה אָמַרְתָּ הֵיטֵב אֵיטִיב עִמָּךְ וְשַׂמְתִּי אֶת־זַרְעֲךָ כְּחוֹל הַיָּם אֲשֶׁר לֹא־יִסָּפֵר מֵרֹב:

יד וַיָּלֶן שָׁם בַּלַּיְלָה הַהוּא וַיִּקַּח מִן־הַבָּא בְיָדוֹ מִנְחָה לְעֵשָׂו אָחִיו:

טו עִזִּים מָאתַיִם וּתְיָשִׁים עֶשְׂרִים רְחֵלִים מָאתַיִם וְאֵילִים עֶשְׂרִים:

טז גְּמַלִּים מֵינִיקוֹת וּבְנֵיהֶם שְׁלֹשִׁים פָּרוֹת אַרְבָּעִים וּפָרִים עֲשָׂרָה אֲתֹנֹת עֶשְׂרִים וַעְיָרִם עֲשָׂרָה:

יז וַיִּתֵּן בְּיַד־עֲבָדָיו עֵדֶר עֵדֶר לְבַדּוֹ וַיֹּאמֶר אֶל־עֲבָדָיו עִבְרוּ לְפָנַי וְרֶוַח תָּשִׂימוּ בֵּין עֵדֶר וּבֵין עֵדֶר:

יח וַיְצַו אֶת־הָרִאשׁוֹן לֵאמֹר כִּי יִפְגָּשְׁךָ עֵשָׂו אָחִי וּשְׁאֵלְךָ לֵאמֹר לְמִי־אַתָּה וְאָנָה תֵלֵךְ וּלְמִי אֵלֶּה לְפָנֶיךָ:

יט וְאָמַרְתָּ לְעַבְדְּךָ לְיַעֲקֹב מִנְחָה הִוא שְׁלוּחָה לַאדֹנִי לְעֵשָׂו וְהִנֵּה גַם־הוּא אַחֲרֵינוּ:

כ וַיְצַו גַּם אֶת־הַשֵּׁנִי גַּם אֶת־הַשְּׁלִישִׁי גַּם אֶת־כָּל־הַהֹלְכִים אַחֲרֵי הָעֲדָרִים לֵאמֹר כַּדָּבָר הַזֶּה תְּדַבְּרוּן אֶל־עֵשָׂו בְּמֹצַאֲכֶם אֹתוֹ:

כא וַאֲמַרְתֶּם גַּם הִנֵּה עַבְדְּךָ יַעֲקֹב אַחֲרֵינוּ כִּי־אָמַר אֲכַפְּרָה פָנָיו בַּמִּנְחָה הַהֹלֶכֶת לְפָנָי וְאַחֲרֵי־כֵן אֶרְאֶה פָנָיו אוּלַי יִשָּׂא פָנָי:

כב וַתַּעֲבֹר הַמִּנְחָה עַל־פָּנָיו וְהוּא לָן בַּלַּיְלָה־הַהוּא בַּמַּחֲנֶה:

²³ That same night he arose, and taking his two wives, his two maidservants, and his eleven children, he crossed the ford of the Jabbok.

²⁴ After taking them across the stream, he sent across all his possessions.

²⁵ *Yaakov* was left alone. And a man wrestled with him until the break of dawn.

²⁶ When he saw that he had not prevailed against him, he wrenched *Yaakov*'s hip at its socket, so that the socket of his hip was strained as he wrestled with him.

²⁷ Then he said, "Let me go, for dawn is breaking." But he answered, "I will not let you go, unless you bless me."

²⁸ Said the other, "What is your name?" He replied, "*Yaakov*."

²⁹ Said he, "Your name shall no longer be *Yaakov*, but *Yisrael*, for you have striven with beings divine and human, and have prevailed."

³⁰ *Yaakov* asked, "Pray tell me your name." But he said, "You must not ask my name!" And he took leave of him there.

³¹ So *Yaakov* named the place Peniel, meaning, "I have seen a divine being face to face, yet my life has been preserved."

³² The sun rose upon him as he passed Penuel, limping on his hip.

³³ That is why the children of *Yisrael* to this day do not eat the thigh muscle that is on the socket of the hip, since *Yaakov*'s hip socket was wrenched at the thigh muscle.

33 ¹ Looking up, *Yaakov* saw Esau coming, accompanied by four hundred men. He divided the children among *Leah*, *Rachel*, and the two maids,

² putting the maids and their children first, *Leah* and her children next, and *Rachel* and *Yosef* last.

³ He himself went on ahead and bowed low to the ground seven times until he was near his brother.

כג וַיָּ֣קָם ׀ בַּלַּ֣יְלָה ה֗וּא וַיִּקַּ֞ח אֶת־שְׁתֵּ֤י נָשָׁיו֙ וְאֶת־שְׁתֵּ֣י שִׁפְחֹתָ֔יו וְאֶת־אַחַ֥ד עָשָׂ֖ר יְלָדָ֑יו וַֽיַּעֲבֹ֔ר אֵ֖ת מַעֲבַ֥ר יַבֹּֽק:

כד וַיִּ֨קָּחֵ֔ם וַיַּֽעֲבִרֵ֖ם אֶת־הַנָּ֑חַל וַֽיַּעֲבֵ֖ר אֶת־אֲשֶׁר־לֽוֹ:

כה וַיִּוָּתֵ֥ר יַעֲקֹ֖ב לְבַדּ֑וֹ וַיֵּֽאָבֵ֥ק אִישׁ֙ עִמּ֔וֹ עַ֖ד עֲל֥וֹת הַשָּֽׁחַר:

כו וַיַּ֗רְא כִּ֣י לֹ֤א יָכֹל֙ ל֔וֹ וַיִּגַּ֖ע בְּכַף־יְרֵכ֑וֹ וַתֵּ֨קַע֙ כַּף־יֶ֣רֶךְ יַעֲקֹ֔ב בְּהֵאָֽבְק֖וֹ עִמּֽוֹ:

כז וַיֹּ֣אמֶר שַׁלְּחֵ֔נִי כִּ֥י עָלָ֖ה הַשָּׁ֑חַר וַיֹּ֨אמֶר֙ לֹ֣א אֲשַֽׁלֵּֽחֲךָ֔ כִּ֖י אִם־בֵּֽרַכְתָּֽנִי:

כח וַיֹּ֥אמֶר אֵלָ֖יו מַה־שְּׁמֶ֑ךָ וַיֹּ֖אמֶר יַעֲקֹֽב:

כט וַיֹּ֗אמֶר לֹ֤א יַֽעֲקֹב֙ יֵֽאָמֵ֥ר עוֹד֙ שִׁמְךָ֔ כִּ֖י אִם־יִשְׂרָאֵ֑ל כִּֽי־שָׂרִ֧יתָ עִם־אֱלֹהִ֛ים וְעִם־אֲנָשִׁ֖ים וַתּוּכָֽל:

ל וַיִּשְׁאַ֣ל יַעֲקֹ֗ב וַיֹּ֨אמֶר֙ הַגִּֽידָה־נָּ֣א שְׁמֶ֔ךָ וַיֹּ֕אמֶר לָ֥מָּה זֶּ֖ה תִּשְׁאַ֣ל לִשְׁמִ֑י וַיְבָ֥רֶךְ אֹת֖וֹ שָֽׁם:

לא וַיִּקְרָ֧א יַעֲקֹ֛ב שֵׁ֥ם הַמָּק֖וֹם פְּנִיאֵ֑ל כִּֽי־רָאִ֤יתִי אֱלֹהִים֙ פָּנִ֣ים אֶל־פָּנִ֔ים וַתִּנָּצֵ֖ל נַפְשִֽׁי:

לב וַיִּֽזְרַֽח־ל֣וֹ הַשֶּׁ֔מֶשׁ כַּֽאֲשֶׁ֥ר עָבַ֖ר אֶת־פְּנוּאֵ֑ל וְה֥וּא צֹלֵ֖עַ עַל־יְרֵכֽוֹ:

לג עַל־כֵּ֡ן לֹֽא־יֹֽאכְל֨וּ בְנֵֽי־יִשְׂרָאֵ֜ל אֶת־גִּ֣יד הַנָּשֶׁ֗ה אֲשֶׁר֙ עַל־כַּ֣ף הַיָּרֵ֔ךְ עַ֖ד הַיּ֣וֹם הַזֶּ֑ה כִּ֤י נָגַע֙ בְּכַף־יֶ֣רֶךְ יַעֲקֹ֔ב בְּגִ֖יד הַנָּשֶֽׁה:

גלג א וַיִּשָּׂ֨א יַעֲקֹ֜ב עֵינָ֗יו וַיַּרְא֙ וְהִנֵּ֣ה עֵשָׂ֣ו בָּ֔א וְעִמּ֕וֹ אַרְבַּ֥ע מֵא֖וֹת אִ֑ישׁ וַיַּ֣חַץ אֶת־הַיְלָדִ֗ים עַל־לֵאָה֙ וְעַל־רָחֵ֔ל וְעַ֖ל שְׁתֵּ֥י הַשְּׁפָחֽוֹת:

ב וַיָּ֧שֶׂם אֶת־הַשְּׁפָח֛וֹת וְאֶת־יַלְדֵיהֶ֖ן רִֽאשֹׁנָ֑ה וְאֶת־לֵאָ֤ה וִֽילָדֶ֨יהָ֙ אַֽחֲרֹנִ֔ים וְאֶת־רָחֵ֥ל וְאֶת־יוֹסֵ֖ף אַֽחֲרֹנִֽים:

ג וְה֖וּא עָבַ֣ר לִפְנֵיהֶ֑ם וַיִּשְׁתַּ֤חוּ אַ֨רְצָה֙ שֶׁ֣בַע פְּעָמִ֔ים עַד־גִּשְׁתּ֖וֹ עַד־אָחִֽיו:

4 Esau ran to greet him. He embraced him and, falling on his neck, he kissed him; and they wept.

ד וַיָּרָץ עֵשָׂו לִקְרָאתוֹ וַיְחַבְּקֵהוּ וַיִּפֹּל עַל־צַוָּארָו וַיִּשָּׁקֵהוּ וַיִּבְכּוּ:

5 Looking about, he saw the women and the children. "Who," he asked, "are these with you?" He answered, "The children with whom *Hashem* has favored your servant."

ה וַיִּשָּׂא אֶת־עֵינָיו וַיַּרְא אֶת־הַנָּשִׁים וְאֶת־הַיְלָדִים וַיֹּאמֶר מִי־אֵלֶּה לָּךְ וַיֹּאמַר הַיְלָדִים אֲשֶׁר־חָנַן אֱלֹהִים אֶת־עַבְדֶּךָ:

6 Then the maids, with their children, came forward and bowed low;

ו וַתִּגַּשְׁןָ הַשְּׁפָחוֹת הֵנָּה וְיַלְדֵיהֶן וַתִּשְׁתַּחֲוֶיןָ:

7 next *Leah*, with her children, came forward and bowed low; and last, *Yosef* and *Rachel* came forward and bowed low;

ז וַתִּגַּשׁ גַּם־לֵאָה וִילָדֶיהָ וַיִּשְׁתַּחֲווּ וְאַחַר נִגַּשׁ יוֹסֵף וְרָחֵל וַיִּשְׁתַּחֲווּ:

8 And he asked, "What do you mean by all this company which I have met?" He answered, "To gain my lord's favor."

ח וַיֹּאמֶר מִי לְךָ כָּל־הַמַּחֲנֶה הַזֶּה אֲשֶׁר פָּגָשְׁתִּי וַיֹּאמֶר לִמְצֹא־חֵן בְּעֵינֵי אֲדֹנִי:

9 Esau said, "I have enough, my brother; let what you have remain yours."

ט וַיֹּאמֶר עֵשָׂו יֶשׁ־לִי רָב אָחִי יְהִי לְךָ אֲשֶׁר־לָךְ:

10 But *Yaakov* said, "No, I pray you; if you would do me this favor, accept from me this gift; for to see your face is like seeing the face of *Hashem*, and you have received me favorably.

י וַיֹּאמֶר יַעֲקֹב אַל־נָא אִם־נָא מָצָאתִי חֵן בְּעֵינֶיךָ וְלָקַחְתָּ מִנְחָתִי מִיָּדִי כִּי עַל־כֵּן רָאִיתִי פָנֶיךָ כִּרְאֹת פְּנֵי אֱלֹהִים וַתִּרְצֵנִי:

11 Please accept my present which has been brought to you, for *Hashem* has favored me and I have plenty." And when he urged him, he accepted.

יא קַח־נָא אֶת־בִּרְכָתִי אֲשֶׁר הֻבָאת לָךְ כִּי־חַנַּנִי אֱלֹהִים וְכִי יֶשׁ־לִי־כֹל וַיִּפְצַר־בּוֹ וַיִּקָּח:

12 And [Esau] said, "Let us start on our journey, and I will proceed at your pace."

יב וַיֹּאמֶר נִסְעָה וְנֵלֵכָה וְאֵלְכָה לְנֶגְדֶּךָ:

13 But he said to him, "My lord knows that the children are frail and that the flocks and herds, which are nursing, are a care to me; if they are driven hard a single day, all the flocks will die.

יג וַיֹּאמֶר אֵלָיו אֲדֹנִי יֹדֵעַ כִּי־הַיְלָדִים רַכִּים וְהַצֹּאן וְהַבָּקָר עָלוֹת עָלָי וּדְפָקוּם יוֹם אֶחָד וָמֵתוּ כָּל־הַצֹּאן:

14 Let my lord go on ahead of his servant, while I travel slowly, at the pace of the cattle before me and at the pace of the children, until I come to my lord in Seir."

יד יַעֲבָר־נָא אֲדֹנִי לִפְנֵי עַבְדּוֹ וַאֲנִי אֶתְנָהֲלָה לְאִטִּי לְרֶגֶל הַמְּלָאכָה אֲשֶׁר־לְפָנַי וּלְרֶגֶל הַיְלָדִים עַד אֲשֶׁר־אָבֹא אֶל־אֲדֹנִי שֵׂעִירָה:

15 Then Esau said, "Let me assign to you some of the men who are with me." But he said, "Oh no, my lord is too kind to me!"

טו וַיֹּאמֶר עֵשָׂו אַצִּיגָה־נָּא עִמְּךָ מִן־הָעָם אֲשֶׁר אִתִּי וַיֹּאמֶר לָמָּה זֶּה אֶמְצָא־חֵן בְּעֵינֵי אֲדֹנִי:

16 So Esau started back that day on his way to Seir.

טז וַיָּשָׁב בַּיּוֹם הַהוּא עֵשָׂו לְדַרְכּוֹ שֵׂעִירָה:

17 But *Yaakov* journeyed on to Succoth, and built a house for himself and made stalls for his cattle; that is why the place was called Succoth.

יז וְיַעֲקֹב נָסַע סֻכֹּתָה וַיִּבֶן לוֹ בָּיִת וּלְמִקְנֵהוּ עָשָׂה סֻכֹּת עַל־כֵּן קָרָא שֵׁם־הַמָּקוֹם סֻכּוֹת:

18 *Yaakov* arrived safe in the city of Shechem which is in the land of Canaan – having come thus from Paddan-aram – and he encamped before the city.

יח וַיָּבֹא יַעֲקֹב שָׁלֵם עִיר שְׁכֶם אֲשֶׁר בְּאֶרֶץ כְּנַעַן בְּבֹאוֹ מִפַּדַּן אֲרָם וַיִּחַן אֶת־פְּנֵי הָעִיר:

19 The parcel of land where he pitched his tent he purchased from the children of Hamor, Shechem's father, for a hundred *kesitah.*

יט וַיִּקֶן אֶת־חֶלְקַת הַשָּׂדֶה אֲשֶׁר נָטָה־שָׁם אָהֳלוֹ מִיַּד בְּנֵי־חֲמוֹר אֲבִי שְׁכֶם בְּמֵאָה קְשִׂיטָה:

va-YI-ken et khel-KAT ha-sa-DEH a-SHER na-tah SHAM a-ha-LO mi-YAD b'-nay kha-MOR a-VEE sh'-KHEM b'-may-AH k'-see-TAH

20 He set up a *Mizbayach* there, and called it *El*-elohe-yisrael.

כ וַיַּצֶּב־שָׁם מִזְבֵּחַ וַיִּקְרָא־לוֹ אֵל אֱלֹהֵי יִשְׂרָאֵל:

34 1 Now *Dina*, the daughter whom *Leah* had borne to *Yaakov*, went out to visit the daughters of the land.

ד א וַתֵּצֵא דִינָה בַּת־לֵאָה אֲשֶׁר יָלְדָה לְיַעֲקֹב לִרְאוֹת בִּבְנוֹת הָאָרֶץ:

2 Shechem son of Hamor the Hivite, chief of the country, saw her, and took her and lay with her by force.

ב וַיַּרְא אֹתָהּ שְׁכֶם בֶּן־חֲמוֹר הַחִוִּי נְשִׂיא הָאָרֶץ וַיִּקַּח אֹתָהּ וַיִּשְׁכַּב אֹתָהּ וַיְעַנֶּהָ:

3 Being strongly drawn to *Dina* daughter of *Yaakov*, and in love with the maiden, he spoke to the maiden tenderly.

ג וַתִּדְבַּק נַפְשׁוֹ בְּדִינָה בַּת־יַעֲקֹב וַיֶּאֱהַב אֶת־הַנַּעֲרָ וַיְדַבֵּר עַל־לֵב הַנַּעֲרָ:

4 So Shechem said to his father Hamor, "Get me this girl as a wife."

ד וַיֹּאמֶר שְׁכֶם אֶל־חֲמוֹר אָבִיו לֵאמֹר קַח־לִי אֶת־הַיַּלְדָּה הַזֹּאת לְאִשָּׁה:

5 *Yaakov* heard that he had defiled his daughter *Dina*; but since his sons were in the field with his cattle, *Yaakov* kept silent until they came home.

ה וְיַעֲקֹב שָׁמַע כִּי טִמֵּא אֶת־דִּינָה בִתּוֹ וּבָנָיו הָיוּ אֶת־מִקְנֵהוּ בַּשָּׂדֶה וְהֶחֱרִשׁ יַעֲקֹב עַד־בֹּאָם:

6 Then Shechem's father Hamor came out to *Yaakov* to speak to him.

ו וַיֵּצֵא חֲמוֹר אֲבִי־שְׁכֶם אֶל־יַעֲקֹב לְדַבֵּר אִתּוֹ:

7 Meanwhile *Yaakov*'s sons, having heard the news, came in from the field. The men were distressed and very angry, because he had committed an outrage in *Yisrael* by lying with *Yaakov*'s daughter – a thing not to be done.

ז וּבְנֵי יַעֲקֹב בָּאוּ מִן־הַשָּׂדֶה כְּשָׁמְעָם וַיִּתְעַצְּבוּ הָאֲנָשִׁים וַיִּחַר לָהֶם מְאֹד כִּי־נְבָלָה עָשָׂה בְיִשְׂרָאֵל לִשְׁכַּב אֶת־בַּת־יַעֲקֹב וְכֵן לֹא יֵעָשֶׂה:

8 And Hamor spoke with them, saying, "My son Shechem longs for your daughter. Please give her to him in marriage.

ח וַיְדַבֵּר חֲמוֹר אִתָּם לֵאמֹר שְׁכֶם בְּנִי חָשְׁקָה נַפְשׁוֹ בְּבִתְּכֶם תְּנוּ נָא אֹתָהּ לוֹ לְאִשָּׁה:

33:19 The parcel of land where he pitched his tent After escaping unscathed from Esau's clutches, *Yaakov* enters Canaan and purchases the land he has chosen to settle. This is a message for all of eternity. To ensure survival amidst countless enemies, the Children of Israel must build up their only true safe haven, the Land of Israel. Like his grandfather *Avraham*, *Yaakov* then builds an altar to *Hashem*. Rabbi Ovadya Seforno, a sixteenth century Italian commentator, points out that after spending time in exile, *Yaakov* appreciates that service of *Hashem* is most fitting in *Eretz Yisrael*, and he immediately makes every possible effort to worship the one true God of Israel there.

View of the landscape of *Shechem*

9   Intermarry with us: give your daughters to us, and
     take our daughters for yourselves:

10   You will dwell among us, and the land will be
     open before you; settle, move about, and acquire
     holdings in it."

11   Then Shechem said to her father and brothers, "Do
     me this favor, and I will pay whatever you tell me.

12   Ask of me a bride-price ever so high, as well as gifts,
     and I will pay what you tell me; only give me the
     maiden for a wife."

13   *Yaakov*'s sons answered Shechem and his father
     Hamor – speaking with guile because he had
     defiled their sister *Dina*

14   and said to them, "We cannot do this thing, to give
     our sister to a man who is uncircumcised, for that is
     a disgrace among us.

15   Only on this condition will we agree with you; that
     you will become like us in that every male among
     you is circumcised.

16   Then we will give our daughters to you and take
     your daughters to ourselves; and we will dwell
     among you and become as one kindred.

17   But if you will not listen to us and become
     circumcised, we will take our daughter and go."

18   Their words pleased Hamor and Hamor's son
     Shechem.

19   And the youth lost no time in doing the thing, for
     he wanted *Yaakov*'s daughter. Now he was the most
     respected in his father's house.

20   So Hamor and his son Shechem went to the public
     place of their town and spoke to their fellow
     townsmen, saying,

21   "These people are our friends; let them settle in
     the land and move about in it, for the land is large
     enough for them; we will take their daughters to
     ourselves as wives and give our daughters to them.

22   But only on this condition will the men agree
     with us to dwell among us and be as one kindred:
     that all our males become circumcised as they are
     circumcised.

ט וְהִתְחַתְּנ֖וּ אֹתָ֑נוּ בְּנֹֽתֵיכֶם֙ תִּתְּנוּ־לָ֔נוּ
    וְאֶת־בְּנֹתֵ֖ינוּ תִּקְח֥וּ לָכֶֽם׃

י וְאִתָּ֖נוּ תֵּשֵׁ֑בוּ וְהָאָ֙רֶץ֙ תִּהְיֶ֣ה לִפְנֵיכֶ֔ם
    שְׁבוּ֙ וּסְחָר֔וּהָ וְהֵאָֽחֲז֖וּ בָּֽהּ׃

יא וַיֹּ֤אמֶר שְׁכֶם֙ אֶל־אָבִ֣יהָ וְאֶל־אַחֶ֔יהָ
     אֶמְצָא־חֵ֖ן בְּעֵֽינֵיכֶ֑ם וַאֲשֶׁ֥ר תֹּֽאמְר֛וּ אֵלַ֖י
     אֶתֵּֽן׃

יב הַרְבּ֙וּ עָלַ֤י מְאֹד֙ מֹ֣הַר וּמַתָּ֔ן וְאֶ֨תְּנָ֔ה
     כַּאֲשֶׁ֥ר תֹּֽאמְר֖וּ אֵלָ֑י וּתְנוּ־לִ֥י אֶת־הַֽנַּעֲרָ֖
     לְאִשָּֽׁה׃

יג וַיַּֽעֲנ֨וּ בְנֵֽי־יַעֲקֹ֜ב אֶת־שְׁכֶ֨ם וְאֶת־חֲמ֤וֹר
     אָבִיו֙ בְּמִרְמָ֔ה וַיְדַבֵּ֑רוּ אֲשֶׁ֣ר טִמֵּ֔א אֵ֖ת
     דִּינָ֥ה אֲחֹתָֽם׃

יד וַיֹּֽאמְר֣וּ אֲלֵיהֶ֗ם לֹ֤א נוּכַל֙ לַֽעֲשׂוֹת֙ הַדָּבָ֣ר
     הַזֶּ֔ה לָתֵת֙ אֶת־אֲחֹתֵ֔נוּ לְאִ֖ישׁ אֲשֶׁר־ל֣וֹ
     עָרְלָ֑ה כִּֽי־חֶרְפָּ֥ה הִ֖וא לָֽנוּ׃

טו אַךְ־בְּזֹ֖את נֵא֣וֹת לָכֶ֑ם אִ֚ם תִּהְי֣וּ כָמֹ֔נוּ
     לְהִמֹּ֥ל לָכֶ֖ם כׇּל־זָכָֽר׃

טז וְנָתַ֤נּוּ אֶת־בְּנֹתֵ֙ינוּ֙ לָכֶ֔ם וְאֶת־בְּנֹֽתֵיכֶ֖ם
     נִֽקַּח־לָ֑נוּ וְיָשַׁ֣בְנוּ אִתְּכֶ֔ם וְהָיִ֖ינוּ לְעַ֥ם
     אֶחָֽד׃

יז וְאִם־לֹ֧א תִשְׁמְע֛וּ אֵלֵ֖ינוּ לְהִמּ֑וֹל וְלָקַ֥חְנוּ
     אֶת־בִּתֵּ֖נוּ וְהָלָֽכְנוּ׃

יח וַיִּֽיטְב֥וּ דִבְרֵיהֶ֖ם בְּעֵינֵ֣י חֲמ֑וֹר וּבְעֵינֵ֖י
     שְׁכֶ֥ם בֶּן־חֲמֽוֹר׃

יט וְלֹֽא־אֵחַ֤ר הַנַּ֙עַר֙ לַֽעֲשׂ֣וֹת הַדָּבָ֔ר כִּ֥י חָפֵ֖ץ
     בְּבַֽת־יַעֲקֹ֑ב וְה֣וּא נִכְבָּ֔ד מִכֹּ֖ל בֵּ֥ית אָבִֽיו׃

כ וַיָּבֹ֥א חֲמ֛וֹר וּשְׁכֶ֥ם בְּנ֖וֹ אֶל־שַׁ֣עַר עִירָ֑ם
    וַיְדַבְּר֛וּ אֶל־אַנְשֵׁ֥י עִירָ֖ם לֵאמֹֽר׃

כא הָאֲנָשִׁ֨ים הָאֵ֜לֶּה שְׁלֵמִ֧ים הֵ֣ם אִתָּ֗נוּ
     וְיֵשְׁב֤וּ בָאָ֙רֶץ֙ וְיִסְחֲר֣וּ אֹתָ֔הּ וְהָאָ֛רֶץ הִנֵּ֥ה
     רַֽחֲבַת־יָדַ֖יִם לִפְנֵיהֶ֑ם אֶת־בְּנֹתָ֞ם נִקַּֽח־
     לָ֣נוּ לְנָשִׁ֔ים וְאֶת־בְּנֹתֵ֖ינוּ נִתֵּ֥ן לָהֶֽם׃

כב אַךְ־בְּ֠זֹ֠את יֵאֹ֨תוּ לָ֤נוּ הָֽאֲנָשִׁים֙ לָשֶׁ֣בֶת
     אִתָּ֔נוּ לִֽהְי֖וֹת לְעַ֣ם אֶחָ֑ד בְּהִמּ֥וֹל לָ֙נוּ֙ כׇּל־
     זָכָ֔ר כַּאֲשֶׁ֖ר הֵ֥ם נִמֹּלִֽים׃

23 Their cattle and substance and all their beasts will be ours, if we only agree to their terms, so that they will settle among us."

כג מִקְנֵהֶם וְקִנְיָנָם וְכָל־בְּהֶמְתָּם הֲלוֹא לָנוּ הֵם אַךְ נֵאוֹתָה לָהֶם וְיֵשְׁבוּ אִתָּנוּ:

24 All who went out of the gate of his town heeded Hamor and his son Shechem, and all males, all those who went out of the gate of his town, were circumcised.

כד וַיִּשְׁמְעוּ אֶל־חֲמוֹר וְאֶל־שְׁכֶם בְּנוֹ כָּל־יֹצְאֵי שַׁעַר עִירוֹ וַיִּמֹּלוּ כָּל־זָכָר כָּל־יֹצְאֵי שַׁעַר עִירוֹ:

25 On the third day, when they were in pain, *Shimon* and *Levi*, two of *Yaakov*'s sons, brothers of *Dina*, took each his sword, came upon the city unmolested, and slew all the males.

כה וַיְהִי בַיּוֹם הַשְּׁלִישִׁי בִּהְיוֹתָם כֹּאֲבִים וַיִּקְחוּ שְׁנֵי־בְנֵי־יַעֲקֹב שִׁמְעוֹן וְלֵוִי אֲחֵי דִינָה אִישׁ חַרְבּוֹ וַיָּבֹאוּ עַל־הָעִיר בֶּטַח וַיַּהַרְגוּ כָּל־זָכָר:

26 They put Hamor and his son Shechem to the sword, took *Dina* out of Shechem's house, and went away.

כו וְאֶת־חֲמוֹר וְאֶת־שְׁכֶם בְּנוֹ הָרְגוּ לְפִי־חָרֶב וַיִּקְחוּ אֶת־דִּינָה מִבֵּית שְׁכֶם וַיֵּצֵאוּ:

27 The other sons of *Yaakov* came upon the slain and plundered the town, because their sister had been defiled.

כז בְּנֵי יַעֲקֹב בָּאוּ עַל־הַחֲלָלִים וַיָּבֹזּוּ הָעִיר אֲשֶׁר טִמְּאוּ אֲחוֹתָם:

28 They seized their flocks and herds and asses, all that was inside the town and outside;

כח אֶת־צֹאנָם וְאֶת־בְּקָרָם וְאֶת־חֲמֹרֵיהֶם וְאֵת אֲשֶׁר־בָּעִיר וְאֶת־אֲשֶׁר בַּשָּׂדֶה לָקָחוּ:

29 all their wealth, all their children, and their wives, all that was in the houses, they took as captives and booty.

כט וְאֶת־כָּל־חֵילָם וְאֶת־כָּל־טַפָּם וְאֶת־נְשֵׁיהֶם שָׁבוּ וַיָּבֹזּוּ וְאֵת כָּל־אֲשֶׁר בַּבָּיִת:

30 *Yaakov* said to *Shimon* and *Levi*, "You have brought trouble on me, making me odious among the inhabitants of the land, the Canaanites and the Perizzites; my men are few in number, so that if they unite against me and attack me, I and my house will be destroyed."

ל וַיֹּאמֶר יַעֲקֹב אֶל־שִׁמְעוֹן וְאֶל־לֵוִי עֲכַרְתֶּם אֹתִי לְהַבְאִישֵׁנִי בְּיֹשֵׁב הָאָרֶץ בַּכְּנַעֲנִי וּבַפְּרִזִּי וַאֲנִי מְתֵי מִסְפָּר וְנֶאֶסְפוּ עָלַי וְהִכּוּנִי וְנִשְׁמַדְתִּי אֲנִי וּבֵיתִי:

31 But they answered, "Should our sister be treated like a whore?"

לא וַיֹּאמְרוּ הַכְזוֹנָה יַעֲשֶׂה אֶת־אֲחוֹתֵנוּ:

va-yo-m'-RU hakh-zo-NAH ya-a-SEH et a-kho-TAY-nu

35 1 *Hashem* said to *Yaakov*, "Arise, go up to *Beit El* and remain there; and build a *Mizbayach* there to the God who appeared to you when you were fleeing from your brother Esau."

א וַיֹּאמֶר אֱלֹהִים אֶל־יַעֲקֹב קוּם עֲלֵה בֵית־אֵל וְשֶׁב־שָׁם וַעֲשֵׂה־שָׁם מִזְבֵּחַ לָאֵל הַנִּרְאֶה אֵלֶיךָ בְּבָרְחֲךָ מִפְּנֵי עֵשָׂו אָחִיךָ:

34:31 Should our sister be treated like a whore *Yaakov*'s sons argue with their father, who personifies peace and mercy, maintaining that in order to protect the family's honor, there are times when use of the sword is necessary. It is through the *Torah*'s education, says Rabbi Samson Raphael Hirsch, that the Jewish people have learned gentleness and human- ity. But, this has not made the Jews a weak or cowardly nation. With *Ha-shem*'s help, the tiny State of Israel has time and again stood up successfully to her numerous enemies, through the courageous men and women of the Israel Defense Forces.

Israeli soldiers praying at the Western Wall

2 So *Yaakov* said to his household and to all who were with him, "Rid yourselves of the alien gods in your midst, purify yourselves, and change your clothes.

ב וַיֹּאמֶר יַעֲקֹב אֶל־בֵּיתוֹ וְאֶל כָּל־אֲשֶׁר עִמּוֹ הָסִרוּ אֶת־אֱלֹהֵי הַנֵּכָר אֲשֶׁר בְּתֹכְכֶם וְהִטַּהֲרוּ וְהַחֲלִיפוּ שִׂמְלֹתֵיכֶם:

3 Come, let us go up to *Beit El*, and I will build a *Mizbayach* there to the God who answered me when I was in distress and who has been with me wherever I have gone."

ג וְנָקוּמָה וְנַעֲלֶה בֵּית־אֵל וְאֶעֱשֶׂה־שָּׁם מִזְבֵּחַ לָאֵל הָעֹנֶה אֹתִי בְּיוֹם צָרָתִי וַיְהִי עִמָּדִי בַּדֶּרֶךְ אֲשֶׁר הָלָכְתִּי:

4 They gave to *Yaakov* all the alien gods that they had, and the rings that were in their ears, and *Yaakov* buried them under the terebinth that was near Shechem.

ד וַיִּתְּנוּ אֶל־יַעֲקֹב אֵת כָּל־אֱלֹהֵי הַנֵּכָר אֲשֶׁר בְּיָדָם וְאֶת־הַנְּזָמִים אֲשֶׁר בְּאָזְנֵיהֶם וַיִּטְמֹן אֹתָם יַעֲקֹב תַּחַת הָאֵלָה אֲשֶׁר עִם־שְׁכֶם:

5 As they set out, a terror from *Hashem* fell on the cities round about, so that they did not pursue the sons of *Yaakov*.

ה וַיִּסָּעוּ וַיְהִי חִתַּת אֱלֹהִים עַל־הֶעָרִים אֲשֶׁר סְבִיבֹתֵיהֶם וְלֹא רָדְפוּ אַחֲרֵי בְּנֵי יַעֲקֹב:

6 Thus *Yaakov* came to Luz – that is, *Beit El* – in the land of Canaan, he and all the people who were with him.

ו וַיָּבֹא יַעֲקֹב לוּזָה אֲשֶׁר בְּאֶרֶץ כְּנַעַן הִוא בֵּית־אֵל הוּא וְכָל־הָעָם אֲשֶׁר־עִמּוֹ:

7 There he built a *Mizbayach* and named the site *El-Beit El*, for it was there that *Hashem* had revealed Himself to him when he was fleeing from his brother.

ז וַיִּבֶן שָׁם מִזְבֵּחַ וַיִּקְרָא לַמָּקוֹם אֵל בֵּית־אֵל כִּי שָׁם נִגְלוּ אֵלָיו הָאֱלֹהִים בְּבָרְחוֹ מִפְּנֵי אָחִיו:

8 *Devora*, *Rivka*'s nurse, died, and was buried under the oak below *Beit El*; so it was named Allon-bacuth.

ח וַתָּמָת דְּבֹרָה מֵינֶקֶת רִבְקָה וַתִּקָּבֵר מִתַּחַת לְבֵית־אֵל תַּחַת הָאַלּוֹן וַיִּקְרָא שְׁמוֹ אַלּוֹן בָּכוּת:

9 *Hashem* appeared again to *Yaakov* on his arrival from Paddan-aram, and He blessed him.

ט וַיֵּרָא אֱלֹהִים אֶל־יַעֲקֹב עוֹד בְּבֹאוֹ מִפַּדַּן אֲרָם וַיְבָרֶךְ אֹתוֹ:

10 *Hashem* said to him, "You whose name is *Yaakov*, You shall be called *Yaakov* no more, But *Yisrael* shall be your name." Thus He named him *Yisrael*.

י וַיֹּאמֶר לוֹ אֱלֹהִים שִׁמְךָ יַעֲקֹב לֹא־יִקָּרֵא שִׁמְךָ עוֹד יַעֲקֹב כִּי אִם־יִשְׂרָאֵל יִהְיֶה שְׁמֶךָ וַיִּקְרָא אֶת־שְׁמוֹ יִשְׂרָאֵל:

11 And *Hashem* said to him, "I am El Shaddai. Be fertile and increase; A nation, yea an assembly of nations, Shall descend from you. Kings shall issue from your loins.

יא וַיֹּאמֶר לוֹ אֱלֹהִים אֲנִי אֵל שַׁדַּי פְּרֵה וּרְבֵה גּוֹי וּקְהַל גּוֹיִם יִהְיֶה מִמֶּךָּ וּמְלָכִים מֵחֲלָצֶיךָ יֵצֵאוּ:

12 The land that I assigned to *Avraham* and *Yitzchak* I assign to you; And to your offspring to come Will I assign the land."

יב וְאֶת־הָאָרֶץ אֲשֶׁר נָתַתִּי לְאַבְרָהָם וּלְיִצְחָק לְךָ אֶתְּנֶנָּה וּלְזַרְעֲךָ אַחֲרֶיךָ אֶתֵּן אֶת־הָאָרֶץ:

v'-et ha-A-retz a-SHER na-TA-tee l'-av-ra-HAM ul-yitz-KHAK l'-KHA e-t'-NE-nah ul-zar-a-KHA a-kha-RE-kha e-TAYN et ha-A-retz

13 *Hashem* parted from him at the spot where He had spoken to him;

יג וַיַּעַל מֵעָלָיו אֱלֹהִים בַּמָּקוֹם אֲשֶׁר־דִּבֶּר אִתּוֹ:

14 and *Yaakov* set up a pillar at the site where He had
spoken to him, a pillar of stone, and he offered a
libation on it and poured oil upon it.

יד וַיַּצֵּב יַעֲקֹב מַצֵּבָה בַּמָּקוֹם אֲשֶׁר־דִּבֶּר
אִתּוֹ מַצֶּבֶת אָבֶן וַיַּסֵּךְ עָלֶיהָ נֶסֶךְ וַיִּצֹק
עָלֶיהָ שָׁמֶן:

15 *Yaakov* gave the site, where *Hashem* had spoken to
him, the name of *Beit El*.

טו וַיִּקְרָא יַעֲקֹב אֶת־שֵׁם הַמָּקוֹם אֲשֶׁר
דִּבֶּר אִתּוֹ שָׁם אֱלֹהִים בֵּית־אֵל:

16 They set out from *Beit El*; but when they were
still some distance short of *Efrat*, *Rachel* was in
childbirth, and she had hard labor.

טז וַיִּסְעוּ מִבֵּית אֵל וַיְהִי־עוֹד כִּבְרַת־
הָאָרֶץ לָבוֹא אֶפְרָתָה וַתֵּלֶד רָחֵל וַתְּקַשׁ
בְּלִדְתָּהּ:

17 When her labor was at its hardest, the midwife said
to her, "Have no fear, for it is another boy for you."

יז וַיְהִי בְהַקְשֹׁתָהּ בְּלִדְתָּהּ וַתֹּאמֶר לָהּ
הַמְיַלֶּדֶת אַל־תִּירְאִי כִּי־גַם־זֶה לָךְ בֵּן:

18 But as she breathed her last – for she was dying –
she named him Ben-oni; but his father called him
Binyamin.

יח וַיְהִי בְּצֵאת נַפְשָׁהּ כִּי מֵתָה וַתִּקְרָא
שְׁמוֹ בֶּן־אוֹנִי וְאָבִיו קָרָא־לוֹ בִנְיָמִין:

19 Thus *Rachel* died. She was buried on the road to
Efrat – now *Beit Lechem*.

יט וַתָּמָת רָחֵל וַתִּקָּבֵר בְּדֶרֶךְ אֶפְרָתָה
הִוא בֵּית לָחֶם:

va-TA-mot ra-KHAYL va-ti-ka-VAYR b'-DE-rekh ef-RA-tah HEE BAYT LA-khem

20 Over her grave *Yaakov* set up a pillar; it is the pillar
at *Rachel*'s grave to this day.

כ וַיַּצֵּב יַעֲקֹב מַצֵּבָה עַל־קְבֻרָתָהּ הִוא
מַצֶּבֶת קְבֻרַת־רָחֵל עַד־הַיּוֹם:

21 *Yisrael* journeyed on, and pitched his tent beyond
Migdal-eder.

כא וַיִּסַּע יִשְׂרָאֵל וַיֵּט אָהֳלֹה מֵהָלְאָה
לְמִגְדַּל־עֵדֶר:

22 While *Yisrael* stayed in that land, *Reuven* went and
lay with *Bilha*, his father's concubine; and *Yisrael*
found out. Now the sons of *Yaakov* were twelve in
number.

כב וַיְהִי בִּשְׁכֹּן יִשְׂרָאֵל בָּאָרֶץ הַהִוא וַיֵּלֶךְ
רְאוּבֵן וַיִּשְׁכַּב אֶת־בִּלְהָה פִּילֶגֶשׁ אָבִיו
וַיִּשְׁמַע יִשְׂרָאֵל וַיִּהְיוּ בְנֵי־יַעֲקֹב שְׁנֵים
עָשָׂר:

23 The sons of *Leah*: Reuven – *Yaakov*'s first-born –
Shimon, *Levi*, *Yehuda*, *Yissachar*, and *Zevulun*.

כג בְּנֵי לֵאָה בְּכוֹר יַעֲקֹב רְאוּבֵן וְשִׁמְעוֹן
וְלֵוִי וִיהוּדָה וְיִשָּׂשכָר וּזְבוּלֻן:

24 The sons of *Rachel*: *Yosef* and *Binyamin*.

כד בְּנֵי רָחֵל יוֹסֵף וּבִנְיָמִן:

25 The sons of *Bilha*, *Rachel*'s maid: *Dan* and *Naftali*.

כה וּבְנֵי בִלְהָה שִׁפְחַת רָחֵל דָּן וְנַפְתָּלִי:

35:19 She was buried on the road to *Efrat* *Yaakov*
did not bury his beloved wife *Rachel* in the
family plot in *Chevron*, but rather in nearby *Beit
Lechem*. Rashi explains that *Rachel*
was intentionally buried there in *Beit
Lechem*, on the side of the road on
which the Jews were forcibly
marched into exile following the destruction of the first *Beit Hamikdash*.
At that devastating moment in Jewish history, the downtrodden people
found comfort in *Rachel*'s holy resting
spot as she entreated God's mercy
towards His people. This is alluded to in *Yirmiyahu*'s
prophecy (Jeremiah 31:15–17) "A cry is heard in *Rama* –
wailing, bitter weeping – *Rachel* is weeping for her children." According to the *Zohar*, the *Mashiach* will ultimately
lead the dispersed Jews along that same route, again
passing *Rachel*'s grave as they are led back to their land
and thus fulfilling the continuation of *Yirmiyahu*'s prophecy, "they shall return from the enemy's land… the children shall return to their country." Today, *Rachel*'s Tomb
on the outskirts of contemporary Bethlehem remains a
popular destination for people to pour out their hearts in
prayer for the day when all of *Rachel*'s descendants will
pass her grave, on their way back home into *Eretz Yisrael*.

Rachel's Tomb in *Beit Lechem*, c. 1890

26 And the sons of *Zilpa*, *Leah*'s maid: *Gad* and *Asher*.
These are the sons of *Yaakov* who were born to him
in Paddan-aram.

כו וּבְנֵי זִלְפָּה שִׁפְחַת לֵאָה גָּד וְאָשֵׁר אֵלֶּה
בְּנֵי יַעֲקֹב אֲשֶׁר יֻלַּד־לוֹ בְּפַדַּן אֲרָם:

27 And *Yaakov* came to his father *Yitzchak* at Mamre,
at *Kiryat Arba* – now *Chevron* – where *Avraham* and
Yitzchak had sojourned.

כז וַיָּבֹא יַעֲקֹב אֶל־יִצְחָק אָבִיו מַמְרֵא
קִרְיַת הָאַרְבַּע הִוא חֶבְרוֹן אֲשֶׁר־גָּר־
שָׁם אַבְרָהָם וְיִצְחָק:

28 *Yitzchak* was a hundred and eighty years old

כח וַיִּהְיוּ יְמֵי יִצְחָק מְאַת שָׁנָה וּשְׁמֹנִים
שָׁנָה:

29 when he breathed his last and died. He was
gathered to his kin in ripe old age; and he was
buried by his sons Esau and *Yaakov*.

כט וַיִּגְוַע יִצְחָק וַיָּמָת וַיֵּאָסֶף אֶל־עַמָּיו זָקֵן
וּשְׂבַע יָמִים וַיִּקְבְּרוּ אֹתוֹ עֵשָׂו וְיַעֲקֹב
בָּנָיו:

6 1 This is the line of Esau – that is, Edom.

לו א וְאֵלֶּה תֹּלְדוֹת עֵשָׂו הוּא אֱדוֹם:

2 Esau took his wives from among the Canaanite
women – Adah daughter of Elon the Hittite, and
Oholibamah daughter of Anah daughter of Zibeon
the Hivite

ב עֵשָׂו לָקַח אֶת־נָשָׁיו מִבְּנוֹת כְּנָעַן אֶת־
עָדָה בַּת־אֵילוֹן הַחִתִּי וְאֶת־אָהֳלִיבָמָה
בַּת־עֲנָה בַּת־צִבְעוֹן הַחִוִּי:

3 and also Basemath daughter of Ishmael and sister of
Nebaioth.

ג וְאֶת־בָּשְׂמַת בַּת־יִשְׁמָעֵאל אֲחוֹת
נְבָיוֹת:

4 Adah bore to Esau Eliphaz; Basemath bore Reuel;

ד וַתֵּלֶד עָדָה לְעֵשָׂו אֶת־אֱלִיפָז וּבָשְׂמַת
יָלְדָה אֶת־רְעוּאֵל:

5 and Oholibamah bore Jeush, Jalam, and Korah.
Those were the sons of Esau, who were born to him
in the land of Canaan.

ה וְאָהֳלִיבָמָה יָלְדָה אֶת־יעיש [יְעוּשׁ]
וְאֶת־יַעְלָם וְאֶת־קֹרַח אֵלֶּה בְּנֵי עֵשָׂו
אֲשֶׁר יֻלְּדוּ־לוֹ בְּאֶרֶץ כְּנָעַן:

6 Esau took his wives, his sons and daughters, and all
the members of his household, his cattle and all his
livestock, and all the property that he had acquired
in the land of Canaan, and went to another land
because of his brother *Yaakov*.

ו וַיִּקַּח עֵשָׂו אֶת־נָשָׁיו וְאֶת־בָּנָיו וְאֶת־
בְּנֹתָיו וְאֶת־כָּל־נַפְשׁוֹת בֵּיתוֹ וְאֶת־
מִקְנֵהוּ וְאֶת־כָּל־בְּהֶמְתּוֹ וְאֶת כָּל־קִנְיָנוֹ
אֲשֶׁר רָכַשׁ בְּאֶרֶץ כְּנָעַן וַיֵּלֶךְ אֶל־אֶרֶץ
מִפְּנֵי יַעֲקֹב אָחִיו:

*va-yi-KAKH ay-SAV et na-SHAV v'-et ba-NAV v'-et b'-no-TAV
v'-et kol naf-SHOT bay-TO v'-et mik-NAY-hu v'-et kol b'-hem-TO
v'-AYT kol kin-ya-NO a-SHER ra-KHASH b'-E-retz k'-NA-an
va-YAY-lekh el E-retz mi-p'-NAY ya-a-KOV a-KHEEV*

36:6 Went to another land because of his brother
Yaakov Esau moves away from *Yaakov* and the
Land of Israel to a foreign land. Rabbi Zalman
Sorotzkin explains that Esau is interested in "a land," meaning a physical territory. He does not want the spiritual and
moral responsibilities that come with *Eretz Yisrael*, since
he understands the unique spiritual sensitivity of the land,
and wants to live without worry that the land may "vomit"
him out (see Leviticus 18:28) The Sages comment that
Esau deferred to his brother in recognition of *Yaakov*'s

rightful acquisition of the
birthright, thereby ac-
knowledging his right to
the Promised Land. With
this fateful decision, Esau
decided to release himself
of the responsibilities inher-
ent in ownership of the
Land of Israel and relin-
quished them to *Yaakov*.

Man holding the four species overlooking Jerusalem's Old City

7 For their possessions were too many for them to dwell together, and the land where they sojourned could not support them because of their livestock.

כִּי־הָיָה רְכוּשָׁם רָב מִשֶּׁבֶת יַחְדָּו וְלֹא יָכְלָה אֶרֶץ מְגוּרֵיהֶם לָשֵׂאת אֹתָם מִפְּנֵי מִקְנֵיהֶם: ז

8 So Esau settled in the hill country of Seir – Esau being Edom.

וַיֵּשֶׁב עֵשָׂו בְּהַר שֵׂעִיר עֵשָׂו הוּא אֱדוֹם: ח

9 This, then, is the line of Esau, the ancestor of the Edomites, in the hill country of Seir.

וְאֵלֶּה תֹּלְדוֹת עֵשָׂו אֲבִי אֱדוֹם בְּהַר שֵׂעִיר: ט

10 These are the names of Esau's sons: Eliphaz, the son of Esau's wife Adah; Reuel, the son of Esau's wife Basemath.

אֵלֶּה שְׁמוֹת בְּנֵי־עֵשָׂו אֱלִיפַז בֶּן־עָדָה אֵשֶׁת עֵשָׂו רְעוּאֵל בֶּן־בָּשְׂמַת אֵשֶׁת עֵשָׂו: י

11 The sons of Eliphaz were Teman, Omar, Zepho, Gatam, and Kenaz.

וַיִּהְיוּ בְּנֵי אֱלִיפָז תֵּימָן אוֹמָר צְפוֹ וְגַעְתָּם וּקְנַז: יא

12 Timna was a concubine of Esau's son Eliphaz; she bore Amalek to Eliphaz. Those were the descendants of Esau's wife Adah.

וְתִמְנַע הָיְתָה פִילֶגֶשׁ לֶאֱלִיפַז בֶּן־עֵשָׂו וַתֵּלֶד לֶאֱלִיפַז אֶת־עֲמָלֵק אֵלֶּה בְּנֵי עָדָה אֵשֶׁת עֵשָׂו: יב

13 And these were the sons of Reuel: Nahath, Zerah, Shammah, and Mizzah. Those were the descendants of Esau's wife Basemath.

וְאֵלֶּה בְּנֵי רְעוּאֵל נַחַת וָזֶרַח שַׁמָּה וּמִזָּה אֵלֶּה הָיוּ בְּנֵי בָשְׂמַת אֵשֶׁת עֵשָׂו: יג

14 And these were the sons of Esau's wife Oholibamah, daughter of Anah daughter of Zibeon: she bore to Esau Jeush, Jalam, and Korah.

וְאֵלֶּה הָיוּ בְּנֵי אָהֳלִיבָמָה בַת־עֲנָה בַּת־צִבְעוֹן אֵשֶׁת עֵשָׂו וַתֵּלֶד לְעֵשָׂו אֶת־יעיש [יְעוּשׁ] וְאֶת־יַעְלָם וְאֶת־קֹרַח: יד

15 These are the clans of the children of Esau. The descendants of Esau's first-born Eliphaz: the clans Teman, Omar, Zepho, Kenaz,

אֵלֶּה אַלּוּפֵי בְנֵי־עֵשָׂו בְּנֵי אֱלִיפַז בְּכוֹר עֵשָׂו אַלּוּף תֵּימָן אַלּוּף אוֹמָר אַלּוּף צְפוֹ אַלּוּף קְנַז: טו

16 Korah, Gatam, and Amalek; these are the clans of Eliphaz in the land of Edom. Those are the descendants of Adah.

אַלּוּף־קֹרַח אַלּוּף גַּעְתָּם אַלּוּף עֲמָלֵק אֵלֶּה אַלּוּפֵי אֱלִיפַז בְּאֶרֶץ אֱדוֹם אֵלֶּה בְּנֵי עָדָה: טז

17 And these are the descendants of Esau's son Reuel: the clans Nahath, Zerah, Shammah, and Mizzah; these are the clans of Reuel in the land of Edom. Those are the descendants of Esau's wife Basemath.

וְאֵלֶּה בְּנֵי רְעוּאֵל בֶּן־עֵשָׂו אַלּוּף נַחַת אַלּוּף זֶרַח אַלּוּף שַׁמָּה אַלּוּף מִזָּה אֵלֶּה אַלּוּפֵי רְעוּאֵל בְּאֶרֶץ אֱדוֹם אֵלֶּה בְּנֵי בָשְׂמַת אֵשֶׁת עֵשָׂו: יז

18 And these are the descendants of Esau's wife Oholibamah: the clans Jeush, Jalam, and Korah; these are the clans of Esau's wife Oholibamah, the daughter of Anah.

וְאֵלֶּה בְּנֵי אָהֳלִיבָמָה אֵשֶׁת עֵשָׂו אַלּוּף יְעוּשׁ אַלּוּף יַעְלָם אַלּוּף קֹרַח אֵלֶּה אַלּוּפֵי אָהֳלִיבָמָה בַּת־עֲנָה אֵשֶׁת עֵשָׂו: יח

19 Those were the sons of Esau – that is, Edom – and those are their clans.

אֵלֶּה בְנֵי־עֵשָׂו וְאֵלֶּה אַלּוּפֵיהֶם הוּא אֱדוֹם: יט

20 These were the sons of Seir the Horite, who were settled in the land: Lotan, Shobal, Zibeon, Anah,

אֵלֶּה בְנֵי־שֵׂעִיר הַחֹרִי יֹשְׁבֵי הָאָרֶץ לוֹטָן וְשׁוֹבָל וְצִבְעוֹן וַעֲנָה: כ

²¹ Dishon, Ezer, and Dishan. Those are the clans of the Horites, the descendants of Seir, in the land of Edom.

כא וְדִשׁוֹן וְאֵצֶר וְדִישָׁן אֵלֶּה אַלּוּפֵי הַחֹרִי בְּנֵי שֵׂעִיר בְּאֶרֶץ אֱדוֹם:

²² The sons of Lotan were Hori and Hemam; and Lotan's sister was Timna.

כב וַיִּהְיוּ בְנֵי־לוֹטָן חֹרִי וְהֵימָם וַאֲחוֹת לוֹטָן תִּמְנָע:

²³ The sons of Shobal were these: Alvan, Manahath, Ebal, Shepho, and Onam.

כג וְאֵלֶּה בְּנֵי שׁוֹבָל עַלְוָן וּמָנַחַת וְעֵיבָל שְׁפוֹ וְאוֹנָם:

²⁴ The sons of Zibeon were these: Aiah and Anah – that was the Anah who discovered the hot springs in the wilderness while pasturing the asses of his father Zibeon.

כד וְאֵלֶּה בְנֵי־צִבְעוֹן וְאַיָּה וַעֲנָה הוּא עֲנָה אֲשֶׁר מָצָא אֶת־הַיֵּמִם בַּמִּדְבָּר בִּרְעֹתוֹ אֶת־הַחֲמֹרִים לְצִבְעוֹן אָבִיו:

²⁵ The children of Anah were these: Dishon and Anah's daughter Oholibamah.

כה וְאֵלֶּה בְנֵי־עֲנָה דִּשֹׁן וְאָהֳלִיבָמָה בַּת־עֲנָה:

²⁶ The sons of Dishon were these: Hemdan, Eshban, Ithran, and Cheran.

כו וְאֵלֶּה בְּנֵי דִישָׁן חֶמְדָּן וְאֶשְׁבָּן וְיִתְרָן וּכְרָן:

²⁷ The sons of Ezer were these: Bilhan, Zaavan, and Akan.

כז אֵלֶּה בְּנֵי־אֵצֶר בִּלְהָן וְזַעֲוָן וַעֲקָן:

²⁸ And the sons of Dishan were these: Uz and Aran.

כח אֵלֶּה בְנֵי־דִישָׁן עוּץ וַאֲרָן:

²⁹ These are the clans of the Horites: the clans Lotan, Shobal, Zibeon, Anah,

כט אֵלֶּה אַלּוּפֵי הַחֹרִי אַלּוּף לוֹטָן אַלּוּף שׁוֹבָל אַלּוּף צִבְעוֹן אַלּוּף עֲנָה:

³⁰ Dishon, Ezer, and Dishan. Those are the clans of the Horites, clan by clan, in the land of Seir.

ל אַלּוּף דִּשֹׁן אַלּוּף אֵצֶר אַלּוּף דִּישָׁן אֵלֶּה אַלּוּפֵי הַחֹרִי לְאַלֻּפֵיהֶם בְּאֶרֶץ שֵׂעִיר:

³¹ These are the kings who reigned in the land of Edom before any king reigned over the Israelites.

לא וְאֵלֶּה הַמְּלָכִים אֲשֶׁר מָלְכוּ בְּאֶרֶץ אֱדוֹם לִפְנֵי מְלָךְ־מֶלֶךְ לִבְנֵי יִשְׂרָאֵל:

³² Bela son of Beor reigned in Edom, and the name of his city was Dinhabah.

לב וַיִּמְלֹךְ בֶּאֱדוֹם בֶּלַע בֶּן־בְּעוֹר וְשֵׁם עִירוֹ דִּנְהָבָה:

³³ When Bela died, Jobab son of Zerah, from Bozrah, succeeded him as king.

לג וַיָּמָת בָּלַע וַיִּמְלֹךְ תַּחְתָּיו יוֹבָב בֶּן־זֶרַח מִבָּצְרָה:

³⁴ When Jobab died, Husham of the land of the Temanites succeeded him as king.

לד וַיָּמָת יוֹבָב וַיִּמְלֹךְ תַּחְתָּיו חֻשָׁם מֵאֶרֶץ הַתֵּימָנִי:

³⁵ When Husham died, Hadad son of Bedad, who defeated the Midianites in the country of Moab, succeeded him as king; the name of his city was Avith.

לה וַיָּמָת חֻשָׁם וַיִּמְלֹךְ תַּחְתָּיו הֲדַד בֶּן־בְּדַד הַמַּכֶּה אֶת־מִדְיָן בִּשְׂדֵה מוֹאָב וְשֵׁם עִירוֹ עֲוִית:

³⁶ When Hadad died, Samlah of Masrekah succeeded him as king.

לו וַיָּמָת הֲדָד וַיִּמְלֹךְ תַּחְתָּיו שַׂמְלָה מִמַּשְׂרֵקָה:

³⁷ When Samlah died, Saul of Rehoboth-on-the-river succeeded him as king.

לז וַיָּמָת שַׂמְלָה וַיִּמְלֹךְ תַּחְתָּיו שָׁאוּל מֵרְחֹבוֹת הַנָּהָר:

³⁸ When Saul died, Baal-hanan son of Achbor succeeded him as king.

לח וַיָּמָת שָׁאוּל וַיִּמְלֹךְ תַּחְתָּיו בַּעַל חָנָן בֶּן־עַכְבּוֹר:

39 And when Baal-hanan son of Achbor died, Hadar succeeded him as king; the name of his city was Pau, and his wife's name was Mehetabel daughter of Matred daughter of Me-zahab.

לט וַיָּמָת בַּעַל חָנָן בֶּן־עַכְבּוֹר וַיִּמְלֹךְ תַּחְתָּיו הֲדַר וְשֵׁם עִירוֹ פָּעוּ וְשֵׁם אִשְׁתּוֹ מְהֵיטַבְאֵל בַּת־מַטְרֵד בַּת מֵי זָהָב:

40 These are the names of the clans of Esau, each with its families and locality, name by name: the clans Timna, Alvah, Jetheth,

מ וְאֵלֶּה שְׁמוֹת אַלּוּפֵי עֵשָׂו לְמִשְׁפְּחֹתָם לִמְקֹמֹתָם בִּשְׁמֹתָם אַלּוּף תִּמְנָע אַלּוּף עַלְוָה אַלּוּף יְתֵת:

41 Oholibamah, Elah, Pinon,

מא אַלּוּף אָהֳלִיבָמָה אַלּוּף אֵלָה אַלּוּף פִּינֹן:

42 Kenaz, Teman, Mibzar,

מב אַלּוּף קְנַז אַלּוּף תֵּימָן אַלּוּף מִבְצָר:

43 Magdiel, and Iram. Those are the clans of Edom – that is, of Esau, father of the Edomites – by their settlements in the land which they hold.

מג אַלּוּף מַגְדִּיאֵל אַלּוּף עִירָם אֵלֶּה אַלּוּפֵי אֱדוֹם לְמֹשְׁבֹתָם בְּאֶרֶץ אֲחֻזָּתָם הוּא עֵשָׂו אֲבִי אֱדוֹם:

37 1 Now *Yaakov* was settled in the land where his father had sojourned, the land of Canaan.

לז א וַיֵּשֶׁב יַעֲקֹב בְּאֶרֶץ מְגוּרֵי אָבִיו בְּאֶרֶץ כְּנָעַן:

2 This, then, is the line of *Yaakov*: At seventeen years of age, *Yosef* tended the flocks with his brothers, as a helper to the sons of his father's wives *Bilha* and *Zilpa*. And *Yosef* brought bad reports of them to their father.

ב אֵלֶּה תֹּלְדוֹת יַעֲקֹב יוֹסֵף בֶּן־שְׁבַע־עֶשְׂרֵה שָׁנָה הָיָה רֹעֶה אֶת־אֶחָיו בַּצֹּאן וְהוּא נַעַר אֶת־בְּנֵי בִלְהָה וְאֶת־בְּנֵי זִלְפָּה נְשֵׁי אָבִיו וַיָּבֵא יוֹסֵף אֶת־דִּבָּתָם רָעָה אֶל־אֲבִיהֶם:

AY-leh tol-DOT ya-a-KOV yo-SAYF ben sh'-va es-RAY sha-NAH ha-YAH ro-EH et e-KHAV ba-TZON v'-HU NA-ar et b'-NAY bil-HAH v'-et b'-NAY zil-PAH n'-SHAY a-VEEV va-ya-VAY yo-SAYF et di-ba-TAM ra-AH el a-vee-HEM

3 Now *Yisrael* loved *Yosef* best of all his sons, for he was the child of his old age; and he had made him an ornamented tunic.

ג וְיִשְׂרָאֵל אָהַב אֶת־יוֹסֵף מִכָּל־בָּנָיו כִּי־בֶן־זְקֻנִים הוּא לוֹ וְעָשָׂה לוֹ כְּתֹנֶת פַּסִּים:

4 And when his brothers saw that their father loved him more than any of his brothers, they hated him so that they could not speak a friendly word to him.

ד וַיִּרְאוּ אֶחָיו כִּי־אֹתוֹ אָהַב אֲבִיהֶם מִכָּל־אֶחָיו וַיִּשְׂנְאוּ אֹתוֹ וְלֹא יָכְלוּ דַּבְּרוֹ לְשָׁלֹם:

5 Once *Yosef* had a dream which he told to his brothers; and they hated him even more.

ה וַיַּחֲלֹם יוֹסֵף חֲלוֹם וַיַּגֵּד לְאֶחָיו וַיּוֹסִפוּ עוֹד שְׂנֹא אֹתוֹ:

6 He said to them, "Hear this dream which I have dreamed:

ו וַיֹּאמֶר אֲלֵיהֶם שִׁמְעוּ־נָא הַחֲלוֹם הַזֶּה אֲשֶׁר חָלָמְתִּי:

37:2 *Yosef* **tended the flocks with his brothers** It is no coincidence that so many biblical heroes are shepherds. The Sages point out that this simple profession is excellent spiritually, for two reasons. On one hand, the abundance of time for quiet reflection and meditation allows the shepherd to develop an intimate relationship with *Hashem*. On the other hand, a shepherd who excels in his work acquires a deep sensitivity to the needs of each and every sheep in his flock. What *Yosef* learns as a young shepherd enables him to become a paradigm of leadership for all future generations in the service of God and the service of man.

A shepherd in traditional dress leads a ram in the Galilee

7 There we were binding sheaves in the field, when suddenly my sheaf stood up and remained upright; then your sheaves gathered around and bowed low to my sheaf."

ז וְהִנֵּה אֲנַחְנוּ מְאַלְּמִים אֲלֻמִּים בְּתוֹךְ הַשָּׂדֶה וְהִנֵּה קָמָה אֲלֻמָּתִי וְגַם־נִצָּבָה וְהִנֵּה תְסֻבֶּינָה אֲלֻמֹּתֵיכֶם וַתִּשְׁתַּחֲוֶיןָ לַאֲלֻמָּתִי:

8 His brothers answered, "Do you mean to reign over us? Do you mean to rule over us?" And they hated him even more for his talk about his dreams.

ח וַיֹּאמְרוּ לוֹ אֶחָיו הֲמָלֹךְ תִּמְלֹךְ עָלֵינוּ אִם־מָשׁוֹל תִּמְשֹׁל בָּנוּ וַיּוֹסִפוּ עוֹד שְׂנֹא אֹתוֹ עַל־חֲלֹמֹתָיו וְעַל־דְּבָרָיו:

9 He dreamed another dream and told it to his brothers, saying, "Look, I have had another dream: And this time, the sun, the moon, and eleven stars were bowing down to me."

ט וַיַּחֲלֹם עוֹד חֲלוֹם אַחֵר וַיְסַפֵּר אֹתוֹ לְאֶחָיו וַיֹּאמֶר הִנֵּה חָלַמְתִּי חֲלוֹם עוֹד וְהִנֵּה הַשֶּׁמֶשׁ וְהַיָּרֵחַ וְאַחַד עָשָׂר כּוֹכָבִים מִשְׁתַּחֲוִים לִי:

10 And when he told it to his father and brothers, his father berated him. "What," he said to him, "is this dream you have dreamed? Are we to come, I and your mother and your brothers, and bow low to you to the ground?"

י וַיְסַפֵּר אֶל־אָבִיו וְאֶל־אֶחָיו וַיִּגְעַר־בּוֹ אָבִיו וַיֹּאמֶר לוֹ מָה הַחֲלוֹם הַזֶּה אֲשֶׁר חָלָמְתָּ הֲבוֹא נָבוֹא אֲנִי וְאִמְּךָ וְאַחֶיךָ לְהִשְׁתַּחֲוֹת לְךָ אָרְצָה:

11 So his brothers were wrought up at him, and his father kept the matter in mind.

יא וַיְקַנְאוּ־בוֹ אֶחָיו וְאָבִיו שָׁמַר אֶת־הַדָּבָר:

12 One time, when his brothers had gone to pasture their father's flock at Shechem,

יב וַיֵּלְכוּ אֶחָיו לִרְעוֹת אֶת־צֹאן אֲבִיהֶם בִּשְׁכֶם:

13 *Yisrael* said to *Yosef*, "Your brothers are pasturing at Shechem. Come, I will send you to them." He answered, "I am ready."

יג וַיֹּאמֶר יִשְׂרָאֵל אֶל־יוֹסֵף הֲלוֹא אַחֶיךָ רֹעִים בִּשְׁכֶם לְכָה וְאֶשְׁלָחֲךָ אֲלֵיהֶם וַיֹּאמֶר לוֹ הִנֵּנִי:

14 And he said to him, "Go and see how your brothers are and how the flocks are faring, and bring me back word." So he sent him from the valley of *Chevron*. When he reached Shechem,

יד וַיֹּאמֶר לוֹ לֶךְ־נָא רְאֵה אֶת־שְׁלוֹם אַחֶיךָ וְאֶת־שְׁלוֹם הַצֹּאן וַהֲשִׁבֵנִי דָּבָר וַיִּשְׁלָחֵהוּ מֵעֵמֶק חֶבְרוֹן וַיָּבֹא שְׁכֶמָה:

15 a man came upon him wandering in the fields. The man asked him, "What are you looking for?"

טו וַיִּמְצָאֵהוּ אִישׁ וְהִנֵּה תֹעֶה בַּשָּׂדֶה וַיִּשְׁאָלֵהוּ הָאִישׁ לֵאמֹר מַה־תְּבַקֵּשׁ:

16 He answered, "I am looking for my brothers. Could you tell me where they are pasturing?"

טז וַיֹּאמֶר אֶת־אַחַי אָנֹכִי מְבַקֵּשׁ הַגִּידָה־נָּא לִי אֵיפֹה הֵם רֹעִים:

17 The man said, "They have gone from here, for I heard them say: Let us go to Dothan." So *Yosef* followed his brothers and found them at Dothan.

יז וַיֹּאמֶר הָאִישׁ נָסְעוּ מִזֶּה כִּי שָׁמַעְתִּי אֹמְרִים נֵלְכָה דֹּתָיְנָה וַיֵּלֶךְ יוֹסֵף אַחַר אֶחָיו וַיִּמְצָאֵם בְּדֹתָן:

18 They saw him from afar, and before he came close to them they conspired to kill him.

יח וַיִּרְאוּ אֹתוֹ מֵרָחֹק וּבְטֶרֶם יִקְרַב אֲלֵיהֶם וַיִּתְנַכְּלוּ אֹתוֹ לַהֲמִיתוֹ:

19 They said to one another, "Here comes that dreamer!

יט וַיֹּאמְרוּ אִישׁ אֶל־אָחִיו הִנֵּה בַּעַל הַחֲלֹמוֹת הַלָּזֶה בָּא:

20 Come now, let us kill him and throw him into one of the pits; and we can say, 'A savage beast devoured him.' We shall see what comes of his dreams!"

כ וְעַתָּה לְכוּ וְנַהַרְגֵהוּ וְנַשְׁלִכֵהוּ בְּאַחַד הַבֹּרוֹת וְאָמַרְנוּ חַיָּה רָעָה אֲכָלָתְהוּ וְנִרְאֶה מַה־יִּהְיוּ חֲלֹמֹתָיו:

21 But when *Reuven* heard it, he tried to save him from them. He said, "Let us not take his life."

כא וַיִּשְׁמַע רְאוּבֵן וַיַּצִּלֵהוּ מִיָּדָם וַיֹּאמֶר לֹא נַכֶּנּוּ נָפֶשׁ:

22 And *Reuven* went on, "Shed no blood! Cast him into that pit out in the wilderness, but do not touch him yourselves" – intending to save him from them and restore him to his father.

כב וַיֹּאמֶר אֲלֵהֶם רְאוּבֵן אַל־תִּשְׁפְּכוּ־דָם הַשְׁלִיכוּ אֹתוֹ אֶל־הַבּוֹר הַזֶּה אֲשֶׁר בַּמִּדְבָּר וְיָד אַל־תִּשְׁלְחוּ־בוֹ לְמַעַן הַצִּיל אֹתוֹ מִיָּדָם לַהֲשִׁיבוֹ אֶל־אָבִיו:

*va-YO-mer a-lay-HEM r'-u-VAYN al tish-p'-khu DAM hash-LEE-khu
o-TO el ha-BOR ha-ZEH a-SHER ba-mid-BAR v'-YAD al tish-l'-khu VO
l'-MA-an ha-TZEEL o-TO mi-ya-DAM la-ha-shee-VO el a-VEEV*

23 When *Yosef* came up to his brothers, they stripped *Yosef* of his tunic, the ornamented tunic that he was wearing,

כג וַיְהִי כַּאֲשֶׁר־בָּא יוֹסֵף אֶל־אֶחָיו וַיַּפְשִׁיטוּ אֶת־יוֹסֵף אֶת־כֻּתָּנְתּוֹ אֶת־כְּתֹנֶת הַפַּסִּים אֲשֶׁר עָלָיו:

24 and took him and cast him into the pit. The pit was empty; there was no water in it.

כד וַיִּקָּחֻהוּ וַיַּשְׁלִכוּ אֹתוֹ הַבֹּרָה וְהַבּוֹר רֵק אֵין בּוֹ מָיִם:

25 Then they sat down to a meal. Looking up, they saw a caravan of Ishmaelites coming from *Gilad*, their camels bearing gum, balm, and ladanum to be taken to Egypt.

כה וַיֵּשְׁבוּ לֶאֱכָל־לֶחֶם וַיִּשְׂאוּ עֵינֵיהֶם וַיִּרְאוּ וְהִנֵּה אֹרְחַת יִשְׁמְעֵאלִים בָּאָה מִגִּלְעָד וּגְמַלֵּיהֶם נֹשְׂאִים נְכֹאת וּצְרִי וָלֹט הוֹלְכִים לְהוֹרִיד מִצְרָיְמָה:

26 Then *Yehuda* said to his brothers, "What do we gain by killing our brother and covering up his blood?

כו וַיֹּאמֶר יְהוּדָה אֶל־אֶחָיו מַה־בֶּצַע כִּי נַהֲרֹג אֶת־אָחִינוּ וְכִסִּינוּ אֶת־דָּמוֹ:

27 Come, let us sell him to the Ishmaelites, but let us not do away with him ourselves. After all, he is our brother, our own flesh." His brothers agreed.

כז לְכוּ וְנִמְכְּרֶנּוּ לַיִּשְׁמְעֵאלִים וְיָדֵנוּ אַל־תְּהִי־בוֹ כִּי־אָחִינוּ בְשָׂרֵנוּ הוּא וַיִּשְׁמְעוּ אֶחָיו:

28 When Midianite traders passed by, they pulled *Yosef* up out of the pit. They sold *Yosef* for twenty pieces of silver to the Ishmaelites, who brought *Yosef* to Egypt.

כח וַיַּעַבְרוּ אֲנָשִׁים מִדְיָנִים סֹחֲרִים וַיִּמְשְׁכוּ וַיַּעֲלוּ אֶת־יוֹסֵף מִן־הַבּוֹר וַיִּמְכְּרוּ אֶת־יוֹסֵף לַיִּשְׁמְעֵאלִים בְּעֶשְׂרִים כָּסֶף וַיָּבִיאוּ אֶת־יוֹסֵף מִצְרָיְמָה:

29 When *Reuven* returned to the pit and saw that *Yosef* was not in the pit, he rent his clothes.

כט וַיָּשָׁב רְאוּבֵן אֶל־הַבּוֹר וְהִנֵּה אֵין־יוֹסֵף בַּבּוֹר וַיִּקְרַע אֶת־בְּגָדָיו:

30 Returning to his brothers, he said, "The boy is gone! Now, what am I to do?"

ל וַיָּשָׁב אֶל־אֶחָיו וַיֹּאמַר הַיֶּלֶד אֵינֶנּוּ וַאֲנִי אָנָה אֲנִי־בָא:

31 Then they took *Yosef*'s tunic, slaughtered a kid, and dipped the tunic in the blood.

לא וַיִּקְחוּ אֶת־כְּתֹנֶת יוֹסֵף וַיִּשְׁחֲטוּ שְׂעִיר עִזִּים וַיִּטְבְּלוּ אֶת־הַכֻּתֹּנֶת בַּדָּם:

37:22 Cast him into that pit *Reuven* suggests throwing *Yosef* into a pit filled with dangerous snakes and scorpions, whereas *Yehuda* recommends selling *Yosef* to merchants. It would seem that *Yehuda*'s plan was likelier to save *Yosef*'s life and ensure a better outcome. Nevertheless, Rabbi Chaim of Volozhin, the nineteenth century author of *Nefesh Hachaim* and founder of the Volozhin Yeshiva, explains that one is safer in *Eretz Yisrael*, despite apparent imminent dangers, than in a foreign land with the illusion of physical security.

Mevo Dotan, named for biblical Dothan

32 They had the ornamented tunic taken to their father, and they said, "We found this. Please examine it; is it your son's tunic or not?"

וַיְשַׁלְּחוּ אֶת־כְּתֹנֶת הַפַּסִּים וַיָּבִיאוּ אֶל־ לב
אֲבִיהֶם וַיֹּאמְרוּ זֹאת מָצָאנוּ הַכֶּר־נָא
הַכְּתֹנֶת בִּנְךָ הִוא אִם־לֹא:

33 He recognized it, and said, "My son's tunic! A savage beast devoured him! *Yosef* was torn by a beast!"

וַיַּכִּירָהּ וַיֹּאמֶר כְּתֹנֶת בְּנִי חַיָּה רָעָה לג
אֲכָלָתְהוּ טָרֹף טֹרַף יוֹסֵף:

34 *Yaakov* rent his clothes, put sackcloth on his loins, and observed mourning for his son many days.

וַיִּקְרַע יַעֲקֹב שִׂמְלֹתָיו וַיָּשֶׂם שַׂק לד
בְּמָתְנָיו וַיִּתְאַבֵּל עַל־בְּנוֹ יָמִים רַבִּים:

35 All his sons and daughters sought to comfort him; but he refused to be comforted, saying, "No, I will go down mourning to my son in Sheol." Thus his father bewailed him.

וַיָּקֻמוּ כָל־בָּנָיו וְכָל־בְּנֹתָיו לְנַחֲמוֹ וַיְמָאֵן לה
לְהִתְנַחֵם וַיֹּאמֶר כִּי־אֵרֵד אֶל־בְּנִי אָבֵל
שְׁאֹלָה וַיֵּבְךְּ אֹתוֹ אָבִיו:

36 The Midianites, meanwhile, sold him in Egypt to Potiphar, a courtier of Pharaoh and his chief steward.

וְהַמְּדָנִים מָכְרוּ אֹתוֹ אֶל־מִצְרָיִם לו
לְפוֹטִיפַר סְרִיס פַּרְעֹה שַׂר הַטַּבָּחִים:

8 1 About that time *Yehuda* left his brothers and camped near a certain Adullamite whose name was Hirah.

וַיְהִי בָּעֵת הַהִוא וַיֵּרֶד יְהוּדָה מֵאֵת א **לח**
אֶחָיו וַיֵּט עַד־אִישׁ עֲדֻלָּמִי וּשְׁמוֹ
חִירָה:

vai-HEE ba-AYT ha-HEE va-YAY-red y'-hu-DAH may-AYT e-KHAV va-YAYT ad EESH a-du-la-MEE ush-MO khee-RAH

2 There *Yehuda* saw the daughter of a certain Canaanite whose name was Shua, and he married her and cohabited with her.

וַיַּרְא־שָׁם יְהוּדָה בַּת־אִישׁ כְּנַעֲנִי וּשְׁמוֹ ב
שׁוּעַ וַיִּקָּחֶהָ וַיָּבֹא אֵלֶיהָ:

3 She conceived and bore a son, and he named him *Er.*

וַתַּהַר וַתֵּלֶד בֵּן וַיִּקְרָא אֶת־שְׁמוֹ עֵר: ג

4 She conceived again and bore a son, and named him *Onan.*

וַתַּהַר עוֹד וַתֵּלֶד בֵּן וַתִּקְרָא אֶת־שְׁמוֹ ד
אוֹנָן:

5 Once again she bore a son, and named him *Sheila;* he was at Chezib when she bore him.

וַתֹּסֶף עוֹד וַתֵּלֶד בֵּן וַתִּקְרָא אֶת־שְׁמוֹ ה
שֵׁלָה וְהָיָה בִכְזִיב בְּלִדְתָּהּ אֹתוֹ:

6 *Yehuda* got a wife for *Er* his first-born; her name was *Tamar.*

וַיִּקַּח יְהוּדָה אִשָּׁה לְעֵר בְּכוֹרוֹ וּשְׁמָהּ ו
תָּמָר:

A valley in the Adullam region of Israel

38:1 *Yehuda* left his brothers Though the story of *Yehuda* and his daughter-in-law *Tamar* seems to interrupt the narrative of the *Yosef* stories, Jewish tradition teaches that its placement here is deliberate. In beautiful shorthand, the Midrash explains the connection: "While the tribes were busy with the sale of *Yosef, Reuven, Yosef* and *Yaakov* were busy with their sackcloth and mourning; *Yehuda* was busy taking a wife; and God was busy creating the light of the *Mashiach*." Like a puppet master operating behind the scenes and hidden from view, *Hashem* is pulling the strings and directing events without the knowledge or understanding of the participants themselves. From the union between *Yehuda* and *Tamar*, the Davidic dynasty and ultimately the *Mashiach* himself would emerge. Precisely when life seems to be completely unraveling, *Hashem* is directing events with His infinite wisdom, and is carefully nurturing our redemption.

7 But *Er*, *Yehuda*'s first-born, was displeasing to *Hashem*, and *Hashem* took his life.

ז וַיְהִי עֵר בְּכוֹר יְהוּדָה רַע בְּעֵינֵי יְהֹוָה וַיְמִתֵהוּ יְהֹוָה:

8 Then *Yehuda* said to *Onan*, "Join with your brother's wife and do your duty by her as a brother-in-law, and provide offspring for your brother."

ח וַיֹּאמֶר יְהוּדָה לְאוֹנָן בֹּא אֶל־אֵשֶׁת אָחִיךָ וְיַבֵּם אֹתָהּ וְהָקֵם זֶרַע לְאָחִיךָ:

9 But *Onan*, knowing that the seed would not count as his, let it go to waste whenever he joined with his brother's wife, so as not to provide offspring for his brother.

ט וַיֵּדַע אוֹנָן כִּי לֹּא לוֹ יִהְיֶה הַזָּרַע וְהָיָה אִם־בָּא אֶל־אֵשֶׁת אָחִיו וְשִׁחֵת אַרְצָה לְבִלְתִּי נְתָן־זֶרַע לְאָחִיו:

10 What he did was displeasing to *Hashem*, and He took his life also.

י וַיֵּרַע בְּעֵינֵי יְהֹוָה אֲשֶׁר עָשָׂה וַיָּמֶת גַּם־אֹתוֹ:

11 Then *Yehuda* said to his daughter-in-law *Tamar*, "Stay as a widow in your father's house until my son *Sheila* grows up" – for he thought, "He too might die like his brothers." So *Tamar* went to live in her father's house.

יא וַיֹּאמֶר יְהוּדָה לְתָמָר כַּלָּתוֹ שְׁבִי אַלְמָנָה בֵית־אָבִיךְ עַד־יִגְדַּל שֵׁלָה בְנִי כִּי אָמַר פֶּן־יָמוּת גַּם־הוּא כְּאֶחָיו וַתֵּלֶךְ תָּמָר וַתֵּשֶׁב בֵּית אָבִיהָ:

12 A long time afterward, Shua's daughter, the wife of *Yehuda*, died. When his period of mourning was over, *Yehuda* went up to Timnah to his sheepshearers, together with his friend Hirah the Adullamite.

יב וַיִּרְבּוּ הַיָּמִים וַתָּמָת בַּת־שׁוּעַ אֵשֶׁת־יְהוּדָה וַיִּנָּחֶם יְהוּדָה וַיַּעַל עַל־גֹּזֲזֵי צֹאנוֹ הוּא וְחִירָה רֵעֵהוּ הָעֲדֻלָּמִי תִּמְנָתָה:

13 And *Tamar* was told, "Your father-in-law is coming up to Timnah for the sheepshearing."

יג וַיֻּגַּד לְתָמָר לֵאמֹר הִנֵּה חָמִיךְ עֹלֶה תִמְנָתָה לָגֹז צֹאנוֹ:

14 So she took off her widow's garb, covered her face with a veil, and, wrapping herself up, sat down at the entrance to Enaim, which is on the road to Timnah; for she saw that *Sheila* was grown up, yet she had not been given to him as wife.

יד וַתָּסַר בִּגְדֵי אַלְמְנוּתָהּ מֵעָלֶיהָ וַתְּכַס בַּצָּעִיף וַתִּתְעַלָּף וַתֵּשֶׁב בְּפֶתַח עֵינַיִם אֲשֶׁר עַל־דֶּרֶךְ תִּמְנָתָה כִּי רָאֲתָה כִּי־גָדַל שֵׁלָה וְהִוא לֹא־נִתְּנָה לוֹ לְאִשָּׁה:

15 When *Yehuda* saw her, he took her for a harlot; for she had covered her face.

טו וַיִּרְאֶהָ יְהוּדָה וַיַּחְשְׁבֶהָ לְזוֹנָה כִּי כִסְּתָה פָּנֶיהָ:

16 So he turned aside to her by the road and said, "Here, let me sleep with you" – for he did not know that she was his daughter-in-law. "What," she asked, "will you pay for sleeping with me?"

טז וַיֵּט אֵלֶיהָ אֶל־הַדֶּרֶךְ וַיֹּאמֶר הָבָה־נָּא אָבוֹא אֵלַיִךְ כִּי לֹא יָדַע כִּי כַלָּתוֹ הִוא וַתֹּאמֶר מַה־תִּתֶּן־לִי כִּי תָבוֹא אֵלָי:

17 He replied, "I will send a kid from my flock." But she said, "You must leave a pledge until you have sent it."

יז וַיֹּאמֶר אָנֹכִי אֲשַׁלַּח גְּדִי־עִזִּים מִן־הַצֹּאן וַתֹּאמֶר אִם־תִּתֵּן עֵרָבוֹן עַד שָׁלְחֶךָ:

18 And he said, "What pledge shall I give you?" She replied, "Your seal and cord, and the staff which you carry." So he gave them to her and slept with her, and she conceived by him.

יח וַיֹּאמֶר מָה הָעֵרָבוֹן אֲשֶׁר אֶתֶּן־לָךְ וַתֹּאמֶר חֹתָמְךָ וּפְתִילֶךָ וּמַטְּךָ אֲשֶׁר בְּיָדֶךָ וַיִּתֶּן־לָהּ וַיָּבֹא אֵלֶיהָ וַתַּהַר לוֹ:

19 Then she went on her way. She took off her veil and again put on her widow's garb.

יט וַתָּקָם וַתֵּלֶךְ וַתָּסַר צְעִיפָהּ מֵעָלֶיהָ וַתִּלְבַּשׁ בִּגְדֵי אַלְמְנוּתָהּ:

²⁰ *Yehuda* sent the kid by his friend the Adullamite, to redeem the pledge from the woman; but he could not find her.

²¹ He inquired of the people of that town, "Where is the cult prostitute, the one at Enaim, by the road?" But they said, "There has been no prostitute here."

²² So he returned to *Yehuda* and said, "I could not find her; moreover, the townspeople said: There has been no prostitute here."

²³ *Yehuda* said, "Let her keep them, lest we become a laughingstock. I did send her this kid, but you did not find her."

²⁴ About three months later, *Yehuda* was told, "Your daughter-in-law *Tamar* has played the harlot; in fact, she is with child by harlotry." "Bring her out," said *Yehuda*, "and let her be burned."

²⁵ As she was being brought out, she sent this message to her father-in-law, "I am with child by the man to whom these belong." And she added, "Examine these: whose seal and cord and staff are these?"

²⁶ *Yehuda* recognized them, and said, "She is more in the right than I, inasmuch as I did not give her to my son *Sheila*." And he was not intimate with her again.

²⁷ When the time came for her to give birth, there were twins in her womb!

²⁸ While she was in labor, one of them put out his hand, and the midwife tied a crimson thread on that hand, to signify: This one came out first.

²⁹ But just then he drew back his hand, and out came his brother; and she said, "What a breach you have made for yourself!" So he was named *Peretz*.

³⁰ Afterward his brother came out, on whose hand was the crimson thread; he was named *Zerach*.

39 ¹ When *Yosef* was taken down to Egypt, a certain Egyptian, Potiphar, a courtier of Pharaoh and his chief steward, bought him from the Ishmaelites who had brought him there.

כ וַיִּשְׁלַ֤ח יְהוּדָה֙ אֶת־גְּדִ֣י הָֽעִזִּ֔ים בְּיַד֙ רֵעֵ֣הוּ הָֽעֲדֻלָּמִ֔י לָקַ֥חַת הָֽעֵרָב֖וֹן מִיַּ֣ד הָֽאִשָּׁ֑ה וְלֹ֖א מְצָאָֽהּ׃

כא וַיִּשְׁאַ֣ל אֶת־אַנְשֵׁ֤י מְקֹמָהּ֙ לֵאמֹ֔ר אַיֵּ֧ה הַקְּדֵשָׁ֛ה הִ֥וא בָֽעֵינַ֖יִם עַל־הַדָּ֑רֶךְ וַיֹּ֣אמְר֔וּ לֹא־הָֽיְתָ֥ה בָזֶ֖ה קְדֵשָֽׁה׃

כב וַיָּ֙שָׁב֙ אֶל־יְהוּדָ֔ה וַיֹּ֖אמֶר לֹ֣א מְצָאתִ֑יהָ וְגַ֨ם אַנְשֵׁ֤י הַמָּקוֹם֙ אָֽמְר֔וּ לֹא־הָֽיְתָ֥ה בָזֶ֖ה קְדֵשָֽׁה׃

כג וַיֹּ֤אמֶר יְהוּדָה֙ תִּֽקַּֽח־לָ֔הּ פֶּ֖ן נִֽהְיֶ֣ה לָב֑וּז הִנֵּ֤ה שָׁלַ֙חְתִּי֙ הַגְּדִ֣י הַזֶּ֔ה וְאַתָּ֖ה לֹ֥א מְצָאתָֽהּ׃

כד וַיְהִ֣י ׀ כְּמִשְׁלֹ֣שׁ חֳדָשִׁ֗ים וַיֻּגַּ֨ד לִֽיהוּדָ֤ה לֵֽאמֹר֙ זָֽנְתָה֙ תָּמָ֣ר כַּלָּתֶ֔ךָ וְגַ֛ם הִנֵּ֥ה הָרָ֖ה לִזְנוּנִ֑ים וַיֹּ֣אמֶר יְהוּדָ֔ה הֽוֹצִיא֖וּהָ וְתִשָּׂרֵֽף׃

כה הִ֣וא מוּצֵ֗את וְהִ֨יא שָֽׁלְחָ֤ה אֶל־חָמִ֙יהָ֙ לֵאמֹ֔ר לְאִישׁ֙ אֲשֶׁר־אֵ֣לֶּה לּ֔וֹ אָֽנֹכִ֖י הָרָ֑ה וַתֹּ֙אמֶר֙ הַכֶּר־נָ֔א לְמִ֞י הַֽחֹתֶ֧מֶת וְהַפְּתִילִ֛ים וְהַמַּטֶּ֖ה הָאֵֽלֶּה׃

כו וַיַּכֵּ֣ר יְהוּדָ֗ה וַיֹּ֙אמֶר֙ צָֽדְקָ֣ה מִמֶּ֔נִּי כִּֽי־עַל־כֵּ֥ן לֹֽא־נְתַתִּ֖יהָ לְשֵׁלָ֣ה בְנִ֑י וְלֹֽא־יָסַ֥ף ע֖וֹד לְדַעְתָּֽהּ׃

כז וַיְהִ֖י בְּעֵ֣ת לִדְתָּ֑הּ וְהִנֵּ֥ה תְאוֹמִ֖ים בְּבִטְנָֽהּ׃

כח וַיְהִ֣י בְלִדְתָּ֔הּ וַיִּתֶּן־יָ֑ד וַתִּקַּ֣ח הַֽמְיַלֶּ֗דֶת וַתִּקְשֹׁ֨ר עַל־יָד֤וֹ שָׁנִי֙ לֵאמֹ֔ר זֶ֖ה יָצָ֥א רִֽאשֹׁנָֽה׃

כט וַיְהִ֣י ׀ כְּמֵשִׁ֣יב יָד֗וֹ וְהִנֵּה֙ יָצָ֣א אָחִ֔יו וַתֹּ֕אמֶר מַה־פָּרַ֖צְתָּ עָלֶ֣יךָ פָּ֑רֶץ וַיִּקְרָ֥א שְׁמ֖וֹ פָּֽרֶץ׃

ל וְאַחַר֙ יָצָ֣א אָחִ֔יו אֲשֶׁ֥ר עַל־יָד֖וֹ הַשָּׁנִ֑י וַיִּקְרָ֥א שְׁמ֖וֹ זָֽרַח׃

לט א וְיוֹסֵ֖ף הוּרַ֣ד מִצְרָ֑יְמָה וַיִּקְנֵ֡הוּ פּֽוֹטִיפַר֩ סְרִ֨יס פַּרְעֹ֜ה שַׂ֤ר הַטַּבָּחִים֙ אִ֣ישׁ מִצְרִ֔י מִיַּד֙ הַיִּשְׁמְעֵאלִ֔ים אֲשֶׁ֥ר הֽוֹרִדֻ֖הוּ שָֽׁמָּה׃

v'-yo-SAYF hu-RAD mitz-RA-y'-mah va-yik-NAY-hu po-tee-FAR
s'-REES par-OH SAR ha-ta-ba-KHEEM EESH mitz-REE mi-YAD
ha-yish-m'-ay-LEEM a-SHER ho-ri-DU-hu SHA-mah

ב וַיְהִי יְהוָֹה אֶת־יוֹסֵף וַיְהִי אִישׁ מַצְלִיחַ
וַיְהִי בְּבֵית אֲדֹנָיו הַמִּצְרִי:

2 *Hashem* was with *Yosef*, and he was a successful man; and he stayed in the house of his Egyptian master.

ג וַיַּרְא אֲדֹנָיו כִּי יְהוָֹה אִתּוֹ וְכֹל אֲשֶׁר־
הוּא עֹשֶׂה יְהוָֹה מַצְלִיחַ בְּיָדוֹ:

3 And when his master saw that *Hashem* was with him and that *Hashem* lent success to everything he undertook,

ד וַיִּמְצָא יוֹסֵף חֵן בְּעֵינָיו וַיְשָׁרֶת אֹתוֹ
וַיַּפְקִדֵהוּ עַל־בֵּיתוֹ וְכָל־יֶשׁ־לוֹ נָתַן
בְּיָדוֹ:

4 he took a liking to *Yosef*. He made him his personal attendant and put him in charge of his household, placing in his hands all that he owned.

ה וַיְהִי מֵאָז הִפְקִיד אֹתוֹ בְּבֵיתוֹ וְעַל
כָּל־אֲשֶׁר יֶשׁ־לוֹ וַיְבָרֶךְ יְהוָֹה אֶת־בֵּית
הַמִּצְרִי בִּגְלַל יוֹסֵף וַיְהִי בִּרְכַּת יְהוָֹה
בְּכָל־אֲשֶׁר יֶשׁ־לוֹ בַּבַּיִת וּבַשָּׂדֶה:

5 And from the time that the Egyptian put him in charge of his household and of all that he owned, *Hashem* blessed his house for *Yosef*'s sake, so that the blessing of *Hashem* was upon everything that he owned, in the house and outside.

ו וַיַּעֲזֹב כָּל־אֲשֶׁר־לוֹ בְּיַד־יוֹסֵף וְלֹא־יָדַע
אִתּוֹ מְאוּמָה כִּי אִם־הַלֶּחֶם אֲשֶׁר־הוּא
אוֹכֵל וַיְהִי יוֹסֵף יְפֵה־תֹאַר וִיפֵה מַרְאֶה:

6 He left all that he had in *Yosef*'s hands and, with him there, he paid attention to nothing save the food that he ate. Now *Yosef* was well built and handsome.

ז וַיְהִי אַחַר הַדְּבָרִים הָאֵלֶּה וַתִּשָּׂא
אֵשֶׁת־אֲדֹנָיו אֶת־עֵינֶיהָ אֶל־יוֹסֵף
וַתֹּאמֶר שִׁכְבָה עִמִּי:

7 After a time, his master's wife cast her eyes upon *Yosef* and said, "Lie with me."

ח וַיְמָאֵן וַיֹּאמֶר אֶל־אֵשֶׁת אֲדֹנָיו הֵן אֲדֹנִי
לֹא־יָדַע אִתִּי מַה־בַּבָּיִת וְכֹל אֲשֶׁר־יֶשׁ־
לוֹ נָתַן בְּיָדִי:

8 But he refused. He said to his master's wife, "Look, with me here, my master gives no thought to anything in this house, and all that he owns he has placed in my hands.

ט אֵינֶנּוּ גָדוֹל בַּבַּיִת הַזֶּה מִמֶּנִּי וְלֹא־חָשַׂךְ
מִמֶּנִּי מְאוּמָה כִּי אִם־אוֹתָךְ בַּאֲשֶׁר
אַתְּ־אִשְׁתּוֹ וְאֵיךְ אֶעֱשֶׂה הָרָעָה הַגְּדֹלָה
הַזֹּאת וְחָטָאתִי לֵאלֹהִים:

9 He wields no more authority in this house than I, and he has withheld nothing from me except yourself, since you are his wife. How then could I do this most wicked thing, and sin before *Hashem*?"

Migrating cranes over the Hula lake nature reserve

39:1 A certain Egyptian The verse here labels Potiphar *ish mitzree* (איש מצרי), 'an Egyptian,' in contrast to *Yosef*, who is called *Ha'Ivri* (העברי), 'the Hebrew' (verse 14). Since we already know the nationalities of these individuals, why are the labels necessary? The Egyptians were known for their arrogance and condescension towards the nomadic tribes. Despite their prejudice, *Yosef* will rise in rank among them. He will succeed at every task presented to him, and subsequently find favor in the eyes of Potiphar, the Egyptian royal official. Only Divine Providence could bring about the success of a mere "Hebrew," as the next verse says "*Hashem* was with *Yosef*, and he was a successful man." *Yosef* demonstrates that when a person puts himself in the hands of God, he can succeed beyond expectation.

10 And much as she coaxed *Yosef* day after day, he did not yield to her request to lie beside her, to be with her.

11 One such day, he came into the house to do his work. None of the household being there inside,

12 she caught hold of him by his garment and said, "Lie with me!" But he left his garment in her hand and got away and fled outside.

13 When she saw that he had left it in her hand and had fled outside,

14 she called out to her servants and said to them, "Look, he had to bring us a Hebrew to dally with us! This one came to lie with me; but I screamed loud.

15 And when he heard me screaming at the top of my voice, he left his garment with me and got away and fled outside."

16 She kept his garment beside her, until his master came home.

17 Then she told him the same story, saying, "The Hebrew slave whom you brought into our house came to me to dally with me;

18 but when I screamed at the top of my voice, he left his garment with me and fled outside."

19 When his master heard the story that his wife told him, namely, "Thus and so your slave did to me," he was furious.

20 So *Yosef*'s master had him put in prison, where the king's prisoners were confined. But even while he was there in prison,

21 *Hashem* was with *Yosef*: He extended kindness to him and disposed the chief jailer favorably toward him.

22 The chief jailer put in *Yosef*'s charge all the prisoners who were in that prison, and he was the one to carry out everything that was done there.

23 The chief jailer did not supervise anything that was in *Yosef*'s charge, because *Hashem* was with him, and whatever he did *Hashem* made successful.

י וַיְהִי כְּדַבְּרָהּ אֶל־יוֹסֵף יוֹם יוֹם וְלֹא־שָׁמַע אֵלֶיהָ לִשְׁכַּב אֶצְלָהּ לִהְיוֹת עִמָּהּ:

יא וַיְהִי כְּהַיּוֹם הַזֶּה וַיָּבֹא הַבַּיְתָה לַעֲשׂוֹת מְלַאכְתּוֹ וְאֵין אִישׁ מֵאַנְשֵׁי הַבַּיִת שָׁם בַּבָּיִת:

יב וַתִּתְפְּשֵׂהוּ בְּבִגְדוֹ לֵאמֹר שִׁכְבָה עִמִּי וַיַּעֲזֹב בִּגְדוֹ בְּיָדָהּ וַיָּנָס וַיֵּצֵא הַחוּצָה:

יג וַיְהִי כִּרְאוֹתָהּ כִּי־עָזַב בִּגְדוֹ בְּיָדָהּ וַיָּנָס הַחוּצָה:

יד וַתִּקְרָא לְאַנְשֵׁי בֵיתָהּ וַתֹּאמֶר לָהֶם לֵאמֹר רְאוּ הֵבִיא לָנוּ אִישׁ עִבְרִי לְצַחֶק בָּנוּ בָּא אֵלַי לִשְׁכַּב עִמִּי וָאֶקְרָא בְּקוֹל גָּדוֹל:

טו וַיְהִי כְשָׁמְעוֹ כִּי־הֲרִימֹתִי קוֹלִי וָאֶקְרָא וַיַּעֲזֹב בִּגְדוֹ אֶצְלִי וַיָּנָס וַיֵּצֵא הַחוּצָה:

טז וַתַּנַּח בִּגְדוֹ אֶצְלָהּ עַד־בּוֹא אֲדֹנָיו אֶל־בֵּיתוֹ:

יז וַתְּדַבֵּר אֵלָיו כַּדְּבָרִים הָאֵלֶּה לֵאמֹר בָּא־אֵלַי הָעֶבֶד הָעִבְרִי אֲשֶׁר־הֵבֵאתָ לָּנוּ לְצַחֶק בִּי:

יח וַיְהִי כַּהֲרִימִי קוֹלִי וָאֶקְרָא וַיַּעֲזֹב בִּגְדוֹ אֶצְלִי וַיָּנָס הַחוּצָה:

יט וַיְהִי כִשְׁמֹעַ אֲדֹנָיו אֶת־דִּבְרֵי אִשְׁתּוֹ אֲשֶׁר דִּבְּרָה אֵלָיו לֵאמֹר כַּדְּבָרִים הָאֵלֶּה עָשָׂה לִי עַבְדֶּךָ וַיִּחַר אַפּוֹ:

כ וַיִּקַּח אֲדֹנֵי יוֹסֵף אֹתוֹ וַיִּתְּנֵהוּ אֶל־בֵּית הַסֹּהַר מְקוֹם אֲשֶׁר־אֲסוּרֵי [אֲסִירֵי] הַמֶּלֶךְ אֲסוּרִים וַיְהִי־שָׁם בְּבֵית הַסֹּהַר:

כא וַיְהִי יְהוָה אֶת־יוֹסֵף וַיֵּט אֵלָיו חָסֶד וַיִּתֵּן חִנּוֹ בְּעֵינֵי שַׂר בֵּית־הַסֹּהַר:

כב וַיִּתֵּן שַׂר בֵּית־הַסֹּהַר בְּיַד־יוֹסֵף אֵת כָּל־הָאֲסִירִם אֲשֶׁר בְּבֵית הַסֹּהַר וְאֵת כָּל־אֲשֶׁר עֹשִׂים שָׁם הוּא הָיָה עֹשֶׂה:

כג אֵין שַׂר בֵּית־הַסֹּהַר רֹאֶה אֶת־כָּל־מְאוּמָה בְּיָדוֹ בַּאֲשֶׁר יְהוָה אִתּוֹ וַאֲשֶׁר־הוּא עֹשֶׂה יְהוָה מַצְלִיחַ:

40 1 Some time later, the cupbearer and the baker of the king of Egypt gave offense to their lord the king of Egypt.

2 Pharaoh was angry with his two courtiers, the chief cupbearer and the chief baker,

3 and put them in custody, in the house of the chief steward, in the same prison house where *Yosef* was confined.

4 The chief steward assigned *Yosef* to them, and he attended them. When they had been in custody for some time,

5 both of them – the cupbearer and the baker of the king of Egypt, who were confined in the prison – dreamed in the same night, each his own dream and each dream with its own meaning.

6 When *Yosef* came to them in the morning, he saw that they were distraught.

7 He asked Pharaoh's courtiers, who were with him in custody in his master's house, saying, "Why do you appear downcast today?"

8 And they said to him, "We had dreams, and there is no one to interpret them." So *Yosef* said to them, "Surely *Hashem* can interpret! Tell me [your dreams]."

9 Then the chief cupbearer told his dream to *Yosef*. He said to him, "In my dream, there was a vine in front of me.

10 On the vine were three branches. It had barely budded, when out came its blossoms and its clusters ripened into grapes.

11 Pharaoh's cup was in my hand, and I took the grapes, pressed them into Pharaoh's cup, and placed the cup in Pharaoh's hand."

12 *Yosef* said to him, "This is its interpretation: The three branches are three days.

13 In three days Pharaoh will pardon you and restore you to your post; you will place Pharaoh's cup in his hand, as was your custom formerly when you were his cupbearer.

14 But think of me when all is well with you again, and do me the kindness of mentioning me to Pharaoh, so as to free me from this place.

א וַיְהִי אַחַר הַדְּבָרִים הָאֵלֶּה חָטְאוּ מַשְׁקֵה מֶלֶךְ־מִצְרַיִם וְהָאֹפֶה לַאֲדֹנֵיהֶם לְמֶלֶךְ מִצְרָיִם:

ב וַיִּקְצֹף פַּרְעֹה עַל שְׁנֵי סָרִיסָיו עַל שַׂר הַמַּשְׁקִים וְעַל שַׂר הָאוֹפִים:

ג וַיִּתֵּן אֹתָם בְּמִשְׁמַר בֵּית שַׂר הַטַּבָּחִים אֶל־בֵּית הַסֹּהַר מְקוֹם אֲשֶׁר יוֹסֵף אָסוּר שָׁם:

ד וַיִּפְקֹד שַׂר הַטַּבָּחִים אֶת־יוֹסֵף אִתָּם וַיְשָׁרֶת אֹתָם וַיִּהְיוּ יָמִים בְּמִשְׁמָר:

ה וַיַּחַלְמוּ חֲלוֹם שְׁנֵיהֶם אִישׁ חֲלֹמוֹ בְּלַיְלָה אֶחָד אִישׁ כְּפִתְרוֹן חֲלֹמוֹ הַמַּשְׁקֶה וְהָאֹפֶה אֲשֶׁר לְמֶלֶךְ מִצְרַיִם אֲשֶׁר אֲסוּרִים בְּבֵית הַסֹּהַר:

ו וַיָּבֹא אֲלֵיהֶם יוֹסֵף בַּבֹּקֶר וַיַּרְא אֹתָם וְהִנָּם זֹעֲפִים:

ז וַיִּשְׁאַל אֶת־סְרִיסֵי פַרְעֹה אֲשֶׁר אִתּוֹ בְמִשְׁמַר בֵּית אֲדֹנָיו לֵאמֹר מַדּוּעַ פְּנֵיכֶם רָעִים הַיּוֹם:

ח וַיֹּאמְרוּ אֵלָיו חֲלוֹם חָלַמְנוּ וּפֹתֵר אֵין אֹתוֹ וַיֹּאמֶר אֲלֵהֶם יוֹסֵף הֲלוֹא לֵאלֹהִים פִּתְרֹנִים סַפְּרוּ־נָא לִי:

ט וַיְסַפֵּר שַׂר־הַמַּשְׁקִים אֶת־חֲלֹמוֹ לְיוֹסֵף וַיֹּאמֶר לוֹ בַּחֲלוֹמִי וְהִנֵּה־גֶפֶן לְפָנָי:

י וּבַגֶּפֶן שְׁלֹשָׁה שָׂרִיגִם וְהִיא כְפֹרַחַת עָלְתָה נִצָּהּ הִבְשִׁילוּ אַשְׁכְּלֹתֶיהָ עֲנָבִים:

יא וְכוֹס פַּרְעֹה בְּיָדִי וָאֶקַּח אֶת־הָעֲנָבִים וָאֶשְׂחַט אֹתָם אֶל־כּוֹס פַּרְעֹה וָאֶתֵּן אֶת־הַכּוֹס עַל־כַּף פַּרְעֹה:

יב וַיֹּאמֶר לוֹ יוֹסֵף זֶה פִּתְרֹנוֹ שְׁלֹשֶׁת הַשָּׂרִגִים שְׁלֹשֶׁת יָמִים הֵם:

יג בְּעוֹד שְׁלֹשֶׁת יָמִים יִשָּׂא פַרְעֹה אֶת־רֹאשֶׁךָ וַהֲשִׁיבְךָ עַל־כַּנֶּךָ וְנָתַתָּ כוֹס־פַּרְעֹה בְּיָדוֹ כַּמִּשְׁפָּט הָרִאשׁוֹן אֲשֶׁר הָיִיתָ מַשְׁקֵהוּ:

יד כִּי אִם־זְכַרְתַּנִי אִתְּךָ כַּאֲשֶׁר יִיטַב לָךְ וְעָשִׂיתָ־נָּא עִמָּדִי חָסֶד וְהִזְכַּרְתַּנִי אֶל־פַּרְעֹה וְהוֹצֵאתַנִי מִן־הַבַּיִת הַזֶּה:

15 For in truth, I was kidnapped from the land of the Hebrews; nor have I done anything here that they should have put me in the dungeon."

טו כִּי־גֻנֹּב גֻּנַּבְתִּי מֵאֶרֶץ הָעִבְרִים וְגַם־פֹּה לֹא־עָשִׂיתִי מְאוּמָה כִּי־שָׂמוּ אֹתִי בַּבּוֹר:

kee gu-NOV gu-NAV-tee may-E-retz ha-iv-REEM v'-gam POH
lo a-SEE-tee m'-U-mah kee sa-MU o-TEE ba-BOR

16 When the chief baker saw how favorably he had interpreted, he said to *Yosef*, "In my dream, similarly, there were three openwork baskets on my head.

טז וַיַּרְא שַׂר־הָאֹפִים כִּי טוֹב פָּתָר וַיֹּאמֶר אֶל־יוֹסֵף אַף־אֲנִי בַּחֲלוֹמִי וְהִנֵּה שְׁלֹשָׁה סַלֵּי חֹרִי עַל־רֹאשִׁי:

17 In the uppermost basket were all kinds of food for Pharaoh that a baker prepares; and the birds were eating it out of the basket above my head."

יז וּבַסַּל הָעֶלְיוֹן מִכֹּל מַאֲכַל פַּרְעֹה מַעֲשֵׂה אֹפֶה וְהָעוֹף אֹכֵל אֹתָם מִן־הַסַּל מֵעַל רֹאשִׁי:

18 *Yosef* answered, "This is its interpretation: The three baskets are three days.

יח וַיַּעַן יוֹסֵף וַיֹּאמֶר זֶה פִּתְרֹנוֹ שְׁלֹשֶׁת הַסַּלִּים שְׁלֹשֶׁת יָמִים הֵם:

19 In three days Pharaoh will lift off your head and impale you upon a pole; and the birds will pick off your flesh."

יט בְּעוֹד שְׁלֹשֶׁת יָמִים יִשָּׂא פַרְעֹה אֶת־רֹאשְׁךָ מֵעָלֶיךָ וְתָלָה אוֹתְךָ עַל־עֵץ וְאָכַל הָעוֹף אֶת־בְּשָׂרְךָ מֵעָלֶיךָ:

20 On the third day – his birthday – Pharaoh made a banquet for all his officials, and he singled out his chief cupbearer and his chief baker from among his officials.

כ וַיְהִי בַּיּוֹם הַשְּׁלִישִׁי יוֹם הֻלֶּדֶת אֶת־פַּרְעֹה וַיַּעַשׂ מִשְׁתֶּה לְכָל־עֲבָדָיו וַיִּשָּׂא אֶת־רֹאשׁ שַׂר הַמַּשְׁקִים וְאֶת־רֹאשׁ שַׂר הָאֹפִים בְּתוֹךְ עֲבָדָיו:

21 He restored the chief cupbearer to his cupbearing, and he placed the cup in Pharaoh's hand;

כא וַיָּשֶׁב אֶת־שַׂר הַמַּשְׁקִים עַל־מַשְׁקֵהוּ וַיִּתֵּן הַכּוֹס עַל־כַּף פַּרְעֹה:

22 but the chief baker he impaled – just as *Yosef* had interpreted to them.

כב וְאֵת שַׂר הָאֹפִים תָּלָה כַּאֲשֶׁר פָּתַר לָהֶם יוֹסֵף:

23 Yet the chief cupbearer did not think of *Yosef*; he forgot him.

כג וְלֹא־זָכַר שַׂר־הַמַּשְׁקִים אֶת־יוֹסֵף וַיִּשְׁכָּחֵהוּ:

1 ¹ After two years' time, Pharaoh dreamed that he was standing by the Nile,

מא **א** וַיְהִי מִקֵּץ שְׁנָתַיִם יָמִים וּפַרְעֹה חֹלֵם וְהִנֵּה עֹמֵד עַל־הַיְאֹר:

² when out of the Nile there came up seven cows, handsome and sturdy, and they grazed in the reed grass.

ב וְהִנֵּה מִן־הַיְאֹר עֹלֹת שֶׁבַע פָּרוֹת יְפוֹת מַרְאֶה וּבְרִיאֹת בָּשָׂר וַתִּרְעֶינָה בָּאָחוּ:

40:15 I was kidnapped from the land of the Hebrews It is remarkable, notes Rabbi Samson Raphael Hirsch, that at this early date, the Land of Israel was already known as the 'Land of the Hebrews.' While the *Torah* chronicles and elaborates on events in the lives of the Patriarchs and other monumental occurrences that influence all of Jewish history, it provides little commentary on the surrounding nations' reactions to these events. Through this reference, though, it becomes clear that the Hebrew people was emerging as a recognized entity, important enough for the land to be referenced as theirs.

An Israeli flag flies over *Yerushalayim*

3 But presently, seven other cows came up from the Nile close behind them, ugly and gaunt, and stood beside the cows on the bank of the Nile;

ג וְהִנֵּה שֶׁבַע פָּרוֹת אֲחֵרוֹת עֹלוֹת אַחֲרֵיהֶן מִן־הַיְאֹר רָעוֹת מַרְאֶה וְדַקּוֹת בָּשָׂר וַתַּעֲמֹדְנָה אֵצֶל הַפָּרוֹת עַל־שְׂפַת הַיְאֹר:

4 and the ugly gaunt cows ate up the seven handsome sturdy cows. And Pharaoh awoke.

ד וַתֹּאכַלְנָה הַפָּרוֹת רָעוֹת הַמַּרְאֶה וְדַקֹּת הַבָּשָׂר אֵת שֶׁבַע הַפָּרוֹת יְפֹת הַמַּרְאֶה וְהַבְּרִיאֹת וַיִּיקַץ פַּרְעֹה:

5 He fell asleep and dreamed a second time: Seven ears of grain, solid and healthy, grew on a single stalk.

ה וַיִּישָׁן וַיַּחֲלֹם שֵׁנִית וְהִנֵּה שֶׁבַע שִׁבֳּלִים עֹלוֹת בְּקָנֶה אֶחָד בְּרִיאוֹת וְטֹבוֹת:

6 But close behind them sprouted seven ears, thin and scorched by the east wind.

ו וְהִנֵּה שֶׁבַע שִׁבֳּלִים דַּקּוֹת וּשְׁדוּפֹת קָדִים צֹמְחוֹת אַחֲרֵיהֶן:

7 And the thin ears swallowed up the seven solid and full ears. Then Pharaoh awoke: it was a dream!

ז וַתִּבְלַעְנָה הַשִּׁבֳּלִים הַדַּקּוֹת אֵת שֶׁבַע הַשִּׁבֳּלִים הַבְּרִיאוֹת וְהַמְּלֵאוֹת וַיִּיקַץ פַּרְעֹה וְהִנֵּה חֲלוֹם:

8 Next morning, his spirit was agitated, and he sent for all the magicians of Egypt, and all its wise men; and Pharaoh told them his dreams, but none could interpret them for Pharaoh.

ח וַיְהִי בַבֹּקֶר וַתִּפָּעֶם רוּחוֹ וַיִּשְׁלַח וַיִּקְרָא אֶת־כָּל־חַרְטֻמֵּי מִצְרַיִם וְאֶת־כָּל־חֲכָמֶיהָ וַיְסַפֵּר פַּרְעֹה לָהֶם אֶת־חֲלֹמוֹ וְאֵין־פּוֹתֵר אוֹתָם לְפַרְעֹה:

9 The chief cupbearer then spoke up and said to Pharaoh, "I must make mention today of my offenses.

ט וַיְדַבֵּר שַׂר הַמַּשְׁקִים אֶת־פַּרְעֹה לֵאמֹר אֶת־חֲטָאַי אֲנִי מַזְכִּיר הַיּוֹם:

10 Once Pharaoh was angry with his servants, and placed me in custody in the house of the chief steward, together with the chief baker.

י פַּרְעֹה קָצַף עַל־עֲבָדָיו וַיִּתֵּן אֹתִי בְּמִשְׁמַר בֵּית שַׂר הַטַּבָּחִים אֹתִי וְאֵת שַׂר הָאֹפִים:

11 We had dreams the same night, he and I, each of us a dream with a meaning of its own.

יא וַנַּחַלְמָה חֲלוֹם בְּלַיְלָה אֶחָד אֲנִי וָהוּא אִישׁ כְּפִתְרוֹן חֲלֹמוֹ חָלָמְנוּ:

12 A Hebrew youth was there with us, a servant of the chief steward; and when we told him our dreams, he interpreted them for us, telling each of the meaning of his dream.

יב וְשָׁם אִתָּנוּ נַעַר עִבְרִי עֶבֶד לְשַׂר הַטַּבָּחִים וַנְּסַפֶּר־לוֹ וַיִּפְתָּר־לָנוּ אֶת־חֲלֹמֹתֵינוּ אִישׁ כַּחֲלֹמוֹ פָּתָר:

13 And as he interpreted for us, so it came to pass: I was restored to my post, and the other was impaled."

יג וַיְהִי כַּאֲשֶׁר פָּתַר־לָנוּ כֵּן הָיָה אֹתִי הֵשִׁיב עַל־כַּנִּי וְאֹתוֹ תָלָה:

14 Thereupon Pharaoh sent for *Yosef*, and he was rushed from the dungeon. He had his hair cut and changed his clothes, and he appeared before Pharaoh.

יד וַיִּשְׁלַח פַּרְעֹה וַיִּקְרָא אֶת־יוֹסֵף וַיְרִיצֻהוּ מִן־הַבּוֹר וַיְגַלַּח וַיְחַלֵּף שִׂמְלֹתָיו וַיָּבֹא אֶל־פַּרְעֹה:

15 And Pharaoh said to *Yosef*, "I have had a dream, but no one can interpret it. Now I have heard it said of you that for you to hear a dream is to tell its meaning."

טו וַיֹּאמֶר פַּרְעֹה אֶל־יוֹסֵף חֲלוֹם חָלַמְתִּי וּפֹתֵר אֵין אֹתוֹ וַאֲנִי שָׁמַעְתִּי עָלֶיךָ לֵאמֹר תִּשְׁמַע חֲלוֹם לִפְתֹּר אֹתוֹ:

16 *Yosef* answered Pharaoh, saying, "Not I! *Hashem* will see to Pharaoh's welfare."

17 Then Pharaoh said to *Yosef*, "In my dream, I was standing on the bank of the Nile,

18 when out of the Nile came up seven sturdy and well-formed cows and grazed in the reed grass.

19 Presently there followed them seven other cows, scrawny, ill-formed, and emaciated – never had I seen their likes for ugliness in all the land of Egypt!

20 And the seven lean and ugly cows ate up the first seven cows, the sturdy ones;

21 but when they had consumed them, one could not tell that they had consumed them, for they looked just as bad as before. And I awoke.

22 In my other dream, I saw seven ears of grain, full and healthy, growing on a single stalk;

23 but right behind them sprouted seven ears, shriveled, thin, and scorched by the east wind.

24 And the thin ears swallowed the seven healthy ears. I have told my magicians, but none has an explanation for me."

25 And *Yosef* said to Pharaoh, "Pharaoh's dreams are one and the same: *Hashem* has told Pharaoh what He is about to do.

26 The seven healthy cows are seven years, and the seven healthy ears are seven years; it is the same dream.

27 The seven lean and ugly cows that followed are seven years, as are also the seven empty ears scorched by the east wind; they are seven years of famine.

28 It is just as I have told Pharaoh: *Hashem* has revealed to Pharaoh what He is about to do.

29 Immediately ahead are seven years of great abundance in all the land of Egypt.

30 After them will come seven years of famine, and all the abundance in the land of Egypt will be forgotten. As the land is ravaged by famine,

טז וַיַּעַן יוֹסֵף אֶת־פַּרְעֹה לֵאמֹר בִּלְעָדָי אֱלֹהִים יַעֲנֶה אֶת־שְׁלוֹם פַּרְעֹה:

יז וַיְדַבֵּר פַּרְעֹה אֶל־יוֹסֵף בַּחֲלֹמִי הִנְנִי עֹמֵד עַל־שְׂפַת הַיְאֹר:

יח וְהִנֵּה מִן־הַיְאֹר עֹלֹת שֶׁבַע פָּרוֹת בְּרִיאוֹת בָּשָׂר וִיפֹת תֹּאַר וַתִּרְעֶינָה בָּאָחוּ:

יט וְהִנֵּה שֶׁבַע־פָּרוֹת אֲחֵרוֹת עֹלוֹת אַחֲרֵיהֶן דַּלּוֹת וְרָעוֹת תֹּאַר מְאֹד וְרַקּוֹת בָּשָׂר לֹא־רָאִיתִי כָהֵנָּה בְּכָל־אֶרֶץ מִצְרַיִם לָרֹעַ:

כ וַתֹּאכַלְנָה הַפָּרוֹת הָרַקּוֹת וְהָרָעוֹת אֵת שֶׁבַע הַפָּרוֹת הָרִאשֹׁנוֹת הַבְּרִיאֹת:

כא וַתָּבֹאנָה אֶל־קִרְבֶּנָה וְלֹא נוֹדַע כִּי־בָאוּ אֶל־קִרְבֶּנָה וּמַרְאֵיהֶן רַע כַּאֲשֶׁר בַּתְּחִלָּה וָאִיקָץ:

כב וָאֵרֶא בַּחֲלֹמִי וְהִנֵּה שֶׁבַע שִׁבֳּלִים עֹלֹת בְּקָנֶה אֶחָד מְלֵאֹת וְטֹבוֹת:

כג וְהִנֵּה שֶׁבַע שִׁבֳּלִים צְנֻמוֹת דַּקּוֹת שְׁדֻפוֹת קָדִים צֹמְחוֹת אַחֲרֵיהֶם:

כד וַתִּבְלַעְןָ הַשִּׁבֳּלִים הַדַּקֹּת אֵת שֶׁבַע הַשִּׁבֳּלִים הַטֹּבוֹת וָאֹמַר אֶל־הַחַרְטֻמִּים וְאֵין מַגִּיד לִי:

כה וַיֹּאמֶר יוֹסֵף אֶל־פַּרְעֹה חֲלוֹם פַּרְעֹה אֶחָד הוּא אֵת אֲשֶׁר הָאֱלֹהִים עֹשֶׂה הִגִּיד לְפַרְעֹה:

כו שֶׁבַע פָּרֹת הַטֹּבֹת שֶׁבַע שָׁנִים הֵנָּה וְשֶׁבַע הַשִּׁבֳּלִים הַטֹּבֹת שֶׁבַע שָׁנִים הֵנָּה חֲלוֹם אֶחָד הוּא:

כז וְשֶׁבַע הַפָּרוֹת הָרַקּוֹת וְהָרָעֹת הָעֹלֹת אַחֲרֵיהֶן שֶׁבַע שָׁנִים הֵנָּה וְשֶׁבַע הַשִּׁבֳּלִים הָרֵקוֹת שְׁדֻפוֹת הַקָּדִים יִהְיוּ שֶׁבַע שְׁנֵי רָעָב:

כח הוּא הַדָּבָר אֲשֶׁר דִּבַּרְתִּי אֶל־פַּרְעֹה אֲשֶׁר הָאֱלֹהִים עֹשֶׂה הֶרְאָה אֶת־פַּרְעֹה:

כט הִנֵּה שֶׁבַע שָׁנִים בָּאוֹת שָׂבָע גָּדוֹל בְּכָל־אֶרֶץ מִצְרָיִם:

ל וְקָמוּ שֶׁבַע שְׁנֵי רָעָב אַחֲרֵיהֶן וְנִשְׁכַּח כָּל־הַשָּׂבָע בְּאֶרֶץ מִצְרָיִם וְכִלָּה הָרָעָב אֶת־הָאָרֶץ:

³¹ no trace of the abundance will be left in the land because of the famine thereafter, for it will be very severe.

לא וְלֹא־יִוָּדַע הַשָּׂבָע בָּאָרֶץ מִפְּנֵי הָרָעָב הַהוּא אַחֲרֵי־כֵן כִּי־כָבֵד הוּא מְאֹד:

³² As for Pharaoh having had the same dream twice, it means that the matter has been determined by *Hashem*, and that *Hashem* will soon carry it out.

לב וְעַל הִשָּׁנוֹת הַחֲלוֹם אֶל־פַּרְעֹה פַּעֲמָיִם כִּי־נָכוֹן הַדָּבָר מֵעִם הָאֱלֹהִים וּמְמַהֵר הָאֱלֹהִים לַעֲשֹׂתוֹ:

³³ "Accordingly, let Pharaoh find a man of discernment and wisdom, and set him over the land of Egypt.

לג וְעַתָּה יֵרֶא פַרְעֹה אִישׁ נָבוֹן וְחָכָם וִישִׁיתֵהוּ עַל־אֶרֶץ מִצְרָיִם:

³⁴ And let Pharaoh take steps to appoint overseers over the land, and organize the land of Egypt in the seven years of plenty.

לד יַעֲשֶׂה פַרְעֹה וְיַפְקֵד פְּקִדִים עַל־הָאָרֶץ וְחִמֵּשׁ אֶת־אֶרֶץ מִצְרַיִם בְּשֶׁבַע שְׁנֵי הַשָּׂבָע:

³⁵ Let all the food of these good years that are coming be gathered, and let the grain be collected under Pharaoh's authority as food to be stored in the cities.

לה וְיִקְבְּצוּ אֶת־כָּל־אֹכֶל הַשָּׁנִים הַטֹּבֹת הַבָּאֹת הָאֵלֶּה וְיִצְבְּרוּ־בָר תַּחַת יַד־פַּרְעֹה אֹכֶל בֶּעָרִים וְשָׁמָרוּ:

³⁶ Let that food be a reserve for the land for the seven years of famine which will come upon the land of Egypt, so that the land may not perish in the famine."

לו וְהָיָה הָאֹכֶל לְפִקָּדוֹן לָאָרֶץ לְשֶׁבַע שְׁנֵי הָרָעָב אֲשֶׁר תִּהְיֶיןָ בְּאֶרֶץ מִצְרָיִם וְלֹא־תִכָּרֵת הָאָרֶץ בָּרָעָב:

³⁷ The plan pleased Pharaoh and all his court

לז וַיִּיטַב הַדָּבָר בְּעֵינֵי פַרְעֹה וּבְעֵינֵי כָּל־עֲבָדָיו:

³⁸ And Pharaoh said to his courtiers, "Could we find another like him, a man in whom is the spirit of *Hashem*?"

לח וַיֹּאמֶר פַּרְעֹה אֶל־עֲבָדָיו הֲנִמְצָא כָזֶה אִישׁ אֲשֶׁר רוּחַ אֱלֹהִים בּוֹ:

³⁹ So Pharaoh said to *Yosef*, "Since *Hashem* has made all this known to you, there is none so discerning and wise as you.

לט וַיֹּאמֶר פַּרְעֹה אֶל־יוֹסֵף אַחֲרֵי הוֹדִיעַ אֱלֹהִים אוֹתְךָ אֶת־כָּל־זֹאת אֵין־נָבוֹן וְחָכָם כָּמוֹךָ:

⁴⁰ You shall be in charge of my court, and by your command shall all my people be directed; only with respect to the throne shall I be superior to you."

מ אַתָּה תִּהְיֶה עַל־בֵּיתִי וְעַל־פִּיךָ יִשַּׁק כָּל־עַמִּי רַק הַכִּסֵּא אֶגְדַּל מִמֶּךָּ:

⁴¹ Pharaoh further said to *Yosef*, "See, I put you in charge of all the land of Egypt."

מא וַיֹּאמֶר פַּרְעֹה אֶל־יוֹסֵף רְאֵה נָתַתִּי אֹתְךָ עַל כָּל־אֶרֶץ מִצְרָיִם:

⁴² And removing his signet ring from his hand, Pharaoh put it on *Yosef*'s hand; and he had him dressed in robes of fine linen, and put a gold chain about his neck.

מב וַיָּסַר פַּרְעֹה אֶת־טַבַּעְתּוֹ מֵעַל יָדוֹ וַיִּתֵּן אֹתָהּ עַל־יַד יוֹסֵף וַיַּלְבֵּשׁ אֹתוֹ בִּגְדֵי־שֵׁשׁ וַיָּשֶׂם רְבִד הַזָּהָב עַל־צַוָּארוֹ:

⁴³ He had him ride in the chariot of his second-in-command, and they cried before him, "Abrek!" Thus he placed him over all the land of Egypt.

מג וַיַּרְכֵּב אֹתוֹ בְּמִרְכֶּבֶת הַמִּשְׁנֶה אֲשֶׁר־לוֹ וַיִּקְרְאוּ לְפָנָיו אַבְרֵךְ וְנָתוֹן אֹתוֹ עַל כָּל־אֶרֶץ מִצְרָיִם:

⁴⁴ Pharaoh said to *Yosef*, "I am Pharaoh; yet without you, no one shall lift up hand or foot in all the land of Egypt."

מד וַיֹּאמֶר פַּרְעֹה אֶל־יוֹסֵף אֲנִי פַרְעֹה וּבִלְעָדֶיךָ לֹא־יָרִים אִישׁ אֶת־יָדוֹ וְאֶת־רַגְלוֹ בְּכָל־אֶרֶץ מִצְרָיִם:

⁴⁵ Pharaoh then gave *Yosef* the name Zaphenath-paneah; and he gave him for a wife Asenath daughter of Poti-phera, priest of On. Thus *Yosef* emerged in charge of the land of Egypt.

מה וַיִּקְרָא פַרְעֹה שֵׁם־יוֹסֵף צָפְנַת פַּעְנֵחַ וַיִּתֶּן־לוֹ אֶת־אָסְנַת בַּת־פּוֹטִי פֶרַע כֹּהֵן אֹן לְאִשָּׁה וַיֵּצֵא יוֹסֵף עַל־אֶרֶץ מִצְרָיִם:

⁴⁶ *Yosef* was thirty years old when he entered the service of Pharaoh king of Egypt. – Leaving Pharaoh's presence, *Yosef* traveled through all the land of Egypt.

מו וְיוֹסֵף בֶּן־שְׁלֹשִׁים שָׁנָה בְּעָמְדוֹ לִפְנֵי פַּרְעֹה מֶלֶךְ־מִצְרָיִם וַיֵּצֵא יוֹסֵף מִלִּפְנֵי פַרְעֹה וַיַּעֲבֹר בְּכָל־אֶרֶץ מִצְרָיִם:

⁴⁷ During the seven years of plenty, the land produced in abundance.

מז וַתַּעַשׂ הָאָרֶץ בְּשֶׁבַע שְׁנֵי הַשָּׂבָע לִקְמָצִים:

⁴⁸ And he gathered all the grain of the seven years that the land of Egypt was enjoying, and stored the grain in the cities; he put in each city the grain of the fields around it.

מח וַיִּקְבֹּץ אֶת־כָּל־אֹכֶל שֶׁבַע שָׁנִים אֲשֶׁר הָיוּ בְּאֶרֶץ מִצְרַיִם וַיִּתֶּן־אֹכֶל בֶּעָרִים אֹכֶל שְׂדֵה־הָעִיר אֲשֶׁר סְבִיבֹתֶיהָ נָתַן בְּתוֹכָהּ:

⁴⁹ So *Yosef* collected produce in very large quantity, like the sands of the sea, until he ceased to measure it, for it could not be measured.

מט וַיִּצְבֹּר יוֹסֵף בָּר כְּחוֹל הַיָּם הַרְבֵּה מְאֹד עַד כִּי־חָדַל לִסְפֹּר כִּי־אֵין מִסְפָּר:

⁵⁰ Before the years of famine came, *Yosef* became the father of two sons, whom Asenath daughter of Poti-phera, priest of On, bore to him.

נ וּלְיוֹסֵף יֻלַּד שְׁנֵי בָנִים בְּטֶרֶם תָּבוֹא שְׁנַת הָרָעָב אֲשֶׁר יָלְדָה־לּוֹ אָסְנַת בַּת־פּוֹטִי פֶרַע כֹּהֵן אוֹן:

⁵¹ *Yosef* named the first-born *Menashe*, meaning, "*Hashem* has made me forget completely my hardship and my parental home."

נא וַיִּקְרָא יוֹסֵף אֶת־שֵׁם הַבְּכוֹר מְנַשֶּׁה כִּי־נַשַּׁנִי אֱלֹהִים אֶת־כָּל־עֲמָלִי וְאֵת כָּל־בֵּית אָבִי:

⁵² And the second he named *Efraim*, meaning, "*Hashem* has made me fertile in the land of my affliction."

נב וְאֵת שֵׁם הַשֵּׁנִי קָרָא אֶפְרָיִם כִּי־הִפְרַנִי אֱלֹהִים בְּאֶרֶץ עָנְיִי:

*v'-AYT SHAYM ha-shay-NEE ka-RA ef-RA-yim kee
hif-RA-nee e-lo-HEEM b'-E-retz on-YEE*

⁵³ The seven years of abundance that the land of Egypt enjoyed came to an end,

נג וַתִּכְלֶינָה שֶׁבַע שְׁנֵי הַשָּׂבָע אֲשֶׁר הָיָה בְּאֶרֶץ מִצְרָיִם:

⁵⁴ and the seven years of famine set in, just as *Yosef* had foretold. There was famine in all lands, but throughout the land of Egypt there was bread.

נד וַתְּחִלֶּינָה שֶׁבַע שְׁנֵי הָרָעָב לָבוֹא כַּאֲשֶׁר אָמַר יוֹסֵף וַיְהִי רָעָב בְּכָל־הָאֲרָצוֹת וּבְכָל־אֶרֶץ מִצְרַיִם הָיָה לָחֶם:

41:52 ***Hashem* has made me forget completely my hardship** As the name of his first son indicates, *Yosef* is finally comforted after his troubling experience with his brothers. Yet, with the name of his second son, *Yosef* indicates that even after being appointed viceroy to Pharaoh, Egypt is still a land of affliction to him. Rabbi Yitzchak Abrabanel, a fifteenth century Bible commentator, points out that despite his elevated status, *Yosef* never forgot where he truly belonged. Though he was comforted over his loss, *Yosef* still yearned to return to his father's household in Eretz Yisrael.

Area of *Chevron*, where *Yosef's* family lived

⁵⁵ And when all the land of Egypt felt the hunger, the people cried out to Pharaoh for bread; and Pharaoh said to all the Egyptians, "Go to Jo-seph; whatever he tells you, you shall do."

נה וַתִּרְעַב כָּל־אֶרֶץ מִצְרַיִם וַיִּצְעַק הָעָם אֶל־פַּרְעֹה לַלָּחֶם וַיֹּאמֶר פַּרְעֹה לְכָל־מִצְרַיִם לְכוּ אֶל־יוֹסֵף אֲשֶׁר־יֹאמַר לָכֶם תַּעֲשׂוּ:

⁵⁶ Accordingly, when the famine became severe in the land of Egypt, *Yosef* laid open all that was within, and rationed out grain to the Egyptians. The famine, however, spread over the whole world.

נו וְהָרָעָב הָיָה עַל כָּל־פְּנֵי הָאָרֶץ וַיִּפְתַּח יוֹסֵף אֶת־כָּל־אֲשֶׁר בָּהֶם וַיִּשְׁבֹּר לְמִצְרַיִם וַיֶּחֱזַק הָרָעָב בְּאֶרֶץ מִצְרָיִם:

⁵⁷ So all the world came to *Yosef* in Egypt to procure rations, for the famine had become severe throughout the world.

נז וְכָל־הָאָרֶץ בָּאוּ מִצְרַיְמָה לִשְׁבֹּר אֶל־יוֹסֵף כִּי־חָזַק הָרָעָב בְּכָל־הָאָרֶץ:

42 ¹ When *Yaakov* saw that there were food rations to be had in Egypt, he said to his sons, "Why do you keep looking at one another?

ב א וַיַּרְא יַעֲקֹב כִּי יֶשׁ־שֶׁבֶר בְּמִצְרָיִם וַיֹּאמֶר יַעֲקֹב לְבָנָיו לָמָּה תִּתְרָאוּ:

² Now I hear," he went on, "that there are rations to be had in Egypt. Go down and procure rations for us there, that we may live and not die."

ב וַיֹּאמֶר הִנֵּה שָׁמַעְתִּי כִּי יֶשׁ־שֶׁבֶר בְּמִצְרָיִם רְדוּ־שָׁמָּה וְשִׁבְרוּ־לָנוּ מִשָּׁם וְנִחְיֶה וְלֹא נָמוּת:

³ So ten of *Yosef's* brothers went down to get grain rations in Egypt;

ג וַיֵּרְדוּ אֲחֵי־יוֹסֵף עֲשָׂרָה לִשְׁבֹּר בָּר מִמִּצְרָיִם:

⁴ for *Yaakov* did not send *Yosef's* brother *Binyamin* with his brothers, since he feared that he might meet with disaster.

ד וְאֶת־בִּנְיָמִין אֲחִי יוֹסֵף לֹא־שָׁלַח יַעֲקֹב אֶת־אֶחָיו כִּי אָמַר פֶּן־יִקְרָאֶנּוּ אָסוֹן:

⁵ Thus the sons of *Yisrael* were among those who came to procure rations, for the famine extended to the land of Canaan.

ה וַיָּבֹאוּ בְּנֵי יִשְׂרָאֵל לִשְׁבֹּר בְּתוֹךְ הַבָּאִים כִּי־הָיָה הָרָעָב בְּאֶרֶץ כְּנָעַן:

⁶ Now *Yosef* was the vizier of the land; it was he who dispensed rations to all the people of the land. And *Yosef's* brothers came and bowed low to him, with their faces to the ground.

ו וְיוֹסֵף הוּא הַשַּׁלִּיט עַל־הָאָרֶץ הוּא הַמַּשְׁבִּיר לְכָל־עַם הָאָרֶץ וַיָּבֹאוּ אֲחֵי יוֹסֵף וַיִּשְׁתַּחֲווּ־לוֹ אַפַּיִם אָרְצָה:

⁷ When *Yosef* saw his brothers, he recognized them; but he acted like a stranger toward them and spoke harshly to them. He asked them, "Where do you come from?" And they said, "From the land of Canaan, to procure food."

ז וַיַּרְא יוֹסֵף אֶת־אֶחָיו וַיַּכִּרֵם וַיִּתְנַכֵּר אֲלֵיהֶם וַיְדַבֵּר אִתָּם קָשׁוֹת וַיֹּאמֶר אֲלֵהֶם מֵאַיִן בָּאתֶם וַיֹּאמְרוּ מֵאֶרֶץ כְּנַעַן לִשְׁבָּר־אֹכֶל:

va-YAR yo-SAYF et e-KHAV va-ya-ki-RAYM va-yit-na-KAYR a-lay-HEM
vai-da-BAYR i-TAM ka-SHOT va-YO-mer a-lay-HEM may-A-yin
ba-TEM va-YO-m'-RU may-E-retz k'-NA-an lish-bor O-khel

42:7 From the land of *Canaan*, to procure food
Many commentators point out the incongruity between *Yosef's* question and the brothers' answer. *Yosef* asked only about their origin; why, then, did the brothers supply a reason for their travels? The question is strengthened by the fact that assumedly, their reason for coming to Egypt was self-evident. Rabbi Zalman Sorotzkin answers that

Sunrise over Masada

8 For though *Yosef* recognized his brothers, they did not recognize him.

ח וַיַּכֵּר יוֹסֵף אֶת־אֶחָיו וְהֵם לֹא הִכִּרֻהוּ:

9 Recalling the dreams that he had dreamed about them, *Yosef* said to them, "You are spies, you have come to see the land in its nakedness."

ט וַיִּזְכֹּר יוֹסֵף אֵת הַחֲלֹמוֹת אֲשֶׁר חָלַם לָהֶם וַיֹּאמֶר אֲלֵהֶם מְרַגְּלִים אַתֶּם לִרְאוֹת אֶת־עֶרְוַת הָאָרֶץ בָּאתֶם:

10 But they said to him, "No, my lord! Truly, your servants have come to procure food.

י וַיֹּאמְרוּ אֵלָיו לֹא אֲדֹנִי וַעֲבָדֶיךָ בָּאוּ לִשְׁבָּר־אֹכֶל:

11 We are all of us sons of the same man; we are honest men; your servants have never been spies!

יא כֻּלָּנוּ בְּנֵי אִישׁ־אֶחָד נָחְנוּ כֵּנִים אֲנַחְנוּ לֹא־הָיוּ עֲבָדֶיךָ מְרַגְּלִים:

12 And he said to them, "No, you have come to see the land in its nakedness!"

יב וַיֹּאמֶר אֲלֵהֶם לֹא כִּי־עֶרְוַת הָאָרֶץ בָּאתֶם לִרְאוֹת:

13 And they replied, "We your servants were twelve brothers, sons of a certain man in the land of Canaan; the youngest, however, is now with our father, and one is no more."

יג וַיֹּאמְרוּ שְׁנֵים עָשָׂר עֲבָדֶיךָ אַחִים אֲנַחְנוּ בְּנֵי אִישׁ־אֶחָד בְּאֶרֶץ כְּנָעַן וְהִנֵּה הַקָּטֹן אֶת־אָבִינוּ הַיּוֹם וְהָאֶחָד אֵינֶנּוּ:

14 But *Yosef* said to them, "It is just as I have told you: You are spies!

יד וַיֹּאמֶר אֲלֵהֶם יוֹסֵף הוּא אֲשֶׁר דִּבַּרְתִּי אֲלֵכֶם לֵאמֹר מְרַגְּלִים אַתֶּם:

15 By this you shall be put to the test: unless your youngest brother comes here, by Pharaoh, you shall not depart from this place!

טו בְּזֹאת תִּבָּחֵנוּ חֵי פַרְעֹה אִם־תֵּצְאוּ מִזֶּה כִּי אִם־בְּבוֹא אֲחִיכֶם הַקָּטֹן הֵנָּה:

16 Let one of you go and bring your brother, while the rest of you remain confined, that your words may be put to the test whether there is truth in you. Else, by Pharaoh, you are nothing but spies!"

טז שִׁלְחוּ מִכֶּם אֶחָד וְיִקַּח אֶת־אֲחִיכֶם וְאַתֶּם הֵאָסְרוּ וְיִבָּחֲנוּ דִּבְרֵיכֶם הַאֱמֶת אִתְּכֶם וְאִם־לֹא חֵי פַרְעֹה כִּי מְרַגְּלִים אַתֶּם:

17 And he confined them in the guardhouse for three days.

יז וַיֶּאֱסֹף אֹתָם אֶל־מִשְׁמָר שְׁלֹשֶׁת יָמִים:

18 On the third day *Yosef* said to them, "Do this and you shall live, for I am a *Hashem*-fearing man.

יח וַיֹּאמֶר אֲלֵהֶם יוֹסֵף בַּיּוֹם הַשְּׁלִישִׁי זֹאת עֲשׂוּ וִחְיוּ אֶת־הָאֱלֹהִים אֲנִי יָרֵא:

19 If you are honest men, let one of you brothers be held in your place of detention, while the rest of you go and take home rations for your starving households;

יט אִם־כֵּנִים אַתֶּם אֲחִיכֶם אֶחָד יֵאָסֵר בְּבֵית מִשְׁמַרְכֶם וְאַתֶּם לְכוּ הָבִיאוּ שֶׁבֶר רַעֲבוֹן בָּתֵּיכֶם:

20 but you must bring me your youngest brother, that your words may be verified and that you may not die." And they did accordingly.

כ וְאֶת־אֲחִיכֶם הַקָּטֹן תָּבִיאוּ אֵלַי וְיֵאָמְנוּ דִבְרֵיכֶם וְלֹא תָמוּתוּ וַיַּעֲשׂוּ־כֵן:

the brothers were accustomed to the need to apologize and offer an explanation for leaving the Holy Land of Israel. Although they could presume that the Egyptian would not think in these terms, they nevertheless felt the need to excuse their absence from their spiritual homeland.

²¹ They said to one another, "Alas, we are being punished on account of our brother, because we looked on at his anguish, yet paid no heed as he pleaded with us. That is why this distress has come upon us."

כא וַיֹּאמְרוּ אִישׁ אֶל־אָחִיו אֲבָל אֲשֵׁמִים אֲנַחְנוּ עַל־אָחִינוּ אֲשֶׁר רָאִינוּ צָרַת נַפְשׁוֹ בְּהִתְחַנְנוֹ אֵלֵינוּ וְלֹא שָׁמָעְנוּ עַל־כֵּן בָּאָה אֵלֵינוּ הַצָּרָה הַזֹּאת:

²² Then *Reuven* spoke up and said to them, "Did I not tell you, 'Do no wrong to the boy'? But you paid no heed. Now comes the reckoning for his blood."

כב וַיַּעַן רְאוּבֵן אֹתָם לֵאמֹר הֲלוֹא אָמַרְתִּי אֲלֵיכֶם לֵאמֹר אַל־תֶּחֶטְאוּ בַיֶּלֶד וְלֹא שְׁמַעְתֶּם וְגַם־דָּמוֹ הִנֵּה נִדְרָשׁ:

²³ They did not know that *Yosef* understood, for there was an interpreter between him and them.

כג וְהֵם לֹא יָדְעוּ כִּי שֹׁמֵעַ יוֹסֵף כִּי הַמֵּלִיץ בֵּינֹתָם:

²⁴ He turned away from them and wept. But he came back to them and spoke to them; and he took *Shimon* from among them and had him bound before their eyes.

כד וַיִּסֹּב מֵעֲלֵיהֶם וַיֵּבְךְּ וַיָּשָׁב אֲלֵהֶם וַיְדַבֵּר אֲלֵהֶם וַיִּקַּח מֵאִתָּם אֶת־שִׁמְעוֹן וַיֶּאֱסֹר אֹתוֹ לְעֵינֵיהֶם:

²⁵ Then *Yosef* gave orders to fill their bags with grain, return each one's money to his sack, and give them provisions for the journey; and this was done for them.

כה וַיְצַו יוֹסֵף וַיְמַלְאוּ אֶת־כְּלֵיהֶם בָּר וּלְהָשִׁיב כַּסְפֵּיהֶם אִישׁ אֶל־שַׂקּוֹ וְלָתֵת לָהֶם צֵדָה לַדָּרֶךְ וַיַּעַשׂ לָהֶם כֵּן:

²⁶ So they loaded their asses with the rations and departed from there.

כו וַיִּשְׂאוּ אֶת־שִׁבְרָם עַל־חֲמֹרֵיהֶם וַיֵּלְכוּ מִשָּׁם:

²⁷ As one of them was opening his sack to give feed to his ass at the night encampment, he saw his money right there at the mouth of his bag.

כז וַיִּפְתַּח הָאֶחָד אֶת־שַׂקּוֹ לָתֵת מִסְפּוֹא לַחֲמֹרוֹ בַּמָּלוֹן וַיַּרְא אֶת־כַּסְפּוֹ וְהִנֵּה־הוּא בְּפִי אַמְתַּחְתּוֹ:

²⁸ And he said to his brothers, "My money has been returned! It is here in my bag!" Their hearts sank; and, trembling, they turned to one another, saying, "What is this that *Hashem* has done to us?"

כח וַיֹּאמֶר אֶל־אֶחָיו הוּשַׁב כַּסְפִּי וְגַם הִנֵּה בְאַמְתַּחְתִּי וַיֵּצֵא לִבָּם וַיֶּחֶרְדוּ אִישׁ אֶל־אָחִיו לֵאמֹר מַה־זֹּאת עָשָׂה אֱלֹהִים לָנוּ:

²⁹ When they came to their father *Yaakov* in the land of Canaan, they told him all that had befallen them, saying,

כט וַיָּבֹאוּ אֶל־יַעֲקֹב אֲבִיהֶם אַרְצָה כְּנָעַן וַיַּגִּידוּ לוֹ אֵת כָּל־הַקֹּרֹת אֹתָם לֵאמֹר:

³⁰ "The man who is lord of the land spoke harshly to us and accused us of spying on the land.

ל דִּבֶּר הָאִישׁ אֲדֹנֵי הָאָרֶץ אִתָּנוּ קָשׁוֹת וַיִּתֵּן אֹתָנוּ כִּמְרַגְּלִים אֶת־הָאָרֶץ:

³¹ We said to him, 'We are honest men; we have never been spies!

לא וַנֹּאמֶר אֵלָיו כֵּנִים אֲנָחְנוּ לֹא הָיִינוּ מְרַגְּלִים:

³² There were twelve of us brothers, sons by the same father; but one is no more, and the youngest is now with our father in the land of Canaan.'

לב שְׁנֵים־עָשָׂר אֲנַחְנוּ אַחִים בְּנֵי אָבִינוּ הָאֶחָד אֵינֶנּוּ וְהַקָּטֹן הַיּוֹם אֶת־אָבִינוּ בְּאֶרֶץ כְּנָעַן:

³³ But the man who is lord of the land said to us, 'By this I shall know that you are honest men: leave one of your brothers with me, and take something for your starving households and be off.

לג וַיֹּאמֶר אֵלֵינוּ הָאִישׁ אֲדֹנֵי הָאָרֶץ בְּזֹאת אֵדַע כִּי כֵנִים אַתֶּם אֲחִיכֶם הָאֶחָד הַנִּיחוּ אִתִּי וְאֶת־רַעֲבוֹן בָּתֵּיכֶם קְחוּ וָלֵכוּ:

34 And bring your youngest brother to me, that I may know that you are not spies but honest men. I will then restore your brother to you, and you shall be free to move about in the land.'"

לד וְהָבִיאוּ אֶת־אֲחִיכֶם הַקָּטֹן אֵלַי וְאֵדְעָה כִּי לֹא מְרַגְּלִים אַתֶּם כִּי כֵנִים אַתֶּם אֶת־אֲחִיכֶם אֶתֵּן לָכֶם וְאֶת־הָאָרֶץ תִּסְחָרוּ:

35 As they were emptying their sacks, there, in each one's sack, was his money-bag! When they and their father saw their money-bags, they were dismayed.

לה וַיְהִי הֵם מְרִיקִים שַׂקֵּיהֶם וְהִנֵּה־אִישׁ צְרוֹר־כַּסְפּוֹ בְּשַׂקּוֹ וַיִּרְאוּ אֶת־צְרֹרוֹת כַּסְפֵּיהֶם הֵמָּה וַאֲבִיהֶם וַיִּירָאוּ:

36 Their father *Yaakov* said to them, "It is always me that you bereave: *Yosef* is no more and *Shimon* is no more, and now you would take away *Binyamin*. These things always happen to me!"

לו וַיֹּאמֶר אֲלֵהֶם יַעֲקֹב אֲבִיהֶם אֹתִי שִׁכַּלְתֶּם יוֹסֵף אֵינֶנּוּ וְשִׁמְעוֹן אֵינֶנּוּ וְאֶת־בִּנְיָמִן תִּקָּחוּ עָלַי הָיוּ כֻלָּנָה:

37 Then *Reuven* said to his father, "You may kill my two sons if I do not bring him back to you. Put him in my care, and I will return him to you."

לז וַיֹּאמֶר רְאוּבֵן אֶל־אָבִיו לֵאמֹר אֶת־שְׁנֵי בָנַי תָּמִית אִם־לֹא אֲבִיאֶנּוּ אֵלֶיךָ תְּנָה אֹתוֹ עַל־יָדִי וַאֲנִי אֲשִׁיבֶנּוּ אֵלֶיךָ:

38 But he said, "My son must not go down with you, for his brother is dead and he alone is left. If he meets with disaster on the journey you are taking, you will send my white head down to Sheol in grief."

לח וַיֹּאמֶר לֹא־יֵרֵד בְּנִי עִמָּכֶם כִּי־אָחִיו מֵת וְהוּא לְבַדּוֹ נִשְׁאָר וּקְרָאָהוּ אָסוֹן בַּדֶּרֶךְ אֲשֶׁר תֵּלְכוּ־בָהּ וְהוֹרַדְתֶּם אֶת־שֵׂיבָתִי בְּיָגוֹן שְׁאוֹלָה:

43 1 But the famine in the land was severe.

מג א וְהָרָעָב כָּבֵד בָּאָרֶץ:

2 And when they had eaten up the rations which they had brought from Egypt, their father said to them, "Go again and procure some food for us."

ב וַיְהִי כַּאֲשֶׁר כִּלּוּ לֶאֱכֹל אֶת־הַשֶּׁבֶר אֲשֶׁר הֵבִיאוּ מִמִּצְרָיִם וַיֹּאמֶר אֲלֵיהֶם אֲבִיהֶם שֻׁבוּ שִׁבְרוּ־לָנוּ מְעַט־אֹכֶל:

3 But *Yehuda* said to him, "The man warned us, 'Do not let me see your faces unless your brother is with you.'

ג וַיֹּאמֶר אֵלָיו יְהוּדָה לֵאמֹר הָעֵד הֵעִד בָּנוּ הָאִישׁ לֵאמֹר לֹא־תִרְאוּ פָנַי בִּלְתִּי אֲחִיכֶם אִתְּכֶם:

4 If you will let our brother go with us, we will go down and procure food for you;

ד אִם־יֶשְׁךָ מְשַׁלֵּחַ אֶת־אָחִינוּ אִתָּנוּ נֵרְדָה וְנִשְׁבְּרָה לְךָ אֹכֶל:

5 but if you will not let him go, we will not go down, for the man said to us, 'Do not let me see your faces unless your brother is with you.'"

ה וְאִם־אֵינְךָ מְשַׁלֵּחַ לֹא נֵרֵד כִּי־הָאִישׁ אָמַר אֵלֵינוּ לֹא־תִרְאוּ פָנַי בִּלְתִּי אֲחִיכֶם אִתְּכֶם:

6 And *Yisrael* said, "Why did you serve me so ill as to tell the man that you had another brother?"

ו וַיֹּאמֶר יִשְׂרָאֵל לָמָה הֲרֵעֹתֶם לִי לְהַגִּיד לָאִישׁ הַעוֹד לָכֶם אָח:

7 They replied, "But the man kept asking about us and our family, saying, 'Is your father still living? Have you another brother?' And we answered him accordingly. How were we to know that he would say, 'Bring your brother here'?"

ז וַיֹּאמְרוּ שָׁאוֹל שָׁאַל־הָאִישׁ לָנוּ וּלְמוֹלַדְתֵּנוּ לֵאמֹר הַעוֹד אֲבִיכֶם חַי הֲיֵשׁ לָכֶם אָח וַנַּגֶּד־לוֹ עַל־פִּי הַדְּבָרִים הָאֵלֶּה הֲיָדוֹעַ נֵדַע כִּי יֹאמַר הוֹרִידוּ אֶת־אֲחִיכֶם:

8 Then *Yehuda* said to his father *Yisrael*, "Send the boy in my care, and let us be on our way, that we may live and not die – you and we and our children.

ח וַיֹּאמֶר יְהוּדָה אֶל־יִשְׂרָאֵל אָבִיו שִׁלְחָה הַנַּעַר אִתִּי וְנָקוּמָה וְנֵלֵכָה וְנִחְיֶה וְלֹא נָמוּת גַּם־אֲנַחְנוּ גַם־אַתָּה גַּם־טַפֵּנוּ:

9 I myself will be surety for him; you may hold me responsible: if I do not bring him back to you and set him before you, I shall stand guilty before you forever.

ט אָנֹכִי אֶעֶרְבֶנּוּ מִיָּדִי תְּבַקְשֶׁנּוּ אִם־לֹא הֲבִיאֹתִיו אֵלֶיךָ וְהִצַּגְתִּיו לְפָנֶיךָ וְחָטָאתִי לְךָ כָּל־הַיָּמִים:

10 For we could have been there and back twice if we had not dawdled."

י כִּי לוּלֵא הִתְמַהְמָהְנוּ כִּי־עַתָּה שַׁבְנוּ זֶה פַעֲמָיִם:

11 Then their father *Yisrael* said to them, "If it must be so, do this: take some of the choice products of the land in your baggage, and carry them down as a gift for the man – some balm and some honey, gum, ladanum, pistachio nuts, and almonds.

יא וַיֹּאמֶר אֲלֵהֶם יִשְׂרָאֵל אֲבִיהֶם אִם־כֵּן אֵפוֹא זֹאת עֲשׂוּ קְחוּ מִזִּמְרַת הָאָרֶץ בִּכְלֵיכֶם וְהוֹרִידוּ לָאִישׁ מִנְחָה מְעַט צֳרִי וּמְעַט דְּבַשׁ נְכֹאת וָלֹט בָּטְנִים וּשְׁקֵדִים:

va-YO-mer a-lay-HEM yis-ra-AYL a-vee-HEM im KAYN ay-FO ZOT a-SU k'-KHU mi-zim-RAT ha-A-retz bikh-lay-KHEM v'-ho-REE-du la-EESH min-KHAH m'-AT tzo-REE um-AT d'-VASH n'-KHOT va-LOT bo-t'-NEEM ush-kay-DEEM

12 And take with you double the money, carrying back with you the money that was replaced in the mouths of your bags; perhaps it was a mistake.

יב וְכֶסֶף מִשְׁנֶה קְחוּ בְיֶדְכֶם וְאֶת־הַכֶּסֶף הַמּוּשָׁב בְּפִי אַמְתְּחֹתֵיכֶם תָּשִׁיבוּ בְיֶדְכֶם אוּלַי מִשְׁגֶּה הוּא:

13 Take your brother too; and go back at once to the man.

יג וְאֶת־אֲחִיכֶם קָחוּ וְקוּמוּ שׁוּבוּ אֶל־הָאִישׁ:

14 And may *El Shaddai* dispose the man to mercy toward you, that he may release to you your other brother, as well as *Binyamin*. As for me, if I am to be bereaved, I shall be bereaved."

יד וְאֵל שַׁדַּי יִתֵּן לָכֶם רַחֲמִים לִפְנֵי הָאִישׁ וְשִׁלַּח לָכֶם אֶת־אֲחִיכֶם אַחֵר וְאֶת־בִּנְיָמִין וַאֲנִי כַּאֲשֶׁר שָׁכֹלְתִּי שָׁכָלְתִּי:

15 So the men took that gift, and they took with them double the money, as well as *Binyamin*. They made their way down to Egypt, where they presented themselves to *Yosef*.

טו וַיִּקְחוּ הָאֲנָשִׁים אֶת־הַמִּנְחָה הַזֹּאת וּמִשְׁנֶה־כֶּסֶף לָקְחוּ בְיָדָם וְאֶת־בִּנְיָמִן וַיָּקֻמוּ וַיֵּרְדוּ מִצְרַיִם וַיַּעַמְדוּ לִפְנֵי יוֹסֵף:

16 When *Yosef* saw *Binyamin* with them, he said to his house steward, "Take the men into the house; slaughter and prepare an animal, for the men will dine with me at noon."

טז וַיַּרְא יוֹסֵף אִתָּם אֶת־בִּנְיָמִין וַיֹּאמֶר לַאֲשֶׁר עַל־בֵּיתוֹ הָבֵא אֶת־הָאֲנָשִׁים הַבָּיְתָה וּטְבֹחַ טֶבַח וְהָכֵן כִּי אִתִּי יֹאכְלוּ הָאֲנָשִׁים בַּצָּהֳרָיִם:

17 The man did as *Yosef* said, and he brought the men into *Yosef*'s house.

יז וַיַּעַשׂ הָאִישׁ כַּאֲשֶׁר אָמַר יוֹסֵף וַיָּבֵא הָאִישׁ אֶת־הָאֲנָשִׁים בֵּיתָה יוֹסֵף:

Fruit and nut stand
in *Yerushalayim*

43:11 Carry them down as a gift for the man *Yaakov* commands his sons to bring an offering to Pharaoh's viceroy of some choice fruits from the land. A *mincha* (מנחה), 'gift,' says Rabbi Samson Raphael Hirsch, indicates a present that benefits the giver more than the receiver. Obviously, a gift could provide a great benefit to the sons of *Yaakov*, if it will cause the viceroy to view them with favor. In addition, as they again descend to Egypt, this particular gift carries the added benefit of reminding them of their homeland and its many blessings. Though it is sometimes necessary to leave *Eretz Yisrael*, it should always be on the forefront of one's mind.

18 But the men were frightened at being brought into *Yosef*'s house. "It must be," they thought, "because of the money replaced in our bags the first time that we have been brought inside, as a pretext to attack us and seize us as slaves, with our pack animals."

יח וַיִּירְאוּ הָאֲנָשִׁים כִּי הוּבְאוּ בֵּית יוֹסֵף וַיֹּאמְרוּ עַל־דְּבַר הַכֶּסֶף הַשָּׁב בְּאַמְתְּחֹתֵינוּ בַּתְּחִלָּה אֲנַחְנוּ מוּבָאִים לְהִתְגֹּלֵל עָלֵינוּ וּלְהִתְנַפֵּל עָלֵינוּ וְלָקַחַת אֹתָנוּ לַעֲבָדִים וְאֶת־חֲמֹרֵינוּ:

19 So they went up to *Yosef*'s house steward and spoke to him at the entrance of the house.

יט וַיִּגְּשׁוּ אֶל־הָאִישׁ אֲשֶׁר עַל־בֵּית יוֹסֵף וַיְדַבְּרוּ אֵלָיו פֶּתַח הַבָּיִת:

20 "If you please, my lord," they said, "we came down once before to procure food.

כ וַיֹּאמְרוּ בִּי אֲדֹנִי יָרֹד יָרַדְנוּ בַּתְּחִלָּה לִשְׁבָּר־אֹכֶל:

21 But when we arrived at the night encampment and opened our bags, there was each one's money in the mouth of his bag, our money in full. So we have brought it back with us.

כא וַיְהִי כִּי־בָאנוּ אֶל־הַמָּלוֹן וַנִּפְתְּחָה אֶת־אַמְתְּחֹתֵינוּ וְהִנֵּה כֶסֶף־אִישׁ בְּפִי אַמְתַּחְתּוֹ כַּסְפֵּנוּ בְּמִשְׁקָלוֹ וַנָּשֶׁב אֹתוֹ בְּיָדֵנוּ:

22 And we have brought down with us other money to procure food. We do not know who put the money in our bags."

כב וְכֶסֶף אַחֵר הוֹרַדְנוּ בְיָדֵנוּ לִשְׁבָּר־אֹכֶל לֹא יָדַעְנוּ מִי־שָׂם כַּסְפֵּנוּ בְּאַמְתְּחֹתֵינוּ:

23 He replied, "All is well with you; do not be afraid. Your God, the God of your father, must have put treasure in your bags for you. I got your payment." And he brought out *Shimon* to them.

כג וַיֹּאמֶר שָׁלוֹם לָכֶם אַל־תִּירָאוּ אֱלֹהֵיכֶם וֵאלֹהֵי אֲבִיכֶם נָתַן לָכֶם מַטְמוֹן בְּאַמְתְּחֹתֵיכֶם כַּסְפְּכֶם בָּא אֵלָי וַיּוֹצֵא אֲלֵהֶם אֶת־שִׁמְעוֹן:

24 Then the man brought the men into *Yosef*'s house; he gave them water to bathe their feet, and he provided feed for their asses.

כד וַיָּבֵא הָאִישׁ אֶת־הָאֲנָשִׁים בֵּיתָה יוֹסֵף וַיִּתֶּן־מַיִם וַיִּרְחֲצוּ רַגְלֵיהֶם וַיִּתֵּן מִסְפּוֹא לַחֲמֹרֵיהֶם:

25 They laid out their gifts to await *Yosef*'s arrival at noon, for they had heard that they were to dine there.

כה וַיָּכִינוּ אֶת־הַמִּנְחָה עַד־בּוֹא יוֹסֵף בַּצָּהֳרָיִם כִּי שָׁמְעוּ כִּי־שָׁם יֹאכְלוּ לָחֶם:

26 When *Yosef* came home, they presented to him the gifts that they had brought with them into the house, bowing low before him to the ground.

כו וַיָּבֹא יוֹסֵף הַבַּיְתָה וַיָּבִיאוּ לוֹ אֶת־הַמִּנְחָה אֲשֶׁר־בְּיָדָם הַבָּיְתָה וַיִּשְׁתַּחֲווּ־לוֹ אָרְצָה:

27 He greeted them, and he said, "How is your aged father of whom you spoke? Is he still in good health?"

כז וַיִּשְׁאַל לָהֶם לְשָׁלוֹם וַיֹּאמֶר הֲשָׁלוֹם אֲבִיכֶם הַזָּקֵן אֲשֶׁר אֲמַרְתֶּם הַעוֹדֶנּוּ חָי:

28 They replied, "It is well with your servant our father; he is still in good health." And they bowed and made obeisance.

כח וַיֹּאמְרוּ שָׁלוֹם לְעַבְדְּךָ לְאָבִינוּ עוֹדֶנּוּ חָי וַיִּקְּדוּ וישתחו [וַיִּשְׁתַּחֲווּ:]

29 Looking about, he saw his brother *Binyamin*, his mother's son, and asked, "Is this your youngest brother of whom you spoke to me?" And he went on, "May *Hashem* be gracious to you, my boy."

כט וַיִּשָּׂא עֵינָיו וַיַּרְא אֶת־בִּנְיָמִין אָחִיו בֶּן־אִמּוֹ וַיֹּאמֶר הֲזֶה אֲחִיכֶם הַקָּטֹן אֲשֶׁר אֲמַרְתֶּם אֵלָי וַיֹּאמַר אֱלֹהִים יָחְנְךָ בְּנִי:

30 With that, *Yosef* hurried out, for he was overcome with feeling toward his brother and was on the verge of tears; he went into a room and wept there.

ל וַיְמַהֵר יוֹסֵף כִּי־נִכְמְרוּ רַחֲמָיו אֶל־אָחִיו וַיְבַקֵּשׁ לִבְכּוֹת וַיָּבֹא הַחַדְרָה וַיֵּבְךְּ שָׁמָּה:

31 Then he washed his face, reappeared, and – now in control of himself – gave the order, "Serve the meal."

לא וַיִּרְחַץ פָּנָיו וַיֵּצֵא וַיִּתְאַפַּק וַיֹּאמֶר שִׂימוּ לָחֶם:

32 They served him by himself, and them by themselves, and the Egyptians who ate with him by themselves; for the Egyptians could not dine with the Hebrews, since that would be abhorrent to the Egyptians.

לב וַיָּשִׂימוּ לוֹ לְבַדּוֹ וְלָהֶם לְבַדָּם וְלַמִּצְרִים הָאֹכְלִים אִתּוֹ לְבַדָּם כִּי לֹא יוּכְלוּן הַמִּצְרִים לֶאֱכֹל אֶת־הָעִבְרִים לֶחֶם כִּי־תוֹעֵבָה הִוא לְמִצְרָיִם:

33 As they were seated by his direction, from the oldest in the order of his seniority to the youngest in the order of his youth, the men looked at one another in astonishment.

לג וַיֵּשְׁבוּ לְפָנָיו הַבְּכֹר כִּבְכֹרָתוֹ וְהַצָּעִיר כִּצְעִרָתוֹ וַיִּתְמְהוּ הָאֲנָשִׁים אִישׁ אֶל־רֵעֵהוּ:

34 Portions were served them from his table; but *Binyamin*'s portion was several times that of anyone else. And they drank their fill with him.

לד וַיִּשָּׂא מַשְׂאֹת מֵאֵת פָּנָיו אֲלֵהֶם וַתֵּרֶב מַשְׂאַת בִּנְיָמִן מִמַּשְׂאֹת כֻּלָּם חָמֵשׁ יָדוֹת וַיִּשְׁתּוּ וַיִּשְׁכְּרוּ עִמּוֹ:

44 1 Then he instructed his house steward as follows, "Fill the men's bags with food, as much as they can carry, and put each one's money in the mouth of his bag.

ד א וַיְצַו אֶת־אֲשֶׁר עַל־בֵּיתוֹ לֵאמֹר מַלֵּא אֶת־אַמְתְּחֹת הָאֲנָשִׁים אֹכֶל כַּאֲשֶׁר יוּכְלוּן שְׂאֵת וְשִׂים כֶּסֶף־אִישׁ בְּפִי אַמְתַּחְתּוֹ:

2 Put my silver goblet in the mouth of the bag of the youngest one, together with his money for the rations." And he did as *Yosef* told him.

ב וְאֶת־גְּבִיעִי גְּבִיעַ הַכֶּסֶף תָּשִׂים בְּפִי אַמְתַּחַת הַקָּטֹן וְאֵת כֶּסֶף שִׁבְרוֹ וַיַּעַשׂ כִּדְבַר יוֹסֵף אֲשֶׁר דִּבֵּר:

3 With the first light of morning, the men were sent off with their pack animals.

ג הַבֹּקֶר אוֹר וְהָאֲנָשִׁים שֻׁלְּחוּ הֵמָּה וַחֲמֹרֵיהֶם:

4 They had just left the city and had not gone far, when *Yosef* said to his steward, "Up, go after the men! And when you overtake them, say to them, 'Why did you repay good with evil?

ד הֵם יָצְאוּ אֶת־הָעִיר לֹא הִרְחִיקוּ וְיוֹסֵף אָמַר לַאֲשֶׁר עַל־בֵּיתוֹ קוּם רְדֹף אַחֲרֵי הָאֲנָשִׁים וְהִשַּׂגְתָּם וְאָמַרְתָּ אֲלֵהֶם לָמָּה שִׁלַּמְתֶּם רָעָה תַּחַת טוֹבָה:

5 It is the very one from which my master drinks and which he uses for divination. It was a wicked thing for you to do!'"

ה הֲלוֹא זֶה אֲשֶׁר יִשְׁתֶּה אֲדֹנִי בּוֹ וְהוּא נַחֵשׁ יְנַחֵשׁ בּוֹ הֲרֵעֹתֶם אֲשֶׁר עֲשִׂיתֶם:

6 He overtook them and spoke those words to them.

ו וַיַּשִּׂגֵם וַיְדַבֵּר אֲלֵהֶם אֶת־הַדְּבָרִים הָאֵלֶּה:

7 And they said to him, "Why does my lord say such things? Far be it from your servants to do anything of the kind!

ז וַיֹּאמְרוּ אֵלָיו לָמָּה יְדַבֵּר אֲדֹנִי כַּדְּבָרִים הָאֵלֶּה חָלִילָה לַעֲבָדֶיךָ מֵעֲשׂוֹת כַּדָּבָר הַזֶּה:

8 Here we brought back to you from the land of Canaan the money that we found in the mouths of our bags. How then could we have stolen any silver or gold from your master's house!

ח הֵן כֶּסֶף אֲשֶׁר מָצָאנוּ בְּפִי אַמְתְּחֹתֵינוּ הֱשִׁיבֹנוּ אֵלֶיךָ מֵאֶרֶץ כְּנָעַן וְאֵיךְ נִגְנֹב מִבֵּית אֲדֹנֶיךָ כֶּסֶף אוֹ זָהָב:

> HAYN KE-sef a-SHER ma-TZA-nu b'-FEE am-t'-kho-TAY-nu
> he-shee-VO-nu ay-LE-kha may-E-retz k'-NA-an v'-AYKH
> nig-NOV mi-BAYT a-do-NE-kha KE-sef O za-HAV

9 Whichever of your servants it is found with shall die; the rest of us, moreover, shall become slaves to my lord."

ט אֲשֶׁר יִמָּצֵא אִתּוֹ מֵעֲבָדֶיךָ וָמֵת וְגַם־ אֲנַחְנוּ נִהְיֶה לַאדֹנִי לַעֲבָדִים:

10 He replied, "Although what you are proposing is right, only the one with whom it is found shall be my slave; but the rest of you shall go free."

י וַיֹּאמֶר גַּם־עַתָּה כְדִבְרֵיכֶם כֶּן־הוּא אֲשֶׁר יִמָּצֵא אִתּוֹ יִהְיֶה־לִּי עָבֶד וְאַתֶּם תִּהְיוּ נְקִיִּם:

11 So each one hastened to lower his bag to the ground, and each one opened his bag.

יא וַיְמַהֲרוּ וַיּוֹרִדוּ אִישׁ אֶת־אַמְתַּחְתּוֹ אָרְצָה וַיִּפְתְּחוּ אִישׁ אַמְתַּחְתּוֹ:

12 He searched, beginning with the oldest and ending with the youngest; and the goblet turned up in *Binyamin*'s bag.

יב וַיְחַפֵּשׂ בַּגָּדוֹל הֵחֵל וּבַקָּטֹן כִּלָּה וַיִּמָּצֵא הַגָּבִיעַ בְּאַמְתַּחַת בִּנְיָמִן:

13 At this they rent their clothes. Each reloaded his pack animal, and they returned to the city.

יג וַיִּקְרְעוּ שִׂמְלֹתָם וַיַּעֲמֹס אִישׁ עַל־ חֲמֹרוֹ וַיָּשֻׁבוּ הָעִירָה:

14 When *Yehuda* and his brothers reentered the house of *Yosef*, who was still there, they threw themselves on the ground before him.

יד וַיָּבֹא יְהוּדָה וְאֶחָיו בֵּיתָה יוֹסֵף וְהוּא עוֹדֶנּוּ שָׁם וַיִּפְּלוּ לְפָנָיו אָרְצָה:

15 *Yosef* said to them, "What is this deed that you have done? Do you not know that a man like me practices divination?"

טו וַיֹּאמֶר לָהֶם יוֹסֵף מָה־הַמַּעֲשֶׂה הַזֶּה אֲשֶׁר עֲשִׂיתֶם הֲלוֹא יְדַעְתֶּם כִּי־נַחֵשׁ יְנַחֵשׁ אִישׁ אֲשֶׁר כָּמֹנִי:

16 *Yehuda* replied, "What can we say to my lord? How can we plead, how can we prove our innocence? *Hashem* has uncovered the crime of your servants. Here we are, then, slaves of my lord, the rest of us as much as he in whose possession the goblet was found."

טז וַיֹּאמֶר יְהוּדָה מַה־נֹּאמַר לַאדֹנִי מַה־ נְּדַבֵּר וּמַה־נִּצְטַדָּק הָאֱלֹהִים מָצָא אֶת־עֲוֹן עֲבָדֶיךָ הִנֶּנּוּ עֲבָדִים לַאדֹנִי גַּם־ אֲנַחְנוּ גַּם אֲשֶׁר־נִמְצָא הַגָּבִיעַ בְּיָדוֹ:

17 But he replied, "Far be it from me to act thus! Only he in whose possession the goblet was found shall be my slave; the rest of you go back in peace to your father."

יז וַיֹּאמֶר חָלִילָה לִּי מֵעֲשׂוֹת זֹאת הָאִישׁ אֲשֶׁר נִמְצָא הַגָּבִיעַ בְּיָדוֹ הוּא יִהְיֶה־לִּי עָבֶד וְאַתֶּם עֲלוּ לְשָׁלוֹם אֶל־אֲבִיכֶם:

44:8 From the land of *Canaan* The brothers attempt to exonerate themselves from the accusations of theft by mentioning that they had already returned the extra money they found in their sacks after the previous trip. Why must the brothers specify that they returned the money from the land of Canaan? It seems that in the brothers' minds, this detail adds a further verification of their honesty. As they brought the money back from the Land of Israel, known for its spiritual heights, they must surely have noble intentions. Since antiquity, *Eretz Yisrael* has been synonymous with morality, and the land itself demands a high level of ethical responsibility from its inhabitants.

Rabbi Tuly Weisz helping Israeli victims of terror

18 Then *Yehuda* went up to him and said, "Please, my lord, let your servant appeal to my lord, and do not be impatient with your servant, you who are the equal of Pharaoh.

יח וַיִּגַּשׁ אֵלָיו יְהוּדָה וַיֹּאמֶר בִּי אֲדֹנִי יְדַבֶּר־נָא עַבְדְּךָ דָבָר בְּאָזְנֵי אֲדֹנִי וְאַל־יִחַר אַפְּךָ בְּעַבְדֶּךָ כִּי כָמוֹךָ כְּפַרְעֹה:

19 My lord asked his servants, 'Have you a father or another brother?'

יט אֲדֹנִי שָׁאַל אֶת־עֲבָדָיו לֵאמֹר הֲיֵשׁ־לָכֶם אָב אוֹ־אָח:

20 We told my lord, 'We have an old father, and there is a child of his old age, the youngest; his full brother is dead, so that he alone is left of his mother, and his father dotes on him.'

כ וַנֹּאמֶר אֶל־אֲדֹנִי יֶשׁ־לָנוּ אָב זָקֵן וְיֶלֶד זְקֻנִים קָטָן וְאָחִיו מֵת וַיִּוָּתֵר הוּא לְבַדּוֹ לְאִמּוֹ וְאָבִיו אֲהֵבוֹ:

21 Then you said to your servants, 'Bring him down to me, that I may set eyes on him.'

כא וַתֹּאמֶר אֶל־עֲבָדֶיךָ הוֹרִדֻהוּ אֵלָי וְאָשִׂימָה עֵינִי עָלָיו:

22 We said to my lord, 'The boy cannot leave his father; if he were to leave him, his father would die.'

כב וַנֹּאמֶר אֶל־אֲדֹנִי לֹא־יוּכַל הַנַּעַר לַעֲזֹב אֶת־אָבִיו וְעָזַב אֶת־אָבִיו וָמֵת:

23 But you said to your servants, 'Unless your youngest brother comes down with you, do not let me see your faces.'

כג וַתֹּאמֶר אֶל־עֲבָדֶיךָ אִם־לֹא יֵרֵד אֲחִיכֶם הַקָּטֹן אִתְּכֶם לֹא תֹסִפוּן לִרְאוֹת פָּנָי:

24 When we came back to your servant my father, we reported my lord's words to him.

כד וַיְהִי כִּי עָלִינוּ אֶל־עַבְדְּךָ אָבִי וַנַּגֶּד־לוֹ אֵת דִּבְרֵי אֲדֹנִי:

25 "Later our father said, 'Go back and procure some food for us.'

כה וַיֹּאמֶר אָבִינוּ שֻׁבוּ שִׁבְרוּ־לָנוּ מְעַט־אֹכֶל:

26 We answered, 'We cannot go down; only if our youngest brother is with us can we go down, for we may not show our faces to the man unless our youngest brother is with us.'

כו וַנֹּאמֶר לֹא נוּכַל לָרֶדֶת אִם־יֵשׁ אָחִינוּ הַקָּטֹן אִתָּנוּ וְיָרַדְנוּ כִּי־לֹא נוּכַל לִרְאוֹת פְּנֵי הָאִישׁ וְאָחִינוּ הַקָּטֹן אֵינֶנּוּ אִתָּנוּ:

27 Your servant my father said to us, 'As you know, my wife bore me two sons.

כז וַיֹּאמֶר עַבְדְּךָ אָבִי אֵלֵינוּ אַתֶּם יְדַעְתֶּם כִּי שְׁנַיִם יָלְדָה־לִּי אִשְׁתִּי:

28 But one is gone from me, and I said: Alas, he was torn by a beast! And I have not seen him since.

כח וַיֵּצֵא הָאֶחָד מֵאִתִּי וָאֹמַר אַךְ טָרֹף טֹרָף וְלֹא רְאִיתִיו עַד־הֵנָּה:

29 If you take this one from me, too, and he meets with disaster, you will send my white head down to Sheol in sorrow.'

כט וּלְקַחְתֶּם גַּם־אֶת־זֶה מֵעִם פָּנַי וְקָרָהוּ אָסוֹן וְהוֹרַדְתֶּם אֶת־שֵׂיבָתִי בְּרָעָה שְׁאֹלָה:

30 "Now, if I come to your servant my father and the boy is not with us – since his own life is so bound up with his

ל וְעַתָּה כְּבֹאִי אֶל־עַבְדְּךָ אָבִי וְהַנַּעַר אֵינֶנּוּ אִתָּנוּ וְנַפְשׁוֹ קְשׁוּרָה בְנַפְשׁוֹ:

31 when he sees that the boy is not with us, he will die, and your servants will send the white head of your servant our father down to Sheol in grief.

לא וְהָיָה כִּרְאוֹתוֹ כִּי־אֵין הַנַּעַר וָמֵת וְהוֹרִידוּ עֲבָדֶיךָ אֶת־שֵׂיבַת עַבְדְּךָ אָבִינוּ בְּיָגוֹן שְׁאֹלָה:

32 Now your servant has pledged himself for the boy to my father, saying, 'If I do not bring him back to you, I shall stand guilty before my father forever.'

לב כִּי עַבְדְּךָ עָרַב אֶת־הַנַּעַר מֵעִם אָבִי לֵאמֹר אִם־לֹא אֲבִיאֶנּוּ אֵלֶיךָ וְחָטָאתִי לְאָבִי כָּל־הַיָּמִים:

³³ Therefore, please let your servant remain as a slave to my lord instead of the boy, and let the boy go back with his brothers.

³⁴ For how can I go back to my father unless the boy is with me? Let me not be witness to the woe that would overtake my father!"

45 ¹ *Yosef* could no longer control himself before all his attendants, and he cried out, "Have everyone withdraw from me!" So there was no one else about when *Yosef* made himself known to his brothers.

² His sobs were so loud that the Egyptians could hear, and so the news reached Pharaoh's palace.

³ *Yosef* said to his brothers, "I am *Yosef*. Is my father still well?" But his brothers could not answer him, so dumbfounded were they on account of him.

⁴ Then *Yosef* said to his brothers, "Come forward to me." And when they came forward, he said, "I am your brother *Yosef*, he whom you sold into Egypt.

⁵ Now, do not be distressed or reproach yourselves because you sold me hither; it was to save life that *Hashem* sent me ahead of you.

⁶ It is now two years that there has been famine in the land, and there are still five years to come in which there shall be no yield from tilling.

⁷ *Hashem* has sent me ahead of you to ensure your survival on earth, and to save your lives in an extraordinary deliverance.

*va-yish-la-KHAY-nee e-lo-HEEM lif-nay-KHEM la-SUM la-KHEM
sh'-ay-REET ba-A-retz ul-ha-kha-YOT la-KHEM lif-lay-TAH g'-do-LAH*

⁸ So, it was not you who sent me here, but *Hashem*; and He has made me a father to Pharaoh, lord of all his household, and ruler over the whole land of Egypt.

לג וְעַתָּה יֵשֶׁב־נָא עַבְדְּךָ תַּחַת הַנַּעַר עֶבֶד לַאדֹנִי וְהַנַּעַר יַעַל עִם־אֶחָיו:

לד כִּי־אֵיךְ אֶעֱלֶה אֶל־אָבִי וְהַנַּעַר אֵינֶנּוּ אִתִּי פֶּן אֶרְאֶה בָרָע אֲשֶׁר יִמְצָא אֶת־אָבִי:

מה א וְלֹא־יָכֹל יוֹסֵף לְהִתְאַפֵּק לְכֹל הַנִּצָּבִים עָלָיו וַיִּקְרָא הוֹצִיאוּ כָל־אִישׁ מֵעָלַי וְלֹא־עָמַד אִישׁ אִתּוֹ בְּהִתְוַדַּע יוֹסֵף אֶל־אֶחָיו:

ב וַיִּתֵּן אֶת־קֹלוֹ בִּבְכִי וַיִּשְׁמְעוּ מִצְרַיִם וַיִּשְׁמַע בֵּית פַּרְעֹה:

ג וַיֹּאמֶר יוֹסֵף אֶל־אֶחָיו אֲנִי יוֹסֵף הַעוֹד אָבִי חָי וְלֹא־יָכְלוּ אֶחָיו לַעֲנוֹת אֹתוֹ כִּי נִבְהֲלוּ מִפָּנָיו:

ד וַיֹּאמֶר יוֹסֵף אֶל־אֶחָיו גְּשׁוּ־נָא אֵלַי וַיִּגָּשׁוּ וַיֹּאמֶר אֲנִי יוֹסֵף אֲחִיכֶם אֲשֶׁר־מְכַרְתֶּם אֹתִי מִצְרָיְמָה:

ה וְעַתָּה אַל־תֵּעָצְבוּ וְאַל־יִחַר בְּעֵינֵיכֶם כִּי־מְכַרְתֶּם אֹתִי הֵנָּה כִּי לְמִחְיָה שְׁלָחַנִי אֱלֹהִים לִפְנֵיכֶם:

ו כִּי־זֶה שְׁנָתַיִם הָרָעָב בְּקֶרֶב הָאָרֶץ וְעוֹד חָמֵשׁ שָׁנִים אֲשֶׁר אֵין־חָרִישׁ וְקָצִיר:

ז וַיִּשְׁלָחֵנִי אֱלֹהִים לִפְנֵיכֶם לָשׂוּם לָכֶם שְׁאֵרִית בָּאָרֶץ וּלְהַחֲיוֹת לָכֶם לִפְלֵיטָה גְּדֹלָה:

ח וְעַתָּה לֹא־אַתֶּם שְׁלַחְתֶּם אֹתִי הֵנָּה כִּי הָאֱלֹהִים וַיְשִׂימֵנִי לְאָב לְפַרְעֹה וּלְאָדוֹן לְכָל־בֵּיתוֹ וּמֹשֵׁל בְּכָל־אֶרֶץ מִצְרָיִם:

45:7 To save your lives in an extraordinary deliverance To allay his brothers' fears that he will take revenge for selling him into slavery, *Yosef* observes that their actions were part of the divine plan, and will undoubtedly bring great salvation. The short term benefit is already clear in that, due to his position, *Yosef* will be able to save his family and the entire region from the famine which has just begun. Further, in the great scheme of history, the sale of *Yosef* brought the entire family down to Egypt, thus beginning the fulfillment of God's promise (Genesis 15:13–14) that *Avraham*'s descendants will be strangers in a strange land. It follows that after the period of enslavement in Egypt specified by the prophecy, they will merit a 'great deliverance,' and ultimately return to the Promised Land.

North American immigrants return to the Promised Land

9 "Now, hurry back to my father and say to him: Thus says your son *Yosef*, '*Hashem* has made me lord of all Egypt; come down to me without delay.

ט מַהֲרוּ וַעֲלוּ אֶל־אָבִי וַאֲמַרְתֶּם אֵלָיו כֹּה אָמַר בִּנְךָ יוֹסֵף שָׂמַנִי אֱלֹהִים לְאָדוֹן לְכָל־מִצְרָיִם רְדָה אֵלַי אַל־תַּעֲמֹד:

10 You will dwell in the region of Goshen, where you will be near me – you and your children and your grandchildren, your flocks and herds, and all that is yours.

י וְיָשַׁבְתָּ בְאֶרֶץ־גֹּשֶׁן וְהָיִיתָ קָרוֹב אֵלַי אַתָּה וּבָנֶיךָ וּבְנֵי בָנֶיךָ וְצֹאנְךָ וּבְקָרְךָ וְכָל־אֲשֶׁר־לָךְ:

11 There I will provide for you – for there are yet five years of famine to come – that you and your household and all that is yours may not suffer want.'

יא וְכִלְכַּלְתִּי אֹתְךָ שָׁם כִּי־עוֹד חָמֵשׁ שָׁנִים רָעָב פֶּן־תִּוָּרֵשׁ אַתָּה וּבֵיתְךָ וְכָל־אֲשֶׁר־לָךְ:

12 You can see for yourselves, and my brother *Binyamin* for himself, that it is indeed I who am speaking to you.

יב וְהִנֵּה עֵינֵיכֶם רֹאוֹת וְעֵינֵי אָחִי בִנְיָמִין כִּי־פִי הַמְדַבֵּר אֲלֵיכֶם:

13 And you must tell my father everything about my high station in Egypt and all that you have seen; and bring my father here with all speed."

יג וְהִגַּדְתֶּם לְאָבִי אֶת־כָּל־כְּבוֹדִי בְּמִצְרַיִם וְאֵת כָּל־אֲשֶׁר רְאִיתֶם וּמִהַרְתֶּם וְהוֹרַדְתֶּם אֶת־אָבִי הֵנָּה:

14 With that he embraced his brother *Binyamin* around the neck and wept, and *Binyamin* wept on his neck.

יד וַיִּפֹּל עַל־צַוְּארֵי בִנְיָמִן־אָחִיו וַיֵּבְךְ וּבִנְיָמִן בָּכָה עַל־צַוָּארָיו:

15 He kissed all his brothers and wept upon them; only then were his brothers able to talk to him.

טו וַיְנַשֵּׁק לְכָל־אֶחָיו וַיֵּבְךְ עֲלֵיהֶם וְאַחֲרֵי כֵן דִּבְּרוּ אֶחָיו אִתּוֹ:

16 The news reached Pharaoh's palace: "*Yosef*'s brothers have come." Pharaoh and his courtiers were pleased.

טז וְהַקֹּל נִשְׁמַע בֵּית פַּרְעֹה לֵאמֹר בָּאוּ אֲחֵי יוֹסֵף וַיִּיטַב בְּעֵינֵי פַרְעֹה וּבְעֵינֵי עֲבָדָיו:

17 And Pharaoh said to *Yosef*, "Say to your brothers, 'Do as follows: load up your beasts and go at once to the land of Canaan.

יז וַיֹּאמֶר פַּרְעֹה אֶל־יוֹסֵף אֱמֹר אֶל־אַחֶיךָ זֹאת עֲשׂוּ טַעֲנוּ אֶת־בְּעִירְכֶם וּלְכוּ־בֹאוּ אַרְצָה כְּנָעַן:

18 Take your father and your households and come to me; I will give you the best of the land of Egypt and you shall live off the fat of the land.'

יח וּקְחוּ אֶת־אֲבִיכֶם וְאֶת־בָּתֵּיכֶם וּבֹאוּ אֵלָי וְאֶתְּנָה לָכֶם אֶת־טוּב אֶרֶץ מִצְרַיִם וְאִכְלוּ אֶת־חֵלֶב הָאָרֶץ:

19 And you are bidden [to add], 'Do as follows: take from the land of Egypt wagons for your children and your wives, and bring your father here.

יט וְאַתָּה צֻוֵּיתָה זֹאת עֲשׂוּ קְחוּ־לָכֶם מֵאֶרֶץ מִצְרַיִם עֲגָלוֹת לְטַפְּכֶם וְלִנְשֵׁיכֶם וּנְשָׂאתֶם אֶת־אֲבִיכֶם וּבָאתֶם:

20 And never mind your belongings, for the best of all the land of Egypt shall be yours.'"

כ וְעֵינְכֶם אַל־תָּחֹס עַל־כְּלֵיכֶם כִּי־טוּב כָּל־אֶרֶץ מִצְרַיִם לָכֶם הוּא:

21 The sons of *Yisrael* did so; *Yosef* gave them wagons as Pharaoh had commanded, and he supplied them with provisions for the journey.

כא וַיַּעֲשׂוּ־כֵן בְּנֵי יִשְׂרָאֵל וַיִּתֵּן לָהֶם יוֹסֵף עֲגָלוֹת עַל־פִּי פַרְעֹה וַיִּתֵּן לָהֶם צֵדָה לַדָּרֶךְ:

22 To each of them, moreover, he gave a change of clothing; but to *Binyamin* he gave three hundred pieces of silver and several changes of clothing.

כב לְכֻלָּם נָתַן לָאִישׁ חֲלִפוֹת שְׂמָלֹת וּלְבִנְיָמִן נָתַן שְׁלֹשׁ מֵאוֹת כֶּסֶף וְחָמֵשׁ חֲלִפֹת שְׂמָלֹת:

²³ And to his father he sent the following: ten he-asses laden with the best things of Egypt, and ten she-asses laden with grain, bread, and provisions for his father on the journey.

²⁴ As he sent his brothers off on their way, he told them, "Do not be quarrelsome on the way."

²⁵ They went up from Egypt and came to their father *Yaakov* in the land of Canaan.

²⁶ And they told him, "*Yosef* is still alive; yes, he is ruler over the whole land of Egypt." His heart went numb, for he did not believe them.

²⁷ But when they recounted all that *Yosef* had said to them, and when he saw the wagons that *Yosef* had sent to transport him, the spirit of their father *Yaakov* revived.

²⁸ "Enough!" said *Yisrael*. "My son *Yosef* is still alive! I must go and see him before I die."

46 ¹ So *Yisrael* set out with all that was his, and he came to *Be'er Sheva*, where he offered sacrifices to the God of his father *Yitzchak*.

² *Hashem* called to *Yisrael* in a vision by night: "*Yaakov! Yaakov!*" He answered, "Here."

³ And He said, "I am *Hashem*, the God of your father. Fear not to go down to Egypt, for I will make you there into a great nation.

⁴ I Myself will go down with you to Egypt, and I Myself will also bring you back; and *Yosef's* hand shall close your eyes."

a-no-KHEE ay-RAYD i-m'-KHA mitz-RAI-ma v'-a-no-KHEE a-al-KHA
gam a-LO v'-yo-SAYF ya-SHEET ya-DO al ay-NE-kha

⁵ So *Yaakov* set out from *Be'er Sheva*. The sons of *Yisrael* put their father *Yaakov* and their children and their wives in the wagons that Pharaoh had sent to transport him;

כג וּלְאָבִיו שָׁלַח כְּזֹאת עֲשָׂרָה חֲמֹרִים נֹשְׂאִים מִטּוּב מִצְרָיִם וְעֶשֶׂר אֲתֹנֹת נֹשְׂאֹת בָּר וָלֶחֶם וּמָזוֹן לְאָבִיו לַדָּרֶךְ:

כד וַיְשַׁלַּח אֶת־אֶחָיו וַיֵּלֵכוּ וַיֹּאמֶר אֲלֵהֶם אַל־תִּרְגְּזוּ בַּדָּרֶךְ:

כה וַיַּעֲלוּ מִמִּצְרָיִם וַיָּבֹאוּ אֶרֶץ כְּנַעַן אֶל־ יַעֲקֹב אֲבִיהֶם:

כו וַיַּגִּדוּ לוֹ לֵאמֹר עוֹד יוֹסֵף חַי וְכִי־הוּא מֹשֵׁל בְּכָל־אֶרֶץ מִצְרָיִם וַיָּפָג לִבּוֹ כִּי לֹא־הֶאֱמִין לָהֶם:

כז וַיְדַבְּרוּ אֵלָיו אֵת כָּל־דִּבְרֵי יוֹסֵף אֲשֶׁר דִּבֶּר אֲלֵהֶם וַיַּרְא אֶת־הָעֲגָלוֹת אֲשֶׁר־ שָׁלַח יוֹסֵף לָשֵׂאת אֹתוֹ וַתְּחִי רוּחַ יַעֲקֹב אֲבִיהֶם:

כח וַיֹּאמֶר יִשְׂרָאֵל רַב עוֹד־יוֹסֵף בְּנִי חָי אֵלְכָה וְאֶרְאֶנּוּ בְּטֶרֶם אָמוּת:

מו א וַיִּסַּע יִשְׂרָאֵל וְכָל־אֲשֶׁר־לוֹ וַיָּבֹא בְּאֵרָה שָּׁבַע וַיִּזְבַּח זְבָחִים לֵאלֹהֵי אָבִיו יִצְחָק:

ב וַיֹּאמֶר אֱלֹהִים לְיִשְׂרָאֵל בְּמַרְאֹת הַלַּיְלָה וַיֹּאמֶר יַעֲקֹב יַעֲקֹב וַיֹּאמֶר הִנֵּנִי:

ג וַיֹּאמֶר אָנֹכִי הָאֵל אֱלֹהֵי אָבִיךָ אַל־ תִּירָא מֵרְדָה מִצְרַיְמָה כִּי־לְגוֹי גָּדוֹל אֲשִׂימְךָ שָׁם:

ד אָנֹכִי אֵרֵד עִמְּךָ מִצְרַיְמָה וְאָנֹכִי אַעַלְךָ גַם־עָלֹה וְיוֹסֵף יָשִׁית יָדוֹ עַל־עֵינֶיךָ:

ה וַיָּקָם יַעֲקֹב מִבְּאֵר שָׁבַע וַיִּשְׂאוּ בְנֵי־ יִשְׂרָאֵל אֶת־יַעֲקֹב אֲבִיהֶם וְאֶת־טַפָּם וְאֶת־נְשֵׁיהֶם בָּעֲגָלוֹת אֲשֶׁר־שָׁלַח פַּרְעֹה לָשֵׂאת אֹתוֹ:

46:4 I Myself will go down with you to Egypt *Yaakov's* family descends to Egypt to escape the famine in *Eretz Yisrael*. In this verse, *Hashem* assures *Yaakov* that when the Children of Israel are in exile, *Hashem's* presence will accompany them. Rabbi Yehuda Lowe, a sixteenth century Talmudic scholar known as the *Maharal*, points out that the word 'descend' in this verse was carefully chosen. It conveys the idea that spiritually speaking, *Eretz Yisrael* is the highest of all places, and hence one who leaves that land is descending. Of course, the opposite is also true. Travel to Israel is repeatedly referred to in the Bible as an 'ascension.' Whenever one enters the Land of Israel, he or she experiences an elevated spiritual state.

Dramatic sunset over *Yerushalayim*

6 and they took along their livestock and the wealth that they had amassed in the land of Canaan. Thus *Yaakov* and all his offspring with him came to Egypt:

א וַיִּקְח֣וּ אֶת־מִקְנֵיהֶ֗ם וְאֶת־רְכוּשָׁם֙ אֲשֶׁ֤ר רָֽכְשׁוּ֙ בְּאֶ֣רֶץ כְּנַ֔עַן וַיָּבֹ֖אוּ מִצְרָ֑יְמָה יַֽעֲקֹ֖ב וְכָל־זַרְע֥וֹ אִתּֽוֹ׃

7 he brought with him to Egypt his sons and grandsons, his daughters and granddaughters – all his offspring.

ז בָּנָ֞יו וּבְנֵ֤י בָנָיו֙ אִתּ֔וֹ בְּנֹתָ֥יו וּבְנ֖וֹת בָּנָ֑יו וְכָל־זַרְע֖וֹ הֵבִ֥יא אִתּ֖וֹ מִצְרָֽיְמָה׃

8 These are the names of the Israelites, *Yaakov* and his descendants, who came to Egypt. *Yaakov's* first-born *Reuven*;

ח וְאֵ֨לֶּה שְׁמ֧וֹת בְּנֵֽי־יִשְׂרָאֵ֛ל הַבָּאִ֥ים מִצְרַ֖יְמָה יַֽעֲקֹ֣ב וּבָנָ֑יו בְּכֹ֥ר יַֽעֲקֹ֖ב רְאוּבֵֽן׃

9 *Reuven's* sons: Enoch, Pallu, *Chetzron*, and Carmi.

ט וּבְנֵ֖י רְאוּבֵ֑ן חֲנ֥וֹךְ וּפַלּ֖וּא וְחֶצְר֥וֹן וְכַרְמִֽי׃

10 *Shimon's* sons: Jemuel, Jamin, Ohad, Jachin, Zohar, and *Shaul* the son of a Canaanite woman.

י וּבְנֵ֣י שִׁמְע֗וֹן יְמוּאֵ֧ל וְיָמִ֛ין וְאֹ֖הַד וְיָכִ֣ין וְצֹ֑חַר וְשָׁא֖וּל בֶּן־הַֽכְּנַֽעֲנִֽית׃

11 *Levi's* sons: *Gershon, Kehat,* and *Merari*.

יא וּבְנֵ֖י לֵוִ֑י גֵּֽרְשׁ֕וֹן קְהָ֖ת וּמְרָרִֽי׃

12 *Yehuda's* sons: *Er, Onan, Sheila, Peretz,* and *Zerach* – but *Er* and *Onan* had died in the land of Canaan; and *Peretz's* sons were *Chetzron* and Hamul.

יב וּבְנֵ֣י יְהוּדָ֗ה עֵ֧ר וְאוֹנָ֛ן וְשֵׁלָ֖ה וָפֶ֣רֶץ וָזָ֑רַח וַיָּ֨מָת עֵ֤ר וְאוֹנָן֙ בְּאֶ֣רֶץ כְּנַ֔עַן וַיִּֽהְי֥וּ בְנֵי־פֶ֖רֶץ חֶצְר֥וֹן וְחָמֽוּל׃

13 *Yissachar's* sons: *Tola,* Puvah, Iob, and Shimron.

יג וּבְנֵ֖י יִשָּׂשכָ֑ר תּוֹלָ֥ע וּפֻוָּ֖ה וְי֥וֹב וְשִׁמְרֹֽן׃

14 *Zevulun's* sons: Sered, *Eilon,* and Jahleel.

יד וּבְנֵ֖י זְבֻל֑וּן סֶ֥רֶד וְאֵל֖וֹן וְיַחְלְאֵֽל׃

15 Those were the sons whom *Leah* bore to *Yaakov* in Paddan-aram, in addition to his daughter *Dina*. Persons in all, male and female: 33.

טו אֵ֣לֶּה ׀ בְּנֵ֣י לֵאָ֗ה אֲשֶׁ֨ר יָֽלְדָ֤ה לְיַֽעֲקֹב֙ בְּפַדַּ֣ן אֲרָ֔ם וְאֵ֖ת דִּינָ֣ה בִתּ֑וֹ כָּל־נֶ֧פֶשׁ בָּנָ֛יו וּבְנוֹתָ֖יו שְׁלֹשִׁ֥ים וְשָׁלֹֽשׁ׃

16 *Gad's* sons: Ziphion, Haggi, Shuni, Ezbon, Eri, Arodi, and Areli.

טז וּבְנֵ֣י גָ֔ד צִפְי֥וֹן וְחַגִּ֖י שׁוּנִ֣י וְאֶצְבֹּ֑ן עֵרִ֥י וַֽאֲרוֹדִ֖י וְאַרְאֵלִֽי׃

17 *Asher's* sons: Imnah, Ishvah, Ishvi, and Beriah, and their sister Serah. Beriah's sons: *Chever* and Malchiel.

יז וּבְנֵ֣י אָשֵׁ֗ר יִמְנָ֧ה וְיִשְׁוָ֛ה וְיִשְׁוִ֥י וּבְרִיעָ֖ה וְשֶׂ֣רַח אֲחֹתָ֑ם וּבְנֵ֣י בְרִיעָ֔ה חֶ֖בֶר וּמַלְכִּיאֵֽל׃

18 These were the descendants of *Zilpa,* whom Laban had given to his daughter *Leah*. These she bore to *Yaakov* – 16 persons.

יח אֵ֚לֶּה בְּנֵ֣י זִלְפָּ֔ה אֲשֶׁר־נָתַ֥ן לָבָ֖ן לְלֵאָ֣ה בִתּ֑וֹ וַתֵּ֤לֶד אֶת־אֵ֨לֶּה֙ לְיַֽעֲקֹ֔ב שֵׁ֥שׁ עֶשְׂרֵ֖ה נָֽפֶשׁ׃

19 The sons of *Yaakov's* wife *Rachel* were *Yosef* and *Binyamin*.

יט בְּנֵ֤י רָחֵל֙ אֵ֣שֶׁת יַֽעֲקֹ֔ב יוֹסֵ֖ף וּבִנְיָמִֽן׃

20 To *Yosef* were born in the land of Egypt *Menashe* and *Efraim,* whom Asenath daughter of Poti-phera priest of On bore to him.

כ וַיִּוָּלֵ֣ד לְיוֹסֵף֮ בְּאֶ֣רֶץ מִצְרַ֒יִם֒ אֲשֶׁ֤ר יָֽלְדָה־לּוֹ֙ אָֽסְנַ֔ת בַּת־פּ֥וֹטִי פֶ֖רַע כֹּהֵ֣ן אֹ֑ן אֶת־מְנַשֶּׁ֖ה וְאֶת־אֶפְרָֽיִם׃

21 *Binyamin's* sons: Bela, Becher, Ashbel, Gera, Naaman, Ehi, Rosh, Muppim, Huppim, and Ard.

כא וּבְנֵ֣י בִנְיָמִ֗ן בֶּ֤לַע וָבֶ֨כֶר֙ וְאַשְׁבֵּ֔ל גֵּרָ֥א וְנַֽעֲמָ֖ן אֵחִ֣י וָרֹ֑אשׁ מֻפִּ֥ים וְחֻפִּ֖ים וָאָֽרְדְּ׃

22 These were the descendants of *Rachel* who were born to *Yaakov* – 14 persons in all.

כב אֵ֚לֶּה בְּנֵ֣י רָחֵ֔ל אֲשֶׁ֥ר יֻלַּ֖ד לְיַֽעֲקֹ֑ב כָּל־נֶ֖פֶשׁ אַרְבָּעָ֥ה עָשָֽׂר׃

23 *Dan's* son: Hushim.

כג וּבְנֵי־דָ֖ן חֻשִֽׁים׃

24 *Naftali's* sons: Jahzeel, Guni, Jezer, and Shillem.

כד וּבְנֵי נַפְתָּלִי יַחְצְאֵל וְגוּנִי וְיֵצֶר וְשִׁלֵּם:

25 These were the descendants of *Bilha,* whom Laban had given to his daughter *Rachel.* These she bore to *Yaakov* – 7 persons in all.

כה אֵלֶּה בְּנֵי בִלְהָה אֲשֶׁר־נָתַן לָבָן לְרָחֵל בִּתּוֹ וַתֵּלֶד אֶת־אֵלֶּה לְיַעֲקֹב כָּל־נֶפֶשׁ שִׁבְעָה:

26 All the persons belonging to *Yaakov* who came to Egypt – his own issue, aside from the wives of *Yaakov's* sons – all these persons numbered 66.

כו כָּל־הַנֶּפֶשׁ הַבָּאָה לְיַעֲקֹב מִצְרַיְמָה יֹצְאֵי יְרֵכוֹ מִלְּבַד נְשֵׁי בְנֵי־יַעֲקֹב כָּל־נֶפֶשׁ שִׁשִּׁים וָשֵׁשׁ:

27 And *Yosef's* sons who were born to him in Egypt were two in number. Thus the total of *Yaakov's* household who came to Egypt was seventy persons.

כז וּבְנֵי יוֹסֵף אֲשֶׁר־יֻלַּד־לוֹ בְמִצְרַיִם נֶפֶשׁ שְׁנָיִם כָּל־הַנֶּפֶשׁ לְבֵית־יַעֲקֹב הַבָּאָה מִצְרַיְמָה שִׁבְעִים:

28 He had sent *Yehuda* ahead of him to *Yosef,* to point the way before him to Goshen. So when they came to the region of Goshen,

כח וְאֶת־יְהוּדָה שָׁלַח לְפָנָיו אֶל־יוֹסֵף לְהוֹרֹת לְפָנָיו גֹּשְׁנָה וַיָּבֹאוּ אַרְצָה גֹּשֶׁן:

29 *Yosef* ordered his chariot and went to Goshen to meet his father *Yisrael;* he presented himself to him and, embracing him around the neck, he wept on his neck a good while.

כט וַיֶּאְסֹר יוֹסֵף מֶרְכַּבְתּוֹ וַיַּעַל לִקְרַאת־יִשְׂרָאֵל אָבִיו גֹּשְׁנָה וַיֵּרָא אֵלָיו וַיִּפֹּל עַל־צַוָּארָיו וַיֵּבְךְּ עַל־צַוָּארָיו עוֹד:

30 Then *Yisrael* said to *Yosef,* "Now I can die, having seen for myself that you are still alive."

ל וַיֹּאמֶר יִשְׂרָאֵל אֶל־יוֹסֵף אָמוּתָה הַפָּעַם אַחֲרֵי רְאוֹתִי אֶת־פָּנֶיךָ כִּי עוֹדְךָ חָי:

31 Then *Yosef* said to his brothers and to his father's household, "I will go up and tell the news to Pharaoh, and say to him, 'My brothers and my father's household, who were in the land of Canaan, have come to me.

לא וַיֹּאמֶר יוֹסֵף אֶל־אֶחָיו וְאֶל־בֵּית אָבִיו אֶעֱלֶה וְאַגִּידָה לְפַרְעֹה וְאֹמְרָה אֵלָיו אַחַי וּבֵית־אָבִי אֲשֶׁר בְּאֶרֶץ־כְּנַעַן בָּאוּ אֵלָי:

32 The men are shepherds; they have always been breeders of livestock, and they have brought with them their flocks and herds and all that is theirs.'

לב וְהָאֲנָשִׁים רֹעֵי צֹאן כִּי־אַנְשֵׁי מִקְנֶה הָיוּ וְצֹאנָם וּבְקָרָם וְכָל־אֲשֶׁר לָהֶם הֵבִיאוּ:

33 So when Pharaoh summons you and asks, 'What is your occupation?'

לג וְהָיָה כִּי־יִקְרָא לָכֶם פַּרְעֹה וְאָמַר מַה־מַּעֲשֵׂיכֶם:

34 you shall answer, 'Your servants have been breeders of livestock from the start until now, both we and our fathers' – so that you may stay in the region of Goshen. For all shepherds are abhorrent to Egyptians."

לד וַאֲמַרְתֶּם אַנְשֵׁי מִקְנֶה הָיוּ עֲבָדֶיךָ מִנְּעוּרֵינוּ וְעַד־עַתָּה גַּם־אֲנַחְנוּ גַּם־אֲבֹתֵינוּ בַּעֲבוּר תֵּשְׁבוּ בְּאֶרֶץ גֹּשֶׁן כִּי־תוֹעֲבַת מִצְרַיִם כָּל־רֹעֵה צֹאן:

47 ¹ Then *Yosef* came and reported to Pharaoh, saying, "My father and my brothers, with their flocks and herds and all that is theirs, have come from the land of Canaan and are now in the region of Goshen."

מז א וַיָּבֹא יוֹסֵף וַיַּגֵּד לְפַרְעֹה וַיֹּאמֶר אָבִי וְאַחַי וְצֹאנָם וּבְקָרָם וְכָל־אֲשֶׁר לָהֶם בָּאוּ מֵאֶרֶץ כְּנָעַן וְהִנָּם בְּאֶרֶץ גֹּשֶׁן:

² And selecting a few of his brothers, he presented them to Pharaoh.

ב וּמִקְצֵה אֶחָיו לָקַח חֲמִשָּׁה אֲנָשִׁים וַיַּצִּגֵם לִפְנֵי פַרְעֹה:

³ Pharaoh said to his brothers, "What is your occupation?" They answered Pharaoh, "We your servants are shepherds, as were also our fathers.

ג וַיֹּ֧אמֶר פַּרְעֹ֛ה אֶל־אֶחָ֖יו מַה־מַּעֲשֵׂיכֶ֑ם וַיֹּאמְר֣וּ אֶל־פַּרְעֹ֗ה רֹעֵ֥ה צֹאן֙ עֲבָדֶ֔יךָ גַּם־אֲנַ֖חְנוּ גַּם־אֲבוֹתֵֽינוּ:

⁴ We have come," they told Pharaoh, "to sojourn in this land, for there is no pasture for your servants' flocks, the famine being severe in the land of Canaan. Pray, then, let your servants stay in the region of Goshen."

ד וַיֹּאמְר֣וּ אֶל־פַּרְעֹ֗ה לָג֣וּר בָּאָרֶץ֮ בָּאנוּ֒ כִּי־אֵ֣ין מִרְעֶ֗ה לַצֹּאן֙ אֲשֶׁ֣ר לַעֲבָדֶ֔יךָ כִּֽי־כָבֵ֥ד הָרָעָ֖ב בְּאֶ֣רֶץ כְּנָ֑עַן וְעַתָּ֛ה יֵֽשְׁבוּ־נָ֥א עֲבָדֶ֖יךָ בְּאֶ֥רֶץ גֹּֽשֶׁן:

⁵ Then Pharaoh said to *Yosef*, "As regards your father and your brothers who have come to you,

ה וַיֹּ֣אמֶר פַּרְעֹ֔ה אֶל־יוֹסֵ֖ף לֵאמֹ֑ר אָבִ֥יךָ וְאַחֶ֖יךָ בָּ֥אוּ אֵלֶֽיךָ:

⁶ the land of Egypt is open before you: settle your father and your brothers in the best part of the land; let them stay in the region of Goshen. And if you know any capable men among them, put them in charge of my livestock."

ו אֶ֤רֶץ מִצְרַ֨יִם֙ לְפָנֶ֣יךָ הִ֔וא בְּמֵיטַ֣ב הָאָ֔רֶץ הוֹשֵׁ֥ב אֶת־אָבִ֖יךָ וְאֶת־אַחֶ֑יךָ יֵֽשְׁב֣וּ בְּאֶ֣רֶץ גֹּ֔שֶׁן וְאִם־יָדַ֗עְתָּ וְיֶשׁ־בָּם֙ אַנְשֵׁי־חַ֔יִל וְשַׂמְתָּ֛ם שָׂרֵ֥י מִקְנֶ֖ה עַל־אֲשֶׁר־לִֽי:

⁷ *Yosef* then brought his father *Yaakov* and presented him to Pharaoh; and *Yaakov* greeted Pharaoh.

ז וַיָּבֵ֤א יוֹסֵף֙ אֶת־יַֽעֲקֹ֣ב אָבִ֔יו וַיַּֽעֲמִדֵ֖הוּ לִפְנֵ֣י פַרְעֹ֑ה וַיְבָ֥רֶךְ יַֽעֲקֹ֖ב אֶת־פַּרְעֹֽה:

⁸ Pharaoh asked *Yaakov*, "How many are the years of your life?"

ח וַיֹּ֥אמֶר פַּרְעֹ֖ה אֶֽל־יַעֲקֹ֑ב כַּמָּ֕ה יְמֵ֖י שְׁנֵ֥י חַיֶּֽיךָ:

⁹ And *Yaakov* answered Pharaoh, "The years of my sojourn [on earth] are one hundred and thirty. Few and hard have been the years of my life, nor do they come up to the life spans of my fathers during their sojourns."

ט וַיֹּ֤אמֶר יַֽעֲקֹב֙ אֶל־פַּרְעֹ֔ה יְמֵי֙ שְׁנֵ֣י מְגוּרַ֔י שְׁלֹשִׁ֥ים וּמְאַ֖ת שָׁנָ֑ה מְעַ֣ט וְרָעִ֗ים הָיוּ֙ יְמֵי֙ שְׁנֵ֣י חַיַּ֔י וְלֹ֣א הִשִּׂ֗יגוּ אֶת־יְמֵי֙ שְׁנֵ֣י חַיֵּ֣י אֲבֹתַ֔י בִּימֵ֖י מְגֽוּרֵיהֶֽם:

¹⁰ Then *Yaakov* bade Pharaoh farewell, and left Pharaoh's presence.

י וַיְבָ֥רֶךְ יַֽעֲקֹ֖ב אֶת־פַּרְעֹ֑ה וַיֵּצֵ֖א מִלִּפְנֵ֥י פַרְעֹֽה:

¹¹ So *Yosef* settled his father and his brothers, giving them holdings in the choicest part of the land of Egypt, in the region of Rameses, as Pharaoh had commanded.

יא וַיּוֹשֵׁ֣ב יוֹסֵף֮ אֶת־אָבִ֣יו וְאֶת־אֶחָיו֒ וַיִּתֵּ֨ן לָהֶ֤ם אֲחֻזָּה֙ בְּאֶ֣רֶץ מִצְרַ֔יִם בְּמֵיטַ֥ב הָאָ֖רֶץ בְּאֶ֣רֶץ רַעְמְסֵ֑ס כַּֽאֲשֶׁ֖ר צִוָּ֥ה פַרְעֹֽה:

¹² *Yosef* sustained his father, and his brothers, and all his father's household with bread, down to the little ones.

יב וַיְכַלְכֵּ֤ל יוֹסֵף֙ אֶת־אָבִ֣יו וְאֶת־אֶחָ֔יו וְאֵ֖ת כָּל־בֵּ֣ית אָבִ֑יו לֶ֖חֶם לְפִ֥י הַטָּֽף:

¹³ Now there was no bread in all the world, for the famine was very severe; both the land of Egypt and the land of Canaan languished because of the famine.

יג וְלֶ֤חֶם אֵין֙ בְּכָל־הָאָ֔רֶץ כִּֽי־כָבֵ֥ד הָרָעָ֖ב מְאֹ֑ד וַתֵּ֜לַהּ אֶ֤רֶץ מִצְרַ֨יִם֙ וְאֶ֣רֶץ כְּנַ֔עַן מִפְּנֵ֖י הָרָעָֽב:

¹⁴ *Yosef* gathered in all the money that was to be found in the land of Egypt and in the land of Canaan, as payment for the rations that were being procured, and *Yosef* brought the money into Pharaoh's palace.

יד וַיְלַקֵּ֣ט יוֹסֵ֗ף אֶת־כָּל־הַכֶּ֨סֶף֙ הַנִּמְצָ֜א בְּאֶֽרֶץ־מִצְרַ֣יִם וּבְאֶ֣רֶץ כְּנַ֔עַן בַּשֶּׁ֖בֶר אֲשֶׁר־הֵ֣ם שֹֽׁבְרִ֑ים וַיָּבֵ֥א יוֹסֵ֛ף אֶת־הַכֶּ֖סֶף בֵּ֥יתָה פַרְעֹֽה:

15 And when the money gave out in the land of Egypt and in the land of Canaan, all the Egyptians came to *Yosef* and said, "Give us bread, lest we die before your very eyes; for the money is gone!"

טו וַיִּתֹּם הַכֶּסֶף מֵאֶרֶץ מִצְרַיִם וּמֵאֶרֶץ כְּנַעַן וַיָּבֹאוּ כָל־מִצְרַיִם אֶל־יוֹסֵף לֵאמֹר הָבָה־לָּנוּ לֶחֶם וְלָמָּה נָמוּת נֶגְדֶּךָ כִּי אָפֵס כָּסֶף:

16 And *Yosef* said, "Bring your livestock, and I will sell to you against your livestock, if the money is gone."

טז וַיֹּאמֶר יוֹסֵף הָבוּ מִקְנֵיכֶם וְאֶתְּנָה לָכֶם בְּמִקְנֵיכֶם אִם־אָפֵס כָּסֶף:

17 So they brought their livestock to *Yosef*, and *Yosef* gave them bread in exchange for the horses, for the stocks of sheep and cattle, and the asses; thus he provided them with bread that year in exchange for all their livestock.

יז וַיָּבִיאוּ אֶת־מִקְנֵיהֶם אֶל־יוֹסֵף וַיִּתֵּן לָהֶם יוֹסֵף לֶחֶם בַּסּוּסִים וּבְמִקְנֵה הַצֹּאן וּבְמִקְנֵה הַבָּקָר וּבַחֲמֹרִים וַיְנַהֲלֵם בַּלֶּחֶם בְּכָל־מִקְנֵהֶם בַּשָּׁנָה הַהִוא:

18 And when that year was ended, they came to him the next year and said to him, "We cannot hide from my lord that, with all the money and animal stocks consigned to my lord, nothing is left at my lord's disposal save our persons and our farmland.

יח וַתִּתֹּם הַשָּׁנָה הַהִוא וַיָּבֹאוּ אֵלָיו בַּשָּׁנָה הַשֵּׁנִית וַיֹּאמְרוּ לוֹ לֹא־נְכַחֵד מֵאֲדֹנִי כִּי אִם־תַּם הַכֶּסֶף וּמִקְנֵה הַבְּהֵמָה אֶל־אֲדֹנִי לֹא נִשְׁאַר לִפְנֵי אֲדֹנִי בִּלְתִּי אִם־גְּוִיָּתֵנוּ וְאַדְמָתֵנוּ:

19 Let us not perish before your eyes, both we and our land. Take us and our land in exchange for bread, and we with our land will be serfs to Pharaoh; provide the seed, that we may live and not die, and that the land may not become a waste."

יט לָמָּה נָמוּת לְעֵינֶיךָ גַּם־אֲנַחְנוּ גַּם אַדְמָתֵנוּ קְנֵה־אֹתָנוּ וְאֶת־אַדְמָתֵנוּ בַּלָּחֶם וְנִהְיֶה אֲנַחְנוּ וְאַדְמָתֵנוּ עֲבָדִים לְפַרְעֹה וְתֶן־זֶרַע וְנִחְיֶה וְלֹא נָמוּת וְהָאֲדָמָה לֹא תֵשָׁם:

20 So *Yosef* gained possession of all the farm land of Egypt for Pharaoh, every Egyptian having sold his field because the famine was too much for them; thus the land passed over to Pharaoh.

כ וַיִּקֶן יוֹסֵף אֶת־כָּל־אַדְמַת מִצְרַיִם לְפַרְעֹה כִּי־מָכְרוּ מִצְרַיִם אִישׁ שָׂדֵהוּ כִּי־חָזַק עֲלֵהֶם הָרָעָב וַתְּהִי הָאָרֶץ לְפַרְעֹה:

21 And he removed the population town by town, from one end of Egypt's border to the other.

כא וְאֶת־הָעָם הֶעֱבִיר אֹתוֹ לֶעָרִים מִקְצֵה גְבוּל־מִצְרַיִם וְעַד־קָצֵהוּ:

22 Only the land of the priests he did not take over, for the priests had an allotment from Pharaoh, and they lived off the allotment which Pharaoh had made to them; therefore they did not sell their land.

כב רַק אַדְמַת הַכֹּהֲנִים לֹא קָנָה כִּי חֹק לַכֹּהֲנִים מֵאֵת פַּרְעֹה וְאָכְלוּ אֶת־חֻקָּם אֲשֶׁר נָתַן לָהֶם פַּרְעֹה עַל־כֵּן לֹא מָכְרוּ אֶת־אַדְמָתָם:

23 Then *Yosef* said to the people, "Whereas I have this day acquired you and your land for Pharaoh, here is seed for you to sow the land.

כג וַיֹּאמֶר יוֹסֵף אֶל־הָעָם הֵן קָנִיתִי אֶתְכֶם הַיּוֹם וְאֶת־אַדְמַתְכֶם לְפַרְעֹה הֵא־לָכֶם זֶרַע וּזְרַעְתֶּם אֶת־הָאֲדָמָה:

24 And when harvest comes, you shall give one-fifth to Pharaoh, and four-fifths shall be yours as seed for the fields and as food for you and those in your households, and as nourishment for your children."

כד וְהָיָה בַּתְּבוּאֹת וּנְתַתֶּם חֲמִישִׁית לְפַרְעֹה וְאַרְבַּע הַיָּדֹת יִהְיֶה לָכֶם לְזֶרַע הַשָּׂדֶה וּלְאָכְלְכֶם וְלַאֲשֶׁר בְּבָתֵּיכֶם וְלֶאֱכֹל לְטַפְּכֶם:

25 And they said, "You have saved our lives! We are grateful to my lord, and we shall be serfs to Pharaoh."

כה וַיֹּאמְרוּ הֶחֱיִתָנוּ נִמְצָא־חֵן בְּעֵינֵי אֲדֹנִי וְהָיִינוּ עֲבָדִים לְפַרְעֹה:

26 And *Yosef* made it into a land law in Egypt, which is still valid, that a fifth should be Pharaoh's; only the land of the priests did not become Pharaoh's.

כו וַיָּשֶׂם אֹתָהּ יוֹסֵף לְחֹק עַד־הַיּוֹם הַזֶּה עַל־אַדְמַת מִצְרַיִם לְפַרְעֹה לַחֹמֶשׁ רַק אַדְמַת הַכֹּהֲנִים לְבַדָּם לֹא הָיְתָה לְפַרְעֹה:

27 Thus *Yisrael* settled in the country of Egypt, in the region of Goshen; they acquired holdings in it, and were fertile and increased greatly.

כז וַיֵּשֶׁב יִשְׂרָאֵל בְּאֶרֶץ מִצְרַיִם בְּאֶרֶץ גֹּשֶׁן וַיֵּאָחֲזוּ בָהּ וַיִּפְרוּ וַיִּרְבּוּ מְאֹד:

28 *Yaakov* lived seventeen years in the land of Egypt, so that the span of *Yaakov's* life came to one hundred and forty-seven years.

כח וַיְחִי יַעֲקֹב בְּאֶרֶץ מִצְרַיִם שְׁבַע עֶשְׂרֵה שָׁנָה וַיְהִי יְמֵי־יַעֲקֹב שְׁנֵי חַיָּיו שֶׁבַע שָׁנִים וְאַרְבָּעִים וּמְאַת שָׁנָה:

29 And when the time approached for *Yisrael* to die, he summoned his son *Yosef* and said to him, "Do me this favor, place your hand under my thigh as a pledge of your steadfast loyalty: please do not bury me in Egypt.

כט וַיִּקְרְבוּ יְמֵי־יִשְׂרָאֵל לָמוּת וַיִּקְרָא לִבְנוֹ לְיוֹסֵף וַיֹּאמֶר לוֹ אִם־נָא מָצָאתִי חֵן בְּעֵינֶיךָ שִׂים־נָא יָדְךָ תַּחַת יְרֵכִי וְעָשִׂיתָ עִמָּדִי חֶסֶד וֶאֱמֶת אַל־נָא תִקְבְּרֵנִי בְּמִצְרָיִם:

30 When I lie down with my fathers, take me up from Egypt and bury me in their burial-place." He replied, "I will do as you have spoken."

ל וְשָׁכַבְתִּי עִם־אֲבֹתַי וּנְשָׂאתַנִי מִמִּצְרַיִם וּקְבַרְתַּנִי בִּקְבֻרָתָם וַיֹּאמַר אָנֹכִי אֶעֱשֶׂה כִדְבָרֶךָ:

*v'-sha-khav-TEE im a-vo-TAI un-sa-TA-nee mi-mitz-RA-yim uk-var-TA-nee
bik-vu-ra-TAM va-yo-MAR a-no-KHEE e-SEH khid-va-RE-kha*

31 And he said, "Swear to me." And he swore to him. Then *Yisrael* bowed at the head of the bed.

לא וַיֹּאמֶר הִשָּׁבְעָה לִי וַיִּשָּׁבַע לוֹ וַיִּשְׁתַּחוּ יִשְׂרָאֵל עַל־רֹאשׁ הַמִּטָּה:

48 1 Some time afterward, *Yosef* was told, "Your father is ill." So he took with him his two sons, *Menashe* and *Efraim*.

א וַיְהִי אַחֲרֵי הַדְּבָרִים הָאֵלֶּה וַיֹּאמֶר לְיוֹסֵף הִנֵּה אָבִיךָ חֹלֶה וַיִּקַּח אֶת־שְׁנֵי בָנָיו עִמּוֹ אֶת־מְנַשֶּׁה וְאֶת־אֶפְרָיִם:

2 When *Yaakov* was told, "Your son *Yosef* has come to see you," *Yisrael* summoned his strength and sat up in bed.

ב וַיַּגֵּד לְיַעֲקֹב וַיֹּאמֶר הִנֵּה בִּנְךָ יוֹסֵף בָּא אֵלֶיךָ וַיִּתְחַזֵּק יִשְׂרָאֵל וַיֵּשֶׁב עַל־הַמִּטָּה:

3 And *Yaakov* said to *Yosef*, "*El Shaddai* appeared to me at Luz in the land of Canaan, and He blessed me,

ג וַיֹּאמֶר יַעֲקֹב אֶל־יוֹסֵף אֵל שַׁדַּי נִרְאָה־אֵלַי בְּלוּז בְּאֶרֶץ כְּנָעַן וַיְבָרֶךְ אֹתִי:

Aeriel view of *Yosef's* tomb in *Shechem*

47:30 Take me up from Egypt
In requesting that he be buried in *Eretz Yisrael* with his father and grandfather, *Yaakov* is instilling in *Yosef* a message to carry through the ages. Though he journeyed to Egypt with God's blessing, *Yaakov* longs to return to the Holy Land – if not during his lifetime then at least after death. No matter how comfortable life may be at this historical juncture, *Yaakov* recognizes that Egypt is not where he belongs. He wants only to return to the land of his fathers. *Yosef* takes his father's message to heart, and later insists that his own bones also be carried back to the Land of Israel when the nation will ultimately be redeemed from Egypt (Genesis 50:25).

4 and said to me, 'I will make you fertile and
numerous, making of you a community of peoples;
and I will assign this land to your offspring to come
for an everlasting possession.'

ד וַיֹּאמֶר אֵלַי הִנְנִי מַפְרְךָ וְהִרְבִּיתִךָ
וּנְתַתִּיךָ לִקְהַל עַמִּים וְנָתַתִּי אֶת־
הָאָרֶץ הַזֹּאת לְזַרְעֲךָ אַחֲרֶיךָ אֲחֻזַּת
עוֹלָם:

*va-YO-mer ay-LAI hi-n'-NEE maf-r'-KHA v'-hir-bee-TI-kha
un-ta-TEE-kha lik-HAL a-MEEM v'-NA-ta-TEE et ha-A-retz
ha-ZOT l'-zar-a-KHA a-kha-RE-kha a-khu-ZAT o-LAM*

5 Now, your two sons, who were born to you in the
land of Egypt before I came to you in Egypt, shall
be mine; *Efraim* and *Menashe* shall be mine no less
than *Reuven* and *Shimon*.

ה וְעַתָּה שְׁנֵי־בָנֶיךָ הַנּוֹלָדִים לְךָ בְּאֶרֶץ
מִצְרַיִם עַד־בֹּאִי אֵלֶיךָ מִצְרַיְמָה לִי־
הֵם אֶפְרַיִם וּמְנַשֶּׁה כִּרְאוּבֵן וְשִׁמְעוֹן
יִהְיוּ־לִי:

6 But progeny born to you after them shall be yours;
they shall be recorded instead of their brothers in
their inheritance.

ו וּמוֹלַדְתְּךָ אֲשֶׁר־הוֹלַדְתָּ אַחֲרֵיהֶם לְךָ
יִהְיוּ עַל שֵׁם אֲחֵיהֶם יִקָּרְאוּ בְּנַחֲלָתָם:

7 I [do this because], when I was returning from
Paddan, *Rachel* died, to my sorrow, while I was
journeying in the land of Canaan, when still some
distance short of *Efrat*; and I buried her there on
the road to *Efrat* – now *Beit Lechem*.

ז וַאֲנִי בְּבֹאִי מִפַּדָּן מֵתָה עָלַי רָחֵל בְּאֶרֶץ
כְּנַעַן בַּדֶּרֶךְ בְּעוֹד כִּבְרַת־אֶרֶץ לָבֹא
אֶפְרָתָה וָאֶקְבְּרֶהָ שָּׁם בְּדֶרֶךְ אֶפְרָת
הִוא בֵּית לָחֶם:

8 Noticing *Yosef*'s sons, *Yisrael* asked, "Who are
these?"

ח וַיַּרְא יִשְׂרָאֵל אֶת־בְּנֵי יוֹסֵף וַיֹּאמֶר מִי־
אֵלֶּה:

9 And *Yosef* said to his father, "They are my sons,
whom *Hashem* has given me here." "Bring them up
to me," he said, "that I may bless them."

ט וַיֹּאמֶר יוֹסֵף אֶל־אָבִיו בָּנַי הֵם אֲשֶׁר־
נָתַן־לִי אֱלֹהִים בָּזֶה וַיֹּאמַר קָחֶם־נָא
אֵלַי וַאֲבָרֲכֵם:

10 Now *Yisrael*'s eyes were dim with age; he could not
see. So [*Yosef*] brought them close to him, and he
kissed them and embraced them.

י וְעֵינֵי יִשְׂרָאֵל כָּבְדוּ מִזֹּקֶן לֹא יוּכַל
לִרְאוֹת וַיַּגֵּשׁ אֹתָם אֵלָיו וַיִּשַּׁק לָהֶם
וַיְחַבֵּק לָהֶם:

11 And *Yisrael* said to *Yosef*, "I never expected to see
you again, and here *Hashem* has let me see your
children as well."

יא וַיֹּאמֶר יִשְׂרָאֵל אֶל־יוֹסֵף רְאֹה פָנֶיךָ לֹא
פִלָּלְתִּי וְהִנֵּה הֶרְאָה אֹתִי אֱלֹהִים גַּם
אֶת־זַרְעֶךָ:

12 *Yosef* then removed them from his knees, and
bowed low with his face to the ground.

יב וַיּוֹצֵא יוֹסֵף אֹתָם מֵעִם בִּרְכָּיו וַיִּשְׁתַּחוּ
לְאַפָּיו אָרְצָה:

13 *Yosef* took the two of them, *Efraim* with his right
hand – to *Yisrael*'s left – and *Menashe* with his left
hand – to *Yisrael*'s right – and brought them close
to him.

יג וַיִּקַּח יוֹסֵף אֶת־שְׁנֵיהֶם אֶת־אֶפְרַיִם
בִּימִינוֹ מִשְּׂמֹאל יִשְׂרָאֵל וְאֶת־מְנַשֶּׁה
בִשְׂמֹאלוֹ מִימִין יִשְׂרָאֵל וַיַּגֵּשׁ אֵלָיו:

14 But *Yisrael* stretched out his right hand and laid it
on *Efraim*'s head, though he was the younger, and
his left hand on *Menashe*'s head – thus crossing his
hands – although *Menashe* was the first-born.

יד וַיִּשְׁלַח יִשְׂרָאֵל אֶת־יְמִינוֹ וַיָּשֶׁת
עַל־רֹאשׁ אֶפְרַיִם וְהוּא הַצָּעִיר וְאֶת־
שְׂמֹאלוֹ עַל־רֹאשׁ מְנַשֶּׁה שִׂכֵּל אֶת־יָדָיו
כִּי מְנַשֶּׁה הַבְּכוֹר:

¹⁵ And he blessed *Yosef*, saying, "The *Hashem* in whose ways my fathers *Avraham* and *Yitzchak* walked, The *Hashem* who has been my shepherd from my birth to this day –

טו וַיְבָ֣רֶךְ אֶת־יוֹסֵ֑ף וַיֹּאמַ֗ר הָֽאֱלֹהִים֙ אֲשֶׁ֨ר הִתְהַלְּכ֤וּ אֲבֹתַי֙ לְפָנָ֔יו אַבְרָהָ֖ם וְיִצְחָ֑ק הָֽאֱלֹהִים֙ הָֽרֹעֶ֣ה אֹתִ֔י מֵֽעוֹדִ֖י עַד־הַיּ֥וֹם הַזֶּֽה:

¹⁶ The Angel who has redeemed me from all harm – the lads. In them may my name be recalled, And the names of my fathers *Avraham* and *Yitzchak*, And may they be teeming multitudes upon the earth."

טז הַמַּלְאָךְ֩ הַגֹּאֵ֨ל אֹתִ֜י מִכָּל־רָ֗ע יְבָרֵךְ֘ אֶת־הַנְּעָרִים֒ וְיִקָּרֵ֤א בָהֶם֙ שְׁמִ֔י וְשֵׁ֥ם אֲבֹתַ֖י אַבְרָהָ֣ם וְיִצְחָ֑ק וְיִדְגּ֥וּ לָרֹ֖ב בְּקֶ֥רֶב הָאָֽרֶץ:

*ha-mal-AKH ha-go-AYL o-TEE mi-kol RA y'-va-RAYKH et
ha-n'-a-REEM v'-yi-ka-RAY va-HEM sh'-MEE v'-SHAYM a-vo-TAI
av-ra-HAM v'-yitz-KHAK v'-yid-GU la-ROV b'-KE-rev ha-A-retz*

¹⁷ When *Yosef* saw that his father was placing his right hand on *Efraim*'s head, he thought it wrong; so he took hold of his father's hand to move it from *Efraim*'s head to *Menashe*'s.

יז וַיַּ֣רְא יוֹסֵ֗ף כִּֽי־יָשִׁ֨ית אָבִ֥יו יַד־יְמִינ֛וֹ עַל־רֹ֥אשׁ אֶפְרַ֖יִם וַיֵּ֣רַע בְּעֵינָ֑יו וַיִּתְמֹ֣ךְ יַד־אָבִ֗יו לְהָסִ֥יר אֹתָ֛הּ מֵעַ֥ל רֹאשׁ־אֶפְרַ֖יִם עַל־רֹ֥אשׁ מְנַשֶּֽׁה:

¹⁸ "Not so, Father," *Yosef* said to his father, "for the other is the first-born; place your right hand on his head."

יח וַיֹּ֧אמֶר יוֹסֵ֛ף אֶל־אָבִ֖יו לֹא־כֵ֣ן אָבִ֑י כִּי־זֶ֣ה הַבְּכֹ֔ר שִׂ֥ים יְמִֽינְךָ֖ עַל־רֹאשֽׁוֹ:

¹⁹ But his father objected, saying, "I know, my son, I know. He too shall become a people, and he too shall be great. Yet his younger brother shall be greater than he, and his offspring shall be plentiful enough for nations."

יט וַיְמָאֵ֣ן אָבִ֗יו וַיֹּ֨אמֶר֙ יָדַ֤עְתִּֽי בְנִי֙ יָדַ֔עְתִּי גַּם־ה֥וּא יִֽהְיֶה־לְּעָ֖ם וְגַם־ה֣וּא יִגְדָּ֑ל וְאוּלָ֗ם אָחִ֤יו הַקָּטֹן֙ יִגְדַּ֣ל מִמֶּ֔נּוּ וְזַרְע֖וֹ יִֽהְיֶ֥ה מְלֹֽא־הַגּוֹיִֽם:

²⁰ So he blessed them that day, saying, "By you shall *Yisrael* invoke blessings, saying: *Hashem* make you like *Efraim* and *Menashe*." Thus he put *Efraim* before *Menashe*.

כ וַיְבָ֨רְכֵ֜ם בַּיּ֣וֹם הַהוּא֮ לֵאמוֹר֒ בְּךָ֗ יְבָרֵ֤ךְ יִשְׂרָאֵל֙ לֵאמֹ֔ר יְשִֽׂמְךָ֣ אֱלֹהִ֔ים כְּאֶפְרַ֖יִם וְכִמְנַשֶּׁ֑ה וַיָּ֥שֶׂם אֶת־אֶפְרַ֖יִם לִפְנֵ֥י מְנַשֶּֽׁה:

*vai-VA-r'-KHAYM ba-YOM ha-HU lay-MOR b'-KHA y'-va-RAYKH
yis-ra-AYL lay-MOR y'-sim-KHA e-lo-HEEM k'-ef-RA-yim
v'-khim-na-SHEH va-YA-sem et ef-RA-yim lif-NAY m'-na-SHEH*

שם

48:16 May my name be recalled The Hebrew word for 'name' is *shem* (שם). The great master of the Hebrew language, Rabbi Samson Raphael Hirsch, explains that the word *shem* is related to the word *sham* (שם), meaning 'there.' Rabbi Hirsch explains that by naming and defining something, one puts it in its proper 'place.' Here, *Yaakov* blesses his grandsons *Efraim* and *Menashe*, by placing their ancestors' names upon them, thereby establishing their 'place' within the spiritual legacy of their forbears.

48:20 By you shall *Yisrael* invoke blessings As dictated by this verse, to this day Jewish parents bless their sons each *Shabbat* with the words, "May *Hashem* make you like *Efraim* and *Menashe*." Out of all the biblical heroes possible to emulate, what is special about *Efraim* and *Menashe*? Rabbi Shlomo Riskin, Chief Rabbi of *Efrat*, explains that the two sons of *Yosef* play a very significant role in the formation of the Jewish people. They are the first of *Avraham*'s family to be born in Egypt, yet despite their physical disconnection from *Eretz Yisrael*, they remain loyal to the traditions of their ancestors. *Efraim* and *Menashe*, therefore, represent a key to the survival of the Jewish people and their return to Israel in the future. For this reason, they are chosen as special role models for the Children of Israel.

Rabbi Shlomo Riskin
(b. 1940)

21 Then *Yisrael* said to *Yosef*, "I am about to die; but *Hashem* will be with you and bring you back to the land of your fathers.

כא וַיֹּאמֶר יִשְׂרָאֵל אֶל־יוֹסֵף הִנֵּה אָנֹכִי מֵת וְהָיָה אֱלֹהִים עִמָּכֶם וְהֵשִׁיב אֶתְכֶם אֶל־אֶרֶץ אֲבֹתֵיכֶם׃

22 And now, I assign to you one portion more than to your brothers, which I wrested from the Amorites with my sword and bow."

כב וַאֲנִי נָתַתִּי לְךָ שְׁכֶם אַחַד עַל־אַחֶיךָ אֲשֶׁר לָקַחְתִּי מִיַּד הָאֱמֹרִי בְּחַרְבִּי וּבְקַשְׁתִּי׃

49 1 And *Yaakov* called his sons and said, "Come together that I may tell you what is to befall you in days to come.

מט א וַיִּקְרָא יַעֲקֹב אֶל־בָּנָיו וַיֹּאמֶר הֵאָסְפוּ וְאַגִּידָה לָכֶם אֵת אֲשֶׁר־יִקְרָא אֶתְכֶם בְּאַחֲרִית הַיָּמִים׃

2 Assemble and hearken, O sons of *Yaakov*; Hearken to *Yisrael* your father:

ב הִקָּבְצוּ וְשִׁמְעוּ בְּנֵי יַעֲקֹב וְשִׁמְעוּ אֶל־יִשְׂרָאֵל אֲבִיכֶם׃

3 *Reuven*, you are my first-born, My might and first fruit of my vigor, Exceeding in rank And exceeding in honor.

ג רְאוּבֵן בְּכֹרִי אַתָּה כֹּחִי וְרֵאשִׁית אוֹנִי יֶתֶר שְׂאֵת וְיֶתֶר עָז׃

4 Unstable as water, you shall excel no longer; For when you mounted your father's bed, You brought disgrace – my couch he mounted!

ד פַּחַז כַּמַּיִם אַל־תּוֹתַר כִּי עָלִיתָ מִשְׁכְּבֵי אָבִיךָ אָז חִלַּלְתָּ יְצוּעִי עָלָה׃

5 *Shimon* and *Levi* are a pair; Their weapons are tools of lawlessness.

ה שִׁמְעוֹן וְלֵוִי אַחִים כְּלֵי חָמָס מְכֵרֹתֵיהֶם׃

6 Let not my person be included in their council, Let not my being be counted in their assembly. For when angry they slay men, And when pleased they maim oxen.

ו בְּסֹדָם אַל־תָּבֹא נַפְשִׁי בִּקְהָלָם אַל־תֵּחַד כְּבֹדִי כִּי בְאַפָּם הָרְגוּ אִישׁ וּבִרְצֹנָם עִקְּרוּ־שׁוֹר׃

7 Cursed be their anger so fierce, And their wrath so relentless. I will divide them in *Yaakov*, Scatter them in *Yisrael*.

ז אָרוּר אַפָּם כִּי עָז וְעֶבְרָתָם כִּי קָשָׁתָה אֲחַלְּקֵם בְּיַעֲקֹב וַאֲפִיצֵם בְּיִשְׂרָאֵל׃

8 You, O *Yehuda*, your brothers shall praise; Your hand shall be on the nape of your foes; Your father's sons shall bow low to you.

ח יְהוּדָה אַתָּה יוֹדוּךָ אַחֶיךָ יָדְךָ בְּעֹרֶף אֹיְבֶיךָ יִשְׁתַּחֲווּ לְךָ בְּנֵי אָבִיךָ׃

9 *Yehuda* is a lion's whelp; On prey, my son, have you grown. He crouches, lies down like a lion, Like the king of beasts – who dare rouse him?

ט גּוּר אַרְיֵה יְהוּדָה מִטֶּרֶף בְּנִי עָלִיתָ כָּרַע רָבַץ כְּאַרְיֵה וּכְלָבִיא מִי יְקִימֶנּוּ׃

10 The scepter shall not depart from *Yehuda*, Nor the ruler's staff from between his feet; So that tribute shall come to him And the homage of peoples be his.

י לֹא־יָסוּר שֵׁבֶט מִיהוּדָה וּמְחֹקֵק מִבֵּין רַגְלָיו עַד כִּי־יָבֹא שִׁילוֹ [שִׁילֹה] וְלוֹ יִקְּהַת עַמִּים׃

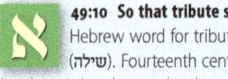

49:10 So that tribute shall come to him The Hebrew word for tribute in this verse is *Shilo* (שילה). Fourteenth century scholar Rabbi Yaakov ben Asher, known by the name of his Bible commentary as the *Baal Haturim*, reveals a hidden connection between the word *Shilo* (שילה) and *Mashiach* (משיח), the Hebrew word for 'Messiah.' According to the mystical study of *gematriya*, every Hebrew letter corresponds to a

שילה
משיח

lo ya-SUR SHAY-vet mee-hu-DAH um-kho-KAYK mi-BAYN rag-LAV
AD kee ya-VO shee-LOH v'-LO yi-k-HAHT a-MEEM

¹¹ He tethers his ass to a vine, His ass's foal to a choice vine; He washes his garment in wine, His robe in blood of grapes.

יא אֹסְרִי לַגֶּפֶן עִירֹה [עִירוֹ] וְלַשֹּׂרֵקָה בְּנִי אֲתֹנוֹ כִּבֵּס בַּיַּיִן לְבֻשׁוֹ וּבְדַם־עֲנָבִים סוּתֹה [סוּתוֹ]:

¹² His eyes are darker than wine; His teeth are whiter than milk.

יב חַכְלִילִי עֵינַיִם מִיָּיִן וּלְבֶן־שִׁנַּיִם מֵחָלָב:

¹³ *Zevulun* shall dwell by the seashore; He shall be a haven for ships, And his flank shall rest on Sidon.

יג זְבוּלֻן לְחוֹף יַמִּים יִשְׁכֹּן וְהוּא לְחוֹף אֳנִיֹּת וְיַרְכָתוֹ עַל־צִידֹן:

z'-vu-LUN l'-KHOF ya-MEEM yish-KON v'-HU l'-KHOF
a-ni-YOT v'-yar-kha-TO al tzee-DON

¹⁴ *Yissachar* is a strong-boned ass, Crouching among the sheepfolds.

יד יִשָּׂשכָר חֲמֹר גָּרֶם רֹבֵץ בֵּין הַמִּשְׁפְּתָיִם:

¹⁵ When he saw how good was security, And how pleasant was the country, He bent his shoulder to the burden, And became a toiling serf.

טו וַיַּרְא מְנֻחָה כִּי טוֹב וְאֶת־הָאָרֶץ כִּי נָעֵמָה וַיֵּט שִׁכְמוֹ לִסְבֹּל וַיְהִי לְמַס־עֹבֵד:

¹⁶ *Dan* shall govern his people, As one of the tribes of *Yisrael.*

טז דָּן יָדִין עַמּוֹ כְּאַחַד שִׁבְטֵי יִשְׂרָאֵל:

¹⁷ *Dan* shall be a serpent by the road, A viper by the path, That bites the horse's heels So that his rider is thrown backward.

יז יְהִי־דָן נָחָשׁ עֲלֵי־דֶרֶךְ שְׁפִיפֹן עֲלֵי־אֹרַח הַנֹּשֵׁךְ עִקְּבֵי־סוּס וַיִּפֹּל רֹכְבוֹ אָחוֹר:

¹⁸ I wait for Your deliverance, *Hashem!*

יח לִישׁוּעָתְךָ קִוִּיתִי יְהוָה:

¹⁹ *Gad* shall be raided by raiders, But he shall raid at their heels.

יט גָּד גְּדוּד יְגוּדֶנּוּ וְהוּא יָגֻד עָקֵב:

²⁰ *Asher*'s bread shall be rich, And he shall yield royal dainties.

כ מֵאָשֵׁר שְׁמֵנָה לַחְמוֹ וְהוּא יִתֵּן מַעֲדַנֵּי־מֶלֶךְ:

Mediterranean Sea

different number. With this understanding, if the numerical values of diverse words and ideas match each other, this means they are secretly connected. Amazingly, the numerical value of the words *yavo shilo* (יבא שילה), '*Shilo* shall come,' is to 358 which is exactly the same value as the word *Mashiach.* With prophetic foresight, *Yaakov* blesses *Yehuda* not only with the monarchy, but with the eventual emergence of the Messiah through his lineage.

49:13 *Zevulun* **shall dwell by the seashore**
Each of the twelve tribes of Israel is to receive a specific portion of the land, corresponding to that tribe's unique spiritual attributes. According to Jewish tradition, the sons of *Zevulun*, who were given a coastal territory as their inheritance, became successful sea merchants and entered into a special partnership with the tribe of *Yissachar*, descendants of *Zevulun*'s closest brother. According to the arrangement they forged, members of the tribe of *Zevulun* would use some of their commercial profits to financially support the sons of *Yissachar*, noted scholars who would devote their energies to full time *Torah* study. In turn, they would share the spiritual revenue and heavenly reward of the joint venture with their brethren from *Zevulun*. Today as well, in many Israeli communities it is a common practice for business people to seek out a spiritual partner, supporting the learning of a *Torah* scholar in a mutually-beneficial partnership modeled after the original *Yissachar-Zevulun* agreement.

21 *Naftali* is a hind let loose, Which yields lovely fawns.

כא נַפְתָּלִי אַיָּלָה שְׁלֻחָה הַנֹּתֵן אִמְרֵי־שָׁפֶר:

22 *Yosef* is a wild ass, A wild ass by a spring – Wild colts on a hillside.

כב בֵּן פֹּרָת יוֹסֵף בֵּן פֹּרָת עֲלֵי־עָיִן בָּנוֹת צָעֲדָה עֲלֵי־שׁוּר:

23 Archers bitterly assailed him; They shot at him and harried him.

כג וַיְמָרֲרֻהוּ וָרֹבּוּ וַיִּשְׂטְמֻהוּ בַּעֲלֵי חִצִּים:

24 Yet his bow stayed taut, And his arms were made firm By the hands of the Mighty One of *Yaakov* – There, the Shepherd, the Rock of *Yisrael* –

כד וַתֵּשֶׁב בְּאֵיתָן קַשְׁתּוֹ וַיָּפֹזּוּ זְרֹעֵי יָדָיו מִידֵי אֲבִיר יַעֲקֹב מִשָּׁם רֹעֶה אֶבֶן יִשְׂרָאֵל:

25 The God of your father who helps you, And *Shaddai* who blesses you With blessings of heaven above, Blessings of the deep that couches below, Blessings of the breast and womb.

כה מֵאֵל אָבִיךָ וְיַעְזְרֶךָּ וְאֵת שַׁדַּי וִיבָרֲכֶךָּ בִּרְכֹת שָׁמַיִם מֵעָל בִּרְכֹת תְּהוֹם רֹבֶצֶת תָּחַת בִּרְכֹת שָׁדַיִם וָרָחַם:

26 The blessings of your father Surpass the blessings of my ancestors, To the utmost bounds of the eternal hills. May they rest on the head of *Yosef*, On the brow of the elect of his brothers.

כו בִּרְכֹת אָבִיךָ גָּבְרוּ עַל־בִּרְכֹת הוֹרַי עַד־תַּאֲוַת גִּבְעֹת עוֹלָם תִּהְיֶיןָ לְרֹאשׁ יוֹסֵף וּלְקָדְקֹד נְזִיר אֶחָיו:

27 *Binyamin* is a ravenous wolf; In the morning he consumes the foe, And in the evening he divides the spoil."

כז בִּנְיָמִין זְאֵב יִטְרָף בַּבֹּקֶר יֹאכַל עַד וְלָעֶרֶב יְחַלֵּק שָׁלָל:

28 All these were the tribes of *Yisrael*, twelve in number, and this is what their father said to them as he bade them farewell, addressing to each a parting word appropriate to him.

כח כָּל־אֵלֶּה שִׁבְטֵי יִשְׂרָאֵל שְׁנֵים עָשָׂר וְזֹאת אֲשֶׁר־דִּבֶּר לָהֶם אֲבִיהֶם וַיְבָרֶךְ אוֹתָם אִישׁ אֲשֶׁר כְּבִרְכָתוֹ בֵּרַךְ אֹתָם:

29 Then he instructed them, saying to them, "I am about to be gathered to my kin. Bury me with my fathers in the cave which is in the field of Ephron the Hittite,

כט וַיְצַו אוֹתָם וַיֹּאמֶר אֲלֵהֶם אֲנִי נֶאֱסָף אֶל־עַמִּי קִבְרוּ אֹתִי אֶל־אֲבֹתָי אֶל־הַמְּעָרָה אֲשֶׁר בִּשְׂדֵה עֶפְרוֹן הַחִתִּי:

30 the cave which is in the field of Machpelah, facing Mamre, in the land of Canaan, the field that *Avraham* bought from Ephron the Hittite for a burial site

ל בַּמְּעָרָה אֲשֶׁר בִּשְׂדֵה הַמַּכְפֵּלָה אֲשֶׁר עַל־פְּנֵי־מַמְרֵא בְּאֶרֶץ כְּנָעַן אֲשֶׁר קָנָה אַבְרָהָם אֶת־הַשָּׂדֶה מֵאֵת עֶפְרֹן הַחִתִּי לַאֲחֻזַּת־קָבֶר:

31 there *Avraham* and his wife *Sara* were buried; there *Yitzchak* and his wife *Rivka* were buried; and there I buried *Leah*

לא שָׁמָּה קָבְרוּ אֶת־אַבְרָהָם וְאֵת שָׂרָה אִשְׁתּוֹ שָׁמָּה קָבְרוּ אֶת־יִצְחָק וְאֵת רִבְקָה אִשְׁתּוֹ וְשָׁמָּה קָבַרְתִּי אֶת־לֵאָה:

32 the field and the cave in it, bought from the Hittites."

לב מִקְנֵה הַשָּׂדֶה וְהַמְּעָרָה אֲשֶׁר־בּוֹ מֵאֵת בְּנֵי־חֵת:

33 When *Yaakov* finished his instructions to his sons, he drew his feet into the bed and, breathing his last, he was gathered to his people.

לג וַיְכַל יַעֲקֹב לְצַוֹּת אֶת־בָּנָיו וַיֶּאֱסֹף רַגְלָיו אֶל־הַמִּטָּה וַיִּגְוַע וַיֵּאָסֶף אֶל־עַמָּיו:

50 ¹ *Yosef* flung himself upon his father's face and wept over him and kissed him.

² Then *Yosef* ordered the physicians in his service to embalm his father, and the physicians embalmed *Yisrael*.

³ It required forty days, for such is the full period of embalming. The Egyptians bewailed him seventy days;

⁴ and when the wailing period was over, *Yosef* spoke to Pharaoh's court, saying, "Do me this favor, and lay this appeal before Pharaoh:

⁵ 'My father made me swear, saying, "I am about to die. Be sure to bury me in the grave which I made ready for myself in the land of Canaan." Now, therefore, let me go up and bury my father; then I shall return.'"

⁶ And Pharaoh said, "Go up and bury your father, as he made you promise on oath."

⁷ So *Yosef* went up to bury his father; and with him went up all the officials of Pharaoh, the senior members of his court, and all of Egypt's dignitaries,

⁸ together with all of *Yosef*'s household, his brothers, and his father's household; only their children, their flocks, and their herds were left in the region of Goshen.

⁹ Chariots, too, and horsemen went up with him; it was a very large troop.

¹⁰ When they came to Goren ha-Atad, which is beyond the *Yarden*, they held there a very great and solemn lamentation; and he observed a mourning period of seven days for his father.

¹¹ And when the Canaanite inhabitants of the land saw the mourning at Goren ha-Atad, they said, "This is a solemn mourning on the part of the Egyptians." That is why it was named Abel-mizraim, which is beyond the *Yarden*.

¹² Thus his sons did for him as he had instructed them.

¹³ His sons carried him to the land of Canaan, and buried him in the cave of the field of Machpelah, the field near Mamre, which *Avraham* had bought for a burial site from Ephron the Hittite.

נ א וַיִּפֹּל יוֹסֵף עַל־פְּנֵי אָבִיו וַיֵּבְךְּ עָלָיו וַיִּשַּׁק־לֽוֹ:

ב וַיְצַו יוֹסֵף אֶת־עֲבָדָיו אֶת־הָרֹפְאִים לַחֲנֹט אֶת־אָבִיו וַיַּחַנְטוּ הָרֹפְאִים אֶת־יִשְׂרָאֵֽל:

ג וַיִּמְלְאוּ־לוֹ אַרְבָּעִים יוֹם כִּי כֵּן יִמְלְאוּ יְמֵי הַחֲנֻטִים וַיִּבְכּוּ אֹתוֹ מִצְרַיִם שִׁבְעִים יֽוֹם:

ד וַיַּעַבְרוּ יְמֵי בְכִיתוֹ וַיְדַבֵּר יוֹסֵף אֶל־בֵּית פַּרְעֹה לֵאמֹר אִם־נָא מָצָאתִי חֵן בְּעֵינֵיכֶם דַּבְּרוּ־נָא בְּאָזְנֵי פַרְעֹה לֵאמֹֽר:

ה אָבִי הִשְׁבִּיעַנִי לֵאמֹר הִנֵּה אָנֹכִי מֵת בְּקִבְרִי אֲשֶׁר כָּרִיתִי לִי בְּאֶרֶץ כְּנַעַן שָׁמָּה תִּקְבְּרֵנִי וְעַתָּה אֶעֱלֶה־נָּא וְאֶקְבְּרָה אֶת־אָבִי וְאָשֽׁוּבָה:

ו וַיֹּאמֶר פַּרְעֹה עֲלֵה וּקְבֹר אֶת־אָבִיךָ כַּאֲשֶׁר הִשְׁבִּיעֶֽךָ:

ז וַיַּעַל יוֹסֵף לִקְבֹּר אֶת־אָבִיו וַיַּעֲלוּ אִתּוֹ כָּל־עַבְדֵי פַרְעֹה זִקְנֵי בֵיתוֹ וְכֹל זִקְנֵי אֶֽרֶץ־מִצְרָֽיִם:

ח וְכֹל בֵּית יוֹסֵף וְאֶחָיו וּבֵית אָבִיו רַק טַפָּם וְצֹאנָם וּבְקָרָם עָזְבוּ בְּאֶרֶץ גֹּֽשֶׁן:

ט וַיַּעַל עִמּוֹ גַּם־רֶכֶב גַּם־פָּרָשִׁים וַיְהִי הַֽמַּחֲנֶה כָּבֵד מְאֹֽד:

י וַיָּבֹאוּ עַד־גֹּרֶן הָאָטָד אֲשֶׁר בְּעֵבֶר הַיַּרְדֵּן וַיִּסְפְּדוּ־שָׁם מִסְפֵּד גָּדוֹל וְכָבֵד מְאֹד וַיַּעַשׂ לְאָבִיו אֵבֶל שִׁבְעַת יָמִֽים:

יא וַיַּרְא יוֹשֵׁב הָאָרֶץ הַכְּנַעֲנִי אֶת־הָאֵבֶל בְּגֹרֶן הָאָטָד וַיֹּאמְרוּ אֵֽבֶל־כָּבֵד זֶה לְמִצְרָיִם עַל־כֵּן קָרָא שְׁמָהּ אָבֵל מִצְרַיִם אֲשֶׁר בְּעֵבֶר הַיַּרְדֵּֽן:

יב וַיַּעֲשׂוּ בָנָיו לוֹ כֵּן כַּאֲשֶׁר צִוָּֽם:

יג וַיִּשְׂאוּ אֹתוֹ בָנָיו אַרְצָה כְּנַעַן וַיִּקְבְּרוּ אֹתוֹ בִּמְעָרַת שְׂדֵה הַמַּכְפֵּלָה אֲשֶׁר קָנָה אַבְרָהָם אֶת־הַשָּׂדֶה לַאֲחֻזַּת־קֶבֶר מֵאֵת עֶפְרֹן הַחִתִּי עַל־פְּנֵי מַמְרֵֽא:

Vayechi

ויחי

14 After burying his father, *Yosef* returned to Egypt, he and his brothers and all who had gone up with him to bury his father.

יד וַיָּשָׁב יוֹסֵף מִצְרַיְמָה הוּא וְאֶחָיו וְכָל־הָעֹלִים אִתּוֹ לִקְבֹּר אֶת־אָבִיו אַחֲרֵי קָבְרוֹ אֶת־אָבִיו:

15 When *Yosef's* brothers saw that their father was dead, they said, "What if *Yosef* still bears a grudge against us and pays us back for all the wrong that we did him!"

טו וַיִּרְאוּ אֲחֵי־יוֹסֵף כִּי־מֵת אֲבִיהֶם וַיֹּאמְרוּ לוּ יִשְׂטְמֵנוּ יוֹסֵף וְהָשֵׁב יָשִׁיב לָנוּ אֵת כָּל־הָרָעָה אֲשֶׁר גָּמַלְנוּ אֹתוֹ:

16 So they sent this message to *Yosef*, "Before his death your father left this instruction:

טז וַיְצַוּוּ אֶל־יוֹסֵף לֵאמֹר אָבִיךָ צִוָּה לִפְנֵי מוֹתוֹ לֵאמֹר:

17 So shall you say to *Yosef*, 'Forgive, I urge you, the offense and guilt of your brothers who treated you so harshly.' Therefore, please forgive the offense of the servants of the God of your father." And *Yosef* was in tears as they spoke to him.

יז כֹּה־תֹאמְרוּ לְיוֹסֵף אָנָּא שָׂא נָא פֶּשַׁע אַחֶיךָ וְחַטָּאתָם כִּי־רָעָה גְמָלוּךָ וְעַתָּה שָׂא נָא לְפֶשַׁע עַבְדֵי אֱלֹהֵי אָבִיךָ וַיֵּבְךְּ יוֹסֵף בְּדַבְּרָם אֵלָיו:

18 His brothers went to him themselves, flung themselves before him, and said, "We are prepared to be your slaves."

יח וַיֵּלְכוּ גַּם־אֶחָיו וַיִּפְּלוּ לְפָנָיו וַיֹּאמְרוּ הִנֶּנּוּ לְךָ לַעֲבָדִים:

19 But *Yosef* said to them, "Have no fear! Am I a substitute for *Hashem*?

יט וַיֹּאמֶר אֲלֵהֶם יוֹסֵף אַל־תִּירָאוּ כִּי הֲתַחַת אֱלֹהִים אָנִי:

20 Besides, although you intended me harm, *Hashem* intended it for good, so as to bring about the present result – the survival of many people.

כ וְאַתֶּם חֲשַׁבְתֶּם עָלַי רָעָה אֱלֹהִים חֲשָׁבָהּ לְטֹבָה לְמַעַן עֲשֹׂה כַּיּוֹם הַזֶּה לְהַחֲיֹת עַם־רָב:

21 And so, fear not. I will sustain you and your children." Thus he reassured them, speaking kindly to them.

כא וְעַתָּה אַל־תִּירָאוּ אָנֹכִי אֲכַלְכֵּל אֶתְכֶם וְאֶת־טַפְּכֶם וַיְנַחֵם אוֹתָם וַיְדַבֵּר עַל־לִבָּם:

22 So *Yosef* and his father's household remained in Egypt. *Yosef* lived one hundred and ten years.

כב וַיֵּשֶׁב יוֹסֵף בְּמִצְרַיִם הוּא וּבֵית אָבִיו וַיְחִי יוֹסֵף מֵאָה וָעֶשֶׂר שָׁנִים:

23 *Yosef* lived to see children of the third generation of *Efraim*; the children of *Machir* son of *Menashe* were likewise born upon *Yosef's* knees.

כג וַיַּרְא יוֹסֵף לְאֶפְרַיִם בְּנֵי שִׁלֵּשִׁים גַּם בְּנֵי מָכִיר בֶּן־מְנַשֶּׁה יֻלְּדוּ עַל־בִּרְכֵּי יוֹסֵף:

24 At length, *Yosef* said to his brothers, "I am about to die. *Hashem* will surely take notice of you and bring you up from this land to the land that He promised on oath to *Avraham*, to *Yitzchak*, and to *Yaakov*."

כד וַיֹּאמֶר יוֹסֵף אֶל־אֶחָיו אָנֹכִי מֵת וֵאלֹהִים פָּקֹד יִפְקֹד אֶתְכֶם וְהֶעֱלָה אֶתְכֶם מִן־הָאָרֶץ הַזֹּאת אֶל־הָאָרֶץ אֲשֶׁר נִשְׁבַּע לְאַבְרָהָם לְיִצְחָק וּלְיַעֲקֹב:

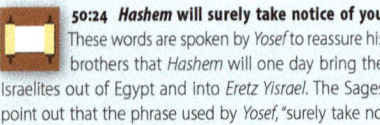

50:24 Hashem will surely take notice of you These words are spoken by *Yosef* to reassure his brothers that *Hashem* will one day bring the Israelites out of Egypt and into *Eretz Yisrael*. The Sages point out that the phrase used by *Yosef*, "surely take no- tice," is repeated many years later by *Moshe* when he tells the Jewish people that the time had come for their re- demption (see Exodus 3:16). *Yosef* initiated an oral tradi- tion among the descendants of *Yaakov*; the words "surely take notice" became a code for their national redemption.

va-YO-mer yo-SAYF el e-KHAV a-no-KHEE MAYT vay-lo-HEEM pa-KOD
yif-KOD et-KHEM v'-he-e-LAH et-KHEM min ha-A-retz ha-ZOT el
ha-A-retz a-SHER nish-BA l'-av-ra-HAM l'-yitz-KHAHK ul-ya-a-KOV

²⁵ So *Yosef* made the sons of *Yisrael* swear, saying, "When *Hashem* has taken notice of you, you shall carry up my bones from here."

²⁶ *Yosef* died at the age of one hundred and ten years; and he was embalmed and placed in a coffin in Egypt.

כה וַיַּשְׁבַּע יוֹסֵף אֶת־בְּנֵי יִשְׂרָאֵל לֵאמֹר פָּקֹד יִפְקֹד אֱלֹהִים אֶתְכֶם וְהַעֲלִתֶם אֶת־עַצְמֹתַי מִזֶּה:

כו וַיָּמָת יוֹסֵף בֶּן־מֵאָה וָעֶשֶׂר שָׁנִים וַיַּחַנְטוּ אֹתוֹ וַיִּישֶׂם בָּאָרוֹן בְּמִצְרָיִם:

When later generations hear this phrase uttered by *Moshe*, they understand that their redemption is imminent.

50:24 To *Avraham*, to *Yitzchak*, and to *Yaakov*. The story of the origins of the Jewish nation through God's selection of *Avraham*, *Yitzchak*, and *Yaakov* is timeless. Though God indeed fulfilled His promise to redeem *Avraham*'s children from Egypt, the story does not end there; it continues to unfold over thousands of years. *Hashem* made an eternal promise to *Avraham* and to his descendants, the Jewish people. While there are many difficult times along the way – persecution, slavery, exile, pogroms, and even the horrors of the twentieth century – the Jewish people will ultimately emerge as a great nation residing in *Eretz Yisrael*.

Israeli soldiers saluting the flag

List of Transliterated Words in *The Israel Bible*

The following is a list of nouns which have been transliterated into Hebrew in the English translation and commentary of *The Israel Bible*:

Hebrew Name	English Name	Pronunciation	Hebrew
Achan	Achan	a-KHAN	עָכָן
Achav	Ahab	akh-AV	אַחְאָב
Achaz	Ahaz	a-KHAZ	אָחָז
Achazyahu	Ahaziah	a-khaz-YA-hu	אֲחַזְיָהוּ
Achiezer	Ahiezer	a-khee-E-zer	אֲחִיעֶזֶר
Achihud	Ahihud	a-khee-HUD	אֲחִיהוּד
Achikam	Ahikam	a-khee-KAM	אֲחִיקָם
Achilud	Ahilud	a-khee-LUD	אֲחִילוּד
Achimelech	Ahimelech	a-khee-ME-lekh	אֲחִימֶלֶךְ
Achira	Ahira	a-khee-RA	אֲחִירַע
Achisamach	Ahisamach	a-khee-sa-MAKH	אֲחִיסָמָךְ
Achitofel	Ahithophel	a-khee-TO-fel	אֲחִיתֹפֶל
Achituv	Ahitub	a-khee-TUV	אֲחִיטוּב
Achiya	Ahijah	a-khi-YAH	אֲחִיָּה
Adam	Adam	a-DAM	אָדָם
Adar	Adar	a-DAR	אֲדָר
Adoniyahu	Adonijah	a-do-ni-YA-hu	אֲדֹנִיָּהוּ
Adulam	Adullam	a-du-LAM	עֲדֻלָּם
Agur	Agur	a-GUR	אָגוּר
Aharon	Aaron	a-ha-RON	אַהֲרֹן
Amasa	Amasa	a-ma-SA	עֲמָשָׂא
Amatzya	Amaziah	a-matz-YAH	אֲמַצְיָה
Amen	Amen	a-MAYN	אָמֵן
Amiel	Ammiel	a-mee-AYL	עֲמִיאֵל
Aminadav	Amminadab	a-mee-na-DAV	עֲמִינָדָב
Amitai	Amittai	a-mi-TAI	אֲמִתַּי
Amnon	Amnon	am-NON	אַמְנֹן

Hebrew Name	English Name	Pronunciation	Hebrew
Amon	Amon	a-MON	אָמוֹן
Amos	Amos	a-MOS	עָמוֹס
Amotz	Amoz	a-MOTZ	אָמוֹץ
Amram	Amram	am-RAM	עַמְרָם
Anatot	Anathoth	a-na-TOT	עֲנָתוֹת
Aron	Ark	a-RON	אֲרוֹן
Aron HaBrit	Ark of the Covenant	a-RON ha-b'-REET	אֲרוֹן הַבְּרִית
Arpachshad	Arpachshad	ar-pakh-SHAD	אַרְפַּכְשָׁד
Asa	Asa	a-SA	אָסָא
Asael	Asahel	a-sah-AYL	עֲשָׂהאֵל
Asaf	Asaph	a-SAF	אָסָף
Ashdod	Ashdod	ash-DOD	אַשְׁדוֹד
Asher	Asher	a-SHAYR	אָשֵׁר
Ashkelon	Ashkelon	ash-k'-LON	אַשְׁקְלוֹן
Atalya	Athaliah	a-tal-YAH	עֲתַלְיָה
Avdon	Abdon	av-DON	עַבְדּוֹן
Avichayil	Abihail	a-vee-KHA-yil	אֲבִיחַיִל
Avidan	Abidan	a-vee-DAN	אֲבִידָן
Avigail	Abigail	a-vee-GA-yil	אֲבִיגַיִל
Avihu	Abihu	a-vee-HU	אֲבִיהוּא
Avimelech	Abimelech	a-vee-ME-lekh	אֲבִימֶלֶךְ
Avinadav	Abinadab	a-vee-na-DAV	אֲבִינָדָב
Aviram	Abiram	a-vee-RAM	אֲבִירָם
Avishai	Abishai	a-vee-SHAI	אֲבִישַׁי
Aviya	Abijah	a-vi-YAH	אֲבִיָּה
Aviyam	Abijam	a-vi-YAM	אֲבִיָּם
Avner	Abner	av-NAYR	אַבְנֵר
Avraham	Abraham	av-ra-HAM	אַבְרָהָם
Avram	Abram	av-RAM	אַבְרָם
Avshalom	Absalom	av-sha-LOM	אַבְשָׁלוֹם
Azarya	Azariah	a-zar-YAH	עֲזַרְיָה
Azeika	Azekah	a-zay-KAH	עֲזֵקָה
Azza	Gaza	a-ZAH	עַזָּה

Hebrew Name	English Name	Pronunciation	Hebrew
B'nei Yisrael	The Children of Israel	b'-NAY yis-ra-AYL	בְּנֵי יִשְׂרָאֵל
Barak	Barak	ba-rakh-AYL	בָּרָק
Baruch	Baruch	ba-RUKH	בָּרוּךְ
Barzilai	Barzillai	bar-zi-LAI	בַּרְזִלַּי
Basha	Baasa	ba-SHA	בַּעְשָׁא
Batsheva	Bath-sheba	bat-SHE-va	בַּת־שֶׁבַע
Be'er Sheva	Beer-sheba	b'-AYR SHE-va	בְּאֵר שֶׁבַע
Be'eri	Beeri	b'-ay-REE	בְּאֵרִי
Beit Aven	Beth-aven	bayt A-ven	בֵּית אָוֶן
Beit El	Beth-el	bayt el	בֵּית אֵל
Beit Hamikdash	Temple	bayt ha-mik-DASH	בֵּית הַמִּקְדָּשׁ
Beit Lechem	Beth-lehem	bayt LE-khem	בֵּית לָחֶם
Beit Shean	Beth-shean	bayt sh'-AN	בֵּית שְׁאָן
Beit Shemesh	Beth-shemesh	bayt SHE-mesh	בֵּית שֶׁמֶשׁ
Berechya	Berechiah	be-rekh-YAH	בֶּרֶכְיָה
Betzalel	Bezalel	b'-tzal-AYL	בְּצַלְאֵל
Bilha	Bilhah	bil-HAH	בִּלְהָה
Binyamin	Benjamin	bin-ya-MIN	בִּנְיָמִין
Boaz	Boaz	BO-az	בֹּעַז
Buki	Bukki	bu-KEE	בֻּקִּי
Buzi	Buzi	bu-ZEE	בּוּזִי
Carmel	Carmel	kar-MEL	כַּרְמֶל
Chachalya	Hacaliah	kha-khal-YAH	חֲכַלְיָה
Chagai	Haggai	kha-GAI	חַגַּי
Chana	Hannah	kha-NAH	חַנָּה
Chanamel	Hanamel	kha-nam-AYL	חֲנַמְאֵל
Chanani	Hanani	kha-NA-nee	חֲנָנִי
Chananya	Hananiah	kha-nan-YAH	חֲנַנְיָה
Chaniel	Hanniel	kha-nee-AYL	חַנִּיאֵל
Chanoch	Enoch	kha-NOKH	חֲנוֹךְ
Chava	Eve	kha-VAH	חַוָּה
Chavakuk	Habakkuk	kha-va-KUK	חֲבַקּוּק
Chermon	Hermon	kher-MON	חֶרְמוֹן

Hebrew Name	English Name	Pronunciation	Hebrew
Chetzron	Hezron	khetz-RON	חֶצְרוֹן
Chever	Heber	KHE-ver	חֶבֶר
Chevron	Hebron	khev-RON	חֶבְרוֹן
Chilkiyahu	Hilkiah	khil-ki-YA-hu	חִלְקִיָּהוּ
Chizkiyahu	Hezekiah	khiz-ki-YA-hu	חִזְקִיָּהוּ
Chofni	Hophni	khof-NEE	חָפְנִי
Chogla	Hoglah	khog-LAH	חָגְלָה
Chulda	Hulda	khul-DAH	חֻלְדָּה
Chur	Hur	Khur	חוּר
Dan	Dan	Dan	דָּן
Daniel	Daniel	da-ni-YAYL	דָּנִיֵּאל
Datan	Dathan	da-TAN	דָּתָן
David	David	da-VID	דָּוִד
Devora	Deborah	d'-vo-RAH	דְּבוֹרָה
Dina	Dinah	DEE-nah	דִּינָה
Doeg Ha'adomi	Doeg the Edomite	do-AYG ha-a-do-MEE	דּוֹאֵג הָאֲדֹמִי
Efraim	Ephraim	ef-RA-yim	אֶפְרַיִם
Efrat	Ephrat	ef-RAT	אֶפְרָתָה
Efrat	Ephrathah	ef-RA-tah	אֶפְרָתָה
Ehud	Ehud	ay-HUD	אֵהוּד
Eila	Elah	AY-lah	אֵלָה
Eilon	Elon	ay-LON	אֵילוֹן
Ein Gedi	En-gedi	ayn GE-dee	עֵין גֶּדִי
Elazar	Eleazar	el-a-ZAR	אֶלְעָזָר
Elchanan	Elhanan	el-kha-NAN	אֶלְחָנָן
Eli	Eli	ay-LEE	עֵלִי
Eliav	Eliab	e-lee-AV	אֱלִיאָב
Elidad	Elidad	e-lee-DAD	אֱלִידָד
Eliezer	Eliezer	e-lee-E-zer	אֱלִיעֶזֶר
Elimelech	Elimelech	e-lee-ME-lekh	אֱלִימֶלֶךְ
Elisha	Elisha	e-lee-SHA	אֱלִישָׁע
Elishama	Elishama	e-lee-sha-MA	אֱלִישָׁמָע
Elisheva	Elisheba	e-lee-SHE-va	אֱלִישֶׁבַע

Hebrew Name	English Name	Pronunciation	Hebrew
Elitzafan	Eli-zaphan	e-lee-tza-FAN	אֱלִיצָפָן
Elitzur	Elizur	e-lee-TZUR	אֱלִיצוּר
Eliyahu	Elijah	ay-li-YA-hu	אֵלִיָּהוּ
Elkana	Elkanah	el-ka-NAH	אֶלְקָנָה
Elyasaf	Eliasaph	el-ya-SAF	אֶלְיָסָף
Elyashiv	Eliashib	el-ya-SHEEV	אֶלְיָשִׁיב
Enosh	Enosh	e-NOSH	אֱנוֹשׁ
Er	Er	ayr	עֵר
Eshtaol	Eshtaol	esh-ta-OL	אֶשְׁתָּאֹל
Esther	Esther	es-TAYR	אֶסְתֵּר
Eved Melech	Ebed-melech	E-ved ME-lekh	עֶבֶד־מֶלֶךְ
Even Ha-Ezer	Eben-Ezer	E-ven ha-E-zer	אֶבֶן הָעֶזֶר
Ever	Eber	AY-ver	עֵבֶר
Evyatar	Abiathar	ev-ya-TAR	אֶבְיָתָר
Ezra	Ezra	ez-RA	עֶזְרָא
Gad	Gad	gad	גָּד
Gadi	Gaddi	ga-DEE	גַּדִּי
Gadiel	Gaddiel	ga-dee-AYL	גַּדִּיאֵל
Gamliel	Gamaliel	gam-lee-AYL	גַּמְלִיאֵל
Gedalia	Gedaliah	g'-dal-YA (hu)	גְּדַלְיָהוּ
Gedera	Gederah	g'-day-RAH	גְּדֵרָה
Gershom	Gershom	gay-r'-SHOM	גֵּרְשׁוֹם
Gershon	Gershon	gay-r'-SHON	גֵּרְשׁוֹן
Geshem	Geshem	GE-shem	גֶּשֶׁם
Geuel	Geuel	g'-u-AYL	גְּאוּאֵל
Gidon	Gideon	gid-ON	גִּדְעוֹן
Gilad	Gilead	gil-AD	גִּלְעָד
Gilgal	Gilgal	gil-GAL	גִּלְגָּל
Giva	Gibeah	giv-AH	גִּבְעָה
Givon	Gibeon	giv-ON	גִּבְעוֹן
Hadassa	Hadassah	ha-da-SAH	הֲדַסָּה
Har Eival	Mount Ebal	ay-VAL	הַר עֵיבָל
Har Gerizim	Mount Gerizim	g'-ri-ZEEM	הַר גְּרִזִים

Hebrew Name	English Name	Pronunciation	Hebrew
Har HaBayit	Temple Mount	har ha-BA-yit	הַר הַבַּיִת
Har HaZeitim	the Mount of Olives	har ha-zay-TEEM	הַר הַזֵּיתִים
Hashem	Lord/God		
Hayman	Heman	hay-MAN	הֵימָן
Hoshea	Hosea	ho-SHAY-a	הוֹשֵׁעַ
Ido	Iddo	i-DO	עִדּוֹ
Imanu-El	Immanuel	i-MA-nu ayl	עִמָּנוּ אֵל
Ish-boshet	Ish-bosheth	eesh BO-shet	אִישׁ־בֹּשֶׁת
Itamar	Ithamar	ee-ta-MAR	אִיתָמָר
Itiel	Ithiel	ee-tee-AYL	אִיתִיאֵל
Ivtzan	Ibzan	iv-TZAN	אִבְצָן
Iyov	Job	i-YOV	אִיּוֹב
Kadmiel	Kadmiel	kad-mee-AYL	קַדְמִיאֵל
Kalev	Caleb	ka-LAYV	כָּלֵב
Keesh	Kish	keesh	קִישׁ
Kehat	Kohath	k'-HAT	קְהָת
Keinan	Kenan	kay-NAN	קֵינָן
Kemuel	Kemuel	k'-mu-AYL	קְמוּאֵל
Keruvim	Cherubim	k'-ru-VEEM	כְּרוּבִים
Kilyon	Chilion	kil-YON	כִּלְיוֹן
Kiryat Arba	Kiriath-arba	keer-YAT AR-bah	קִרְיַת אַרְבַּע
Kiryat Sefer	Kiriath-sepher	keer-YAT SAY-fer	קִרְיַת־סֵפֶר
Kiryat Ye'arim	Kiriath-jearim	keer-YAT y'-a-REEM	קִרְיַת יְעָרִים
Kislev	Chislev	kis-LAYV	כִּסְלֵו
Kohanim	Priests	ko-ha-NEEM	כֹּהֲנִים
Kohelet	Koheleth	ko-HE-let	קֹהֶלֶת
Kohen	Priest	ko-HAYN	כֹּהֵן
Kohen Gadol	High Priest	ko-HAYN ga-DOL	כֹּהֵן גָּדוֹל
Korach	Korah	KO-rakh	קֹרַח
Kushi	Cushi	ku-SHEE	כּוּשִׁי
Lachish	Lachish	la-KHEESH	לָכִישׁ
Leah	Leah	lay-AH	לֵאָה
Lemech	Lamech	LE-mekh	לֶמֶךְ

Hebrew Name	English Name	Pronunciation	Hebrew
Lemuel	Lemuel	l'-mu-AYL	לְמוּאֵל
Levi	Levi	lay-VEE	לֵוִי
Leviim	Levites	l'-vee-IM	לְוִיִם
Machla	Mahlah	makh-LAH	מַחְלָה
Machlon	Mahlon	makh-LON	מַחְלוֹן
Machseya	Mahseiah	makh-say-YAH	מַחְסֵיָה
Malachi	Malachi	mal-a-KHEE	מַלְאָכִי
Manoach	Manoah	ma-NO-akh	מָנוֹחַ
Mashiach	Messiah	ma-SHEE-akh	מָשִׁיחַ
Mefiboshet	Mephibosheth	m'-fee-VO-shet	מְפִיבֹשֶׁת
Mehalalel	Mahalalel	ma-ha-lal-AYL	מַהֲלַלְאֵל
Menachem	Menahem	m'-na-KHAYM	מְנַחֵם
Menashe	Menasseh	m'-na-SHEH	מְנַשֶּׁה
Menorah	Candlestick	m'-no-RAH	מְנֹרָה
Merari	Merari	m'-ra-REE	מְרָרִי
Metushelach	Methusaleh	m'-tu-SHE-lakh	מְתוּשֶׁלַח
Micha	Micah	mee-KHAH	מִיכָה
Michael	Michael	mee-kha-AYL	מִיכָאֵל
Michaihu	Micaiah	mee-KHAI-hu	מִיכָיְהוּ
Michal	Michal	mee-KHAL	מִיכַל
Milka	Milcah	mil-KAH	מִלְכָּה
Miriam	Miriam	mir-YAM	מִרְיָם
Mishael	Mishael	mee-sha-AYL	מִישָׁאֵל
Mishkan	Tabernacle	mish-KAN	מִשְׁכַּן
Mitzpa	Mizpah	mitz-PAH	מִצְפָּה
Mizbayach	Altar	miz-BAY-akh	מִזְבֵּחַ
Mordechai	Mordecai	mor-d'-KHAI	מָרְדֳּכַי
Moriah	Moriah	mo-ri-YAH	מוֹרִיָּה
Moshe	Moses	mo-SHEH	מֹשֶׁה
Nachbi	Nahbi	nakh-BEE	נַחְבִּי
Nachor	Nahor	na-KHOR	נָחוֹר
Nachshon	Nahshon	nakh-SHON	נַחְשׁוֹן
Nachum	Nahum	na-KHUM	נַחוּם

Hebrew Name	English Name	Pronunciation	Hebrew
Nadav	Nadab	na-DAV	נָדָב
Naftali	Naphtali	naf-ta-LEE	נַפְתָּלִי
Naomi	Naomi	na-o-MEE	נָעֳמִי
Natan	Nathan	na-TAN	נָתָן
Naval	Nabal	na-VAL	נָבָל
Navi	Prophet	na-VEE	נָבִיא
Navot	Naboth	na-VAL	נָבָל
Nechemya	Nehemiah	n'-khem-YAH	נְחֶמְיָה
Negev	Negeb	NE-gev	נֶגֶב
Nerya	Neriah	nay-ri-YAH	נֵרִיָּה
Netanel	Nethanel	n'-tan-AYL	נְתַנְאֵל
Neviah	Prophetess	n'-vee-AH	נְבִיאָה
Neviim	Prophets	n'-vee-EEM	נְבִיאִים
Nisan	Nisan	nee-SAN	נִיסָן
Noa	Noah	no-AH	נֹעָה
Noach	Noah	NO-akh	נֹחַ
Nov	Nob	nov	נֹב
Nun	Nun	nun	נוּן
Oded	Oded	o-DAYD	עוֹדֵד
Ohola	Oholah	a-ho-LAH	אָהֳלָה
Oholiav	Oholiab	o-ha-lee-AV	אָהֳלִיאָב
Oholiva	Oholibah	a-ho-lee-VAH	אָהֳלִיבָה
Omri	Omri	om-REE	עָמְרִי
Onan	Onan	o-NAN	אוֹנָן
Otniel	Othniel	ot-nee-AYL	עָתְנִיאֵל
Ovadya	Obadiah	o-vad-YAH	עֹבַדְיָה
Oved	Obed	o-VAYD	עוֹבֵד
Oved Edom	Obed Edom	o-VAYD e-DOM	עוֹבֵד אֱדֹם
Pagiel	Pagiel	pag-ee-AYL	פַּגְעִיאֵל
Palti	Palti	pal-TEE	פַּלְטִי
Paltiel	Paltiel	pal-tee-AYL	פַּלְטִיאֵל
Pekach	Pekah	PE-kakh	פֶּקַח
Pedael	Pedahel	p'-da-AYL	פְּדַהְאֵל

135

Hebrew Name	English Name	Pronunciation	Hebrew
Pekachya	Pekahiah	p'-kakh-YAH	פְּקַחְיָה
Peleg	Peleg	PE-leg	פֶּלֶג
Penina	Peninnah	p'-ni-NAH	פְּנִנָּה
Peretz	Perez	PE-retz	פֶּרֶץ
Petuel	Pethuel	p'-tu-AYL	פְּתוּאֵל
Pinchas	Phinehas	peen-KHAS	פִּינְחָס
Rachel	Rachel	ra-KHAYL	רָחֵל
Ram	Ram	ram	רָם
Rama	Ramah	ra-MAH	רָמָה
Re'u	Reu	r'-U	רְעוּ
Rechovam	Rehoboam	r'-khav-AM	רְחַבְעָם
Reuven	Reuben	r'-u-VAYN	רְאוּבֵן
Rivka	Rebecca	riv-KAH	רִבְקָה
Rut	Ruth	rut	רוּת
Salma	Salmon/Salmah	sal-MAH	שַׂלְמָה
Salmon	Salmon	sal-MON	שַׂלְמוֹן
Sara	Sarah	sa-RAH	שָׂרָה
Sarai	Sarai	sa-RAI	שָׂרַי
Selah	Selah	SE-lah	סֶלָה
Seraya	Seraiah	s'-ra-YAH	שְׂרָיָה
Serug	Serug	s'-RUG	שְׂרוּג
Setur	Sethur	s'-TUR	סְתוּר
Shaarayim	Shaaraim	sha-a-RA-yim	שַׁעֲרַיִם
Shabbat	Sabbath	sha-BAT	שַׁבַּת
Shabbatot	Sabbaths	sha-ba-TOT	שַׁבָּתוֹת
Shafan	Shaphan	sha-FAN	שָׁפָן
Shafat	Shaphat	sha-FAT	שָׁפָט
Shalem	Salem	sha-LAYM	שָׁלֵם
Shalum	Shallum	sha-LUM	שַׁלּוּם
Shamgar	Shamgar	sham-GAR	שַׁמְגַּר
Shamua	Shammua	sha-MU-a	שַׁמּוּעַ
Shaul	Saul	sha-UL	שָׁאוּל
Shealtiel	Shealtiel	sh'-al-tee-AYL	שְׁאַלְתִּיאֵל

Hebrew Name	English Name	Pronunciation	Hebrew
Shear Yashuv	Shear-Jashub	sh'-AR ya-SHUV	שְׁאָר יָשׁוּב
Shechanya	Shecaniah	sh'-khan-YAH	שְׁכַנְיָה
Shechem	Shechem	sh'-KHEM	שְׁכֶם
Sheila	Shelah	shay-LAH	שֵׁלָה
Shelach	Shelah	SHE-lakh	שֶׁלַח
Shelumiel	Shelumiel	sh'-lu-mee-AYL	שְׁלֻמִיאֵל
Shem	Shem	Shaym	שֵׁם
Shemaya	Shemaiah	sh'-ma-YAH	שְׁמַעְיָה
Sheshbatzar	Sheshbazzar	shaysh-ba-TZAR	שֵׁשְׁבַּצַּר
Shet	Seth	Shayt	שֵׁת
Shevat	Shebat	sh'-VAT	שְׁבָט
Shilo	Shiloh	shi-LOH	שִׁלה
Shim'i	Shimei	shim-EE	שִׁמְעִי
Shimon	Simeon	shim-ON	שִׁמְעוֹן
Shimshon	Samson	shim-SHON	שִׁמְשׁוֹן
Shlomo	Solomon	sh'-lo-MOH	שְׁלמה
Shmuel	Samuel	sh'-mu-AYL	שְׁמוּאֵל
Shofar	Horn	sho-FAR	שׁוֹפָר
Shofarot	Horns	sho-fa-ROT	שׁוֹפָרוֹת
Shomron	Samaria	sho-m'-RON	שׁמְרוֹן
Sivan	Sivan	see-VAN	סִיוָן
Tamar	Tamar	ta-MAR	תָמָר
Tanakh	Hebrew Bible	ta-NAKH	תָּנַ"ךְ
Tapuach	Tappuah	ta-PU-akh	תַּפּוּחַ
Tavor	Tabor	ta-VOR	תָּבוֹר
Tekoa	Tekoa	t'-KO-a	תְקוֹעָה
Terach	Terah	TE-rakh	תֶרַח
Teveria	Tiberias	t'-ver-YAH	טְבֶרְיָה
Tevet	Tebeth	tay-VAYT	טֵבֵת
Tirtza	Tirzah	tir-TZAH	תִּרְצָה
Tola	Tola	to-LA	תוֹלָע
Tzadok	Zadok	tza-DOK	צָדוֹק
Tzefanya	Zephaniah	tz'-fan-YAH	צְפַנְיָה

Hebrew Name	English Name	Pronunciation	Hebrew
Tzelofchad	Zelophehad	tz'-la-f'-KHAD	צְלָפְחָד
Tzeruya	Zeruiah	tz'-ru-YAH	צְרוּיָה
Tzfat	Safed	tz'-FAT	צְפַת
Tzidkiyahu	Zedekiah	tzid-ki-YA-hu	צִדְקִיָהוּ
Tziklag	Ziklag	tzi-k'-LAG	צִקְלַג
Tzion	Zion	tzi-YON	צִיּוֹן
Tzipora	Zipporah	tzi-po-RAH	צִפֹּרָה
Tzora	Zorah	tzor-AH	צָרְעָה
Tzuriel	Zuriel	tzu-ree-AYL	צוּרִיאֵל
Ukal	Ucal	u-KAL	אֻכָל
Uri	Uri	u-REE	אוּרִי
Uriya	Uriah	u-ri-YAH	אוּרִיָה
Utz	Uz	Utz	עוּץ
Uzziyahu	Uzziah	u-zi-YA-hu	עֻזִּיָהוּ
Yaakov	Jacob	ya-a-KOV	יַעֲקֹב
Yachaziel	Jahaziel	ya-kha-zee-AYL	יַחֲזִיאֵל
Yael	Jael	ya-AYL	יָעֵל
Yaffo	Joppa/Jaffa	ya-FO	יָפוֹ
Yair	Jair	ya-EER	יָאִיר
Yakeh	Jakeh	ya-KEH	יָקֶה
Yarden	Jordan	yar-DAYN	יַרְדֵּן
Yarmut	Jarmuth	yar-MUT	יַרְמוּת
Yechezkel	Ezekiel	y'-khez-KAYL	יְחֶזְקֵאל
Yechiel	Jehiel	y'-khee-AYL	יְחִיאֵל
Yechonya	Jeconiah	y'-khon-YAH	יְכָנְיָה
Yedutun	Jeduthun	y'-du-TUN	יְדוּתוּן
Yehoachaz	Jehoahaz	y'-ho-a-KHAZ	יְהוֹאָחָז
Yehoash	Jehoash	y'-ho-ASH	יְהוֹאָשׁ
Yehochanan	Jehohanan	y'-ho-kha-NAN	יְהוֹחָנָן
Yehonatan	Jonathan	y'-ho-na-TAN	יְהוֹנָתָן
Yehoram	Jehoram	y'-ho-RAM	יְהוֹרָם
Yehoshafat	Jehoshaphat	y'-ho-sha-FAT	יְהוֹשָׁפָט
Yehoshavat	Jehoshabeath	y'-ho-shav-AT	יְהוֹשַׁבְעַת

Hebrew Name	English Name	Pronunciation	Hebrew
Yehosheva	Jehosheba	y-ho-SHE-va	יְהוֹשֶׁבַע
Yehoshua	Joshua	y'-ho-SHU-a	יְהוֹשֻׁעַ
Yehotzadak	Jehozadak	y'-ho-tza-DAK	יְהוֹצָדָק
Yehoyachin	Jehoiachin	y'-ho-ya-KHEEN	יְהוֹיָכִין
Yehoyada	Jehoiada	y'-ho-ya-DA	יְהוֹיָדָע
Yehoyakim	Jehoiakim	y'-ho-ya-KEEM	יְהוֹיָקִים
Yehu	Jehu	yay-HU	יֵהוּא
Yehuda	Judah	y'-hu-DAH	יְהוּדָה
Yehudi	Jew	y'-hu-DEE	יְהוּדִי
Yehudim	Jews	y'-hu-DEEM	יְהוּדִים
Yered	Jared	YE-red	יֶרֶד
Yericho	Jericho	y'-ree-KHO	יְרִיחוֹ
Yerovam	Jeroboam	ya-rov-AM	יָרָבְעָם
Yerubaal	Jerubbaal	y'-ru-BA-al	יְרֻבַּעַל
Yerushalayim	Jerusalem	y'-ru-sha-LA-yim	יְרוּשָׁלַיִם
Yeshayahu	Isaiah	y'-sha-YA-hu	יְשַׁעְיָהוּ
Yeshua	Jeshua	yay-SHU-a	יֵשׁוּעַ
Yiftach	Jephthah	yif-TAKH	יִפְתָּח
Yigal	Igal	yig-AL	יִגְאָל
Yirmiyahu	Jeremiah	yir-m'-YA-hu	יִרְמִיָהוּ
Yishai	Jesse	yi-SHAI	יִשַׁי
Yisrael	Israel	yis-ra-AYL	יִשְׂרָאֵל
Yissachar	Issachar	yi-sa-KHAR	יִשָׂשכָר
Yitzchak	Issac	yitz-KHAK	יִצְחָק
Yizrael	Jezreel	yiz-r'-EL	יִזְרְעָאל
Yoash	Joash	yo-ASH	יוֹאָשׁ
Yoav	Joab	yo-AV	יוֹאָב
Yochanan	Johanan	yo-kha-NAN	יוֹחָנָן
Yocheved	Jochebed	yo-KHE-ved	יוֹכֶבֶד
Yoel	Joel	yo-AYL	יוֹאֵל
Yona	Jonah	yo-NAH	יוֹנָה
Yonadav	Jonadab	yo-na-DAV	יוֹנָדָב
Yonatan	Jonathan	yo-na-TAN	יוֹנָתָן

Hebrew Name	English Name	Pronunciation	Hebrew
Yoram	Joram	yo-RAM	יוֹרָם
Yosef	Joseph	yo-SAYF	יוֹסֵף
Yoshiyahu	Josiah	yo-shi-YA-hu	יֹאשִׁיָּהוּ
Yotam	Jotham	yo-TAM	יוֹתָם
Yotzadak	Jozadak	yo-tza-DAK	יוֹצָדָק
Yozavad	Jozabad	yo-za-VAD	יוֹזָבָד
Zanoach	Zanoah	za-NO-akh	זָנוֹחַ
Zecharya	Zechariah	z'-khar-YAH	זְכַרְיָה
Zerach	Zerah	ZE-rakh	זֶרַח
Zerubavel	Zerubbabel	z'-ru-ba-VEL	זְרֻבָּבֶל
Zevulun	Zebulun	z'-vu-LUN	זְבוּלֻן
Zilpa	Zilpah	zil-PAH	זִלְפָּה
Zimri	Zimri	zim-REE	זִמְרִי

Jewish Holidays

Chanukah	Hanukkah	kha-nu-KAH	חֲנוּכָּה
Pesach	Passover	PE-sakh	פֶּסַח
Purim	Purim	pu-REEM	פּוּרִים
Rosh Hashana	Jewish New Year	rosh ha-sha-NAH	רֹאשׁ הַשָּׁנָה
Shavuot	Feast of Weeks	sha-vu-OT	שָׁבוּעוֹת
Shemini Atzeret	Eight Day of Assembly	sh'-mee-NEE a-TZE-ret	שְׁמִינִי עֲצֶרֶת
Sukkot	Feast of Tabernacles	su-KOT	סֻכּוֹת
Yom Kippur	Day of Atonement	yom kee-PUR	יוֹם כִּיפּוּר

Biblical Measurements

Amah	Cubit	a-MAH	אַמָה
Amot	Cubits	a-MOT	אַמוֹת
Bat	Bath	bat	בַּת
Batim	Baths	ba-TEEM	בָּתִּים
Beka	half-shekel	BE-ka	בֶּקַע
Chomarim	Homers	kho-ma-REEM	חֳמָרִים
Chomer	Homer	KHO-mer	חֹמֶר
Efah	Ephah	ay-FAH	אֵיפָה
Geira	Gerah	gay-RAH	גֵּרָה

140

Hebrew Name	English Name	Pronunciation	Hebrew
Gomed	Gomed	GO- med	גֹּמֶד
Hin	Hin	heen	הִין
Kav	kab	kav	קַב
Kesita	kesitah	k'-see-TAH	קְשִׂיטָה
Kikar	talent	ki-KAR	כִּכָּר
Kikarim	talents	ki-ka-RIM	כִּכָּרִים
Kor	kor	kor	כֹּר
Letek	lethech	LE-tek	לֶתֶךְ
Log	Log	log	לֹג
Maneh	Mina	ma-NEH	מָנֶה
Manim	Minas	ma-NEEM	מָנִים
Omer	Omer	O-mer	עֹמֶר
Pim	Pim	peem	פִּים
Se'ah	Seah	say-AH	סְאָה
Se'eem	Seahs	s'-EEM	סְאִים
Shekalim	Shekels	sh'-ka-LEEM	שְׁקָלִים
Shekel	Shekel	SHE-kel	שֶׁקֶל
Tefach	Handbreadth	TE-fakh	טֶפַח
Zeret	Span	ZE-ret	זֶרֶת

Photo Credits

1:1 Mark Neyman, GPO, 2:5 Mark Neyman, GPO, 3:17 kavram/Shutterstock.com, 4:12 The World in HDR/Shutterstock.com, 5:3 John Theodor/Shutterstock.com, 6:13 Dmitriy Feldman svarshik/Shutterstock.com, 7:19 Nathan Alpert' GPO, 8:9 Ryan Rodrick Beiler/Shutterstock.com, 9:26 Jason Busa/Shutterstock.com, 10:5 mikhail/Shutterstock.com, 11:1 VenturaStock/Shutterstock.com, 12:3 Wikimedia Commons, 12:7 G Allen Penton/Shutterstock.com, 13:10 Bill Rice, Wikimedia Commons, 14:18 Stefano Rocca/Shutterstock.com, 15:18 ECOSY/Shutterstock.com, 16:14 John Theodor/Shutterstock.com, 17:21 Yuri Dondish/Shutterstock.com, 18:1 Eitan F., Wikimedia Commons, 19:25 Polyanska Lyubov, 21:31 Dr. Avishai Teicher, Wikimedia Commons, 22:18 Moshe Milner, GPO 23:19 Avi Ohayon, GPO, 24:10 Elbud/Shutterstock.com, 25:9 David Rabkim/Shutterstock.com, 26:3 Olgysha/Shutterstock.com, 26:4 Dotan Beck/Shutterstock.com, 26:16 Elena Dijour/Shutterstock.com, 27:28 Ay PhotoGrapher/Shutterstock.com, 28:11 John Theodor/Shutterstock.com, 28:17 Andrew Shiva, Wikipedia, 28:19 Dvirraz, Wikimedia Commons, 29:1 Lev Levin/Shutterstock.com, 30:25 pioneerka888/Shutterstock.com, 31:3 Barbarajo/Shutterstock.com, 32:9 Seth Aronstam/Shutterstock.com, 33:19 Mark Neyman, GPO, 34:31 Roniuru/Shutterstock.com, 35:10 Wikimedia Commons, 36:6 John Theodor/Shutterstock.com, 37:2 Noel Powell/Shutterstock.com, 37:22 By לין משפחת – received from author, CC BY-SA 3.0, https://commons.wikimedia.org/w/index.php?curid=15907178, 38:1 Moshe EINHORN/Shutterstock.com, 39:1 max shamota/Shutterstock.com, 40:15 John Theodor/Shutterstock.com, 41:52 S1001/Shutterstock.com, 42:7 vvvita/Shutterstock.com, 43:11 Noel Powell/Shutterstock.com 44:8 Courtesy of Israel365, 45:7 Mark Neyman, GPO, 46:4 John Theodor/Shutterstock.com, 47:30 Moshe Milner, GPO, 49:13 Mark Neyman, GPO, 50:24 KrispelSlaven/Shutterstock.com

Map of Modern-Day Israel and its Neighbors

The following is a map of modern-day Israel and the surrounding countries

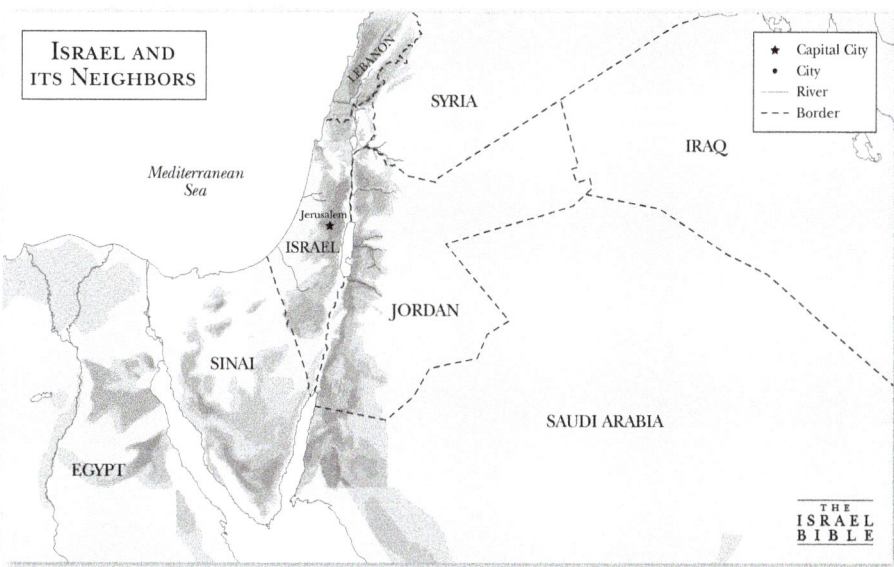

NOTES

NOTES

NOTES

NOTES

NOTES

NOTES

For more inspiring commentary,
interactive maps, educational videos,
vivid photographs and more,
please visit our website

www.TheIsraelBible.com

THE
ISRAEL
BIBLE